THE BRITISH SCHOOL OF OSTEOPATHY
1-4 SUFFOLK ST., LONDON. SW1Y 4HG
TEL. 01 - 930 9254-8

KU-451-985

THE MILLIONAIRE GIVERS

GIVERS

Wealth and Philanthropy in Britain

By

Howard Hurd & Mark Lattimer

**with a contribution from
Redmond Mullin**

A DIRECTORY OF SOCIAL CHANGE PUBLICATION

THE MILLIONAIRE GIVERS
Wealth and Philanthropy in Britain
by Howard Hurd and Mark Lattimer

Published by the Directory of Social Change, Radius Works,
Back Lane, London NW3 1HL

© 1994 Directory of Social Change

No part of this publication may be reproduced in any form
whatsoever without prior written permission from the publisher.

Cartoons by David Lewis
Designed and typeset by Diarmuid Burke & Kate Bass
Printed by Page Bros, Norwich

British Library Cataloguing-in-Publication Data
A catalogue record for this book is available from the British Library

ISBN 1 873860 35 8

KEY TO COVER PHOTOGRAPHS

Front cover (clockwise from bottom left):
Lord Palumbo *(Hanya Chalala)*; Graham Kirkham; Paul Hamlyn
(Ashok Dilwali); The Queen *(Kester Eddy/Barnaby's)*; Julian Hodge
(Hylton Warner); Michael Heseltine; Swraj Paul *(Madan Arora)*;
J Paul Getty *(Julian Calder)*; Anita Roddick *(UPPA)*; Alan Sugar; Raj
Bagri *(Madan Arora)*; Andrew Lloyd Webber.

Back cover (clockwise from bottom left):
Ken Follett *(Marc Raboy)*; Gopi Hinduja *(Madan Arora)*; Andrew
Cohen; Richard Branson; Peter Rigby; Bernard Ashley; Shirley Porter
(UPPA); Hugh Sykes; Norman Stoller *(Paul Francis)*; Paul Channon.

DISCLAIMER

Wherever possible the entries contained within this publication were sent to
the individuals/families concerned in order to allow feedback, comment
and correction. Any errors or inaccuracies which remain are inadvertent,
and no liability of any kind is accepted by the publisher in respect of them.
If informed of any such errors or inaccuracies, the Directory of Social
Change will make suitable corrections in future editions of the publication.

CONTENTS

FROM THE RICH MAN'S TABLE

The 500 richest people in Britain are worth about £60 billion. They did very well indeed out of the 1980s and now, at the end of the recession, they're doing even better. Their fabulous wealth makes them courted by politicians, salespeople, business partners – and charities.

For the first time, *The Millionaire Givers* uncovers how much they do in fact give away, and why. It looks at the reasons, emotional and financial, altruistic and self-interested, why they give might give more or less. And, following a decade which preached the philosophy of individual responsibility, it compares the generosity of the present generation of multi-millionaires with that of philanthropists ten, twenty or more years ago.

The first thing to note is that most of the philanthropists in these pages are men. Although the handful of women givers include some of the most generous, it comes as no surprise that wealth-holding, and therefore philanthropy, in this country is heavily dominated by the boys.

Rich people give in a number of different ways. Like anyone else, they may make a number of 'out-of-pocket' donations in cash. For donations of any size, however, they are likely to be advised to make donations tax-effectively. This may mean making a covenant to a charity for four years or more, or taking advantage of the Gift Aid scheme for larger one-off donations. In each case, the recipient charity is able to reclaim tax at the basic rate paid by the donor, and the donor herself benefits from higher rate relief. With a marginal rate of tax at 40 per cent, this means that a £100 donation only costs the giver £60.

Wealthy businesspeople frequently give through their companies, where tax reliefs are similarly available. More organised than occasional covenants or Gift Aid payments, this typically involves a higher level of giving. It is particularly appropriate for the entrepreneur who wants to put something back into the community but whose wealth is still largely tied up in his company. Once such a tradition of giving has been established, it will often continue and grow after the company goes public, when the entrepreneur will be effectively giving away other shareholders' money as well as his own.

There are many examples of people in the entertainment world donating rights or services to charity. Probably the most common example is that of the pop star playing a benefit concert, although few do so on quite as dedicated a basis as Elton John (see page 79). George Michael is one of the rare stars who has donated the proceeds of a hit single to charity, the money going – as with Elton – to the fight against AIDS. Novelist Catherine Cookson vested her trust with the rights to one of her books, *Bill Bailey's Lot*, and income from royalties is donated to charities.

But most of all, the rich give through foundations. These are charitable trusts which are endowed with a sum of money or a block of shares and which then serve as a tax-free vehicle for making donations. For regular donors such a vehicle simplifies the process considerably, meaning that tax administration only has to be performed once a year rather than for each separate gift, and making it easy for the donor to give to charity not just cash but also shares in a company or some other income producing asset. One wealthy donor also pointed out that having a foundation means you have to make the difficult decision *how much* to give only once a year (or even once in a lifetime), with the subsequent decisions on whom to give to being comparatively painless.

Often tipped off by a media report of a big gift or an acknowledgement by a charity, we have uncovered a large number of major donors in this book. It is significant that nearly all chose to organise their giving through a foundation. Looking at the growth and decay of foundations in the country thus provides an unparalleled insight into the patterns of philanthropy among Britain's rich.

Setting up foundations

Endowing a foundation is a major decision in someone's life, and as with other major decisions like choosing a career in the family company, getting married, and buying your first yacht, it has its allotted time and place. The classic time is on the flotation or sale of a company.

Frequently, foundations are endowed with a block of shares in a company when it is first floated on the market. This was the case with Martyn Arbib and with John and Michael Thornton, to pick just two examples from this book. While wealth is still tied up in a private company, making donations out of profits is usually most convenient; but on flotation it is easy to place a parcel of the newly-issued shares in a trust.

The sale of a company is another moment when foundations have been established, illustrated spectacularly in 1987 by Paul Hamlyn. It is notable that the flotation or sale of their company is often the first point in their lives when entrepreneurs really start to think of themselves as wealthy. The creation of foundations is thus linked to the generation of cash or the liquidity of assets – possibly the main reason why so few wealthy landowners, with little surplus cash, feature highly in our list of givers. But other factors are also significant in what motivates people to create foundations.

The table opposite illustrates the rate of establishment of new foundations every decade since the 1930s. The figures are taken from the Charities Aid Foundation's *Directory of Grant-Making Trusts*, the most comprehensive current listing of grant-making foundations. What is most noticeable from our point of view is that a small drop in the number of foundations created during the 1970s (which may have been due to the prolonged recession) quickly accelerates to a steep decline during the 1980s.

This decline is, to say the least, strange. Acknowledged across the political spectrum as the time when some people in society never had it so good, it was also the period when assets had never been so liquid: the mid-years strewn with takeovers, flotations, sales and associated wheeling and dealing. With the political climate emphasising the importance of individual responsibility in addition to, or indeed over and above, the responsibility of the state to society, the logic would seem to suggest that there should have been a big rise in foundation formation, rather than an abrupt decline.

Two potential explanations might be advanced. The first is that other methods of giving tax-effectively may have been preferred to the establishment of foundations. The one most often quoted is Gift Aid, which enables larger one-off donations to be made tax-free. However, Gift Aid was not introduced until October 1990, and in any case would prove cumbersome with the large

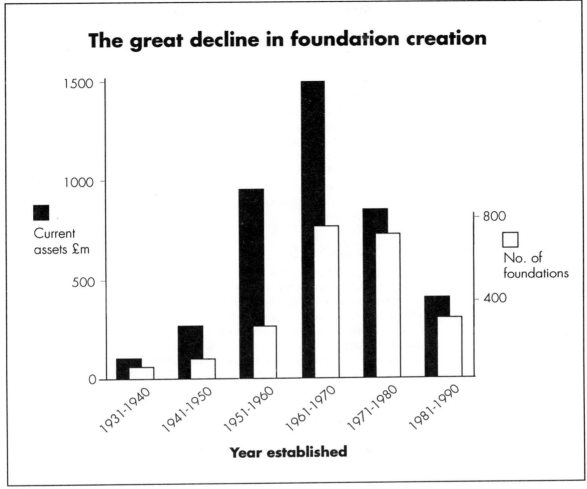

The great decline in foundation creation

Source: CAF Directory of Grant-Making Trusts 1993/94

numbers of donations that foundations customarily make. Much the same is true of covenants. The Association of Charitable Foundations has also argued in the past that the introduction of schemes such as Gift Aid actually make it easier for people to give through foundations, enabling them to regulate the amount they put into the foundation every year. Company giving to charity did rise during the 1980s, but on nothing like the scale required to compensate for the decimation in the numbers of new foundations.

The second explanation is that the figures we have quoted might themselves be misleading, because they refer to the *establishment* of foundations, rather than their endowment or start of operations. There is on occasion a lag of several years between the point at which the lawyers are asked to set up a foundation and the time when it is endowed; this may not be, for example, until after the settlor's death. As foundations are only likely to be included in the CAF *Directory of Grant-Making Trusts* once they are in operation, this factor could be expected to weigh down the figures for the most recent decades. However, using data from previous editions of the Directory produced in the early 1980s, it is clear that this weighting is probably negligible, or in any case as likely to be positive as negative, given that some foundations expire and are removed from the register of charities. The number given in the Directory for foundations established in the 1970s, for example, actually *fell* from 795 to 733 between 1985 and 1993.

This squares with our own impressions gained through research on this book. Many of the new foundations we discovered had not been settled with an endowment but simply served as tax-free vehicles for the founder's giving. A block donation covenanted to the foundation from the individual or his or her company would be split between a number of charities every year. These foundations typically come into operation as soon as they are established. None of the explanations so far advanced, therefore, satisfactorily explains the rapid decline in the number of foundations set up in the 1980s.

Tax breaks

One other thing did take place at the start of the 1980s. There was a marked shift away from direct taxation (from which charities are largely exempt) to indirect taxation (from which they are largely not exempt). Like other charities, gifts to a foundation are exempt from inheritance tax and capital gains tax, and foundations do not pay income or corporation tax on income which is applied for charitable purposes (eg. donated to another charity). We have already noted that charities can reclaim basic rate tax paid by the donor on covenanted donations of four years or more and on single donations made under the Gift Aid scheme, with higher rate taxpayers entitled to higher rate relief.

Cuts in direct taxation are therefore unwelcome to charities. The Charities Aid Foundation estimated in 1988 that when the base rate of income tax fell just from 27 to 25 per cent, charities lost some £11 million in tax reliefs.

But research carried out in the United States in the late 1980s suggests that tax cuts not only reduce the value of donations to charities, they also behave as a disincentive to the act of giving itself. As Mark Lattimer reported in a recent issue of *Trust Monitor* (Directory of Social Change, 1990):

'The analysis of 135 interviews with very wealthy donors undertaken by Dr Teresa Odendahl, and published by the Foundation Center (*America's Wealthy and the Future of Foundations*, 1987), reveals a large measure of agreement in donors' charitable attitudes: "The saving of taxes is not ever far from a person's motivation... it is in mine, and it is in almost everybody's I know. I think if it were not for the savings in taxes – the notion that the government really is participating in a gift – I think there would be an awful lot less giving."

'The majority of millionaires interviewed said that they gave up to the maximum for which they received a deduction. Interestingly, part of the reason for this appears to be a marked antagonism to the idea that their taxes would otherwise be contributing to the maintenance of a welfare state. Creating a foundation is seen as "a way of not giving all your money to the government in taxes". There is also a strong impulse to exercise greater control over the disposition of their wealth. "I am sure I give away more because it is deductible than if it was not because I am sharing it with Uncle Sam. Instead of a Congressman telling me where my dollars are going to go, I am telling them where their dollars can go." The belief among many donors interviewed that a "free-market system fosters a giving environment" thus co-exists rather curiously with the way in which high rates of taxation function as an incentive to give. Odendahl: "The most frequently mentioned reason for starting a foundation was taxes... It is not a coincidence that the greatest number of foundations of all sizes were created during the period of highest tax rates."

'The greater the tax burden, the more pressing the desire for relief. The logic is simple. With a 40 per cent rate of income tax it costs the donor 60p to donate a pound to charity, but with a 65 per cent rate, say, the price of giving is only 35p a pound (assuming full deductability). The steeper the rate of tax, the cheaper it is for the wealthy to give to charity.

'In addition, it should be borne in mind that for the very rich, money that could otherwise be donated to charity is unlikely to be used for personal consumption. Charitable giving is not competing with consumption, but with wealth-holding itself. This is why the issue of donor control is so significant. Creating a foundation enables the donor, in a way, to 'hold onto' all of his or her wealth rather than pay a large part of it in income or capital gains tax, or to 'keep in the family' what would otherwise be lost in inheritance tax. The money has to be applied for charitable purposes but it is still money to be spent at the former owner's discretion. Of the different mechanisms available for tax-effective giving, the charitable foundation is the one which enables the donor to retain most control. Once again, this only really works as an incentive if potential donors feel that tax rates are punitive.'

With the great shift away from direct taxation in the 1980s, this is probably the last thing they felt. In addition, it is notable in any survey of the rich how sophisticated their mechanisms for minimising their general tax burden now are. Many of Britain's richest people are tax exiles, and many of its richest families conserve generational wealth in family trusts that defy many of the greater ambitions of the Inland Revenue. All in all, the fiscal regime in the 1980s did not appear to impose the punitive tax burden which, as we have seen, tends to prompt a further voluntary redistribution of wealth through charitable donation.

How generous are the rich?

The sheer size of the amounts of money involved when considering the richest people in the country often makes it difficult to place in context the value of their contribution to charity. As such, we have looked at the size of individuals' annual giving as a proportion of their net wealth, in order to create an index of generosity. The 40 most 'generous' givers calculated using this method are listed in the table overleaf.

But what of the super-rich as a group? The total annual donations made by people in this book come to £175 million (£75 million if you discount the exceptional George Soros). This covers the evidence we have found for giving by the 500 richest people or families in Britain. The total wealth held by these people has already been quoted as £60 billion (this is simply the figure calculated by the *Sunday Times* in its 1994 survey of Britain's rich, adjusted to reflect our own – considerably more conservative – estimation of the wealth of the Queen). These figures are very rough and ready and it would be unwise to draw firm conclusions from them, but it is nevertheless interesting to see how they compare with the giving and wealth-holding of other groups in society.

● THE 40 MOST GENEROUS† GIVERS

	%
George Soros	14.0
Peter Beckwith	12.3
Vivien Duffield	7.0
J Paul Getty	3.0*
Anthony Hopkins	3.0*
Julian Hodge	2.4
Stanley Kalms	2.2
Lord Rayne	2.2
Sainsbury brothers	2.2
Martyn Arbib	2.1
John Douglas	1.9*
Wates family	1.7
John Zochonis	1.7
Dame Shirley & Leslie Porter	1.7
Lord Leverhulme	1.4
Swraj Paul	1.4
Paul Hamlyn	1.3
Alan Pascoe	1.2*
Kenneth Horne	1.2
Sidney Corob	1.1
George Michael	1.1
Dowager Marchioness of Normanby	1.1
O'Hea family	1.1
John Cleese	1.0*
Michael Thornton	1.0*
Joel Joffe	1.0
Cyril Stein	1.0
Robert Edmiston	1.0
Prince Charles	1.0
Cameron Mackintosh	0.9
Rosemary Bugden	0.8
Benzion Freshwater	0.8
Philip Harris	0.8
Arnold Lee	0.8
David Sainsbury	0.8
Cliff Richard	0.7
William Gredley	0.7
Henry Hoare	0.7
Coral Samuel	0.7
Hugh Sykes	0.7

† *Known charitable donations in last year as percentage of total wealth (using average of Sunday Times and Business Age wealth estimates where available).*

* *Denotes calculation using other wealth estimate, for example provided by individual concerned.*

There are unfortunately few reliable figures on wealth-holding by other groups in society, but it is clear that the most valuable asset owned by many people is the house or flat in which they live, set against the size of their mortgage. Taking the annual giving of the super-rich as a proportion of their net wealth produces a quotient of 0.29 per cent (0.13 per cent without Soros). That is broadly equivalent to a family in socio-economic group C1, with a mortgaged suburban semi-detached house and some savings (making a net worth of £34,000), donating £99 a year, or just under two pounds a week. Taking Mr Soros out of the calculation would give us equivalent figures for our C1 family of £44 in donations a year, or £3.67 a month. The average (mean) donation per month by people in Britain in 1992 was considerably larger at £11.03 (*Individual Giving and Volunteering in Britain*, Charities Aid Foundation, 1993).

These results, rough and ready as they are, are broadly in line with existing research which shows that the wealthier people are, the smaller the proportion of their wealth given away in donations. (The individuals at the top of our generosity table, of course, are the notable exceptions.) John Posnett's analysis of the Family Expenditure Survey in *Charity Trends* (CAF, 11th edition) includes a breakdown of household giving as a percentage of income. The proportion of net income donated to charity showed a significant decline as income increased, and the most 'generous' households were those in the lowest quintile of net income, and those of skilled and unskilled manual workers.

Looking at society as a whole, therefore, the conclusion is that allowing wealth to concentrate in the hands of the few may result in some spectacular individual gifts, but overall it results in a smaller proportion going to charity. It is also the proportion that is most costly to society to obtain, because it involves the granting of expensive tax reliefs. We have certainly found no evidence for the existence of a charitable 'trickle-down' effect. In fact the evidence that does exist – and it is admittedly sketchy – would seem to reject the notion of a trickle-down effect emphatically.

The trickle-down thesis also assumes that the beneficiaries of charitable giving are the less well-off. This is often not the case. A glance through these pages will suffice to show how a significant amount of the giving emanating from the rich is directed towards the fine arts, to heritage, and to other causes which provide enjoyment to many classes in society but from which the least well-off very rarely benefit.

But wealthy people also benefit from charity in other ways. One very noticeable trend that emerged in research for this book was that although the amounts donated by wealthy landowners were very modest, many of them had established charities for the upkeep and maintenance of their family seat or stately home, enabling them to be open to the public. What with the indirect benefit they derive from such charities, the grants received from heritage bodies, and the substantial payments often pocketed under the agricultural set-aside scheme, it is clear that many rich landowners benefit far more from charity and grant-aid than they ever contribute. If the trickle-down effect in our society is ailing, the 'trickle-up effect' is obviously alive and well.

The book they tried to censor

The publication of this book was not welcomed by many of the wealthy individuals concerned, nor, indeed, by some organisations in the charity world.

In fact, we had not anticipated the strength of feeling it would arouse. In some cases, individuals were worried that inclusion in the book would subject them (ie. their staff or advisers) to a flood of appeals from charities. This is clearly a real concern, and we have tried to emphasise repeatedly that it is inappropriate and generally unfruitful for charities to send unsolicited appeals through the post. We rely on their good sense and restraint.

The desire to resist publication runs much deeper than concern over a few appeal letters, however. The following extract is illustrative of a number of letters we received when draft entries were sent to the individuals concerned for comment and correction: 'We hereby formally request that you remove the intended entry from the Directory immediately. The entry is not correct in content and the publication of this information is strictly contrary to the wishes of the company.' Typically, the statement that a draft was in some respects inaccurate would not be accompanied by corrections or even any attempt to specify inaccuracies.

A few individuals, or rather their solicitors, went further:

'We ask you immediately to confirm that you will refrain from making the entry, failing which our client's rights are reserved to refer the matter to the Charity Commission as to whether your proposals are in the interests of charity.'

'Under no circumstances does Mr x wish to have any entry in your book. It is unsolicited and uncalled for. Mr x's activities are his affair... Please confirm by return that you will withdraw any reference to Mr x in your guide, failing which we have instructions to proceed to ensure that you are unable to publish anything.'

It is perhaps to be expected that rich people should have a panoply of paid advisers to protect them, but why the secrecy? The presumption in favour of privacy and confidentiality in British life is obviously very powerful, even when as here people choose to make donations through the mechanism of a public charitable trust whose activities are on public record. And the disposition of such vast wealth in society must be a matter of legitimate public interest. There is, all the same, something about the personal decision to give or not to give to charity which touches an exposed nerve with certain individuals, and leads them to resist disclosure automatically.

But in dwelling too long on the negative reactions we are in danger of obscuring the fact that the vast majority of individuals cooperated with the publication of the book. Some of the more high-profile figures were clearly delighted, if a little surprised, to encounter journalists who went as far as to check their copy with the people they were writing about:

'Thank you very much for your letter and the courtesy of letting me know what my entry is going to be in your book *The Millionaire Givers*. In fact I have a slight advantage over you as I do have the accounts for the ( ) foundation to February 1993...'

The aim of this book was to make detailed information available for the first time on the role of the wealthy in supporting charity, on the motivations that lie behind their individual actions, and on the establishment and development of foundations for the future. It is hoped that one of the results will be to foster giving among wealthy people, both by encouraging charities to treat them sensitively and by showing wealthy people and their advisers a host of examples of what others have done. In opening the door on what was hitherto a somewhat closed world, we hope the light of day may bring figures into relief, and breathe warmth into Britain's philanthropy.

FAME, FORTUNE AND PHILANTHROPY

The ranks of Britain's rich are a very varied bunch, ranging from pop stars and authors, through entrepreneurs, retailers and industrialists, to politicians and aristocrats. Here we highlight some of the famous, and not-so-famous, who grace the pages of this book.

Pop Stars

In this post-Live Aid era it seems that hardly a day goes by without the launch of another charity record or the announcement of another benefit concert. Legions of pop stars have freely given their talents to promote a multiplicity of good causes, ranging from threatened shipyards and homeless people to disaster and famine relief. This high profile support contrasts with their personal charitable donations, which tend to be less well publicised.

Several of the pop stars in this book have set up grant-making trusts through which they direct some of their gifts. One of the longest established, and perhaps the best known, is Cliff Richard's trust, through which he donated over £120,000 in the last year to various causes, with some preference for children's charities and Christian organisations. More recently he has set up another charitable trust to promote his favourite sport, tennis, for the benefit of the general public. George Michael has supported people with disabilities and children with special needs to the tune of £2 million over the past four years through his Platinum Trust, and has set up the Platinum Overseas Trust to fund research into leukaemia, cancer and AIDS. Elton John is another pop star who is personally committed to the fight against AIDS through a foundation created specifically for this purpose. Recently he auctioned his vast record collection and directed the £182,000 proceeds to the Terrence Higgins Trust. He also gives support to good causes through Watside Charities, a company which controls part of his entertainment interests.

Virtuoso guitarists Eric Clapton and Mark Knopfler each have a grant-making trust as part of their philanthropic activities. Clapton gave £20,500 to Chemical Dependency through his trust in the last year, whilst Knopfler concentrates upon helping children and medical causes. George Harrison named his Material World Charitable Foundation after one of his albums, and in the seventies used it to support a concert tour by the Indian sitar player Ravi Shankar, and to purchase Bhaktivedanta Manor in rural Hertfordshire as the British base for the Krishna Movement. His erstwhile Beatles' colleague Paul McCartney, perhaps the country's richest pop star, proved a rather more elusive donor. We did discover that his personal company MPL Communications supported charities to the tune of £104,000 last year. He has also recently announced a £1m gift to the Liverpool Institute of Performing Arts.

Peter Gabriel and Phil Collins, another pair of former associates, also chose a similar route for some of their gifts. The private companies which control their personal performance interests both made charitable donations in the last year – Peter Gabriel Ltd's amounted to £33,000 and Phil Collins Ltd's to £12,000. The majority of Phil Collins' gifts are made on an anonymous basis, however, and come from his personal account to help needy individuals as well as registered charities.

We have been less successful in tracing charitable donations for many of Britain's other wealthy pop stars. Sting is well-known for his crusade against environmental destruction through the Rainforest Foundation, and has also been involved in promoting musical education amongst underprivileged young people through the Outlandos Trust. We have drawn a blank for past and present members of the Rolling Stones, and could find no charitable trusts registered in the names of Mick Jagger – an avid art collector, Keith Richards, or Bill Wyman. Similarly there appear to be no grant-making trusts registered in the names of Tom Jones, Engelbert Humperdinck, Ringo Starr, Rod Stewart, or Dave Stewart (no relation) – all of whom have featured in the lists of the country's richest individuals over recent years.

Actors and Showbiz

Whilst their names are often up in lights along the streets of the West End, other members of the entertainment industry are also big stars on the charities front. The two who give the largest amounts are the multi-millionaire producers of musicals, Sir Andrew Lloyd Webber and Cameron Mackintosh. Composer and impresario Lloyd Webber has launched his own personal crusade to save part of the nation's cultural heritage, both on canvas – by snapping up a Canaletto for a cool £10 million and endowing it to his charitable art foundations – and in bricks and mortar, by setting up a fund to keep churches open to the public. He also puts some of his earnings back into the acting profession with his £150,000 per year sponsorship of the National Youth Music Theatre. Cameron Mackintosh may be less recognisable to members of the general public, but is renowned in the charities world for the activities of his Mackintosh Foundation which in 1992/93 gave £1.9m to causes associated with the theatre, education, children, homeless people, and AIDS.

Some of the country's most highly regarded actors and film-makers, whilst by no means amongst the richest people in this book, are nevertheless relatively generous supporters of charitable causes and students of their profession. Lord (Richard) Attenborough has a long-established trust through which he gave over £220,000 in the last year, and he has a multitude of connections in the voluntary sector. Sir Anthony Hopkins has recently set up a grant-making trust which had an income of nearly £150,000 last year, through which he focuses support on acting students, and alcoholic and drug rehabilitation projects. Sir John Gielgud made donations of over £20,000 last year to various individuals and organisations through his charitable trust, including some involved with acting and animal welfare. Film and television star John Cleese has donated more than one-quarter of a million pounds over the past five years to a select group of causes, with an emphasis on psychotherapy, birth control, ecology and Tibet.

A number of other rich showbiz personalities are not, however, represented in this book because we were unable to trace any personal charitable trusts connected to them. Lyricist Tim Rice is well-known for his work with the Foundation for Sport and the Arts, the massive grant-maker which is funded by various football pools companies. Actor Michael Caine works with a number of charities, including the NSPCC, and director Michael Winner reportedly wishes his London home to become a museum upon his death.

Authors and Artists

A number of our most famous authors have set up charitable trusts through which to make donations. Catherine Cookson has given a total of £400,000 over the past six years through her trust which was funded by the royalties from the sales of *Bill Bailey's Lot*, one of her books. It is now, however, being wound down because Cookson and her elderly husband were being inundated with too many requests for help. Dame Barbara Cartland, the prolific writer of romantic novels, made gifts of £16,000 through her charitable trust last year to various causes around her Hertfordshire home including the local St John Ambulance. Detective novelist Baroness (P D) James has recently established a trust which has yet to get into its grant-making stride. Amongst its aims are the promotion of education into English language and literature, the furtherance of Christianity, and the preservation of churches. The leading novelist and Labour Party supporter Ken Follett gave £40,000 though his trust in the last year, much of which funded education and research charities.

We were not able to trace any charitable trusts registered in the names of many of our other wealthy writers such as Barbara Taylor Bradford, Terry Pratchett, Jackie Collins, Jack Higgins (also known as Harry Patterson), Dick Francis, or Lord Archer. Away from the literary field, we did uncover a pair of trusts set up by artist David Hockney and photographer Lord Lichfield. Whilst by no means as rich as most members of the aristocracy represented in this book, Patrick Lichfield directs some support through his relatively small charitable trust to causes around his West Midlands home, Shugborough Hall. Although he now lives in the US, David Hockney maintains close links with his hometown of Bradford through his grant-making trust. Over recent years he has donated to it several works of art which have been sold to finance grants. His foundation's largest gift in recent years has been £75,000 to his old school, Bradford Grammar.

Sports Stars

The burgeoning salaries and prize monies available to our leading professional sports stars have created a new breed of multi-millionaire. Some of them make gifts through trusts they have established, often with a preference for medical or children's charities. Golfer Nick Faldo has diverted some of the fruits of his success to good causes via his charitable trust, amounting to £12,000 in the last year. Paul Gascoigne, one of our most famous footballing exports, has also set up a grant-making trust which gave away £1,500 in the last year. Two other former England players, who captained both club and country before moving into football management, are also supporters of charitable causes. Bryan Robson, who recently left his long-time club Manchester United in order to take up the challenge as player-manager at Middlesborough, gave £9,000 from his testimonial to start a scanner appeal in the North West. Kevin Keegan has a charitable trust which does not appear to have made any grants in recent years, but in the past has given £6,000 to fund a minibus for underprivileged children in Newcastle-upon-Tyne, and a similar amount to leukaemia research.

Other rich sports stars proved rather more elusive, and we were unable to uncover any grant-making trusts linked with individuals such as Lennox Lewis, Lester Piggott, Ian Woosnam, Steve Davis, Sandy Lyle, Kenny Dalglish, Willie Carson, David Platt, Gary Lineker, or Frank Bruno. Similarly, Nigel Mansell, perhaps Britain's richest active sportsman, has a reputation as a generous donor on the quiet, but has no trust registered in his name in this country.

We have found trusts associated with a couple of the former stars who have made most of their money since retiring from the sport. Jackie Stewart supports the mechanics who work on Grand Prix circuits through a charitable trust he set up a few years ago. Alan Pascoe, the former athlete who has achieved financial success from sports promotion, gave £25,000 in the last year through his charitable trust, much of which went to various sports-related causes.

Politicians

It is not entirely unsurprising that with a single exception all of the wealthy politicians in this book come from the Conservative benches. Lady Thatcher's charitable trust seems to be funded mainly by gifts from sympathetic business leaders and acolytes such as Sir Donald Gosling and Sir Geoffrey Leigh, both of whom have used their own trusts to contribute money to Thatcher's trust. She also has her non-charitable Thatcher Foundation, which aims to spread her own particular free-market gospel around the world. Former Westminster leader Dame Shirley Porter inherited a substantial part of her father's interests in Tesco. She has also amalgamated the assets of her father's grant-making trust into her own Porter Foundation which is now making grants totalling around £1m per year.

Ex-cabinet member Paul Channon and current overseas development minister Mark Lennox-Boyd are both members of the wealthy Guinness family. Channon has a charitable trust, which last year made donations of £8,000 with a preference for the arts; Lennox-Boyd gave £11,000 from his trust in the year before he wound it up. Tim Sainsbury is a member of one of the country's other richest families, who run the successful supermarket chain. Like many of his close relations he diverts part of his personal fortune to good causes, and last year transferred £34m worth of shares in the family company to charitable trusts. Michael Heseltine is one of the few MPs in the book to have made his own fortune, and directs some of it to charities through his eponymous grant-making trust – in the last year it made gifts totalling £10,000.

A more recent entrant to the world of politics is the incredibly rich global entrepreneur, Sir James Goldsmith, who has recently been elected as a French MEP on the *L'Autre Europe* list. His philanthropic impulses exhibit a strong preference for conservation and the environment, and amount to several million pounds each year.

Asian People

Members of ethnic minority groups are not very well represented in the various published lists of wealthy individuals, although those who do feature are all self-made millionaires. Many have set up grant-making trusts sometimes with a preference for the countries from which their family originates.

Swraj Paul, who created the Caparo Industries steel manufacturing group, is perhaps the best known due to his recent £1 million gift to help London Zoo redevelop its children's section. He made this donation in memory of his daughter Ambika, who died from leukaemia in the late 1960s. When he set up a charitable foundation he also named it after his late daughter. It had an income of nearly £0.25 million in the last year it made donations to unspecified causes of £50,000. Raj Bagri is another individual who is well-known in the City as founder of the Metdist group of companies and heads one of its main trading institutions, the London Metal Exchange. His grant-making foundation has assets of over £1.7 million, and made donations of just over £20,000 in the last year.

Nat Puri has also generated his wealth from the industrial sector, and is now a major mover in the East Midlands through his Nottingham-based Melton Medes engineering to textile business. Amongst the aims of his Puri Foundation is the provision of assistance to those in need, especially citizens of Mullan Pur in India, inhabitants of Nottinghamshire, and former and current employees of his companies. The foundation has also committed itself to meeting the £250,000 cost of a new Hindu temple and community centre in Nottingham, and in the last year made charitable donations of just under £10,000 to unspecified causes. Anwar Pervez made his fortune in the wholesale sector through the north London based Bestway cash-and-carry business. The company directs 2.5% of its pre-tax profits to the Bestway Foundation, which Pervez also founded. In the last year the foundation made grants of £245,000 of which just under half went to organisations operating in this country, including £60,000 to a school in Neasden. The remainder was directed at overseas causes, of which the largest gift was £60,000 to a relief fund for Pakistan.

Two other families in the book have become rich through their global business interests. The Hinduja brothers make the top ten of the *Sunday Times'* rich list with a combined wealth estimated at being greater than £1 billion. Part of this has found its way into the Hinduja Foundation, whose primary objective is to grapple with the tricky question of world development. In the last year its charitable expenditure amounted to £68,000, which included £25,000 to the Prince's Youth Business Trust and £28,000 on a project run in conjunction with the International Society for Krishna Consciousness. The Shivdasani family, headed by matriarch Lakshmi along with her children Azad and Bina, support a range of causes, with an emphasis on education, to the tune of around £475,000 last year through various branches of their Inlaks Foundation.

Royal Family

As well as lending their names to numerous good causes, various members of the royal family also provide financial support through well-established grant-making trusts. Apart from the more public side of her philanthropy – the tradition of distributing Maundy money – the Queen also makes donations through the auspices of the Privy Purse Charitable Trust. Last year these amounted to £208,000 with a strong emphasis on the Church. These gifts are somewhat outshone by those of her eldest son, however, who in the last year contributed nearly £1.5m to a wide variety of causes through the Prince of Wales' Charities and the Duke of Cornwall's Benevolent Fund. His wife proffers support on a slightly more modest scale through the Princess of Wales Charities Trust, which made grants totalling £141,000 concentrated upon medical organisations.

The Princess Royal is well-known for her figurehead role at the Save the Children Fund. Her charitable trust, the Princess Anne's Charities, was responsible for gifts amounting to £105,000 in the last year, half of which went to children's causes. Her younger brother, Prince Andrew, made donations of £13,000 last year through his eponymous trust. But we have thus far been unable to trace any grant-making trusts funded by Prince Edward, Prince Philip, the Queen Mother, Princess Margaret of the Duchess of York.

Women

Even the most cursory glance reveals that the women in this book have obtained their wealth from a wide variety of sources. Apart from those mentioned above, some have made their fortune themselves, whilst others have inherited their partner's or their family's fortunes.

In the world of business, perhaps the best-known female entrepreneur is Anita Roddick, the founder of the Body Shop empire and renowned for her outspoken views on the responsibilities of business. Along with her husband, Gordon, she recently sold £8m worth of shares and promised most to charity. Less famous, but equally successful in their own field, are a number of other businesswomen. Rosemary Bugden helps run her son's Interlink Express delivery company, and was one of its initial backers. She funds arts in Avon and the South West through an eponymous charitable trust, which in the last year made donations of £114,000. Margaret Barbour runs the family firm which makes the famous waxed jackets, and supports health and welfare charities in the North East through the Barbour Trust. Clarice Pears heads the family who control the private William Pears commercial property group, and recently helped set up a grant-making trust in the family's name.

A number of the women have diverted part of an inherited fortune to good causes. Perhaps the most notable is Vivien Duffield, daughter of the late Sir Charles Clore who built up the Sears retail empire. The Clore Foundation and Vivien Duffield Foundation received part of the wealth she was bequeathed, and make several million pounds of donations each year. In recent years they have committed a total of £7 million to the Eureka! children's museum in Halifax, and previously had given £6 million to the Tate Gallery. Other women have been left a fortune upon the death of their husband: charitable trusts set up by Coral Samuel and her late husband Basil Samuel made total donations of £660,000 in the last year to a wide variety of causes; Lady Eileen Joseph's foundation made gifts of £23,000 in the last year; and Lady Sheila Butlin continues her late husband's charitable activities through her involvement with his grant-making trust. Lady Grantchester, daughter of the late John Moores, supports good causes through her Fairway Trust.

Two female members of the very wealthy Guinness family also appear in the book. The Dowager Marchioness of Normanby founded a charitable trust along with her late husband which now holds shares in the Guinness company with a value of nearly £3 million. It made grants of £333,000 in the last year, with a preference for welfare, heritage and medical causes, and organisations in North Yorkshire. Viscountess Boyd's charitable trust holds a smaller bundle of Guinness shares, and gave away £38,000 in the last year, including £20,000 to the Bodleian Library at Oxford University.

Three female members of Britain's aristocratic classes also merit a mention. Lady Willoughby de Eresby gives around £15,000 per year to charities through the Ancaster Trust, supporting a range of causes including those active in and around her family's estates in Lincolnshire and Scotland. Countess Sutherland, whose family reportedly owns over 100,000 in the Highlands of Scotland, has a grant-making trust who primary activity is to help preserve the family home Dunrobin Castle for the benefit of the nation, and which spends around £15,000 annually to this end. Lady Juliet de Chair has established an eponymous charitable trust which made donations of nearly £7,000 in the last year with some emphasis on children's causes and the arts.

GIVERS IN THE REGIONS

Many of the individuals in this book clearly believe in that well-worn saying, 'charity begins at home'. Like everyone else, when the wealthy make donations, there is often a strong preference for causes operating in and around the areas they know best – their home, or their workplace, or the areas otherwise responsible for their wealth. This parochial instinct offers clear possibilities for the tuned in fundraiser. With this in mind, we have rounded up the individuals and foundations who focus their efforts in the regions across the country.

North West

The best known philanthropists in the North West are undoubtedly the Moores family of Littlewoods pools fame. This Merseyside-based dynasty direct a major chunk of their charitable funds to causes in and around Liverpool. Lord Leverhulme is another big supporter of charities in the area, thanks to his family's soap-based fortune. Super-rich pop star Paul McCartney recently gave £1m to the Liverpool Institute for Performing Arts. Former retailer Albert Gubay has reportedly promised half of his £250m fortune to the Church in Liverpool when he dies. Down the road in Manchester, John Zochonis, whose cleaning products company makes Imperial Leather, is a major supporter of the voluntary sector through a trust which holds nearly £23m-worth of shares in the firm. In nearby Oldham, Norman Stoller, chair of the Seton Healthcare group, funds causes in and around Manchester to the tune of over £100,000. The Warburton family made donations of £130,000 last year through their company to organisations around Bolton. Elsewhere in the region, donors to local causes include: the Pilkington family around St Helens, the Earl of Derby, the Marquess of Cholmondeley and family, the Duke of Westminster, Peter Emerson Jones, and Peter Hinchcliffe.

North East

The wealthy donors active in the North East can be basically divided into two groups: those in and around Leeds and Bradford, and those whose allegiances lie further up the coast in Tyneside. The first group includes individuals such as former furniture-maker George Moore, property millionaire Tony Clegg, the Shepherd construction family, Arnold Ziff and family, car-seller Tony Bramall, former paint entrepreneur Leslie Silver. Aristocrats Lord Halifax and Lord Harewood make gifts on a slightly smaller scale to causes in the region, and artist David Hockney maintains links to his hometown of Bradford, despite living in the US, by supporting charities through his foundation. Slightly further afield, Hugh Sykes is a major donor in and around Sheffield, and the Dowager

Marchioness of Normanby devotes considerable support to causes close to her Whitby home.

Up in Tyne & Wear, one notable benefactor is the Duke of Northumberland, whose family have major landholdings around Alnwick Castle, and who has recently set up a Percy Family Fund under the auspices of the Tyne & Wear Foundation. Others include the Fenwick family who run the department stores of the same name, and Margaret Barbour who makes the famous waxed-jackets. Car-seller Peter Vardy's company is giving £1m to fund a City Technology College in Gateshead. Catherine Cookson has also been a major donor around the Tyne through a trust funded by royalties from one of her books, but has wound the trust down apparently because she could no longer deal with all the requests for money. In the past Kevin Keegan, former footballer but now manager at Newcastle United FC, has given money to buy a minibus for underprivileged children in the town.

West Midlands

The towns and cities of the West Midlands are the focus of the efforts of a number of rich individuals. These include airline boss Michael Bishop, who combines support for the opera with funding for inner city projects; the Bamford family whose firm makes JCBs and restricts its grants to causes close to its base in Rocester, Staffordshire; vacuum cleaner manufacturer Alan Brazier; the carpet-making Brinton family; the Hereford-based cider-making Bulmer family; investor Lindsay Bury who gives to organisations in Shropshire; and Paul Judge who gives in the Worcestershire area. On the titled front, benefactors range from Lord Aylesford who focuses upon Coventry and Warwickshire, through the Earl of Bradford who concentrates on Shropshire charities, and on a smaller scale photographer Lord Lichfield. When West Midlands-based retailer James Beattie died in 1988 he bequeathed around £1m to his charitable trust, which his family will use to support Wolverhampton charities. Two families maintain strong philanthropic links with the West Midlands despite being mainly based elsewhere in recent years – the newspaper and property Iliffe family, and constructor John Douglas (whose father Sir Robert still lives and donates in Staffordshire).

East Midlands

Over in the East Midlands there are a number of entrepreneurs who restrict the bulk of their support in the areas close to their home and/or their place of work, and their activities are supplemented by a scattering of aristocratic givers. In Northamptonshire we have Kenneth Horne who has used part of his paper-making fortune to endow the Horne Foundation with £6m. Industrialist Sir Humphrey Cripps, and his family, are involved with the long-established Cripps Foundation which annually makes over £1m of donations, many of which are directed to Northampton causes. The timber-selling Travis family have a more recent trust which already holds £2m assets and gave £88,000 to local charities. Some money is also donated to Northamptonshire by members of the MacDonald-Buchanan whisky family who live in the county. The Marquess of Northampton shows some preference for making donations through his Compton Charitable Trust to causes operating around his Castle Ashby stately home.

In Lincolnshire notable givers include the poultry producing Padley family, Lady Willoughby de Eresby (through her Ancaster Trust), and the Nickerson family whose activities are funded by various bequests of the late 'Partridge Joe' Nickerson who made his fortune from seeds. The food fortune of David Samworth and his family finances their charitable activities in Nottinghamshire, and industrialist Nat Puri supports organisations in the county through his foundation which has promised £250,000 to fund a new Hindu temple in Nottingham. Various members of the chocolate-making Thornton family, most prominently Michael and John, make donations to organisations in Derbyshire, as does former newspaper owner Lionel Pickering – also a major backer of Derby County FC.

Wales and the South West

Wales and the South West appear rather more sparsely populated by rich donors, although there are several worthy of note. Perhaps the biggest grant-makers in the South West are the shoe-making Clark family, who concentrate much of the efforts around the town of Street in Somerset where their company is based. Businesswoman Rosemary Bugden devotes considerable support to the arts around Bristol and Bath, and greetings-card mogul Andrew Brownsword has recently set up a charitable trust to support medical and children's organisations in the Avon area. Other givers to causes in the South West include Guinness family member Viscountess Boyd, Lord Margadale in Wiltshire, the Marquess of Salisbury around his estates in Dorset, and the Duke of Beaufort in Avon. Banker Sir Julian Hodge is one of few wealthy philanthropists to direct substantial amounts to causes in Wales, which receive grants of more than £1m each year from him.

Scotland

Partly because of the difficulties in obtaining information about charitable trusts registered with the Inland Revenue in Scotland, we have been able to unearth only a relatively small number of wealthy donors active north of the border. Some of these are aristocrats: Lady Willoughby de Eresby (who supports charities in Scotland as well as those in Lincolnshire); the Duke of Atholl; Lord Mansfield; and Lord Margadale. Other philanthropists who direct some support to Scottish causes are impresario Cameron Mackintosh, the MacDonald-Buchanan family, and the Thomson printing family.

South East

Given the overall concentration of wealth in the hands of those living in the South East, it is not totally unsurprising that a large number of rich individuals show a preference for the region. In East Anglia, donors include Lord Cholmondeley and his family, Sir Nicholas Bacon, Timothy Colman, and Viscount Coke, and in Suffolk a major philanthropist is property millionaire William Gredley. Down on the south coast, causes in Hampshire are supported by former retailer Alan Prince and heating industrialist Philip Baxendale.

Slightly to the east, the nautical fortune of Derek Fawcett benefits causes around Portsmouth. Donors in Sussex include various members of the O'Hea ventilation equipment family, the Duke of Norfolk (based at Arundel Castle), and Lord Egremont.

Closer to the capital, Martyn Arbib is one of Oxfordshire's major philanthropists from his base at Henley-on-Thames, and has given £4m to the local rowing museum. Politician and publisher Michael Heseltine also supports charities around his Oxford home. Berkshire is the focus for the charitable efforts of the Frizzell insurance family and the Iliffe newspaper and property family (who also support causes in the West Midlands). Barbara Cartland, frozen food and wine seller John Apthorp and the Marquess of Salisbury give to organisations in Hertfordshire; the Marquess of Tavistock supports causes near Woburn Abbey; and members of the Whitbread brewing family give to causes in Bedfordshire. Amongst those who have a preference for causes in London are Earl Cadogan and his family, who support charities in the Chelsea area; Richard Attenborough; the Wates building family; Abe Jaffe, though his Currie Motors retail chain; and the Dukes of Westminster and Northumberland through family charitable trusts.

Supporters of overseas projects

In a rather refreshing contrast to the parochial preferences of the majority, a number of the wealthy people in this book devote much of their support to organisations active overseas or to sponsor students from other countries to study in Britain, although often there is some personal or business connection. These include Asian entrepreneurs such as the Hinduja brothers, wholesaler Anwar Pervez, the Shivdasani family, Nat Puri, and Raj Bagri. Other donors to Third World causes include David Sainsbury, Paul Hamlyn, Joel Joffe, and Richard Attenborough. Some focus donations on particular areas: Africa for Tiny Rowland; Hong Kong for the Keswick family; Barbados for Peter Moores; Tibet for John Cleese; and the Arab states for Wafic Said. George Soros also helps this redistribution of wealth by diverting the bulk of his massive largesse to causes in Eastern Europe.

FUNDRAISING FROM THE RICH

by Redmond Mullin

The rich are individuals

There are many people in the UK, with high incomes, who can give thousands of pounds away. Collectively, they can put £100,000, £250,000 or more into a charitable enterprise. Some of them do. I have seen an individual give £50,000 from salary over four years. I categorise these people as 'prosperous' not 'rich'. So what does 'rich' mean here?

My glib definition is this: someone who can sign a cheque for £100,000 (or more) without flinching or getting someone else's permission. That helps to fix our focus and criteria for selection. Its usefulness is limited, because 'rich' does not designate a single type. There is a large variety of people who are rich. The rich are individuals.

Nor is it helpful to position the rich – as many not-for-profit bodies do – simply as the highest segment of the broader category: 'Individuals'. Most trusts or foundations are vehicles used by rich individuals or families for the voluntary redistribution of their wealth. These same individuals and families may determine not only their private allocations of funds, but also the allocations from their trusts or foundations and companies. Their total funding for a single cause can sometimes come from a combination of these sources.

Rich people can be very independently individual; but there are some general points which may help understanding with approaches at these levels. Much 'ancient' wealth was accumulated only since the eighteenth century. Much 'established' wealth was created over the last 100 to 150 years. Great wealth has been accumulated by some families and individuals over the past few decades. This affects attitudes and behaviour.

Take two hugely rich, ennobled families. One is openly philanthropic, in public leadership and giving; the other, almost as rich, is niggardly and infrequent in its disbursements, the head of the family saying that he holds their property in trust for the children. This raises the problem of wealth that is largely held in land, or, for some of the newly rich, wealth that is in corporate paper.

Such dynastic families as the Rothschilds, the Barings, and the Kleinworts have very different traditions and capabilities from most of the senior people and institutions that surround them in the City. Famous philanthropists like Clore, Getty, Hamlyn, Laing, Sainsbury, Weston and Wolfson (or the equally famous philanthropists who are always 'anon') have different interests. They behave differently from each other (although they can co-operate). As new generations have arrived, their family priorities have changed. The ways they make their decisions vary enormously.

There have, over the past ten years, been conspicuous new entrants as rich UK philanthropists, such as Paul Judge, the Beckwiths and many donors of sums above £0.5m, whose names would mean nothing to most readers of this book, many of whom have featured in none of the lists of donors fundraisers use.

Various motives may move rich people to philanthropy. Of course vanity, self-aggrandisement, a bid for advantage or honours are included. This is sometimes explicit, sometimes implied, but it would be stupid to believe that these were the exclusive reasons why rich people gave funds and personal support to charitable causes. It would also insult their idealism, altruism and judgement. These are often people with a sense of public responsibility, whether this was an attitude fostered by a family or induced by reflection. The rich are individuals. Many of them care about people and issues and enjoy creativity and performance; many may want to change or improve the situations they observe, or might be persuaded to do so. Their motives may mix self-interest with altruism.

Are there problems then? I think so. Awkwardness is felt by some charity people as they consider approaching the rich. Scott Fitz Gerald said 'The rich are different'. They are in many ways. They may be free from commonplace anxieties. They can exert exceptional authority and power. They may acquire exceptional sophistication. They may achieve none of these. They may seem alien and daunting. They can be arrogant. They can also be vulnerable, insecure, uncouth, unsophisticated, in need of reassurance and recognition, deeply sensitive and idealistic, caring and generous. It is dangerous and unproductive to carry ill-informed prejudices about any main prospective source for fundraising, particularly perhaps the rich.

There are deeper concerns, both for rich people themselves and for those who want voluntary funds from them. There was discussion in the ancient world – from Aristotle, Cicero and Seneca amongst others – about the civic and private responsibilities of wealth. Except with Seneca, general conclusions tended to be that the poor, except of one's own class, were a vile problem; the poor of one's own class merited aid. There were requirements for the rich on occasion to make conspicuous dispositions of wealth (for public functions and buildings, even for the fleet); but that these should not extend to vulgar excess. Seneca had a kindlier, more fraternal attitude to the poor. A more radical pre-Christian view was that wealth was ridiculous, an evil (from Diogenes) necessarily ill-gained (from Seneca).

Jewish tradition has from earliest times argued that the rich and communities that are prosperous, have earnest responsibilities to counter indigence, amongst gentiles as well as Jews. Evidence for the strength of this tradition is conspicuous in the philanthropy of rich Jewish individuals and families in the UK, giving within their own communities, giving to Israel and giving to non-Jewish causes of all kinds – from learning and the arts to welfare. Christian tradition continued the argument for generosity and responsibility in the handling and distribution of wealth, but added a view that there were intrinsic merits in poverty. It could be argued (by the British Pelagians as well as by more orthodox teachers) that wealth was originally, necessarily ill-gained – echoing some pagan teachings. Post-enlightenment socialisms have endorsed these negative attitudes. Contemporary liberation theology has argued from justice for a redistribution of wealth towards the poor.

So there have been cultural stimulants and strictures, particularly aimed at the rich, on the disposition of their wealth. The reciprocal approaches from those in society who have wanted redistributions of wealth for themselves or on account of their causes have ranged from the statutory imposition of taxes; through persuasions to voluntary philanthropy; to the dogmatic, where the rich are regarded with suspicion and hostility, their wealth requiring sequestration. As I have suggested, such prejudices have been nurtured over ages. I have omitted envy, not knowing how to treat it.

The relevance of this to fundraising is that, in addition to the social inhibitions some people in charities may feel in relation to the rich, there may also be attitudes which are hostile towards them. There can be arrogance in petitioners as well as in providers of funds. My favourite example of this, from a report I wrote for the Gulbenkian Foundation, is an arts body describing the fundraising approach as 'the sting'. This is insulting as well as unproductive.

That brings me to the nub of this introduction, which is about raising funds from rich people. The reason it has taken some paragraphs to get here is that there are real as well as imagined issues involved and both have to be faced. At this point, I assume that you sincerely want to reach the rich. Hence my first point: they are individuals, with diverse means, interests, prejudices, motives, and networks for contacts. Therefore, you need to start with good research to find out everything you can about them, to see if there are any presumptive reasons why they might pay attention to your cause and whether you have any people who might carry you and your arguments to them. Like everybody else, some rich people are or would like to be in networks; others are not and would not. This will help determine whether and how you approach them. The same research should show the variety of ways they might support you – as individuals, but also maybe as trust or corporate decision makers, or even as your best fundraising advocates with their peers.

How can rich people be best approached? I have already said that they are individuals. Are there any useful generalisations to be made? As with the rest of us there are, but they stem from the particular. For example:

● One of the established rich is invited to Buckingham Palace for a major fundraising function. The case is made. He sends £1m the next day.
● A newly-rich individual, identified by research, is at a like function. He is then involved in close discussions on what he could achieve for the cause. He gives several million pounds.
● At a 10 Downing Street reception two committee members approach their chairman. He is committed to £75,000. They say that they are each willing to give £150,000, but will not give more than their chairman. He commits £150,000.
● Recently, someone unlisted nationally decides he must give £500,000 as chairman of a regional appeal. He has never given more than £25,000, but he helped invent the cause. Over dinner, he tells someone else, committed to £100,000, what he is doing. The guest raises his commitment to £500,000. Two others follow. This is more than any of them has done before.
● Someone else you have not heard of has recently given several million pounds to a new venture, because the cause became one he found compelling and its initial promoters had supported it generously.
● As one outcome of a cold mailing, a famous artist sends £100,000 then another £100,000, because he feels he has made more than he needs out of two recent works. He had not formerly given at these levels. No such worthy cause had ever previously asked for such a sum from him.
● One of the great women philanthropists gives £1m on condition that the charity find nine more donations at the same level. They succeed. On another occasion, she puts down £0.5m to avoid taking active part in an appeal and says the people around the table can do likewise to deliver the result needed.
● The same principles apply in village or parish. Where I live there is a great philanthropic leader who has created facilities for everyone by putting up his own funds, challenging people to match and others to exceed him. Because of his commitment, he succeeds.

So some matters have been made clear. There must be the people who can deliver the funds, identified through research or local knowledge. There must be a cause which is convincing and exciting. There is a huge advantage if there are rich, financially committed people prepared to approach their peers to support the cause. Failing this, there must be an approach without such advocates designed with understanding of the prospect's interests, prejudices and means – delivered as personally as can be achieved.

In this, it is crucial that there should be specific indications of the sum (or range of sums) sought and of what these could achieve. At a great function, one of the famous philanthropists approaches a charity's director, takes the cigar out of his mouth, and asks 'What do you want, then?'. 'Oh, sir, only the pleasure of your company, sir'. Philanthropist puts cigar back in mouth. On returning to his office, he removes it again, says, 'Bloody fool didn't ask me for anything. Send him £1,000'. The charity could well have received £100,000 if they had asked, said what they wanted and explained why.

There is a point beyond all of this. As an appeal is building, I will try to engage financially committed rich people in its leadership. The structures and procedures will invite some of these to remain involved as leaders and friends – informed allies – after the appeal has ended, for example through membership of a development foundation or board. In a few instances, one of the major backers who has provided start-up funds may become part of the team which plots and instigates the appeal.

All of this implies that the charity has staff and friends who can be part of its first approach to the rich prospect and who may continue in touch with them, keeping their interest and involvement, after the first support has been achieved. Some charities have staff and departments dedicated to fostering and sustaining these relationships. Different rich patrons will want different kinds of satisfaction and contact if they want such longer-term involvement: to observe the application of their funds; to be fellows at the High Table; to be kept informed by experts about the field concerned; to have someone they like and know with whom they can talk. This does mean that the charity should be equipped for such relationships, not that it should create them artificially. Such benefactors usually want people who know what they are talking about, who will not (or perhaps will) waste their time, and with whom they are comfortable. This does not entail the engineering of contrived social match-making. It may mean that committed charity staff must gain confidence, stop worrying and learn to work with the rich. But that (like my opening description of the rich) may also be too glib.

● *Redmond Mullin* *has worked in research at Masius, in advertising at J Walter Thompson, and in fundraising with Wells. He now runs his own fundraising consultancy and has published, broadcast and taught extensively. He was founder of the Institute of Charity Fundraising Managers and formerly a director of the Charities Aid Foundation. He is a non-executive director of the London Philharmonic Orchestra, executive director of the Charlemagne Institute and chairs the Advisory Committee for the Open University Voluntary Sector Management Programme. His book Foundations for Fundraising is shortly to be published by ICSA Publishing.*

RULES OF ENTRY

This directory provides information on those members of the richest class in society who make donations to charity or are otherwise active in the charitable world. To merit an entry, therefore, the individual or family has to be both very rich *and* charitable. No-one should infer criticism of those well-known millionaires who are not included in the book, however: donations they have made might simply not have come to our attention.

At the start of each entry, there is a list of summary information in the following order:

● Known charitable donations in last year

The figure stated at the top of each entry is for known charitable donations made by the family/individual concerned in the last year, and includes donations from three main sources:

- Gifts made directly from personal reserves.
- Gifts made via closely-linked grant-making trusts or foundations that were set up by the individual/family concerned and whose income comes directly from the individual/family or stems from an original endowment made by the individual concerned or a member of their immediate family, and over the disbursement of which they still hold a significant degree of discretion.
- Gifts made via closely-linked companies, in which the individual/family concerned holds half or more of the equity.

Our figures are therefore drawn mainly from information that is in the public domain, including Charity Commission files on grant-making trusts, accounts held at Companies' House, charity reports and accounts, various directories and publications, and other media coverage. The donations figure does not always include donations made on a private and confidential basis, or through Gift Aid, covenants, or CAF charity accounts, unless we were directly informed about them by the individual/family concerned. The figure also attempts to include only donations made directly to the charitable end-user: it does not normally include, for example, endowments made to foundations for the purposes of generating future income for donating.

Readers familiar with the legal basis of charitable trusts will note that in some cases we have included in the donations figure grants made from a personal charitable trust, despite the fact that the philanthropist is technically no longer the owner of the money held in trust. In nearly all such cases, however, the donor retains *de facto* control of the money and it is noteworthy that of all the philanthropists to whom we wrote to confirm the information in their entry, only one claimed otherwise. The complex patterns of wealth-holding in our society prompted by tax and company law mean that when we speak of someone being rich, or being a philanthropist, we are actually talking about three distinct but overlapping concepts: ownership of wealth, control of wealth, and benefit from wealth.

●

This indicates entries containing information on grant-making trusts or other sources of funds which have not previously been listed in existing publications.

● Preferences

These give an idea of the types of cause supported, based on past donations made by the individual/family, but should not necessarily be taken as a firm indication of future support.

● Wealth

Our wealth estimates are based on published lists and other reported estimates, taking into account any figures provided by the individuals or families concerned. These data were classified according to the following wealth bands:

less than £20m	£75m-£100m
£20m-£35m	£100m-£250m
£35m-£50m	£250m-£500m
£50m-£75m	over £500m

● Trust links

This lists the grant-making trusts or foundations, if any, through which the individual/family concerned make donations.

● Company links

This lists the main companies with which the individual/family concerned are involved, although it does not necessarily indicate that they are major shareholders in that company or control its charitable donations budget, if any.

● Contact

The contact given in each entry is usually either the address for closely-linked grant-making trusts, or companies with which the individual/family are closely involved.

Please note that unsolicited applications for funding often lead to annoyance and are rarely productive. This book should not be used as a mailing list. Inappropriate applications waste money and time and may prejudice future chances of success. Please read Redmond Mullin's chapter on how to approach wealthy donors.

References and sources

Charity Commission computer database and files; *Directory of Grant-Making Trusts*; *Directory of Charity Trustees*; *A Guide to the Major Trusts* Vols. 1 & 2; *The Major Companies Guide*; *A Guide to Company Giving*; *The London Grants Guide*; *The West Midlands Grants Guide*; *The Educational Grants Directory*; *Hendersons Top 2000 Charities*; various charity annual reports and accounts. *Trust Monitor*, *Third Sector*, *Charity* magazine; *Business Age* magazine; *Sunday Times*, *Esquire* magazine; *Economist*; newspaper and media reports.

Who's Who; *Debrett's People of Today*; *Who's Who in the City*; *Who's Who in Industry*; *Who's Who in Scotland*; *Asian's Who's Who International*; *Directory of Directors*; *Birmingham Post & Mail Year Book and Who's Who*; *Nigel Dempster's Address Book*; *Best of British Men*; *Best of British Women*.

Companies House database and files; *FAME (Financial Analysis Made Easy)* Jordans Database of Accounts of Major Public & Private British Companies; *Management Today* magazine; various company annual accounts.

THE MILLIONAIRE GIVERS

GEORGE SOROS

about £100 million

PREFERENCE: Central and Eastern Europe, former Soviet Union, civil rights

AGE: 63

WEALTH: over £500m

TRUST LINKS: Open Society Fund, Soros Foundations

COMPANY LINKS: Soros Fund Management

At the beginning of 1994, George Soros remarked to a *Guardian* journalist that he was not happy with the way his charitable giving had been going. Had they been present, the massed ranks of causes in Eastern Europe and around the world that were benefiting from his largesse would have started to sweat. Was it possible that the world's greatest living philanthropist, the biggest thing to hit Eastern Europe since communism, was having a rethink? They needn't have worried. 'Actually, I'm not spending as much as I would like to,' he said. When the interviewer asked him how much that was, he replied: 'One half of my income'.

That income was estimated by *Financial World* magazine in 1993 at $1.1 billion, exceeding the profits of McDonalds or the GDP of over 40 different countries. The money comes from speculation, or to be precise, the management of hedge funds trading in global currency and stock markets. And Soros is the most successful speculator of all time. His Netherlands Antilles-based Quantum Fund has frequently enjoyed 50 per cent growth *in one year*, and the combined value of the funds he manages is now over $9 billion. Spectacular coups, like the $1 billion Quantum made by taking a massive short position on sterling before it fell out of the Exchange Rate Mechanism in 1992, have made the Hungarian emigré a household name. But for his competitors in the financial world, the really annoying thing about Soros is that he now spends less than a day a week on the job.

The rest of his time is devoted to spending the money he makes in the West on the development of civil societies in the East. A network of some 21 Soros foundations now spans the countries of the former Soviet bloc, pumping money into educational programmes, scholarships and fellowships, as well as initiatives in the fields of culture, civil rights, health and the environment. A Central European University has been established, based in Prague and Budapest. Soros hops from one capital to the next, dining with a President in one, inspecting a project in another, talking with groups of academics and students in a third; sometimes doing all three in one afternoon before jetting off again.

None of this, however, Soros sees as charity. He told another reporter from the *Observer.* 'The truth is that I am not a humanitarian, and that I detest foundations in the conventional sense. My motive has never been charity. You could even say it was self-interest. I wanted to further those societies where people like me could live in peace.'

'People like me' in this case clearly does not refer to the hugely wealthy but to ethnic minorities, immigrants or displaced people, or perhaps mavericks generally. A Jewish boy in Nazi-occupied Hungary, Soros had been given false identity papers by his astute father, and packed off to live with gentiles. After the war, he emigrated to Britain, and then to the US. Half a century later, Soros' triumphant return to his native Hungary and other Eastern European countries has repeatedly come up against a resurgent anti-Semitism and nationalist paranoia. In Hungary he was reviled in an article in a party newspaper headed 'Termites are devouring our nation'; in Serb Belgrade his foundation narrowly escaped being banned from carrying out humanitarian work on account of his support for the independent press.

Soros referred to his status as 'a potential victim of the Holocaust' to explain his widely publicised $50 million donation to aid agencies working in war-torn Bosnia. It was a highly uncharacteristic act, however. Aid in the conventional sense, in the emergency relief and sticking-plaster sense, is not on the Soros agenda. As Bill McAllister, the American who coordinated much of Soros' work in Eastern Europe, puts it: 'If you ask for money for the starving, he'd say no.'

The Soros project is to build the human and institutional structures to sustain pluralist liberal democracies in the former Soviet bloc and elsewhere in the world, to foster the 'open society'. The phrase is borrowed from the late Karl Popper, the philosopher under whose influence the young Soros came when he arrived at the London School of Economics in 1947, and to whom Soros' thinking acknowledges a great debt. The first **Open Society Fund** was established in the US in 1979 and made its initial grants to support civil rights groups and scholarships for black students at Capetown University.

The Open Society Fund in New York continues to co-ordinate much of Soros' philanthropic empire, particularly at those times and places when it has been prudent to keep a low profile. Aryeh Neier, a former director of Human Rights Watch, was appointed president in 1993. The vast

---

THE SOROS FILE
Giving since 1992

$50 million	Aid to Bosnia
$25 million	Aid for Macedonia
$100 million	Scientific research in Russia
$230 million *	Central European University
$10 million	Open Society Institute
$70 million *	Sustain network of Soros Foundations in Eastern Europe
$10 million	Open Society Foundation, South Africa
$6 million	Drug Policy Foundation (US)

*Spread over a number of years

majority of programmes are co-ordinated by the separate foundations in each country, however. Generally, they provide support for Central and Eastern European projects and individuals, only making grants to non-indigenous organisations where Central and Eastern Europeans are direct beneficiaries. A Soros foundation directory and information booklet is available from the address below.

Yet the scope, as well as the scale, of Soros' giving is probably wider than has previously been realised, as recent donations in the US and to South Africa testify. As yet, little seems to be going to the UK, his philosophical birthplace and sometime home, although much of the Bosnian aid was channelled through UK agencies. Soros' secretary in London keeps a low profile.

One thing is for certain. George Soros is not the man to approach for £70 for a new pool table for the youth club. Back in the days before he was a billionaire and Eastern Europe was still very much a 'closed' society, he met a woman running an underground network for dissidents. When he asked her how much she needed, she muttered something about $10,000 being a great help. 'Annette,' he is supposed to have replied, 'you must think larger'.

The question mark that remains over the future scale of Soros' philanthropy relates not to his willingness to give, but to his continued capacity to give. The size of Soros' giving is tied to the size of his income, and that income is, to say the least, risky. In addition, government ministries and central banks throughout the Western world have been devoting a lot of time to working out how the activities of Soros and other hedge fund operators can be regulated, to limit the huge, heavily-geared speculative flows that are currently destabilising world

markets. When the bankers talk of a global financial apocalypse, it is only half in jest.

A recent article in *Trust Monitor* commented on the billionaire giver: 'His foundations are not a gift to the past, nor expiation for worldly greed, but the means by which he, George Soros, can wield an influence in the world that he could not hope to match just by making money'. Ironically, the political consequences of Soros' financial activities – sabotaging European monetary union, for one – may even outlast his gargantuan attempts to keep the velvet revolutions from being stained with the blood and bile of nationalism.

Contact: Open Society Fund,
888 Seventh Avenue, New York,
NY 10106, USA.
Tel: 00 1 212 757 2323.

DAVID SAINSBURY

£11.1 million

PREFERENCE: technical education, management development, plant science, health care, Third World, disadvantaged children

AGE: 54

WEALTH: over £500m

TRUST LINKS: Gatsby Charitable Foundation

COMPANY LINKS: J Sainsbury

When the Sainsbury riches filtered down the generations, David Sainsbury, an only son, ended up with a pot several times the size of his cousins (qv) who had to share theirs out between them. He currently holds over a sixth of the share capital of J Sainsbury plc, the company he now chairs, which makes him on paper easily a billionaire. So long as Sainsbury keeps fighting off those discount retailers, his wealth can only be described as fabulous. Much the same could be said about the magnificent **Gatsby Charitable Foundation**, the charity David Sainsbury set up in the sixties and named after his favourite novel, and which now holds over £0.4 billion in Sainsbury shares.

Sainsbury himself makes an unlikely character for a Scott Fitzgerald novel. The finance director at Sainsbury's for some 20 years while his cousin John was in the chair, he is methodical, unostentatious, and driven by a sense of duty to his family and to society. The only trait he does share with the great Gatsby is a strong dislike of publicity or exposure, unless it is on his own terms.

Rare among givers, he has approached the task of supporting charity with the same energy and professionalism that he brings to his business. The foundation has concentrated its support in specific, often unglamorous, fields and appointed a range of expert advisers and consultants to guide its programmes. The principal adviser is Dr John Ashworth of the London School of Economics, a biologist, businessman and teacher who was formerly chief scientist at the Central Policy Review Staff, *the* government think-tank. Ashworth's experience provides a key to David Sainsbury's interests at the foundation, and to the influence he clearly hopes it will have.

Headline grants from Gatsby in recent years have included some £4 million for a chair in marketing and the centre for business strategy at the London Business School (Sainsbury chairs the school's governing body), ongoing support for the Sainsbury Centre for Mental Health in London and a monstrous £14 million for the establishment of the Sainsbury Laboratory for Plant Science at the John Innes Centre in Norwich. This latter grant will enable basic research to be undertaken which may lead to the development of disease-resistant crops, 'which may therefore need no expensive and possibly harmful chemical protection'. The foundation has also funded agricultural research in Africa. Notably, the official custodians of Gatsby's riches number just two trustees: the Sainsbury family solicitor, Miss J S Portrait, and Christopher Stone, a director of the company Diatech Ltd.

In 1992/93 grants from Gatsby totalled £11.1 million. In addition to the causes noted above, donations were made under the headings of disadvantaged children, health care and service delivery, Third World development, and technical education, with the latter including a grant of £3.4 million to the Royal Academy of Engineering for a programme 'to encourage very able students to study technological subjects and to aspire to leadership positions in engineering industry'. There is a technocratic feel to much of the work supported by Gatsby, and an emphasis on education and training in all its fields of support.

Sainsbury stands out from most of the figures in this book in that he has clearly thought deeply about the role of business in society, about the creation of opportunity and of wealth, and about the contribution government could make to both. Until 1987 he had a venture capital fund which provided risk capital for entrepreneurs with high technology ideas, and he is the author of two books, the last entitled *Wealth Creation and Jobs*. Sainsbury knows only too well the choices that businesspeople make when jobs are seen to conflict with profitability: he recently agreed the shedding of over

600 staff at Sainsbury offices through a programme of voluntary redundancies.

The focus of Sainsbury's political hopes for most of the eighties was the SDP, and in particular David Owen. Sainsbury was an SDP member from the start and reputedly bankrolled Owen's party for up to £1 million (although not, of course, through the Gatsby Charitable Foundation). Since the SDP's demise he has supported the establishment of the Social Market Foundation, a think-tank dedicated to the promotion of an Owenite agenda, but has also attempted to spread his political influence more widely. Gatsby's work has led to him being spoken of approvingly by Tory wets: at the launch of the Sainsbury Mental Health Initiative awards in October 1994 health secretary Virginia Bottomley paid particular tribute to 'the energy and dedication of David Sainsbury'.

Meanwhile, Gatsby is growing in power as each year passes. Not content with having created the largest privately-funded foundation of his generation, Sainsbury pumps in more assets on a regular basis: £4 million in 1991, and a breathtaking £200 million in Sainsbury shares in early 1993. David Sainsbury knows that the next five or so years may prove the most important of his life, and he is going in prepared. Finally holding the reins of the family company, he will be spending his spare time trying to create an industrial strategy for Britain.

Contact: The Administrator, Gatsby Charitable Foundation, 9 Red Lion Court, London EC4A 3EB. Tel: 0171 410 0330.

SAINSBURY brothers

£10.4 million

PREFERENCE: arts, environment, medicine, social welfare
WEALTH: over £500m
TRUST LINKS: Linbury Trust, Headley Trust, Monument Trust
COMPANY LINKS: J Sainsbury

The Prince of Wales has a lot to thank the Sainsbury brothers for. When he complained about the 'monstrous carbuncle' designed to form the new National Gallery extension, they financed the construction of something a little more neo-classical to the tune of over £30 million. In fact, there is much about Lord (John) Sainsbury, Tim Sainsbury and Simon Sainsbury that recalls the philanthropy of an earlier age: patronage of the arts, of the national heritage and (in the case of Tim) support for the spread of Christianity.

Yet the Sainsburys have also supported projects that are at the forefront of social innovation and address new social needs. And although they have collaborated on the National Gallery extension and some other charitable ventures, each of the brothers also exhibits individual interests and concerns in the work he supports.

Lord Sainsbury, at 67 the eldest of the three, was a dynamic chair of J Sainsbury plc for 23 years until 1992 when he was succeeded by his cousin David (qv). Married to the former ballerina Anya Linden, it is the arts that in recent years has dominated the donations made through his **Linbury Trust** (Lin(den-Sains)bury – get it?). The Royal Opera House Covent Garden, which Lord Sainsbury chaired until 1991, and the Royal Ballet School, where he has been a governor, have both benefited handsomely, as has Worcester College, Oxford, his *alma mater*.

In 1992/93 donations actually made by the Linbury Trust came to £2.2 million, although the total of grants *approved* added up to £7.9 million. Of this some £4 million was ear-marked for education, apparently demonstrating something of a shift in priorities, but it is not clear how much of this may have gone to Worcester College. In addition to the arts and education, sizeable amounts were also given to environmental and medical organisations and those working with disadvantaged children, older people and drug abusers. Substantial support was also given for 'social work and research' – note that the term 'social work' is here employed very broadly. A further new development in 1992 was the establishment of a trust by Lord Sainsbury's son Julian. The **J J Charitable Trust** had yet to pay out any money by the end of the financial year, but had approved one grant to the value of £115,000, possibly destined for an arts body in the US.

The Rt Hon Timothy Sainsbury MP was a director at the family firm until he joined the government payroll in 1983. Until recently he was minister of state for industry. Married to a devout Christian, he indulges many of his charitable interests through the **Jerusalem Trust** which supports the advancement of the Christian religion in the UK and overseas. The bulk of the £1.9 million paid out by the trust in 1993 appeared to go to evangelical causes, although some Christian welfare work was also supported.

The main vehicle for Tim Sainsbury's giving, however, is the **Headley Trust**. A total of £1.7 million was paid out by Headley in 1993, most of it to social welfare charities, for arts and the environment, and for charities working in developing countries. A further £512,000 came from the Museums, Galleries and Libraries Fund, most of it believed to have gone to the Ashmolean in Oxford. It was also announced in Autumn 1993 that Tim Sainsbury had transferred some £34 million in Sainsbury shares to charitable trusts of which he was not a trustee. As both Sainsbury and his wife are currently trustees of the Headley and Jerusalem Trusts, the precise destination of the money is unclear.

An accountant, middle-brother Simon Sainsbury keeps a much lower profile than his brothers but he is believed to be the wealthiest and in charitable terms is perhaps the most interesting of the three. His **Monument Trust** paid out over £4.1 million in 1992/93, following a similar level of spend the year before. The largest single chunk went to AIDS organisations: Monument was one of the first organisations in the UK to realise the threat posed by AIDS and together with other Sainsbury trusts has been a strong supporter of AIDS groups. Major support was also given in the fields of health and community care, the built environment and the arts. Other headline grants included £243,000 to the Council for the Protection of Rural England and the latest instalment in a £5 million commitment to the Judge Institute of Management Studies at Cambridge, named after another benefactor, Paul Judge (qv).

Together with cousin David's Gatsby Charitable Foundation, the Sainsbury trusts described above all hold the bulk of their assets in shares of the family company and are administered from the same office. There are also a few other Sainsbury trusts whose giving has not been included in the total given above. These include the **Kay Kendall Leukaemia Fund**, set up in 1984 under the will of the late James Sainsbury, and the much smaller

Ashden Trust, which supports ecological and homelessness projects and of which the trustees are Lord Sainsbury's daughter Mrs S Butler-Sloss and Mr R Butler-Sloss.

The Sainsburys stand out from other philanthropic families in the UK, past and present, not just for the scale of their giving but for the active involvement and generosity of members right across the family. It looks as though these traits have already been cultivated in the next generation.

Contact: The Administrator,
Sainsbury Family Charitable Trusts,
9 Red Lion Court, London EC4A 3EB.
Tel: 0171 410 0330.

PETER BECKWITH
£5,043,000 NEW

PREFERENCE: education, youth, elderly people, general
AGE: 49
WEALTH: £35m-£50m
TRUST LINKS: Peter Beckwith Charitable Trust, Peter Beckwith Harrow Trust
COMPANY LINKS: sold stake in London and Edinburgh Trust

Despite their wealth, Peter Beckwith and his younger brother John (qv) are two of the country's lower-profile entrepreneurs, and as a consequence their philanthropic activities have gone largely unnoticed. Peter has diverted a substantial portion of his wealth to the support of educational establishments, amongst other causes.

Peter Beckwith practised as a solicitor after graduating from Cambridge, and when still only in his mid twenties he founded London and Edinburgh Trust along with his brother. This property development business was to make their fortune. After initial set-backs encountered during the 1973-5 property slump, the company went from strength to strength, and was soon making nearly £20 million a year. With impeccable timing, the Beckwiths sold out at the very peak of the market in 1990 to the Swedish property investors SPP. The current recession then hit hard, and within a year the company had posted losses of £138 million. The brothers stayed on for a while to run the company for the new owners, but eventually resigned in 1992.

The sale of London and Edinburgh netted Peter and John Beckwith around £40 million each. A significant proportion of this has since been redirected towards a variety of charitable causes. Most notably, in 1992 Peter made a gift of £5 million to Cambridge University, where he had studied for his law degree at Emmanuel College. This money was divided between building projects for the departments of biochemistry, law and management studies. The Cambridge fundraisers have clearly been hard at work targeting their wealthy alumni, having also received £8 million from Paul Judge (qv).

Peter Beckwith's philanthropic activities do not end there, as he also makes donations via two charitable trusts. The **Peter Beckwith Charitable Trust** was established in 1989 with Peter and his wife Paula as trustees, and makes donations for general charitable purposes. The trust has no real asset base, receiving most of its income directly from its founder. In 1991 grants totalled £43,000, including £5,000 to the National Council of YMCAs, and £1,700 to BBC Children in Need. Most of the remaining gifts were for either £500 or £1,000, and were mainly directed towards charities dealing with the young and the elderly, disabilities, and sport. Also listed amongst the donations made were a £500 gift to Wimbledon Conservative Association, and £10,300 given to CPC Services Ltd – a private company whose main activities are the supply of car spares and resurfacing tennis courts. More recently, in 1992 he set up the **Peter Beckwith Harrow Trust**, whose objects are primarily to advance the education of pupils at the public school which both Beckwith brothers attended. It also aims to support other charitable organisations concerned with the education of children and young people. As there are no subsequent accounts on file at the Charity Commission, the size of this trust is not clear.

On the business front, Peter is chair of his own investment company, PMB Holdings, is deputy chair of Letinvest plc, and is involved along with his brother in their new company Riverside Holdings, with which they plan to establish a chain of health clubs in Europe.

Contact for Peter Beckwith Charitable Trust and Peter Beckwith Harrow Trust: Peter Beckwith, Trustee, Hill Place House, 55a High St, London SW7 1DH. Tel: 0181 944 1288.

MARTYN ARBIB

£4,089,000

PREFERENCE: museums, education, medicine, youth, elderly people, Thames Valley

AGE: 54

WEALTH: £100m-£250m

TRUST LINKS: Arbib Foundation

COMPANY LINKS: Perpetual

Financial wizard Martyn Arbib, chair of Perpetual, has recently made one of the more generous one-off gifts in this book. In the last year he has given £4 million to the River and Rowing Museum at Henley Foundation, which reflects his close links with the town on the Thames where his company is based. This donation was made via his grant-making charity, the **Arbib Foundation**, and will be recorded in its 1993/94 accounts.

Martyn Arbib created the Arbib Foundation in 1987, the year he floated his award-winning Perpetual fund management group. During its first few months in existence the foundation disposed of a tranche of Perpetual shares which it had acquired at negligible cost, but which fetched over £500,000 when sold. Its shareholding was soon replenished with a further half a million Perpetual shares, again received at no cost. By 1991/92, the foundation's assets had grown to over £700,000 which funded donations of £51,000, and an identical amount in the following year. Apart from the support of charitable purposes, the foundation was established to help finance 'a public museum in the Thames Valley area for the education of the general public.' This was no doubt a reference to the River and Rowing Museum at Henley Foundation, which also received a grant of £22,500 in 1991/92. Other significant donations made in the year were £5,000 to the Dennis Silk Trust (which provides scholarships at St Peter's College, Radley); £2,750 to the NSPCC; £2,000 to the Farriers Appeal; and £1,500 to both Babes in Arms and National ACT. The free market think-tank the Institute of Economic Affairs has been a recipient of an annual grant of £1,000 in recent years. A wide variety of other causes receive support from the foundation, notably leukaemia and cancer research and treatment, young people, the elderly, and organisations in south Oxfordshire and the Thames Valley.

Arbib's links with Henley-on-Thames have been one of the most distinctive features of his business life. He set up the Perpetual unit trust group in 1974 and located it proudly in this Oxfordshire town. Despite its distance from the City, or some would say because of it, Perpetual has been an amazing success in the financial management and investment world, out-performing many of its rivals in both the long- and short-term. When the company was floated, Arbib pocketed over £10 million for a portion of his shares, and he still owns nearly three-quarters of the increasingly valuable stock. The firm reported charitable grants of £38,500 in its 1992/93 accounts, which have been included in Arbib's personal donations figure above, and also gives additional support of charitable functions through sponsorship and advertising. Arbib is also a non-executive director of Kelsey Industries, which apparently gets its title from his mother's maiden name. His money-making talents even extend to his favourite hobby, horse racing. His St Leger winning horse Snurge has earned a record £1.2 million in prize money, a decent return on the £33,000 Arbib paid for it five years ago.

Contact: Mr M Arbib, Arbib Foundation, 17 Thameside, Henley-on-Thames, Oxfordshire, RG9 1LH.

SIR KIRBY and SIR MAURICE LAING
and family
about £3.6 million

Preference: Christian causes, education, youth, medicine, general
Ages: 78 and 76 respectively
Wealth: £20m-£35m

Trust links: Kirby Laing Foundation, Maurice Laing Foundation, Martin Laing Foundation, etc.
Company links: John Laing

The elders of the British construction industry, Sir Kirby and Sir Maurice Laing now only take a backseat role in the business built up by their father, the late Sir John Laing. Having both been company directors since 1939 (Sir Maurice was chair until 1982), it is now Sir Kirby's son Martin who is the current chair of John Laing plc. With the Laings, construction clearly runs in the blood.

● CONSTRUCTION GIVERS

Kirby and Maurice Laing	£3,600,000
Wates family	£1,450,000
Shepherd family	£220,000
McAlpine family	£160,000
John Douglas	£115,000
Robert Douglas	£30,000
Steve Morgan	£18,000
David Wilson	£14,000

And so does charity. Sir Kirby and Sir Maurice each have a foundation, as do Martin and his two brothers. Sir Kirby set up his foundation in 1972; by 1993 it was making donations totalling £1.2 million in the year. The foundation generally makes a very large number of grants to a wide spread of different causes, with perhaps medical and Christian causes particularly noticeable. In 1991 the foundation made an award of £0.5 million each to Oxford and Cambridge Universities. Sir Kirby is president of the board of governors of St Lawrence College, a past president of the Royal Albert Hall, and a trustee of the Inter-Varsity Fellowship and the Crusaders' Union. Sir Maurice Laing's foundation was

THE BRITISH SCHOOL OF OSTEOPATH
1-4 SUFFOLK ST., LONDON. SW1
TEL. 01 930 9254-8

established in the same year as that of his brother. It also made grants of some £1.2 million in 1993/94, following a bumper £5.4 million the year before, made possible by an asset base now worth over £40 million. Like its brother foundation, a large number of grants were made, but they were dominated by awards of £300,000 to the Ocean Youth Club, £85,000 to the London Bible College (of which Sir Maurice is president), £90,000 to the London School of Economics and £50,000 to the North London Hospice. Of note were a number of big grants to complementary medicine causes. In the previous year, the World Humanity Action Trust, the Luis Palau Evangelistic Mission and the University of Exeter had each received £1 million or more. Although Sir Maurice was the foundation's settlor, his son John Hedley Laing recently assigned to it a large stake in another Laing property company.

The big recent increase in giving by these two foundations must be due at least in part to the sale of their respective stakes in Laing Properties, which was taken over in 1990 in a move masterminded by Chelsfield's Elliott Bernerd (qv). The takeover succeeded despite the major stakes in Laing Properties held by the foundations and by Laing family trusts. It is not a move the Laings want repeated with their construction company: the deed of the Maurice Laing Foundation, for example, empowers the trustees 'to retain all the funds in shares of John Laing and Son Ltd or its successor companies, without being answerable for any loss occasioned thereby'. Both the **Kirby and Maurice Laing Foundations** derive a portion of their income from a charitable company, Eskmuir Ltd, which holds just under three million ordinary shares in John Laing plc gifted to it by the Laing brothers. Since its creation in 1973, the only

beneficiaries of grants made by Eskmuir have been the Kirby and Maurice Laing Foundations, and in 1992/93 they received £202,000 and £173,000 respectively.

It is worth noting that both the Kirby and Maurice Laing Foundations are administered jointly with two other foundation set up by the brothers' late parents, and an application to one is considered as an application to all. The **J W Laing Trust** (supporting mainly Christian evangelism) and the **Beatrice Laing Trust** (social welfare) together have assets worth £60 million and distribute donations of over £3 million annually.

Martin Laing, Sir Kirby's son, has many voluntary appointments. He is a council member and past director of Business in the Community, and a member of the UK-Japan 2000 Group, the Business Council for Sustainable Development, and the Archbishop's Council of the Church Urban Fund. He is a director of the Hertfordshire Groundwork Trust and the City of London Sinfonia, and trustee of the Natural Energy Foundation and both the UK and international branches of the World Wide Fund for Nature. He is also involved with education through being a member of the court of the University of London and governor of both the Papplewick School Ascot and St Lawrence College Ramsgate. Martin Laing directs financial support to charities through the **Martin Laing Foundation**, which made donations of £140,000 in 1991/92. The largest grant was of £25,000 to Princess Helena College, with the rest going through the Charities Aid Foundation, probably for onward payment to other charities.

Two other family members, David and Christopher Laing, support charitable causes through their personal foundations. The **David**

Laing Foundation made donations totalling £375,000 in 1991/92, but also made a gift out of capital of £540,000 to MacIntyre. The **Christopher Laing Foundation**'s donations came to £175,000 in 1993, with major gifts of £40,000 to the Chartered Institute of Building, £15,000 to the Save the Children Fund and £25,000 to the Sports Council Trust Company.

Finally, Sir Kirby, Sir Maurice and Martin Laing are also trustees of **Laing's Charitable Trust**, through which John Laing plc channels its £1 million programme of community support. All in all, it's enough to make you agree with the directors' report for one of the Laing charities, which points out that John Laing is 'recognised to be one of the finest of the UK construction companies'.

Contact for the Kirby and Maurice Laing Foundations: R M Harley, Administrator, Box 1, 133 Page Street, Mill Hill, London NW7 2ER. Tel: 0181 906 5200. For the Martin and Christopher Laing Foundations: Mr P Glaessen, Ernst & Young, 400 Capability Green, Luton, Beds LU1 3LU. Tel: 01582 400700. For the David Laing Foundation: The Studio, Mackerye End, Harpenden, Herts AL5 5DR.

ROBERT EDMISTON

about £3 million

PREFERENCE: Christianity
AGE: 48
WEALTH: £250m-£500m
TRUST LINKS: Christian Vision
COMPANY LINKS: IM Group

Bob Edmiston is the sole owner of the IM Group, a company that distributes motor vehicles from the Far East under franchise. He is not, however, the only one to profit, as he reputedly donates ten per cent of the profits he receives to a charity he set up named **Christian Vision**. With IM profits at £32 million in 1992, that would put Edmiston's donations at over £3 million. This ties in well with Christian Vision's income in its latest accounts, which stood at £3,918,000.

Christian Vision is listed at the Charity Commission as making grants to institutions and its objects are the relief of poverty, general welfare of the aged and general charitable purposes. Given Edmiston's Pentecostal leanings, however, it is probable that the bulk of its income is devoted to evangelical causes.

The entry for Edmiston in *Business Age*'s annual listing of the rich says, cryptically: 'We also believe that he has made several multi-million donations to charity in the past 12 months'. This would certainly square with the fact that IM has recently been drowning in cash, having sold off some substantial chunks of the business, including most of its Hyundai franchise. However, the Group has also put money into new pastures recently, diversifying into property and construction. Donations made directly by the company appear minimal, totalling just over £2,000 in 1990.

A management accountant by training, and with work and charity dominating his life, Edmiston is not subject to much public exposure. In 1992 he did pen a classic in the 'My Biggest Mistake' series published by the *Independent on Sunday*, describing how he accepted a job in a company, Jensen Motors, just as it was spiralling to disaster. Practically the last to leave (fickleness is not one of Edmiston's failings), his 'mistake' turns out to be his salvation, as he buys into part of the Jensen business salvaged from the receivers and is alerted to the opportunity of bidding for Fuji's Subaru concession.

Edmiston ends the piece: 'And for all the trauma, it was a valuable experience. For as someone once said: "It's not the length of the experience that counts but the intensity".' Too true, Mr Edmiston, but we're not sure it was car dealing they were talking about.

Contact: R N Edmiston, IM Group, Ryder Street, West Bromwich, West Midlands B70 0EJ. Tel: 0121 522 2000.

J PAUL GETTY, KBE

about £3 million

(*but see below*)

PREFERENCE: art, conservation, social welfare, cricket

AGE: 62

WEALTH: see below

TRUST LINKS: J Paul Getty Jnr Charitable Trust

COMPANY LINKS: None

For most of the millionaires in this book, giving is either a social duty, a grand gesture or the playing out of a personal obsession. With John Paul Getty, it is all three.

A US citizen, Getty has lived in England for nearly a quarter of a century and much of his philanthropy can be traced to his love for his adopted home. Whether it be preventing the UK's artistic heritage from haemorrhaging abroad, shoring up some of the country's oldest communities and some of its newest, or quietly championing the game of cricket as it should to be played, Getty's philanthropy displays an enlightened sense of national pride.

Getty is the eldest son of J Paul Getty Snr, the US oil billionaire who died in 1976. When the family finally sold its 40% stake in Getty Oil in 1984, Getty Jnr went on a charitable spending spree. £30 million went to the National Gallery to set up an endowment fund for acquiring works of art, followed by a further £20 million two years later. The **J Paul Getty Jnr Charitable Trust** was endowed with £20 million at the same time. The British Film Institute pocketed £17 million for its national film archive, and Lord's cricket ground was tossed a friendly £2 million to help build the new Mount Stand.

To say that Getty's philanthropy has slowed down a little since then seems almost to make light of the size of the cheques which he is still prepared to write. Although most commentators put Getty's worth at over £1.5 billion, they make the mistake of ascribing to him a large part of the value of family trusts in which he has a life interest but of which he cannot touch the capital. His solicitor points out that under £50 million is a more accurate figure for the wealth Getty actually holds. He does, however, receive a huge annual income from various Getty Trusts (the bulk of his own resources being also in trust) and his capacity to give is certainly substantial. The Imperial War Museum received £2 million in 1990. In 1994, Getty threatened to withdraw an offer of £1 million to the campaign to keep Canova's sculpture the *Three Graces* from being exported to the Getty museum in California when a fundraiser hinted that the gift was influenced by a grudge between Getty and his late father, who founded the museum.

Quite enough has been written about Getty Jnr's relationship with his father for us to dwell on it here. Suffice it to say that their public images could hardly be more different: the late California oilman was famed for his meanness, exemplified for the media by the existence of a pay-phone for guests at his country house. Notably, previous donations from Getty Jnr – for the acquisition of Duccio's *Crucifixion* and Mantegna's *Adoration of the Magi* – were also given to prevent works of art from leaving the UK. But we can put that down to his open preference for his chosen country over the country of his birth. Certainly, few native Englishmen could have received an honorary knighthood with as much pleasure as Getty did in 1986.

Getty's Englishness is most apparent in his passion for cricket. Introduced to the delights of the game by Mick Jagger, a former neighbour, Getty's enthusiasm has extended to buying John Wisden Ltd., publishers of the cricketers' almanack, and to building his own private cricket ground complete with thatched

pavilion on his estate at Wormsley in the Chilterns. Disgusted at the vulgarities of the modern game, Getty harks back to the time when it was 'the playing out of all those things that are most important in an English gentleman' (*Independent*, 16/5/93).

GETTY'S GIFTS

1984	Manchester City Art Gallery to acquire Duccio's Crucifixion	£300,000
1984	Families of striking miners	£100,000
1985-7	National Gallery acquisition fund	£50 million
1985-7	J Paul Getty Charitable Trust endowment	£20 million
1986	Lord's cricket ground	£3 million
1986-9	British Film Institute	£17 million
1990	Imperial War Museum	£2 million
1994	National Galleries of Scotland Three Graces appeal	£1 million

After a spontaneous donation of £100,000 to help the families of striking miners in 1984, Getty's support for social welfare causes is now largely channelled through the J Paul Getty Charitable Trust. In 1993 the Trust spent £1.3 million on a selection of 'unpopular' causes, including mental health, projects with misusers of drugs and alcohol, mentally handicapped people, ex-offenders, and homeless people, as well as some support for conservation projects. The Trust also supports community groups and self-help groups, with a preference for areas stricken by poverty. Consistently innovative, it is one of the few UK trusts prepared to offer support to projects based in ethnic minority communities. Of over 2,000 applicants for grants in 1993, 129 awards were made.

Getty is himself one of the trustees of the J Paul Getty Charitable Trust. They are chaired by James Ramsden and the other trustees are Vanni Treves of the City law firm Macfarlanes, and Christopher Gibbs, a London art dealer. Retiring rather than reclusive, Getty is still not an easy man to approach (outside the open invitation made by the Trust to relevant applicants). His great wealth has obviously been a source of grief in the past, as the kidnapping tragedy of his eldest son testifies, and some current beneficiaries have been asked not to disclose details of donations. National Gallery director Neil MacGregor, unlike Getty, is giving nothing away: 'Because he's been so outstandingly generous, I've never had to approach him.'

Contact: Bridget O'Brien Twohig, J Paul Getty Charitable Trust, 149 Harley Street, London W1N 2DH, Tel: 071-486 1859

VIVIEN DUFFIELD
and family
about £2.8 million

PREFERENCE: arts and museums, Jewish causes, children, medicine, welfare

AGE: 48

WEALTH: £35m-£50m

TRUST LINKS: Vivien Duffield Foundation, Clore Foundation, Miss V L Clore's 1967 Charitable Trust

COMPANY LINKS: Sears heiress

Vivien Duffield has clearly inherited her father's philanthropic streak. But then she would not find this surprising, because as she says: 'If you're lucky enough to have money, it's your duty to give it away' (*Independent*, 2/2/93). She has intimate connections with two major foundations and a smaller trust, which together give away several million pounds annually.

Duffield is the daughter of the late Sir Charles Clore, the retail and property entrepreneur who made his fortune through the Sears department stores and clothing group. Upon his death in 1979 he left a substantial £123 million estate, of which the Inland Revenue eventually received over half before the family could stake their claim. Much of this fortune has been directed to charities through two grant-making trusts: the **Clore Foundation** and the **Vivien Duffield Foundation** both of which are amongst the top forty largest grant-makers in this country.

Sir Charles established the Clore Foundation in 1964 with an initial settlement of £100,000, and in the late sixties and early seventies it received capital additions totalling £5.8 million from Alan Clore and the then Vivien Clore. By 1993 its assets were worth £26 million, which generated an income of just over £2 million and facilitated donations of £1.3 million. Whilst the recipients of these gifts were not specified, the list for 1991 shows the main beneficiary to be Eureka! – an interactive children's museum created on 12 acres of derelict land in Halifax. Its remaining donations went to variety of causes, but especially to Jewish, arts, medical and children's organisations located in London and the South East. These gifts included £200,000 to both the Royal Marsden and Great Ormond Street hospitals – Duffield is a past-chair of their appeals. Prior to the foundation's support of Eureka! the single largest beneficiary of its support had been the Tate Gallery, which received a total of £6 million to house a collection of paintings by Turner.

Vivien Duffield used over £20 million of her inheritance to finance an eponymous charitable trust which she established in 1987. The Vivien Duffield Foundation also lends the bulk of its support to mainstream arts organisations, Jewish charities, children's causes, and the medical and social welfare sectors. In 1992 it held capital to the value of £21 million which provided income of £1.7 million. It made gifts amounting to £1.5 million, most of which went in a £1.1 million grant to Eureka!, which is to receive a total of £7 million from the two foundations. Other major recipients of grants had close connections with Duffield. The NSPCC received £100,000, and Duffield has served on a couple of the charity's committees in the past. She is also a high profile supporter and director of the Royal Opera House, and is also director of its trust. She is to figurehead its redevelopment appeal, and has been lobbying John Major for funds from the forthcoming National Lottery. The Royal Opera House received £117,000 from the Vivien Duffield Foundation in 1992. In a similar vein, Duffield is also a member of the Royal Ballet's board.

She also has a more personal trust, **Miss V L Clore's 1967 Charitable Trust**. As the name suggests, it was established by Vivien Duffield, née Clore, in 1967. This was the year of her 21st birthday, for which her father had given her a gift of £100,000 to spend as she wished. Rather than fritter it away, she set up a charitable trust. The trust's assets have since grown to over £600,000, generating an income of £31,000 in 1991/92. In that year, donations of £24,000 were made, mainly to Jewish, arts and medical causes, although the largest single donation was £5,100 given to Mencap.

Duffield's long-time partner Jocelyn Stevens is the out-spoken chair of English Heritage. He plays an active part in his companion's charitable activities – not only is he a trustee of

both Miss V L Clore's Charitable Trust and the Vivien Duffield Foundation, he is also a trustee of Eureka! Vivien Duffield returns the favour as trustee of Stevens' own trust, the **Jocelyn Stevens Charitable Trust**, which he set up in 1990. Although recent accounts are not available at the Charity Commission, this trust had a gross income of £15,000 in 1990/91.

Contact: The Clore Foundation, the Vivien Duffield Foundation, and Miss V L Clore's Charitable Trust are all administered by: Mrs Miriam Harris, Unit 3, Chelsea Manor Studios, Flood St, London, SW3 5SR. For the Jocelyn Stevens Charitable Trust: Jocelyn Stevens, 14 Cheyne Walk, London, SW3 5RA. Tel: 0171 351 1191.

MOORES family

about £2.8 million

PREFERENCE: social welfare, arts, education, Merseyside, Barbados
WEALTH: over £500m
TRUST LINKS: Moores Family Charity Foundation, John Moores Foundation, Peter Moores Foundation, Peter Moores Barbados Trust, Fairway Trust, Janatha Stubbs Foundation
COMPANY LINKS: Littlewoods

It is interesting to speculate what would have passed if the principal philanthropic impulse in the Moores family had come from the late multi-millionaire empire builder Sir John Moores, rather than from his children. There might have been just the one foundation, rather than the handful we have now, each as different from the others as foundations could be. The size of that foundation might have made it as well-known as a Wolfson or a Nuffield. And had it been endowed with a major stake in the Littlewoods Organisation, the company Sir John founded, the family battle over control of the company that has lasted more than a decade and a half might never have happened.

As it is, Sir John's younger son Peter is selling his 22 per cent holding in Littlewoods, Britain's largest privately-owned company, having been prevented from taking a more decisive role in its management. Selling the stake, worth over £400 million, will make opera-lover Peter a very wealthy man indeed. It leaves elder brother John, his sister Lady Grantchester, and his cousins in effective control of the company.

The **Peter Moores Foundation** is not currently the richest of the family's grant-making charities, although its total donations in 1992/93, at some £2.15 million, easily outflanked those of the others. Over half of this sum was dedicated to advancing public interest in, and access to, opera and associated activities. Substantial sums were also allocated to the visual arts, community projects and education. The year also saw the establishment of a separate **Peter Moores Barbados Trust**, and £211,000 was allocated in order to pursue similar objectives there. Peter Moores currently divides his time between homes on the Caribbean island and in Lancashire. Back in 1991 his foundation hit the headlines when it announced a £2 million donation to endow a chair in management studies at Oxford, where Peter went to university.

Peter's brother John set up the **John Moores Foundation** in 1964. In 1993 it held assets of £6.4 million and had made donations in the year of £374,000. Unusually for the benefactors described in this book, the foundation is dedicated to addressing poverty and disadvantage, making a large number of small grants to grassroots organisations working in Merseyside and Northern Ireland. These include welfare rights or advice centres, women's health projects, neighbourhood organisations, black groups, and second chance education projects. John also chairs what is now known as the Liverpool John Moores University.

The **Moores Family Charity Foundation** is essentially a conduit for charitable funds from Littlewoods, the bulk of which go to other Moores trusts. In 1991, the last year for which figures are available, the foundation made total donations of £568,000, of which £186,000 was paid to the John Moores Foundation and £119,000 to the Peter Moores Foundation. Lady Grantchester's **Fairway Trust** received £55,000 and £36,000 went to the foundation named after the other Moores sibling, Janatha Stubbs. The remainder was spent on grants to a range of different charities operating in Merseyside: Young Enterprise got £12,000, Merseyside County Scout Council £10,000, Liverpool Playhouse £5,000, and the John Moores Liverpool Exhibition Trust £54,000. Given the Moores family's ownership and control of the company, these donations have been included in the total given above (care was taken to eliminate double counting).

In a bid to head off the threat to their business posed by the new National Lottery, Littlewoods and the other major pools promoters, Vernons and Zetters, set up the massive Foundation for Sport and the Arts in 1991. Grants of some £60 million every year are financed by a reduction in betting duty on the pools and by a percentage of the price of each pools coupon paid to the foundation by the Pools Promoters Association.

Contact: For Peter Moores Foundation: M Johnson, c/o Messrs Wallwork Nelson and Johnson, Derby House, Lytham Road, Fulwood, Preston PR2 4JF. For John Moores Foundation: Linda Lazenby, 79 Gorsey Lane, Wallasey, Merseyside L44 4HF. Tel: 0151 637 0924. For Moores Family Charity Foundation: Mrs Patricia Caton, PO Box 28, Liverpool L23 0XJ. Tel: 0151 949 0117.

PAUL HAMLYN
£2,776,000

PREFERENCE: education, arts, Third World, publishing, elderly people
AGE: 68
WEALTH: £100m–£250m
TRUST LINKS: Paul Hamlyn 1987

Foundation, Helen Hamlyn Foundation
COMPANY LINKS: Reed Elsevier

Paul Hamlyn is out to prove that the great age of philanthropy is not dead – or perhaps that the second age has begun. His foundation, endowed in classic style with £50 million when he sold his publishing company Octopus to Reed International in 1987, is one of the few modern creations with the potential vision, clout and quirkiness to become a new Nuffield or a Rowntree. Hamlyn has even appointed former Nuffield Foundation director James Cornford to head the foundation from 1994.

The early years of the **Paul Hamlyn Foundation** have not been entirely smooth, however. The attempt to develop a programme of work guided by a thought-out policy came up against Hamlyn's own habit of shooting from the hip, reputedly making large awards outside policy areas. Then there was the embarrassing incident in early 1993 when the foundation reported that its offer of subsidised tickets to a *Romeo and Juliet* ballet had been turned down by a Hackney head teacher on account of the ballet's overtly heterosexual nature, among other reasons. Hysterical media coverage ensued.

The foundation's latest report, however, presents a more encouraging picture of recent activities. A total of £2.8 million was spent in 1992/93, although with income at £4.9 million it is still holding back some of its fire. The lion's share went to education (£972,000), followed by the arts (£698,000) and projects in the Third World including the promotion of appropriate medicine (£234,000). The foundation also made grants totalling £73,000 in the field of book publishing, supporting training in publishing in the UK and overseas, including Eastern Europe, and promoting access to and awareness of books.

Promoting access is a common feature of donations from the foundation. Hamlyn Westminster Week at the Royal Opera House finances subsidised tickets to encourage attendance by people who would not or could not go otherwise. A keen opera-goer himself, Paul Hamlyn is apparently one of the very few patrons of the arts in this book who think that high art is for more than just a select few. The Hamlyn Library Awards give support and encouragement to schools committed to developing their libraries. Hamlyn comments in the foundation's annual report: 'The foundation tries, in a small way, to assist those [charities] which work to help others to help themselves.'

Work in the educational field in recent years has been dominated by two projects: a £1 million award to the Bodleian Library in Oxford for the employment of specialised librarians to ensure access to the collections, and the financing of a National Commission on Education, which reported at the end of 1993. Recommendations like the provision of nursery education for all have had limited immediate impact, but may prove influential over the longer term, particularly if there is a change in political climate.

One other big grant the foundation made in 1992/93 was of £675,000 to the **Helen Hamlyn Foundation**, another grant-making charity (Helen being Paul Hamlyn's wife), which directs its support solely for the benefit of elderly people. In particular the foundation has promoted integrated care systems for elderly people and appropriate domestic design and equipment. Helen and Paul Hamlyn sit on the boards of both foundations and on the bigger

foundation they are joined by Paul's son and daughter, Michael and Jane, and Robert Gavron.

Despite the openness with which his foundation operates, there exists considerable confusion about the extent of Paul Hamlyn's giving. The *Sunday Times* puts his total donations to charity at £70 million, and *Business Age* magazines ventures a figure of over £100 million. It is probable, however, that both of these estimates involve significant double counting, with the foundation's endowment counted separately from major gifts since made by the foundation. Of course that £50 million endowment, now worth over £61 million, still represents in financial terms one of the greatest acts of philanthropy in UK history.

Hamlyn retains a large shareholding in Reed, which recently merged with Dutch publishing giant Elsevier. He is a chancellor of Thames Valley University and, rare among the figures in this book, a significant supporter of the Labour Party. German by birth, having arrived in the UK from Hitler's Germany in the thirties, Hamlyn's liberal leanings run deep.

Contact: Paul Hamlyn Foundation: James Cornford, Director, Sussex House, 12 Upper Mall, London W6 9TA. Tel: 0181 741 2812. Helen Hamlyn Foundation: R Hollingbery, 8 Bryanston Mews East, London W1H 7FH. Tel: 0171 402 0815.

SIR JAMES GOLDSMITH
about £2.5 million

PREFERENCE: environment, litigation, protecting Europe
AGE: 61
WEALTH: over £500m

TRUST LINKS: Goldsmith
Foundation, Ecological Foundation
COMPANY LINKS: numerous
overseas interests

Our estimate of £2.5 million for Sir
James Goldsmith's annual giving
includes a large proportion of non-
charitable grants and, like most things
about the entrepreneur-turned-
politician, it is conservative.
Potentially much more finds its way
into environmental projects from Sir
James' fabulous wealth, which is
largely invested, appropriately
enough, in gold.

Goldsmith was one of the most
feared corporate operators in the
1970s and 1980s. From the day he left
Eton school after winning £8,000 on
a three-horse accumulator to his
spectacular £13 billion failed takeover
bid for BAT Industries in 1989, his
eyes have always been on the big one.
His combativeness was not above
resorting to litigation (most famously
against *Private Eye*) and his early
giving took the form of a Goldsmith
Libel Fund to help selected individuals
bring and defend actions for libel. For
all the fight and flair, however,
Goldsmith is a financial conservative
– some would say pessimist – who
always believed in keeping a large
proportion of his assets liquid (hence
the obsession with gold). That
strategy paid off in 1987 when he sold
off almost everything he owned
before the stock market crash and
then reputedly laughed down the
telephone as his business friends
watched the noughts come
tumbling off the value of their
investments.

Back in the early 1970s, about the
time when Goldsmith's Cavenham
Foods was gobbling up Bovril, Home
& Colonial, Maypole and Lipton, his
elder brother Edward founded the
Ecologist magazine. As well as helping
to finance the magazine, Sir James set

up the small **Ecological Foundation**
in 1972, whose charitable expenditure
had gone up to £88,000 by 1992. But
the big environmental grants had to
wait until 1990, when on his retirement
from business he established the
Goldsmith Foundation.

Sir James himself is chief executive
of the Goldsmith Foundation, but his
brother Edward is closely involved.
Financial data on the Foundation,
believed to be based in Switzerland,
are hard to come by. The best
information we have comes from a
letter Edward wrote to the *Guardian*
in May 1994:

'The Foundation hands out several
million pounds a year and is, I think I

can say, the main source of funding today, especially in the UK and France, for action-oriented projects in a number of fields. The first is sustainable agriculture, which not only provides fresh and healthy food but also preserves, rather than destroys our natural environment and rural society.

'The second field is that of sustainable energy, and in particular the war against the nuclear industry, with its highly subsidised, very polluting and incredibly dangerous installations, such as THORP in Cumbria and the Superphénix fast-breeder reactor in France. Our third interest is the encouragement of the local and regional economy in opposition to the global economy as institutionalised by the GATT Uruguay round.'

To these comments, Sir James Goldsmith himself added the following: 'The main purposes of the Goldsmith Foundation are: to promote regional free trade and to oppose global free trade; to fight for a Europe based on its nations and against the supra-national bureaucratic state proposed by Maastricht; to campaign for a transformation of intensive farming practices into a non-intensive farming system; and to transform the use and production of energy, *inter alia*, eliminating nuclear energy.'

Goldsmith's skirmishes in the 'war against the nuclear industry' include a £50,000 grant to an *Ecologist*-run campaign discrediting nuclear power as an answer to the greenhouse effect and underwriting the costs of Greenpeace's legal challenge to the commissioning of THORP in 1994. His extensive mining interests aside, Goldsmith also believes in practising what he preaches: the land on his 16,000-acre Mexican estate is organically farmed and harbours a number of rare and endangered species

of animal. He has also set up a Cuixmala Ecological Foundation in Mexico.

But the Foundation and the estate have not proved enough to occupy the irrepressible Goldsmith since his formal retirement from business, and he has filled in time by writing a best-selling book, *Le Piège* (The Trap), denouncing the politics of global free trade in apocalyptic terms, and getting himself elected as a French MEP (Goldsmith's mother was French and he has dual nationality). Jimmy, as he is known in France, was elected on the *L'Autre Europe* list, a group he helped set up with right-wing maverick Philippe de Villiers and which also includes Charles de Gaulle, grandson of the great general. The politics are anti-Maastricht, anti-GATT and anti-Schengen, calling for a Europe built of strong old nations which is prepared to protect its interests and its people, rich and poor, against cheap labour and competition from outside Europe. Sir James emphasised to us that the objectives were not party political, but were 'well above party politics'.

Characteristically, Goldsmith ensured that his political convictions were argued in the law courts as well as on the hustings by financing Lord Rees-Mogg's High Court challenge to the ratification of the Maastricht Treaty in 1993. It was the sort of high-profile political spanner in the works that he is now threatening to wield on a regular basis. Certainly, election to the European Parliament may be only the first step for a man whose ambition has been likened to that of Ross Perot and whose new motto seems to be: 'Think local, act global'.

Contact: Jon Cracknell, Goldsmith Foundation, Stanhope Administration, Swan House, Madeira Walk, Windsor, Berks SL4 1EU. Tel: 01753 830707.

CAMERON MACKINTOSH

£1,903,000

PREFERENCE: theatre, education, children, AIDS, homeless people, Vietnamese refugees, general
AGE: 47
WEALTH: £100m-£250m
TRUST LINKS: Mackintosh Foundation
COMPANY LINKS: Cameron Mackintosh Ltd

Cameron Mackintosh kept himself down to only a five per cent pay increase last year. But that still meant a rise of £500,000, bringing his annual salary up to a record £10.2 million. Unlike some top executives, Mackintosh can at least claim that his pay rise was performance-related: turnover at his production company was up by almost a quarter.

The productions that have made Mackintosh famous include a number of shows with Andrew Lloyd Webber (qv) including *Cats* and *Phantom of the Opera*, as well as other blockbusters such as *Les Misérables* and *Miss Saigon*. The proceeds of the sale of two tickets for every performance of *Miss Saigon* now go to the Bui-Doi or 'dust for life' Fund, established to support refugees from Vietnam.

The **Mackintosh Foundation** was set up in 1986, and now benefits from covenanted donations of £1.5 million a year from the man who must rank as one of the greatest impresarios of all time. The foundation spends most of its income but also has a permanent endowment of £1 million which will start releasing income for distribution after Autumn 1995.

Theatre dominates the foundation's recent major grants. In 1992/93 it donated £250,000 to the Royal National Theatre's production of *Carousel*, and a further £150,000 later the same year for *Sweeney Todd*, part of a promised £1 million fund to support revivals of classic stage musicals. Nearly £200,000 was given to the Alliance of New American Musicals to encourage the creation of new musicals by American writers and artists, this too part of a £1 million endowment over three years. In previous years it endowed Oxford University with the Cameron Mackintosh Fund for Contemporary Theatre, worth a further £1 million, and paid for the design and construction of a studio theatre for use by students, called the Old Fire Station. Other theatres and the Actors Charitable Trust have also benefited.

With philanthropy on the Mackintosh scale, however, other causes can also get a look in. Centrepoint Soho was paid £160,000 in 1992/93, and other homeless charities, AIDS groups and children's charities are regular beneficiaries. Some hospital charities have also benefited, and while most of the foundation's support falls into the above subject areas, a smattering of further grants covers a wide range of beneficiaries, from Medical Aid for Free Romania to the RNLI.

Given Mackintosh's habit of getting interested in causes related to the subjects of his productions, it may be worth noting that he is currently involved with a new show based around the legend of Frenchman Martin Guerre, written by the authors of *Miss Saigon* and *Les Misérables*.

It is also worth bearing in mind, however, that the Mackintosh Foundation is run with a skeleton administration and the trustees, although active, are unlikely to welcome numerous speculative appeals. The foundation has written to the editors of the *Guide to the Major Trusts*: 'We are a small charity, although with substantial funds, run on a voluntary basis. We operate in a very few specific areas and people within that sector know of our work, and for the moment we are happy to keep it like that.'

Some of Mackintosh's most personal donations concern his patronage of the small fishing village of Mallaig in the western Highlands of Scotland. Mackintosh sometimes retreats to Mallaig, staying in a croft that belonged to his late aunt just outside the village above Loch Nevis, and he considered it right that the village should share in some of his good fortune. Mackintosh followed up a grant of £120,000 to the Mallaig and District Swimming Pool Association with the decision to extend his roots by buying land in the surrounding area. Having bought the local grocers shop, he may also be indirectly providing Mallaig with shopping facilities, although not – as yet – a theatre.

Contact: Appeals Secretary, Mackintosh Foundation, 1 Bedford Square, London WC1B 3RA. Tel: 0171 637 8866.

● BIGGEST DONORS TO JEWISH CAUSES

Lord Rayne	£1,845,000
Benzion Freshwater	£1,600,000
Jack Dellal	£611,000
Evelyn de Rothschild	£605,000
Stanley Kalms	£604,000
Alan Sugar	£538,000
Cyril Stein	£478,000
Lord Weinstock	£333,000
Stephen Rubin	£300,000
Michael Green	£272,000
Elliot Bernerd	£189,000
David Lewis	£164,000
Everard Goodman	£158,000

LORD RAYNE
£1,845,000

PREFERENCE: medicine, education, social welfare, the arts, Jewish charities
AGE: 76
WEALTH: £50m-£75m
TRUST LINKS: Rayne Foundation, Rayne Trust
COMPANY LINKS: London Merchant Securities, First Leisure Corporation.

Lord Rayne can be counted among the most generous philanthropists in the UK, if generosity is measured by donations as a proportion of wealth. Most of the other individuals in the book who are responsible for giving on the same scale as Rayne are two, four or even ten times as wealthy as he is.

Like many others on these pages, his money has come primarily from property, where his speciality was picking areas that would become upwardly mobile, such as the Angel in Islington, and snapping up the property while it was still cheap. He has been around long enough to have the cycle of boom and recession ingrained in his brain, but the downturn still hurts and he has made sure in recent years to diversify his business interests, both within the property sector and in leisure.

A collector of fine art, Rayne has held a string of appointments in the arts field, including serving as chair of the National Theatre for some 15 years. The arts also benefit from the **Rayne Foundation**, which he set up in 1962 and which donated a total of £1.7 million in 1992, including a major grant to the Royal National Theatre Endowment Fund. The foundation's main areas of support, however, are medicine and higher education, with the 1992 grants list including awards of £250,000 to the medical school of King's College Hospital and £50,000 each to Great Ormond Street, Birkbeck College and Wadham College. Welfare causes also got a look in, with major grants to two housing associations. The foundation concentrates support on the London area where Rayne made his fortune and spreads its largesse widely, making some 500 small grants to a bewildering array of charities. Lord Rayne is joined on the foundation's board by his son, Robert, and Lords Goodman and Greenhill.

Other voluntary appointments held by Lord Rayne reflect the interests expressed in his foundation's grants. He is currently vice-president of the Yehudi Menuhin School, honorary vice-president of Jewish Care, and a council member of the King's Fund, RADA, and the South Bank Board.

Rayne also set up the smaller **Rayne Trust** in 1958, which mainly supports Jewish charities. A total of £145,000 was donated in 1991/92, with headline grants to the West London Synagogue, Jewish Care and the Manor House Trust. The Rayne Trust is very much a family affair, with Rayne, his son and his second wife as the trustees.

Contact for both Rayne Foundation and Rayne Trust: R D Lindsay-Rea, 33 Robert Adam Street, London W1M 5AH. Tel: 0171 935 3555.

BENZION FRESHWATER
and family
£1.6 million

PREFERENCE: Jewish causes
AGE: 46
WEALTH: £100m-£250m

TRUST LINKS: Mayfair Charities
COMPANY LINKS: Daejan Holdings

The Freshwater family are major donors to Jewish causes through the **Mayfair Charities Ltd**, a grant-making charitable company set up by Osias Freshwater in 1968. Osias, a refugee from Eastern Europe who came to London in the 1920s, built up the family fortune through his activities on the capital's property market. But it is his son Benzion who is now trustee of the Mayfair Charities, and chair and chief executive of the investment firm Daejan Holdings, which is 80% controlled by the Freshwater family.

The Mayfair Charities has a substantial asset base of over £46 million, and in 1990/91 received an income of £5.9 million. Some of this income comes from three subsidiary undertakings which are wholly owned by Mayfair Charities – Freshwater Property Management, Haysgrans Property Company, and Metropolitan Property Companies (Overseas) – which covenant part of their profits to the trust. Most of the trust's income was retained and added to its capital, but £1.55 million was distributed to various charitable causes, heavily dominated by Jewish organisations operating in Britain and overseas. Examples of the major overseas donations made by the trust are its three large gifts focused on Jerusalem – £518,000 to Yeshiva Ohr Somayach, £100,000 to Yeshiva Ohr Elchonon, and £40,500 to Yad Eliezer. Grants in this country included £173,000 to Beth Jacob Grammar School, £98,000 to Kollel Hibath Jerusalem, £84,000 to Pardes House School, and £83,000 to Society of Friends of the Torah.

Further support for orthodox Jewish charities, especially in the educational and medical fields, comes from Daejan Holdings. In 1992/93 the company supported such causes to the tune of £60,000, but specifically excludes the arts, enterprise and conservation. Payments were made via the Charities Aid Foundation.

Contact: C C Morse, Mayfair Charities, Freshwater House, 158-162 Shaftesbury Ave, London, WC2H 8HR. Tel: 0171 836 1555. Daejan Holdings: same correspondent at same address.

PRINCE CHARLES
£1.48 million

PREFERENCE: youth, social welfare, medicine, conservation
AGE: 46
WEALTH: £100m-£250m
TRUST LINKS: Prince of Wales' Charities, Duke of Cornwall's Benevolent Fund
COMPANY LINKS: Duchy of Cornwall

Prince Charles is well known for his efforts on behalf of fundraising charities such as the Prince's Trust and the Prince's Youth Business Trust, both of which benefit young people – and are well-supported by many of the people in this book. The high public profile afforded the Prince of Wales is essential to the operation of such charities: staff commented that the sympathetic television documentary on the Prince's life broadcast in 1994 made their job easier, although the subsequent publication of Jonathan Dimbleby's biography was welcomed rather less enthusiastically.

Prince Charles also makes his own donations to charity, however. There appear to be two main vehicles for his giving. The **Prince of Wales' Charities**, established in 1979, made donations totalling £1.3 million in 1991/92. The bulk of donations were made to youth and social welfare charities, with medicine, conservation, art, the Church and some other causes also supported. In 1989/90, the last year for which accounts were on file at the Charity Commission, £136,000 was donated, although some £61,500 of this was paid to another trust, the Prince of Wales Charities Trust. Beneficiaries were not listed by name. The trustees are Sir Matthew Farrer, the

Queen's solicitor, and Commander Richard Aylard.

The main source of Prince Charles' income is not the Civil List but the estates of the Duchy of Cornwall. Some of the more unusual receipts that come Charles' way as Duke of Cornwall are those known as 'Bona Vacantia', which are the casual profits of the estates of deceased intestates dying domiciled in Cornwall without kin, after allowing for payments made in relation to claims on any estate. Since 1975 Prince Charles has invested this money in the **Duke of Cornwall's Benevolent Fund**, and grants are made from the income produced. In 1993 the assets of the fund were over £1 million and donations totalling £134,000 had been made in the year. St Anta All Saints Church received £25,000, the Hale Clinic and Marylebone Health Centres £15,000 each, and St Luke's Hospice and the Devon Wildlife Trust £10,000 each. Trustees of the fund include Lord Cairns, vice-chair of S G Warburg, who also sits on the council of the Duchy of Cornwall.

Prince Charles is listed as a patron of over 150 charities, covering every field of voluntary activity.

Contact: For the Prince of Wales' Charities: Commander Aylard, Prince of Wales Office, St James's Palace, London SW1A 1BS. For the Duke of Cornwall's Benevolent Fund: David Landale, Duchy of Cornwall, 10 Buckingham Gate, London SW1E 6LA. Tel: 0171 834 7346.

WATES family

£1.45m

PREFERENCE: young people, the disadvantaged, Christian causes, south London
AGE: 54

WEALTH: £100m-£250m
TRUST LINKS: Wates Foundation, Wates Charitable Trust
COMPANY LINKS: Wates Building Group Ltd

Through their eponymous foundations, the Wates family are major supporters of projects for the young and disadvantaged in inner city areas. The **Wates Foundation** was established in the mid 1960s by members of the family with an endowment in their company, the Wates Building Group. The foundation is still administered from the firm's head office in south London, and the current trustees are all offspring of the founders. Its annual grant total is around £1.4 million, which is directed to a wide range of causes, but with a particular focus upon the problems faced by young people in inner city areas, such as homelessness, drug and alcohol abuse, unemployment and crime. To this end it has committed substantial sums to NACRO, People for Action and Centrepoint. The foundation clearly believes that charity begins at home, as around one-third of its donations are received by organisations operating locally to its south London base.

The two leading family members, Sir Christopher and his cousin Michael, are not directly involved with the Wates Foundation. Perhaps this is because they are busy looking after the family's business interests, notably the private Wates Building Group, which the family totally owns, and the quoted property investment company, Wates City of London, of which they control a large share. They do, however, have time for a range of charitable interests. Michael Wates has close links with King's College Hospital, and in particular its School of Medicine and Dentistry. Sir Christopher Wates is deputy chair and governor of the London House for Overseas Graduates, and is a trustee of the Science Museum, and Lambeth Palace Library, and a past trustee of Chatham Historic Dockyard Trust.

Sir Christopher is also trustee of a smaller and more personal grant-making trust, the **Wates Charitable Trust**. This was registered in 1989, and by 1992 had assets of £192,000 and an income of £133,000 received mainly via Gift Aid donations. Given Sir Christopher's role as a Church Commissioner, it is not altogether surprising that the majority of the grant total of £37,000 went to various churches and Christian organisations.

When contacted, Sir Christopher requested to be left out of this publication as 'it is not helpful to have details of my private grant making trust published in this way.'

Contact: The Director, Wates Foundation, 1260 London Rd, Norbury, London, SW16 4EG. Tel: 0181 764 5000. Wates Charitable Trust, Wates Charitable Trustees Ltd, 16a St James St, London SW1A 1ER.

RICHARD BRANSON

about £1.2 million

(but see below)

PREFERENCE: young people, health, environment, general
AGE: 44
WEALTH: over £500m
TRUST LINKS: Healthcare Foundation
COMPANY LINKS: Virgin Group

The way this book is organised, with its emphasis on cash donations, does not really do justice to figures like Richard Branson whose involvement with charity and social reform is much more complex. Practically the first organisation he ever founded, before all those endlessly successful companies, was the Student Advisory Centre, later renamed Help. Seventeen years later he founded another non-profit group, the **Healthcare Foundation**, together with Michael Grade and Anita Roddick (qv). In its early years the foundation put over £1 million – raised from the sale of Mates condoms – into the fight against AIDS, and has since branched out to support projects in other areas where young people are at risk. In 1990 the foundation paid out £219,000 in grants to beneficiaries including Drug Concern, Positively Women, London Lighthouse, Phoenix House and the Hungerford Drug Project. Branson is now also a trustee of the grant-maker Charity Projects as well as holding a clutch of other voluntary appointments.

But the crowning glory of Branson's philanthropic achievement was to have been the Lottery Foundation, which he set up in 1994 to make an heroic bid to run the National Lottery just in order that all the operating profits could have been given to charity. Despite bearing the customary Branson hallmarks of a strong team and inspired publicity, it lost out to rival Camelot which scooped the franchise prize. Branson has described the decision as his greatest disappointment but, characteristically, hasn't given up. He intends to try again when the license comes up for renewal in seven years' time. His argument, presumably, will be the same: 'In almost every other country, state and city in the world where a lottery operates, the profits are returned to the community. Why not here?' (*Trust Monitor*, 4/94).

Branson's own motives for mounting his charity bid for the National Lottery were the subject of intense speculation and a large dash of cynicism from commentators. The explanation he himself provides for what lies behind his altruism may reveal something meaningful about the motivation of wealthy donors – or just his sense of humour: 'Well I do hope it will make the eye of the needle a little bit larger when I come to the end of my days' (*Independent*, 3/94).

Branson's portfolio of companies are a focus for other needle-widening ventures. Virgin's retail operations gave Greenpeace one per cent of their turnover on the day the album *Rainbow Warriors* was released, and other parts of the group have been involved in sponsorship deals with voluntary organisations. In 1991 the Virgin Group pointed out that it had received about 100,000 requests for donations, but did not make one-off donations as it supported 35 major charities, including the Healthcare Foundation, Help, Parents Against Tobacco, and the Disasters and Emergencies Committee, as well as voluntary groups in the Notting Hill and North Kensington area of London where the Group has its head office. Our estimate for the annual value of this support has been added to a £1 million donation Branson made last year to the Body Shop Foundation (see under 'Anita and Gordon Roddick') to give the donations total quoted above.

Other voluntary jobs held by Branson may provide further clues to his charitable sympathies. He is president of the British Disabled Water Ski Association, honorary vice president of Operation Raleigh and an honorary committee member of Friends of the Earth. He is also a patron of the National Holiday Fund, the Paul O'Gorman Foundation and the London School for Performing Arts and Technology. Branson's own exploits as a performer are well known, particularly his world record crossings of the Atlantic by hot air balloon.

Well on his way to becoming a billionaire, Richard Branson is if anything accelerating the rate of his business activities. Recent boosts include an early victory against British Airways over the 'dirty tricks' affair, and a £560 million cash injection from the sale of the Virgin music business to Thorn EMI. Some of this money was for investing in Virgin Atlantic Airlines, but Branson is also moving into soft drinks, including his own brand of cola, and bidding with a consortium to run the new Channel tunnel fast rail link. If he wins, international passengers may find themselves stepping off a Branson train to stay in a Branson hotel – in this case County Hall near Waterloo, which Branson is planning to turn into a £150 million hotel and leisure complex in partnership with its Japanese owners.

Contact: Anne Leach, Healthcare Foundation, Jevington House, Knotty Green, Beaconsfield, Bucks HP9 2TY. Tel: 01494 673777. W. Whitehorn, Corporate Public Relations, Virgin Group of Companies, 120 Campden Hill Road, London W8 7AR. Tel: 0171 229 1282.

SIR ANDREW LLOYD WEBBER

£1.2 million

PREFERENCE: arts, education, medicine, housing
AGE: 46
WEALTH: £250m-£500m
TRUST LINKS: Open Churches Fund, Andrew Lloyd Webber Art Foundation, Bill Lloyd Webber Memorial Fund

COMPANY LINKS: Really Useful Group

The Conservative Party's favourite composer has many strings to his philanthropic bow, of which perhaps the best known is his crusade to save the nation's cultural heritage. Most recently, in June this year he launched his new charitable venture, the **Open Churches Fund**, with an initial investment of £1 million. Its purpose is to provide funding to enable churches, which are forced for security reasons to be locked, to be open to the public. Sir Andrew spent a great deal of his childhood learning about church architecture, a subject on which he is very knowledgeable, and finds it frustrating to find so many very beautiful churches locked and inaccessible.

He also spent £10.25 million in April 1992 on Canaletto's *View of the Old Horse Guards London from St James's Park*, which is now owned by the **Andrew Lloyd Webber Art Foundation**. Sir Andrew established this charitable foundation in order to advance public appreciation and understanding of painting and the arts at the same time as he bought the Canaletto, and he is a trustee along with his wife. He told the press shortly after the Canaletto purchase that 'it is a plum one for the Foundation, but has slightly wiped things out because it was not my intention to spend so much at one go' (*Sunday Times*, 3/5/92), and that 'I might have to write another musical before I can think of doing this again' (*Independent*, 16/4/92). He has also built up a peerless private collection of pre-Raphaelite paintings and sculptures, which he hopes will one day be put on permanent public display, possibly even in a gallery built at his stately home Sydmonton Court. Lloyd Webber states, however, that this depends upon his future wealth: 'If things continue to go well in my business, which is quite dodgy, I dream that one day the whole collection could be seen together...Access to art is extremely important' (*Sunday Times*, 3/5/92).

Another facet to his charitable activities in the arts field is the **Bill Lloyd Webber Memorial Fund**. Sir Andrew set up this grant-making charity in 1982 to commemorate his late father, who was director of London College of Music. The fund promotes public education in the arts – and in particular drama, dance, music and singing – largely by supporting scholarships for students at the Arts Educational School and Guildhall School of Music and Drama. In 1992/93 it had an income of £39,000, of which two-thirds came from Lloyd Webber's Really Useful Group, and its total charitable expenditure was £51,500. Its trustees currently include Sir Andrew and his cellist-virtuoso brother Julian.

On a wider front, in the past Lloyd Webber has made a £100,000 donation to the Almeida Theatre, and has given £400,000 to diabetes research because his first wife suffered from the illness. He is also vice president of the Royal Theatrical Fund. More recently, in November 1992, Sir Andrew decided to become the major sponsor of the National Youth Music Theatre. This involves about £150,000 a year. His interest in promoting the talent of young composers and performers is well manifested in this company, whose new productions at the Edinburgh Festival and elsewhere have received critical acclaim.

Sir Andrew's wealth has come from his talents at writing catchy tunes, which he has put together in a string of very successful musicals, including *Jesus Christ Superstar* and *Evita* with his former lyricist partner Tim Rice and more recently *Cats*, *Starlight Express*, and *Phantom of the Opera*. His business interests are largely handled by the Really Useful Group which he floated in 1987 for £10 million, took private again in 1990 for £77 million, and a few weeks later sold nearly one-third to Polygram for £78m. The community contributions made by the company, £70,000 this year, can be taken as part of Lloyd Webber's personal charitable support given his majority holding. Sir Andrew appears to be somewhat of an enlightened landowner around his country home, Sydmonton, just outside Newbury in Berkshire. He owns 4,000 acres, including the hills made famous by the book *Watership Down*, and has given some of it to a local housing association. His philanthropic impulses did not extend, however, to a group of New Age travellers which he had evicted from his grounds in 1993.

Contact: Andrew Lloyd Webber Art Foundation, Mr D J M Ward, Speedily Bircham, Bouverie House, 154 Fleet St, London, EC4A 2HX. Tel: 0171 353 3290. Sarah Miller, Charity Administrator, Bill Lloyd Webber Memorial Fund, Escaway Ltd, 22 Tower St, London, WC2H 9NS. Tel: 0171 240 0880. Really Useful Group, 22 Tower St, London, WC2H 9NS. Open Churches Fund: no contact address found, but probably approachable via Really Useful Group's address.

DAVID THOMPSON

£1.2 million

(but see below)

PREFERENCE: education, medicine, homeless people, general
AGE: 58
WEALTH: £250m-£500m
TRUST LINKS: Thompson Family Charitable Trust

COMPANY LINKS: sold stake in Hillsdown Holding

David Thompson made the bulk of his fortune, along with Sir Harry Solomon (qv), from the success of the Hillsdown Holdings food to property conglomerate. The pair had merged their separate business interests in 1974 to create the successful group which was floated in 1985. In the same year Thompson had set up the **Thompson Family Charitable Trust** in order to support general charitable organisations, and had soon endowed it with over 2.5 million shares in Hillsdown. Thompson sold half of his personal stake in the company when he stepped down as chair in 1987, and the trust followed suit and received £7.5 million for its entire shareholding. He later realised the rest of his personal paper wealth when he resigned as a director of Hillsdown and cashed in his remaining shares.

In subsequent years, under the astute investment advice of its founder, the trust has steadily built an asset base of £12 million by retaining most of the income it generates rather than distributing it as donations. This has been the result of a deliberate policy on the part of the trustees to accumulate sufficient capital eventually to enable six or seven figure donations to be made without depleting reserves. They believe that it is better to concentrate the trust's money on substantial projects in this way so that they can make a real difference, rather than supporting a multitude of smaller grants. This plan is now coming to fruition, and in the current year the trust is making a grant of £1.2 million to a school. The trust's secretary told us that the trustees are keen to hear from applicants with suitable projects requiring £1-1.5 million of funding, although educational and medical causes along with proposals to help the homeless stand the greatest chance of success.

Whilst the trust has been consolidating its position during the past six or so years, donations totalling over £0.5 million have been made. A number of these grants went to various horse-racing charities, reflecting Thompson's involvement with the sport, although these causes are not necessarily likely to be major recipients of the trust's largesse in the future. In 1992/93 the trust had a considerable income of £1.4 million, most of which was added to reserves although £34,000 went on donations to a variety of causes. In the subsequent year the grant total has

apparently been much higher, and has included £70,000 to the Save the Children Fund, and this increase is likely to be maintained.

Since leaving Hillsdown Holdings David Thompson has kept active on the business front through a multitude of family-owned companies operating in various sectors including food, leisure, property and commodities. Like a number of the other people in this book, Thompson has also put some of his money into football – the south London club Queens Park Rangers nowrun and owned by his son Richard.

Contact: Mr R B Copus, Secretary, Thompson Family Charitable Trust, 1 Dover St, London, W1X 3PJ. Tel: 0171 491 8839.

Lewis '94

PAUL McCARTNEY

£1,104,000

PREFERENCE: arts, general
AGE: 52
WEALTH: £250m-£500m
TRUST LINKS: none found
COMPANY LINKS: MPL Communications

Paul McCartney has made a fortune from his long-standing success in the music and entertainment business, stemmimg from his involvement with The Beatles. Both the *Sunday Times* and *Business Age* place him amongst the top 25 people in their lists of the Britain's rich, with a fortune estimated at around £400 million, even though he sang in one of The Beatles' best known hits: 'I don't care too much for money – for money can't buy me love'.

So far we have been unable to trace any grant-making trusts registered in McCartney's name, but in September

1994 the *Guardian* reported that he had donated £1 million to the Liverpool Institute of Performing Arts. This has gone towards its £16 million redevelopment so it can install high-tech recording equipment and provide rehearsal rooms. It will also aim to brief its students on the legal aspects of the business, because even someone as wealthy as McCartney says he lost out: 'Lennon and McCartney were pretty neatly ripped off because they didn't know anything about business' (*Guardian*, 29/9/94).

McCartney also make some gifts to charities via **MPL Communications** – the private business which manages and co-ordinates his various entertainment activities, and which he totally owns. The company's accounts record charitable donations of £104,000 in 1992 and £69,000 in 1991, although the beneficiaries are not specified. As chair of the company, Paul McCartney received a relatively modest £315,000 from MPL in 1992, which made a group profit of £181,000.

Linda McCartney, Paul's photographer wife, is a committed vegetarian and is actively involved with animal welfare causes and the promotion of a meat-free lifestyle. She helped raise funds for the anti-fur group Lynx, in an attempt to prevent its untimely demise, and is a now a supporter of Peta, the US-based animal rights group. She reportedly gave £1,000 to the so-called 'McLibel 2' – two unemployed environmentalists who are being sued by McDonald's because of an allegedly defamatory leaflet they distributed outside one of the corporation's London fast food joints.

Contact: Paul McCartney, MPL Communications, 1 Soho Square, London, W1V 6BQ.

DAVID and FREDERICK BARCLAY

£1.08 million

PREFERENCE: medical research, disability
AGE: 60
WEALTH: £250m-£500m
TRUST LINKS: David and Frederick Barclay Foundation
COMPANY LINKS: numerous business interests

Established at the end of 1989, the **David and Frederick Barclay Foundation** has already pumped over £3 million into medical research as well as other health and disability causes. In the foundation's 1992 annual report, the chair, former Tory minister Lord Peyton, points out that: 'David and Frederick Barclay, whose substantial generosity has made all of this possible, would be embarrassed by ritual gratitude or ceremonial thanks. They should, however, obtain joy and satisfaction from the knowledge that they have made possible important research and brought relief to many people who were sick, disabled or distressed.'

The secretive Barclay twins seem in fact to be embarrassed by any sort of publicity. Their extensive business interests include hotels, gaming and brewing, and they made a killing on the brewing-to-shipping Ellerman Group in the eighties. In 1993 they bought a small island off Sark in the Channel Islands, where they can enjoy the ultimate in privacy – and tax efficiency. Their normal domicile is the tax haven of Monaco. The aversion to paying taxes apart, their heart seems to remain in Britain: that is where their charitable donations are made and they have close links with

countenance a modicum of publicity provided it is on their own terms. The purchase of the *European* newspaper in 1992 has raised the profile of their empire in a way which cannot have been entirely unforeseen. And in the same year the Barclay Foundation announced publicly an award of £800,000 to finance research into Alzheimer's disease at St Mary's Hospital Medical School. Partly intended to stem the drain of top scientists to the US, the foundation hoped that the donation would draw attention to the insufficient level of finance made available for such research in this country.

On seeing a draft of this entry, Lord Peyton pointed out that 'the entry as a whole, and particularly the second paragraph, is both misleading and unpleasant. In the world we live in, the combination of success and generosity which the Barclays show is, I would have thought, one to be welcomed.'

Contact: Lord Peyton of Yeovil, David and Frederick Barclay Foundation, 20 St James's Street, London SW1A 1ES. Tel: 0171 915 0915.

members of the Conservative Party. In addition to Lord Peyton, the former Tory fundraiser Lord McAlpine (qv) is a trustee of the Barclays' foundation.

The foundation made donations totalling £1.08 million in 1992, but the accounts record no details of beneficiaries. In the previous year, donations of £50,000 or more had been made to the medical schools at Guy's, Bart's and the London Hospitals. The Thrombosis Research Institute, Moorfields Eye Hospital, the Royal Marsden Cancer Appeal and SANE also received £50,000 each. A handful of much smaller awards went to disability groups including Talking Newspapers for the Blind and John Groom's Association for Disabled People.

As well as being identical, the Barclay twins appear pretty inseparable, operating as equal partners in both their charitable and business ventures. There have been some recent indications that they will

SWRAJ PAUL
£1,050,000

PREFERENCE: children, health, education
AGE: 63
WEALTH: £75m–£100m
TRUST LINKS: Ambika Paul Foundation
COMPANY LINKS: Caparo Group

Last year, Swraj Paul made a gift of £1 million towards the redevelopment of the Children's Zoo at Regents Park in memory of his daughter, who died from leukaemia at the tender age of four in April 1968. He had come to

Britain in the mid-sixties from India with Ambika in order to seek specialised medical treatment, and decided to stay after all efforts proved to be ultimately unsuccessful. Whilst his daughter was alive they spent many happy hours together at the London Zoo, which prompted Paul's offer of help: 'They were having problems and I wrote to them. When Ambika was ill I spent a lot of time here with her. I thought, okay, it would be a nice memorial to her' (*Guardian*, 18/1/94).

As a further tribute to his daughter, ten years after her death he set up the **Ambika Paul Foundation**, with himself, his wife Aruna, and his other daughter Anjli as founding trustees. From relatively small beginnings, this grant-making trust now commands assets of £790,000, and in 1991/92 had an income of £232,000, half of which was from a deed of covenant. In the year donations totalling £50,000 were made by the foundation, which states that 'it is anticipated that the level of donations will increase in the future.' It is not possible to state whether it has any preferred causes as the recipients of the grants made are not listed, and the foundation was established with general charitable purposes.

Paul's other interests may give some indication of his priorities: he is a Fellow of the Royal Society of Arts, founder chair of the Indo-British Association, a governor of Thames Valley University, and patron of Youth Clubs UK.

Paul is one of the most successful Indian entrepreneurs in this country. After he had decided to settle in this country he set himself up in business as a manufacturer in the UK steel market. By continually reinvesting profits, the company prospered and his private Caparo Group, which specialises in the manufacture of steel and engineering products for industry, now has annual sales of £350 million. His lifelong Hindu beliefs have helped him avoid most of the trappings of materialism, and he has said about his substantial personal worth that: 'I have never considered that it belongs to me. I am its trustee and must use it to create more wealth. I believe that you must have respect for money, and should not go about wasting it and showing it off.' (*Times*, 1/9/90).

Contact: Mr Swraj Paul, Ambika Paul Foundation, c/o Caparo House, 103 Baker St, London, W1M 1FD. Tel: 0171 486 1417.

SIR JULIAN HODGE

over £1 million

PREFERENCE: medicine, education, religion, largely in Wales

AGE: 89

WEALTH: £50m-£75m

TRUST LINKS: Jane Hodge Foundation; Sir Julian Hodge Charitable Trust

COMPANY LINKS: sold stakes in Hodge Group, Avana Foods and Bank of Wales

The **Jane Hodge Foundation**, set up by Sir Julian Hodge 42 years ago in memory of his mother, is now the largest grant-making trust in Wales with assets of over £20 million generating an annual income of around £1.5 million. The foundation is a major supporter of charitable projects in the region, and has reserved substantial amounts for several major programmes in the near future. Two chunks of one million have been set aside to provide hospice facilities in Cardiff: half at the Sir Julian Hodge Wing of St Winifrede's Nursing Home, and the rest at a purpose-built hospice. The trustees, all bar one of whom are Hodge family members, have also committed £500,000 to establish a Julian Hodge Home for the Homeless in the same city. Other future projects include the construction of a new Catholic cathedral in Cardiff. The donations made in 1990/91 totalled £319,000, and included £25,000 to Cardiff Royal Infirmary League of Friends, £24,000 to the Sacred Heart Sisters, and £50,000 to the University of Wales for a centre of Japanese Studies. A total of £40,000 was given to various religious causes, mainly churches in Wales.

Hodge also makes donations through a smaller personal trust, the **Sir Julian Hodge Charitable Trust**, which he established in 1964. This trust holds investments to the value of over one-quarter of a million pounds, and had an income in 1990/91 of £35,000. It made donations totalling £11,000 in that year, directed largely at Welsh, medical and religious causes. The largest grants were £2,000 to Rhondda Civic Society, £2,000 to the Philadelphie Methodist Church on Jersey, and various gifts of £1,000 to organisations including Gwent Health Authority, Arts for Disabled People in Wales, a scout group in Llanishen, and the Imperial Society of the Knights Bachelor. Whilst these two trusts together made gifts totalling over £330,000 in 1990/91, Sir Julian has informed us that he made personal charitable donations of over £1 million in 1993.

Sir Julian now lives on Jersey, where he has had a house for about thirty years, having outlived many of his contemporaries. He left school at only fourteen to help his widowed mother, but after studying accountancy at night school he started his own practice and then set up the Hodge Group. His fortune came with the growth of his Wales-based finance business, which he sold in 1973 receiving £35 million personally. However, he did not stop there, and throughout the 1970s built up another two successful companies – the Avana food group, and Bank of Wales, which he sold in 1981 and 1986 respectively, netting further millions. He then moved away from his beloved homeland to the Channel Islands for health reasons. He has not completely retired from the world of finance, and he is chair of two private companies: the Carlyle Trust (Jersey) and St Aubins Investment. He maintains strong links with Wales, not only through the donations made by his trusts, but as a council member of the

University of Wales Cardiff. He is also a patron of Morriston Orpheus Choir.

Contact for both the Jane Hodge Foundation and the Sir Julian Hodge Charitable Trust: Margaret Cason, Secretary to the Trustees, Ty Gwyn, Lisvane Rd, Cardiff, CF4 5SG. Tel: 01222 766521.

ANITA and GORDON RODDICK
see below

PREFERENCE: homeless people, environment, health, youth, tribal peoples
AGE: 52 and 51 respectively
WEALTH: £100m-£250m
TRUST LINKS: Body Shop Foundation,
COMPANY LINKS: Body Shop International

Like her friend Richard Branson (qv), Anita Roddick eschews the conventional approach followed by most of the millionaires in this book of keeping their business interests and their charitable concerns strictly separate. In fact, she is well-known for turning customary priorities on their head by arguing that it is precisely through caring for the environment and for other people(s) that the Roddicks' success in business is derived.

Following some wobbles in recent years, few people now doubt that that success is built on a firm foundation. The Body Shop, of which the Roddicks together own a quarter of the share capital, has some one thousand outlets in 50 countries including 140 in the US, and few Christmas stockings in the UK are considered complete without the bottle of eco-pungent lotion or lip balm that shows you really care. That Anita Roddick herself cares goes without saying. She spends a good part of her time travelling to exotic places and meeting tribal peoples to research new ingredients for her products – not such a bad way to run a company, come to think of it – and when she was filmed doing it for an American Express advertisement, she donated the £35,000 fee to a health clinic.

At times Anita Roddick appears to see her company as more a vehicle for running campaigns than for making money. Rainforests, acid rain, vivisection, saving the whale, recycling, and the Ogoni in Nigeria are just some of the subjects of recent Body Shop campaigns.

Anita's husband Gordon, who chairs the company, is usually described as sharing her ideals. In 1994 both Roddicks cashed in a small part of their stake in Body Shop to raise £8 million, announcing that most of it will go to charity and the rest to finance a film company to make a series on tribal peoples. The largest chunk is going to the Healthcare Foundation (see under 'Richard Branson'), a grant-making charity that supports projects helping young people in danger which was founded in 1987 by Anita together with Branson and Michael Grade.

Anita Roddick had previously indicated her intention of eventually leaving the bulk of her personal fortune – estimated at the time at some £40 million – to the **Body Shop Foundation**. The foundation manages the charitable donations budget of the company but has also received major donations from other sources – notably, £1 million from Richard Branson. In 1992/93 the foundation gave away a total of £753,000 to a wide range of causes, including £162,000 to the Global

53

Lewis '94.

countries, only accounts for a very small percentage of turnover. But the company seems to have weathered that storm, with Anita arguing that trade with the Body Shop gives peoples like the Kayapo Indians (they collect four tons of Brazil nuts a year for Body Shop) a realistic economic alternative to environmentally destructive work such as mining or logging. Crucially the City – not hitherto known for its sympathies with indigenous peoples – came down on the Roddicks' side. The loyal support of the British Union for the Abolition of Vivisection was less important financially, but probably just as gratifying for Anita.

The greatest threat to the Body Shop's continued success is not such sniping, but the growing number of copycat products from competitors, in particular those from US rival Bath & Body Works which has just arrived in Britain. The forthcoming showdown will not just test the Roddicks, but the wider credibility of social and environmental concerns as a basis for making business decisions. And if Body Shop comes out on top, the sum that Anita Roddick eventually leaves to charity may be a lot more than £40 million.

Contact: John Ground, Body Shop Foundation, Hawthorn Road, Wick, Littlehampton, West Sussex BN17 7LR. Tel: 01903 731500.

Communication Foundation, £125,000 to a Brazilian project and £36,000 to Brighton Polytechnic (the Body Shop's head office is based in Littlehampton near Brighton). A grant of £117,000 was made to the *Big Issue*, the magazine produced and sold by homeless people, which the Roddicks had helped to found with a grant of over £200,000.

The size of the Roddick's largesse has still not silenced some critics who surfaced in 1994 to claim that the Body Shop's eco-credentials were exaggerated, pointing out for example that the company's 'Trade not Aid' policy, in which key ingredients are purchased direct from local harvesters in less developed

DAME SHIRLEY and SIR LESLIE PORTER

£966,000

PREFERENCE: Israel, the arts, education, 'excellence and efficiency'

AGE: 63 and 74 respectively
WEALTH: £50m-£75m
TRUST LINKS: Porter Foundation
COMPANY LINKS: Tesco, past links with LBC

Inheritance is the primary source of both the Porters' wealth and their philanthropy. Dame Shirley Porter is the daughter of Sir Jack Cohen, the founder of Tesco, and eventually inherited his fortune which she still holds largely in the form of Tesco shares. The **Porter Foundation** was established by Dame Shirley and her husband as long ago as 1970, but the bulk of its current assets arrived in 1990 in the form of a £15 million injection from her parents' Sir John and Lady Cohen Charitable Foundation.

High profile projects planned on the back of the foundation's new spending power include the endowment of a gallery within the National Portrait Gallery and an 'environmental supercentre' in Israel. These two strands – the arts and Israel – account for many of the foundation's biggest donations in recent years, including £52,000 to the Glyndebourne Opera Trust, £6,800 to the Royal Opera House, £76,500 to British Friends for a Beautiful Israel and a massive £343,000 to the Tel Aviv University Trust. Jewish causes in Britain also figure frequently in the donations list of the foundation, as do a wide range of health and educational charities. The total given by the foundation in 1992/93 was £966,000.

The foundation's policy statement announces that it supports 'projects in the field of education, culture, the environment and health and welfare which encourage excellence, efficiency and innovation and enhance the quality of people's lives'. The pursuit of excellence, and in particular efficiency, readers will recognise as an old Porter obsession from Dame Shirley's most celebrated former role, as leader of Westminster Council. In 1984 she went as far as to set up a company called Efficiency in Local Government Ltd, one of whose primary purposes was to campaign against the now defunct Greater London Council. The Porter Foundation has made grants to the Institute of Economic Affairs and the Foundation for Business Responsibilities, both of which are charities.

Between them the Porters hold a string of voluntary appointments in a wide range of charitable organisations. Dame Shirley is president of the European Standing Conference on the Environment and Tourism, a member of the board of the Tidy Britain Group and of the board of the Oxford Centre for Hebrew and Jewish Studies, and a former director of the English National Ballet.

Sir Leslie is vice president of the National Playing Fields Association, honorary vice president of the Sports Aid Foundation and honorary chair of the board of governors of Tel Aviv University.

Shirley Cohen had married Leslie Porter at the tender age of 19. Now Sir Leslie, he had been managing director of his own family's textile business before joining Tesco and rising to become its chair by 1973. Tesco went through what is recognised as its most successful period while he was at the helm. Now, however, a slide in the Tesco share price has resulted in commentators revising downwards their estimates of the Porter fortune. Dame Shirley's other business interests have also been hit recently; she resigned as chair of the London radio station LBC in March 1994 after it lost its broadcasting franchise to London News Radio.

But the greatest current threat to the Porter wealth comes in the form of legal action. A damning report from the District Auditor in 1994 into Westminster Council's 'designated council house sales policy' alleged that the Council had organised house sales to maximise Tory votes in the impending elections, and Dame Shirley and eight other former councillors and officers together face a surcharge of £21 million. Dame Shirley is preparing an emphatic defence of her record which will probably involve pursuing the District Auditor through the courts.

Contact: Paul Williams, Executive Director, Porter Foundation, 63 Chester Square, London SW1.

SIR DONALD GOSLING

£803,000

PREFERENCE: youth, arts, forces' welfare, general
AGE: 65
WEALTH: £250m–£500m
TRUST LINKS: Gosling Foundation
COMPANY LINKS: National Parking Corporation

Sir Donald Gosling's fortunes have been very closely associated with those of his long-time business partner, Ronald Hobson (qv) with whom he set up the National Parking Corporation. It is entirely fitting, therefore, that their philanthropic activities are also very closely interlinked. Both set up a charitable trust in 1985, administered from the same offices in London, and each is a trustee of the other's grant-maker.

The **Gosling Foundation** is currently the larger of the two trusts, holding 5.5 million ordinary shares in the National Parking Corporation –

which are valued by Gosling and Hobson at £16.6 million – along with £840,000 in the bank. These assets provided an income of £876,000 in 1991/92, which funded charitable donations of £803,000, up from £595,000 in the previous year. A substantial chunk, £200,000, went to the Duke of Edinburgh Award Scheme, and the Fleet Air Arm Memorial Church Fund and the Bodleian Library at Oxford each benefited to the tune of £100,000. Other major gifts included £33,000 to Serenade to a Princess, £30,000 to the Salisbury Spire Appeal, £25,000 to the Prince's Youth Business Trust, and £20,000 to both the National Youth Orchestra and Sunfund.

At the tender age of 15, Sir Donald had seen active service in the navy in the last war, and this is reflected in some of the grants made by his foundation. In 1991/92 donations were made to organisations such as the HMS Repulse Welfare Fund (£20,000), the Fleet Air Arm Museum Appeal (£16,000), the HMS Heron Welfare Fund (£10,000) and the Royal Naval Benevolent Trust (£10,000). On a personal basis, he is closely involved with various causes linked to the Forces: he is patron of the Submarine Memorial Appeal and the HMS Ark Royal Welfare Trust, a trustee of the Fleet Air Arm Museum at Yeovilton, and president and member of the council of management of the White Ensign Association – a frequent recipient of grants from the foundation. Two of the foundation's donations in the previous year are worthy of note: a £200,000 gift was made to Margaret Thatcher's (qv) personal charitable trust, marking Gosling's close support of the former Prime Minister, and £50,000 was received by Saints and Sinners, the charitable club of which Sir Donald is a member.

The National Parking Corporation is the private business through which

Gosling and Hobson have made their fortune. It has its roots in postwar London, where the two ex-servicemen spotted the long-term need for private car parking facilities in busy town centres. The company's National Car Parks subsidiary now controls nearly three-quarters of the private sector parking market thanks to its 650 car parks across Britain. NCP itself made charitable donations of £32,000 in 1990/91, which were directed at charities with which the company was already associated. Another well-known subsidiary of the National Parking Corporation is the car recovery service, National Breakdown. Gosling is also chair of the Palmer & Harvey confectionery and tobacconists firm, and a director of Lovell Holdings. Other charitable activities include his role as chair of the Berkeley Square Ball Charitable Trust and the Selective Employment Scheme, and as trustee of the Royal Yachting Association's Seamanship Foundation.

Sir Donald recently received widespread coverage for his proposal that the country's wealthy business leaders should fund a new boat for the Queen, following the announcement that the Royal Yacht Britannia is to be pensioned-off by 1997. Not afraid to put his money where his mouth is, Gosling put £5 million into the pot to encourage others to follow suit. In a similarly nautical vein, he offered to match any funds raised to turn the HMS Plymouth into a memorial to the Falklands War when he heard that the Government was planning to scrap the vessel.

Contact: Mr A E Bromfield, Secretary to the Trustees, Gosling Foundation, 21 Bryanston St, Marble Arch, London, W1A 4NH. Tel: 0171 499 7050. National Car Parks: Miss A Pell, Sales and Marketing, at same address.

ROLAND 'TINY' ROWLAND

£800,000

PREFERENCE: African charities, children
AGE: 75
WEALTH: £250m-£500m
TRUST LINKS: none found
COMPANY LINKS: Lonrho

Lonrho boss 'Tiny' Rowland and owner of Harrods Mohamed al-Fayed (qv) marked the peaceful settlement of their often acrimonious nine-year battle by each making a donation of £50,000 to the children's welfare charity Childline in December last year. Mr Fayed also gave Mr Rowland a life-size replica of a shark to auction for the charity. It had been named 'Tiny' and hung in Harrods' food hall to represent Lonrho's acquisitive moves towards the department store.

This is not, however, the total extent of his charitable gifts in the last year. We were informed that Tiny Rowland has given away a total of £750,000 of his own money to various African charities in the last twelve months. No doubt this reflects his long-time business activities in the continent.

He was born Roland Walter Fuhrhop, in India, with a German father and an English mother. His fortune stems from the massive Lonrho conglomerate which he has built up over the past three decades, with core activities of international commodity trading and mining. The company is very active in Africa, where Rowland is apparently known as 'Bwana Mkubwa', or 'big man'. Lonrho has recently been divesting itself of various assets, notably the *Observer* newspaper and the Volkswagen franchise in Britain. The company made total charitable donations of £86,000 in 1992, but these are not included in the figure cited above for Tiny Rowland as he does not hold a majority stake. He has also recently announced his decision to retire by the end of 1995.

Contact: Mr R W Rowland, Managing Director & Chief Executive, Lonrho plc, Cheapside House, 138 Cheapside, London, EC2V 6BL.

SIR PHILIP HARRIS

£742,000

PREFERENCE: medicine, education
AGE: 51
WEALTH: £75m-£100m
TRUST LINKS: Philip & Pauline Harris Charitable Trust
COMPANY LINKS: Carpetright, Harris Ventures Ltd

You have to feel a bit sorry for carpet salesman Sir Philip Harris – he has donated a substantial part of his personal fortune to Guy's Hospital, only to have the rug pulled out from under his feet by the government's London NHS restructuring plans. He gave over £4 million towards the £140 million cost of the hospital's new wing which was due to open in September 1994, and his munificence was recognised in the development's name, Philip Harris House. And that is not all – over the years he has donated more than £2 million to the United Medical and Dental Schools of Guy's and St Thomas's, nearly three-quarters of a million to the Generation Trust (which funds its paediatric research unit), and £200,000 for the refurbishment of a lecture theatre in its medical school. But this may all count for nothing as Guy's is hit by the rationalisation of London health services. Virginia Bottomley, the Secretary of State for Health, announced in February 1994 that all would not be lost, and that Philip Harris House should become 'a high quality health and academic campus.' Many of the other contributors to the £44 million raised for the development from charity are not best pleased, as the building may not be used for its original purpose. As a member of the governing council of the United Medical and Dental

Schools, chair of the Generation Trust, and former chair of Guy's itself, Sir Philip may also have something to say about its fate. Press reports indicate that his trust has gone so far as to ask for its money back.

The money he gave to Guy's came from his personal trust, the **Philip and Pauline Harris Charitable Trust**, which he established in 1981 with an endowment of 500,000 shares in Harris Queensway, the company he then controlled. One of the founding trustees was his one-time business associate Hugh Sykes (qv), who has a substantial charitable trust of his own. By the time it exhausts its capital in the year 2000, the trust will have donated over £16 million to various charitable causes. Apart from the Guy's donations, the trust has given substantial support to other medical organisations, most notably over £1 million to Birthright, the appeal arm of the Royal College of Obstetricians and Gynaecologists – Sir Philip is a member of their court of patrons. This was earmarked for research centres at St Mary's Hospital, Sheffield, Oxford and Aberdeen. Over £350,000 has also been given to the National Hospital for Nervous Diseases (of which Philip Harris is governor), £150,000 to Great Ormond Street's 'Wishing Well' appeal, and over £100,000 to South Bromley Hospice. His interests in health and medicine may relate to his past experiences – both his parents died of cancer when he was young.

The other major area of support for the trust is education, and in particular the Harris and Bacon City Technology Colleges, both of which have received a total of three-quarters of a million in recent years. Sir Philip has the closest links with the CTC that bears his name, and both he and his wife, Pauline, are directors of the charitable company that runs it. The trust is the main sponsor of this Croydon-based college which opened in September 1990, having provided the bulk of its £1 million private sponsorship, although this is dwarfed by £7.6 million of capital funding from the Department of Education, which also provided a £3.1 million recurrent grant in 1991. Amongst the other sponsors of the Harris CTC is Great Universal Stores, which has contributed £27,000, and of which Sir Philip is a non-executive director. The Harris CTC's most recent accounts also note that nearly £20,000 worth of carpets were purchased 'at arms length from a company in which Sir Philip Harris has an interest.' Another major educational recipient of Sir Philip's largesse is Oriel College at Oxford, which has been given over £1 million by his trust, and of which he was made an honorary fellow in 1989. Another part of Oxford University, Manchester College, is also to receive £3.6 million from Sir Philip's trust, and in return will change its name to the Manchester Academy and Harris College. In a similar vein, his other charitable activities include chairing the Young Entrepreneurs' Fund.

It clearly takes considerable financial success to be able to give so much money away. At the tender age of fifteen, Sir Philip left school to run his father's three carpet shops. From these modest beginnings he created the massive Harris Queensway chain, which was one of the success stories of the early 1980s. Sir Philip made £69 million when the company was taken-over by Lowndes in 1988. The newly named Lowndes Queensway group eventually collapsed within a couple of years. He has since concentrated his business acumen on a new carpet-selling venture, Carpetright, which he set up with MFI. This chain has gone from strength-to-strength, with rapid expansion fuelled by a merger with Allied and a successful flotation on the stock market in summer last year. Sir Philip's business interests are controlled by his private company Harris Ventures Limited, which is based at Orpington in Kent. He is also a non-executive director of the fertilizer to drugs group Fisons, and is a trustee of its charitable trust. His charitable inclinations have clearly rubbed-off on the rest of his family, who run a string of four near-identical trusts – **the Charles Harris, Martin Harris, Peter Harris, and Susan Sadler Charitable Trusts**. All were established in December 1988 with Pauline Harris as one of the founding trustees, received £50,000 capital later that month, and each donated £12,500 to the Harris CTC in 1991.

Contact: Philip & Pauline Harris Charitable Trust: Donald Bompas, Managing Executive, 187/189 Sevenoaks Way, Orpington, Kent, BR5 3AQ. Tel: 01689 875135. Charles Harris Charitable Trust, Martin Harris Charitable Trust, Peter Harris Charitable Trust, Susan Sadler Charitable Trust – all c/o A.R. Bull, Harris Ventures, Central Court, Knoll Rise, Orpington, Kent, BR6 0JA. Tel: 01689 875135.

ROBERT (ROBIN) FLEMING
and family

£732,000

PREFERENCE: medicine, welfare, conservation, education, arts
AGE: 61
WEALTH: £100m-£250m
TRUST LINKS: P F Charitable Trust
COMPANY LINKS: Robert Fleming Holdings

Robert Fleming – known as Robin to colleagues and friends – is chair of the investment bank Robert Fleming & Co, which was founded by his forefather over one hundred years ago. Thanks to the success of the family firm, the Flemings are able to give substantial financial support to the voluntary sector through the **P F Charitable Trust**, which has distributed over £6.7 million during its life.

This grant-making trust was set up back in 1951 by Robin's late father, Philip – the P F of the title – with an endowment of various shares, including ten thousand in Robert Fleming & Co. His son joined the board of trustees ten years later, and in 1983 Robin Fleming made some valuable additions to the trust's funds.

By 1991/92 the trust held assets in a wide portfolio of shares with a market value of £14.7 million, including 995,000 ordinary shares in Robert Fleming Holdings worth £6.4 million. These helped produce an income of £847,000 which supported total donations of £732,000. Some of this went to charities included on Philip Fleming's original annual personal list, but most were determined by the current trustees. A large chunk of the trust's support went to the medical sector, including research and hospitals. This area received a total of nearly £300,000 including grants of £25,000 to St Thomas' Charitable Trust, £25,000 to Help the Hospices, and £20,000 to the Robert Jones and Agnes Hunt Orthopaedic Hospital. The remaining donations were directed at a wide variety of causes, with some emphasis on conservation, welfare, education, and the arts.

Whilst Robert Fleming Holdings may not be a household name, its principal subsidiary Save & Prosper is well-known in the investment field. The Fleming family hold around 40% of the shares via non-charitable trusts, and many of them work for the company which made total donations of £235,000 in 1993 (these have not, however, been included in the figure cited above). Robin Fleming is a trustee of the British Field Sports Society.

Contact: The Secretary, P F Charitable Trust, Fleming Trustees, 25 Copthall Avenue, London, EC2R 7DR. Tel: 0171 638 5858.

JOHN ZOCHONIS

£663,000

PREFERENCE: general, education, children, North West

AGE: 64

WEALTH: £20m-£35m

TRUST LINKS: Zochonis Charitable Trust

COMPANY LINKS: Paterson Zochonis – recently retired as chair

It would be quite easy to get worked up into a lather about the source of John Zochonis' wealth. He recently retired as chair of Paterson Zochonis, the public company whose subsidiary Cussons produces the famous Imperial Leather brand of soap. The firm was co-founded by his Greek grandfather over a hundred years ago to trade in West Africa. The continued success of this Manchester based company, whose main activities are now the manufacture of toiletries and cleaning products, is good news for the **Zochonis Charitable Trust** which derives its considerable income from a large tranche of almost 4.5 million shares in Paterson Zochonis, having an approximate market value of £22.5 million in 1994.

The Zochonis Charitable Trust was set up in 1977, and in 1993/94 had an income of £750,000 derived mainly from dividends from its shareholding in Paterson Zochonis, although the trust otherwise has no direct connection with the company. Grants of £663,000 were made to a variety of charitable causes, the largest being £100,000 to Greater Manchester Police Community Charity, £40,000 to the Manchester Royal Exchange Theatre and £40,000 to the Westminster Abbey Trust. In the previous year donations totalled £680,000, and included £75,000 to the Royal Commonwealth Society, £71,500 to the University of Salford, and £50,000 to both First Organisation and the Royal Northern School of Music. Smaller grants were directed to a diverse range of organisations, with some focused upon the North West. A regular recipient of gifts in recent years, including £150,000 in 1989/90 and £50,000 in 1992/93, has been Manchester University with which John Zochonis has close links as past chair of its Council.

Contact: The Secretary, Zochonis Charitable Trust, Touche Ross & Co, PO Box 500, Abbey House, 74 Mosley St, Manchester, M60 2AT.

JACK DELLAL

£611,000

PREFERENCE: Jewish causes, drug abuse, education, arts, youth

AGE: 70

WEALTH: £100m-£250m

TRUST LINKS: Dellal Foundation

COMPANY LINKS: Allied Commercial Holdings

Jack Dellal established his fortune in the early seventies when he sold his Manchester-based financial group Dalton Barton for £58 million. Soon afterwards, in 1973, he set up the **Dellal Foundation** with an initial endowment of 100,000 shares in

Court Hotels (London). Over the past twenty years the foundation has built up assets worth over £3 million, which in 1992/93 helped generate an income of £294,000. Donations of £611,000 were made in the year with a clear preference for Jewish and Israeli causes: major grants included £100,000 to the Tel Aviv Foundation, £62,500 to the Jewish Educational Development Trust, and £50,000 to both the Jewish Preparatory School and the Society of Friends of Torah. Other significant gifts included £50,000 to Balliol College at Oxford, and support for drug rehabilitation projects – £100,000 to the Israel Anti Drug Abuse Foundation and £50,000 to Business Against Drugs. These latter donations perhaps reflect personal tragedy, as *Business Age* magazine reported that one of Dellal's daughters died of a drug overdose twelve years ago. Smaller grants were directed at a range of causes, including arts and youth organisations.

● GIVING FROM PROPERTY FORTUNES

Peter Beckwith	£5,040,000
Lord Rayne	£1,845,000
Benzion Freshwater	£1,600,000
Jack Dellal	£611,000
William Gredley	£530,000
Lord Palumbo	£434,000
Sidney Corob	£318,000
Elliot Bernerd	£189,000
Coral Samuel	£178,000
Everard Goodman	£158,000
Arnold Lee	£155,000
Tony Clegg	£151,000

Although his name often appears in the business pages, Jack Dellal hit the headlines in a less usual fashion at the end of last year, after it was confirmed that beleaguered pop star Michael Jackson had stayed at Dellal's Hampshire estate after the cancellation of his world tour. Since first making it rich in the seventies, Dellal has generally increased his fortune on the back of the property market through his main investment company Allied Commercial Holdings, although he has been hard hit by the current recession. He is vice-president of the Anglo-Polish Conservative Association, and an officer of the Order of Polish Restituta.

Contact: Mr J Dellal, Dellal Foundation, 14th Floor, Bowater House, 68 Knightsbridge, London, SW1X 7LT. Tel: 0171 225 0066.

SIR EVELYN DE ROTHSCHILD
£605,000

PREFERENCE: arts, medicine, education
AGE: 63
WEALTH: over £500m
TRUST LINKS: Eranda Foundation, New Court Charitable Trust
COMPANY LINKS: N M Rothschild

Arguably the wealthiest banker in Britain, Sir Evelyn de Rothschild is known for his reticence and his conservative approach to life. As chair of the merchant bank N M Rothschild, these qualities no doubt come in useful when advising governments, as the bank often does, not least our own government during the spate of privatisations in the eighties. When Sir Evelyn set up a charitable trust in 1967 is was under the appropriately cryptic title of the **Eranda Foundation**, 'Eranda' probably being an acronym from his full name, Evelyn Robert Adrian de Rothschild.

Eranda was originally endowed with 200,000 shares in Rothschild Continuation Ltd., the family company that owns N M Rothschild, and now has an annual income worth nearly £0.75 million. In 1990/91, the last year for which accounts were on file at the Charity Commission, the trust made donations totalling £605,000, of which the arts received the lion's share of £348,500. Health, welfare and medical research causes landed £228,500, and educational bodies £28,000. Although details of beneficiaries were not provided in the accounts, a previous set of accounts recorded major donations going to hospitals and medical research charities, to Harrow School for studentships, to the Save the Children Fund, to CBF World Jewish Relief and to the National Trust Ascot Fund. Sir Evelyn was himself a schoolboy at Harrow and is now well known for his love of racing; he has chaired United Racecourses Ltd. since 1977.

N M Rothschild itself made charitable donations totalling nearly £0.5 million in 1992/93.

Sir Evelyn's father, the late Anthony Gustav de Rothschild, set up a charitable trust in 1947 of which his son is now a trustee. The **New Court Charitable Trust**, once again holding a block of shares in Rothschild Continuation, made donations totalling £14,500 in 1990/91, including £2,400 to Toynbee Hall, £1,000 to CBF World Jewish Relief and £2,000 to the Runnymede Trust.

Rather larger is another trust established in the past by a member of the family, Leopold David de Rothschild. The **Leopold de Rothschild (1959) Charitable Trust** gave £61,000 away in 1991, including grants of £8,500 to Glyndebourne, £4,000 to the Liberal Jewish Synagogue, £2,500 to Jewish Care, £2,000 to the English Chamber Orchestra, and further awards to St

Michael's Hospice, Crusaid and the Jewish Association. The trust holds 126,000 shares in Rothschild Continuation. The Charity Commission register also reveals three smaller trusts connected to the family, the **Leopold de Rothschild 1980 Charitable Trust**, the **Edmund de Rothschild Charitable Trust** and the **Edmund de Rothschild 1981 Charitable Trust**.

Sir Evelyn de Rothschild's most famous living cousin, Lord (Jacob) Rothschild, is considered in a separate entry in this book.

Contact: For the Eranda Foundation: The Secretary, New Court, St Swithin's Lane, EC4P 4DU. Tel: 0171 280 5000. For the other trusts: Rothschild Trust Corporation Ltd., at the same address.

STANLEY KALMS

£604,000

PREFERENCE: Jewish causes, education
AGE: 62
WEALTH: £20m-£35m
TRUST LINKS: Stanley Kalms Foundation
COMPANY LINKS: Dixons

Stanley Kalms is a major supporter of charities, and in particular Jewish organisations, through his eponymous grant-making trust. In 1989 he established the **Stanley Kalms Foundation** with his wife Pamela, and later that year it took over the assets of the now defunct Kalms Family Charitable Trust. By 1992/93 the foundation held assets of £2.1 million and had an income of £192,000 which was far outstripped by donations of over £600,000. The accounts for that year do not specify the recipients of donations, but those made in the previous year give a good indication of the foundation's priorities. The bulk of grants went to various Jewish causes, such as £200,000 to the Jewish Educational Development Trust, £10,000 to Nightingale House, £6,000 to Friends of Mifal Hatorah, and £5,000 to each of the Institute of Jewish Affairs, Friends of the Hebrew University and Jewish Philanthropic Association. Apart from making gifts to Jewish organisations, the Kalms Foundation also supports individuals through fellowship grants. Some secular charities were also supported, notably the Ravenswood Foundation which received £10,000, and the Royal Opera House Trust which received £12,500 in 1990/91.

A major recipient of support from the Kalms Foundation has been the **Traditional Alternatives Foundation**, including a grant of £138,000 in 1992/93. This charity, established by Kalms and his wife in 1990, has the object of furthering education, learning and research in Judaism, and over the past few years has funded a conference entitled 'Women and the Jewish Future' as well as a review of the United Synagogue's role in the future.

Kalms is the epitome of the self-made entrepreneurial millionaire so beloved by Thatcherism. He left school at sixteen to work in his father's single north London photographic shop. This family business has since evolved into the public Dixons electronics and photographic retail group chaired by Stanley Kalms, which has a presence in virtually every high street through its Dixons and Currys stores. The company is also heavily involved with the government's programme of City Technology Colleges, as major sponsor of the Dixons Bradford CTC. Kalms is involved on a personal basis with this initiative as a governor of the Dixons College, and a trustee of the

national City Technology Colleges Trust. On a wider front, he is chair of King's Healthcare Trust, and director of the right wing Centre for Policy Studies think-tank. He is also a visiting professor at the University of North London's Business School, and non-executive director of British Gas.

Contact: Mrs O Morgan, Stanley Kalms Foundation, 29 Farm Street, London, W1X 7RD.
Tel: 0171 499 3494.

SIR JOHN and SIR ADRIAN SWIRE

£547,000

PREFERENCE: education, arts, medicine, general
AGE: 67 and 62
WEALTH: over £500m
TRUST LINKS: Swire Charitable Trust, John Swire 1989 Charitable Trust, Adrian Swire Charitable Trust, Swire Educational Trust
COMPANY LINKS: J Swire & Sons

The Swires are one of the two families that have dominated business life in Hong Kong for generations (see also Keswick family), through companies such as Swire Pacific and Cathay Pacific Airways, all controlled by the London-based private company J Swire & Sons. Sir Adrian Swire is the current chair of the company, having taken over from elder brother Sir John in 1987.

Just as you won't go very far in Hong Kong without seeing the name of Swire, so the Charity Commission register in London is scattered with trusts with Swire in their title. One of the first, simply called the **Swire Charitable Trust**, was set up by the two brothers in 1975. By 1992 it was making donations of £77,500 in the year, the money generated by assets worth over £2.2 million, the bulk of it held in Swire companies' shares. The accounts do not specify the beneficiaries in that year, but in 1991 the Glyndebourne Building Fund had received £25,000, the Ashmolean Museum £20,000, the Cystic Fibrosis Research Trust £8,000, and the Ranfurly Library Service £4,500.

Sir John and Sir Adrian also each have a trust in their individual names, both set up in the late eighties. The **John Swire 1989 Charitable Trust** made donations totalling £39,000 in 1992 and the **Adrian Swire Charitable Trust** gave away £20,000. Donations listed from the former trust in 1991 give a good indication of Sir John's charitable interests: £10,000 went to the Cancer Relief Macmillan Fund, £2,500 to the Kent Gardens Trust, and £1,000 each to King's School Canterbury, the National Autistic Care and Training Appeal, and University College and Middlesex Hospitals. The deed for this trust notably specifies that 'the trustees shall have power to retain any Swire shares which are from time to time comprised in the trust fund and shall not be under any duty to diversify the trust fund...' The Swire family currently controls over 60 per cent of J Swire & Sons.

Another trust established in 1989 was the **Swire Educational Trust.** This is principally financed by the four main Swire companies and was set up 'to administer a variety of scholarship schemes... for overseas students to study at universities and colleges in the UK, Hong Kong and elsewhere'. Both Sir John and Sir Adrian Swire sit as trustees. The 1992 accounts reveal some £410,000 spent on student costs. Given the Swire family's close control over J Swire & Sons and their role in setting up the trust, this expenditure has been included in the total given for their

donations above. However, total worldwide donations for the Swire Group, topping £2.5 million in 1992, have not been included as many of these will have been made by subsidiary companies in which the Swires' personal interest is more modest.

We were informed by John Swire & Sons that the numbers we quote 'obviously do not include any charitable donations made personally by Sir John or Sir Adrian (or indeed their immediate family) [who] would want to keep that information private.'

Contact: For the Swire Educational Trust: G C Pope, John Swire & Sons Ltd., Swire House, 59 Buckingham Gate, London SW1E 6AJ.
Tel: 0171 834 7717.
For the other trusts: Mr G D W Swire, at same address.

MOHAMED AL-FAYED and family
£539,000

PREFERENCE: general
AGE: 61
WEALTH: unknown
TRUST LINKS: Alfayed Charitable Foundation
COMPANY LINKS: Harrods

At the end of last year Harrods' boss Mohamed al-Fayed marked the amicable end of his long-running feud with Tiny Rowland (qv) by matching his erstwhile rival's £50,000 donation to the Childline children's charity. This gift may have originated from the **Alfayed Charitable Foundation**, which Mohamed al-Fayed, along with his brothers Salah and Ali Fayed, had created in 1987 to support general charitable causes. The foundation has since received over £1.4 million in covenants, presumably from al-Fayed and his brothers, and has given away nearly £2 million. In 1992, it had an income of £387,000, and made donations of £539,000 to unspecified recipients.

Contact: Miss A Smith, Secretary to the Trustees, Alfayed Charitable Foundation, Suite 5, 55 Park Lane, London, W1Y 3DB.
Tel: 0171 409 9144.

● GIVING BY INDUSTRIALISTS

Swraj Paul	£1,050,000
Tiny Rowland	£800,000
John Zochonis	£663,000
Alan Sugar	£538,000
O'Hea family	£439,000
Kenneth Horne	£359,000
Lord Weinstock	£333,000
Clark family	£300,000
Stephen Rubin	£300,000
George Moore	£291,000
Graham Kirkham	£260,000
Bamford family	£155,000

ALAN SUGAR
£538,000

PREFERENCE: Jewish causes, Essex
AGE: 47
WEALTH: £100m–£250m
TRUST LINKS: Alan Sugar Foundation
COMPANY LINKS: Amstrad, Tottenham Hotspur FC

Alan Sugar is one of the country's best known entrepreneurs, thanks to the popularity of the value-for-money electronics goods produced by his Essex-based company Amstrad. Recently he has reached out to a different audience as chair of the football club Spurs. Over the past few years he has been a generous supporter of Jewish causes through the **Alan Sugar Foundation**, which he set up in 1986. A major beneficiary has been an old people's home in Ilford run by Jewish Care, which has received a total of £1.1 million from the foundation, financed largely by the sale of various Amstrad shares.

The foundation's accounts show charitable donations of over half a million pounds in 1992/93, substantially up on the previous year's £136,000. Over three-quarters went to Redbridge Jewish Youth and Community Centre in a £297,000 grant, and £150,000 to the United Synagogue Educational Trust's Redbridge School. Other gifts included £50,000 to Jewish Care, £25,000 to the Ravenswood Foundation, £10,000 to Jew's College London and £5,000 to the National Youth Theatre. The accounts seem to show a switch in funding, as the foundation derived the bulk of its £388,000 income from gifts and associated tax rebates rather than from share sales as it had done previously.

In the past few years Alan Sugar has rarely been missing from either the business or sports pages due to his continued involvement with Amstrad, and his more recent interests in Tottenham Hotspur Football Club. He incurred the wrath of many Amstrad shareholders when he tried to return the consumer electronics company to his private control, and was faced with a similar reaction when Terry Venables left Spurs. He has since regained the respect of many Spurs fans by fighting the punishment meted out upon the club by the football authorities following alleged financial irregularities prior to his involvement. The current recession has had a harsh impact upon Sugar's personal wealth, which has been adversely affected by the fall in the Amstrad share price – at one stage he was reportedly worth over £500 million, but recent estimates put his worth at only one-quarter of that amount.

Contact: Colin Sandy, Alan Sugar Foundation, 53 Broad Street Green Road, Great Totham, Maldon, Essex, CM9 8NX.

WILLIAM GREDLEY
£530,000 NEW

PREFERENCE: mental health, elderly people, general
AGE: 61
WEALTH: £75m-£100m
TRUST LINKS: Gredley Charitable Trust
COMPANY LINKS: Unex Group

William Gredley is another individual who graces these pages thanks to his involvement with the property and construction industry. The Unex Group of companies, of which he is the principal owner, is one of the leaders in this sector, and operates from offices at Stetchworth, near Newmarket. In 1992/93, the Unex Group made charitable donations and provided other benefits to charities which amounted in aggregate to £530,000. The principal beneficiary was MIND, which received about half a million pounds, as Gredley has a preferred sympathy for the mentally disturbed. Of the remainder, £4,000 went to sundry charities and £26,000 went to the **Gredley Charitable Trust**, which Gredley had set up in 1990 with himself, his son and his late wife as founding trustees.

The trust states that its main activity is 'the organising and financing of an annual summer day trip to the coast, on behalf of the older residents of Newmarket, Suffolk, and of the surrounding villages.' To this end, it spent nearly £25,000 in 1992/93 on day trip expenses, with a similar sum (£21,000) the previous year. The trust also distributes a relatively restricted amount of money in the form of charitable donations, although these totalled less than £700 in the year. The expenditure on day trips and donations is financed by annually reviewed payments from Phylora Limited, a company connected with William Gredley.

Apart from his holdings in Unex, Gredley also owns a string of horses and an 800 acre stud farm at Stetchworth Park. One of his fillies, User Friendly, has bought him considerable recent success by winning her first six races on the trot.

Contact: Mr J V Gredley, Gredley Charitable Trust, Unex House, Church Lane, Stetchworth, Newmarket, Suffolk, CB8 9TN. Tel: 01638 508144.

LADY THATCHER
about £500,000
(but see below)

PREFERENCE: free-market principles, Eastern Europe, general
AGE: 69
WEALTH: £20m-35m
TRUST LINKS: Margaret Thatcher Foundation, Margaret Thatcher Charitable Trust
COMPANY LINKS: none

Margaret Thatcher is rather like the Queen in that much of the money she gives away has been donated by others. The Thatcher roadshow has circled the globe fund-raising for the **Margaret Thatcher Foundation**, reputedly pulling in seven-figure donations from the Sultan of Brunei

and Hong Kong billionaire Li Ka-Shing. The foundation's Washington branch records donations from supporters of $448,000 in 1992. On a more modest scale, the **Margaret Thatcher Charitable Trust** has also benefited from donations from those still faithful to the former prime minister. In 1990, for example, it received £200,000 from Sir Donald Gosling (qv).

The Margaret Thatcher Foundation is established in both the UK, where it is a limited company, in the US, where it is registered as a charity, and in Switzerland. It gives its purposes as: 'to promote the widest possible acceptance of the principles of economic and political freedom, democracy, the rule of law and the importance of strong defence; to assist and work with the peoples of former communist countries and other oppressive regimes throughout the world as they adopt democracy; to encourage strong transatlantic links between Britain, Europe and North America; to foster greater contact between Western nations and those of the Middle East in the region's search for a lasting peace with security; to further free trade throughout the world.'

Set up, in Lady Thatcher's own words, 'to perpetuate all the kinds of things I believe in', the foundation encountered an early hitch in the UK when it was advised by the Charity Commission that it was not eligible for registration as a charity. With a cash balance in 1992 of only £254,000, the foundation's UK arm is now almost certainly its smallest. The names of the directors will be familiar to seasoned Thatcher watchers: Sir Geoffrey Leigh (qv), historian Norman Stone, former arts minister Lord Gowrie, ex-Tory fundraiser Lord McAlpine (qv) and Lord Harris of High Cross, co-founder of the Institute of Economic Affairs.

Most of the work in progress announced by the UK branch of the Thatcher Foundation consists of exchange projects with Central and Eastern Europe and the countries of the former Soviet Union. 'Enterprise Europe' seeks to place young entrepreneurs from the Czech Republic, Poland, Hungary and Slovakia with British companies; 'Window on the World' enabled television professionals from the Baltic States to look at British journalism and broadcasting. The part of its work that is charitable is financed by the foundation through a tax-deductible account held at the Charities Aid Foundation.

The interests of the Margaret Thatcher Charitable Trust are somewhat closer to home, with regular donations to Somerville College (her *alma mater*) and to charities in Finchley, her old parliamentary constituency. Other recipients of grants in 1991 included the NSPCC, St Mary's Hospital Medical School and the Mountbatten Community Trust, out of total spend that year of £18,000. Together with Thatcher on the board of trustees sits Cynthia Crawford, her former personal secretary (familiar to readers of the memoirs as 'Crawfie').

Lady Thatcher has made most of her money since she was toppled from power in 1990. The considerable income she makes from speaking engagements in the US, Japan and elsewhere – the going rate for an hour of free-market fervour is around $30,000 – has been supplemented by the £3.5 million she picked up from publishers Harper Collins for her memoirs. How much of this goes to the Margaret Thatcher Foundation is unclear. Thatcher's 1991 speaking tour was dedicated to the Foundation, with a fund-raising target of £12 million, but that sort of money is yet to show up in Foundation accounts lodged in the UK or the US. The bulk of the Thatcher Foundation's income may well be routed to Switzerland, with its favourable tax regime. The difficulty of obtaining information on the Foundation's Swiss branch means that both its real size and its activities are still shrouded in mystery.

Contact for: Margaret Thatcher Foundation: Julian Seymour, PO Box 1466, London SW1X 8HY, Tel: 0171 259 5363. For the Margaret Thatcher Charitable Trust, Mrs C M Crawford, 73 Chester Square, London SW1W 1DU.

CYRIL STEIN
£478,000

PREFERENCE: Jewish and Israeli charities
AGE: 66
WEALTH: £35m-£50m
TRUST LINKS: Cyril and Betty Stein Charitable Trust
COMPANY LINKS: recently retired from Ladbrokes

Cyril Stein's generosity is almost the stuff of which legends are made. The philanthropic side of his nature was illustrated in a recent profile by the *Guardian* which related the following apocryphal story: 'On a flight to see one of Ladbroke's overseas operations Mr Stein discovered a little girl on the plane needed a £45,000 liver transplant. After immediately digging in his own pocket for £15,000 he raised the rest of the hospital bill from fellow passengers.'

His generosity also finds expression through the **Cyril and Betty Stein Charitable Trust**, which in 1991/92 gave away almost half a million pounds to various Jewish causes and still had assets of £1.6 million. The largest grants made in the year were £105,000 to the Israel Education & Development Corporation, £65,000 to the Victims of Persecution Fund, and £60,000 to the Foundation for Education. This trust is an amalgam of two previously separate trusts, the Cyril Stein Foundation and the Betty Stein Charitable Trust, which have since ceased to exist and been removed from the register of charities. Cyril Stein's other charitable interests include his role as chair of the governors of Carmel College, a Jewish private school. He is also a member of the appeal committee of the Mental Health Foundation.

Until very recently Cyril Stein's

name was synonymous with the Ladbroke betting and leisure group, which he had controlled for nearly forty years. He was part-purchaser of the company with his uncle in 1956, and made his first million eleven years later when a bundle of shares in the company were floated on the stock exchange. He remained at the helm as the firm's turnover grew from only £2 million at flotation to its present level of more than £4 billion. Last year, however, Stein announced that he would step down as chair of the company, and although he was intending to stay on as a non-executive director of the group and non-executive chair of its property division, he has now totally retired. He will be keen to retreat into relative obscurity, as he always shunned the limelight when boss of Ladbrokes, and tried to keep his life outside business private and his wife and family away from publicity.

Contact: Mr D Clayton, Trustee, Cyril and Betty Stein Charitable Trust, Messrs Clayton Stark & Co, 18 St George St, Hanover Sq, London W1R 0LL.
Tel: 0171 493 1205.

SHIVDASANI family
around £475,000

PREFERENCE: education; welfare, blind people and medicine in India and Nigeria
WEALTH: unknown
TRUST LINKS: Inlaks Foundation
COMPANY LINKS: Inlaks Group

Even though the Shivdasani family are not UK based, as their headquarters are in Switzerland and the chair of the Inlaks Group, Azad Shivdasani, is a Swiss resident, they do give significant charitable funds in this country, largely through the UK branch of their **Inlaks Foundation**.

The Inlaks Group of Companies was founded in 1947 by the late Indurkumar Shivdasani. By the time of his death in 1979, the group had become one of West Africa's main trading companies, as well as including substantial agricultural interests in India, France and Nigeria. Indoo Shivdasani was supported throughout his professional career by his wife Lakshmi, who survives him.

After the death of his father, Azad Shivdasani became chair and chief executive of the Inlaks Group. Under his stewardship, the group has continued to grow and diversify, and now has investments in aluminium rolling, brewing, services to the petroleum industry, tea plantations, food packaging, and the distribution of pharmaceuticals. Indoo Shivdasani's other children, Sonu Shivdasani and Countess Bina Sella di Monteluce, have significant investments in real estate development and tourism.

The Inlaks Foundation was created by the late Indoo Shivdasani in 1976 and registered as a charitable trust in Liechtenstein. The foundation concentrates on providing scholarships to outstanding young people from overseas to develop their professional, scientific, artistic or cultural abilities abroad. Each year 10-15 people are sent overseas either to leading institutions mainly in the United States and Britain or to carry out specific projects. Beside the scholarships it also promotes research into blindness and funds eye camps in India and Nigeria. The foundation supports and funds hospital projects and gives donations to homes for the elderly, orphaned and young in India.

The current capital of the Inlaks Foundation's charity trust in Liechtenstein stands at $10.5 million (around £6.6 million), which each year funds scholarships totalling about $500,000 (circa £300,000) depending on the number of scholars selected. The support for the students who come to Britain is directed through the Inlaks Foundation UK, which was registered as a charity in this country in 1982. Donations are given from the foundation in Liechtenstein to the UK foundation to pay for the British scholarships which amounted to £205,000 in 1993.

We were also informed that apart from the foundation, members of the Shivdasani family make personal donations to a wide variety of causes and charitable projects around the world. The figure for these private donations comes somewhere in the region of $200,000-$250,000 (around £125,000-£160,000). Their total charitable gifts, taking into account both these personal grants and those of the foundation, thus come to around $750,000 annually, which is approximately £475,000.

Contact: Hon. Secretary, Inlaks Foundation (UK), 88 Gloucester Terrace, London, W2 3HH. Tel: 0171 351 4929.

O'HEA family
£439,000 NEW

PREFERENCE: occupational health and medical research, Christian causes, West Sussex

WEALTH: £35m-£50m

TRUST LINKS: Colt Foundation, O'Hea Charitable Trust, Ault-O'Hea Charitable Trust

COMPANY LINKS: Colt Group

Many of us can breathe more easily thanks to the O'Hea family. Their company, the Colt Group, is Britain's top supplier of air conditioning, ventilation, and smoke and air pollution control systems. Whilst various members of the family own

shares worth £40m in the business, they have also handed over a large portion of their holding to two grant-making trusts – the **Colt Foundation** and the **O'Hea Charitable Trust**.

The Colt Foundation is the larger of these two trusts, and was set up by various members of the O'Hea family with an endowment of 22% of the shares in the Colt company, which its deed of settlement prevents it from divesting. With an annual income in excess of £300,000, it is now a major supporter of medical research,. At present it has a particular focus upon occupational health, and has committed £100,000 a year for the five years 1990-95 to support research into the toxicity of mineral fibres being undertaken at the Institute of Occupational Medicine at Edinburgh University. In 1991 grants totalling £387,000 were made, including £100,000 for the Institute at Edinburgh. The two other major donations were £61,000 to Strathclyde University to develop automated cervical cancer screening equipment, and £33,000 to Leeds University. The remaining grants all went to bodies undertaking medical research, or to support studentships run in conjunction with various medical bodies.

The O'Hea Charitable Trust appears to be one channel through which the family offers support to personally preferred causes. It was set up in the same year, and shares four of its founding trustees with the Colt Foundation, namely Alan and Jerome O'Hea, Mary Ault and Patricia Lebus. Again, its assets mainly consist of a significant holding in Colt Investments, as well as over £150,000 in a capital account. In 1991/92 the trust had income of £41,000 and made charitable gifts amounting to £52,000. These were directed to a wide variety of causes which are classified in the accounts by trustee name. Most these grants were smaller than £5,000 and show some preference to Christian organisations – with donations of £4,000 to the CREW (Catholic Charismatic Renewal) Trust and the Christian Trust. Medical causes also received a number of donations, with £4,000 to the Royal Flying Doctor Services and £3,000 to Dublin Children's Hospital. Other gifts went to various causes dealing with the disabled, young people, health and medicine, and overseas development. Some grants were also made around Chichester in West Sussex – close to Colt Group's head office in Havant, south east Hampshire.

There is also one other more recent family-linked grant-maker, the **Ault-O'Hea Charitable Trust**. This was established in 1993 by Mary Ault, who is connected with both charities listed above, and who is a trustee along with three other Ault family members. Because it is so new, there are no accounts on file for this trust at the Charity Commission, so we are unable to give any indication of preferences or size. In addition to the support made through these three charitable trusts, the donations made by the Colt Group can also be regarded as coming indirectly from the O'Hea family, given their close control of the company. In comparison, however, it gives relatively little – the most recent figures indicate that it donated just under £6,000 to mainly local charities in 1988.

In response to the draft of this entry, we were informed that the O'Hea family did not wish to be represented in this book, and that their wealth is spread over a very large number of individuals.

Contact: Colt Foundation: Miss V J Hall, Secretary to the Trustees, New Lane, Havant, Hants, PO9 2LY. Tel: 01705 491400. O'Hea Charitable Trust, Mr W McD Morrison, Secretary to the Trustees, Fiddlers, Smugglers Lane, Bosham, Chichester, W Sussex, PO18 8QP. Tel: 01243 572335. Ault-O'Hea Charitable Trust: Mr P D Ault, Secretary, 12 Weybridge Park, Weybridge, Surrey, KT13 8SQ.

LORD PALUMBO
£434,000
(but see below)

PREFERENCE: heritage, arts, education, medicine, general
AGE: 59
WEALTH: £50m-£75m
TRUST LINKS: Rudolph Palumbo Charitable Foundation
COMPANY LINKS: Rugarth Investment Trust, City Acre Property Investment Trust

Peter Palumbo, former chair of the Arts Council, has lived his life in the shadow of two men: his property developer father, Rudolph Palumbo, and the Bauhaus architect Mies van der Rohe. The monument to both of them was to have been a new building designed by Mies for the Mappin & Webb site opposite the Mansion House in the City of London, which the Palumbos had patiently acquired lease-by-lease over the years. Some 36 years later, with both Rudolph Palumbo and Mies van der Rohe dead, the dream is still to be fulfilled.

Lord Palumbo has, however, managed to create a memorial to his father in the shape of a foundation he set up in 1989 and named after him. The **Rudolph Palumbo Charitable Foundation** was the beneficiary of a four-year covenant from Palumbo's City Acre Property Investment Trust, worth an annual £350,000. In 1993 the foundation had assets of £266,000 and had made donations totalling £434,000 in the year.

Big donations included £100,000 to the Painshill Park Trust, £25,000 each to Birkbeck College, the Chicken Shed Theatre, Glyndebourne Productions and the LSE Butler's Wharf Appeal, and £20,000 each to the Natural History Museum and the Royal Marsden Hospital. Various other charities covering a range of causes were also supported, with an emphasis on medical charities. The largest single grant of £123,000 went to St Stephen's Church, Walbrook, the Wren church Palumbo has restored and where he has been a church warden since 1960. In addition to Lord and Lady Palumbo, the foundation's trustees comprise Sir Matthew Farrer, Lord Mishcon, solicitor John Underwood and accountant Thomas Tharby.

Palumbo's involvement with charity does not end there. He is a governor of the London School of Economics, a chancellor of the University of Portsmouth, and a trustee of the Writers' and Scholars' Educational Trust and – naturally – of the Mies van der Rohe Archive. While the Victorian listed buildings on the Mappin & Webb site awaited demolition, he allowed voluntary groups to use the space rent-free. Looking now as though he has finally won the fight over the future of the site, albeit too late for what Prince Charles referred to as Mies van der Rohe's 'glass stump', Palumbo is to replace the Victorian edifice with a bold masterpiece designed by the late James Stirling.

Among the numerous products of Palumbo's legendary vision, it promises to be a rare success. The Arts Foundation that Palumbo launched while at the Arts Council, financed by a £1 million donation from the Swiss banker Francis Hock, has completed its first three years with a lot of clever ideas to its name and very little else. Palumbo's time at the Arts Council was marked by the incompatibility of his own dreams – modelled on Mitterand's *grands projets* – with the pragmatic (some would say penny-pinching) philosophy prevalent in government. When he left in 1994, after swingeing cuts to the arts were announced in the Budget, it was with him complaining about 'irresponsible neglect of a precious national resource'.

In a recent legal case, it was said in court that Lord Palumbo had spent £4.9 million in charitable donations, as well as £263,000 in donations to the Conservative Party. Assuming that the figure is accurate, the destination of these charitable donations, and whether they included some of the money paid through the foundation described above, is unclear.

Contact: Mr T H Tharby, Rudolph Palumbo Charitable Foundation, 37a Walbrook, London EC4N 8BS. Tel: 0171 626 9236.

WARNING
Unsolicited requests for funding often lead to annoyance and are rarely productive. This book should not be used as a mailing list. Inappropriate applications waste time and money and may prejudice chances of future success.

GEORGE MICHAEL

£428,000 NEW

PREFERENCE: disability, children, medicine

AGE: 31

WEALTH: £20m-£35m

TRUST LINKS: Platinum Trust, Platinum Overseas Trust

COMPANY LINKS: Nobby's Hobbies Holdings

On the grounds of the donations he has made through the **Platinum Trust**, George Michael can justifiably claim that 'I've given away a

Lewis '94

People (a total of £24,000), Breakthrough Trust (£15,000), and People First (£7,500).

Since March last year, however, Michael has made no further payments into the trust fund. The Platinum Trust is no longer in a position to accept new applications, as any remaining income is to be allocated to organisations it has previously funded. This does not necessarily mean that George Michael's philanthropic activities have ceased, as we have found another possible outlet. He founded the **Platinum Overseas Trust** in September 1991 with the primary aim of promoting research into, and treatment of, leukaemia, cancer, AIDS and associated diseases, and also to advance general education and public concern regarding these ailments. We were unable to obtain any subsequent accounts for this grant-making trust from the Charity Commission, so we cannot give any indication of its current size or activities.

Although one of Britain's most successful pop stars in the eighties, initially as one-half of Wham! and more recently as a solo artist, George Michael's future earnings are veiled in a cloak of uncertainty due to his on-going legal proceedings against Sony Music. He claimed that the contract with the record company was unfair and that Sony had failed to promote adequately the material of his choice from his last album. He recently lost the expensive initial case, which started in November 1993, but is to appeal against the decision as he has vowed to never record for Sony again. He has, nevertheless, appeared recently on several charity singles, and he organised and headlined the Princess of Wales' *Concert of Hope* in 1993.

George Michael may be ambivalent about appearing in this book, because he believes that: 'Everyone's got really

substantial percentage of what I've earned.' (*Guardian*, 29/11/93). He set up this charitable grant-maker under his real name of Georgios Kyriacos Panayiotou in 1990, the same year as his second solo album – *Listen Without Prejudice, Vol. 1* – topped the UK charts. Over the ensuing four years he paid £2 million into the trust fund, which has made grants totalling £1.3 million, including £428,000 in 1992/93. These gifts have been mainly directed at children with special needs, along with mentally and physically handicapped adults requiring special attention. Recipients in 1992/93 included the British Council of Organisations of Disabled pissed off listening to celebrities patting each other on the back saying how generous they are being. And they are right to.' (*Independent*, 22/4/93).

Contact: Platinum Trust and Platinum Overseas Trust: Mr A D Russell or Mr C D Organ, Regency House, 1/4 Warwick St, London, W1R 5WB. Tel: 0171 439 8692.

VISCOUNT LEVERHULME
£424,000

PREFERENCE: education, general, Merseyside
AGE: 78
WEALTH: £20m-£35m
TRUST LINKS: Lord Leverhulme's Charitable Trust
COMPANY LINKS: Unilever

The 3rd Viscount Leverhulme is the latest in a line of major philanthropists to come from the Lever family. Their charitable impulses initially found expression with the present Viscount's grandfather, the First Lord Leverhulme, who was one of the more enlightened entrepreneurs to make a fortune on the back of the industrial revolution. He set up the Leverhulme Trust, now one of the largest grant-making trusts in the country, which controls assets of over £400 million and made donations of over £11 million in 1991. And, whilst many of his contemporaries were happy to see their workers rot in slums, Lord Leverhulme housed his employees in a model community around his Port Sunlight soap factory near Liverpool. It must have worked, because his small company has grown over the years to ultimately become the massive Unilever conglomerate.

The current Lord Leverhulme has followed in his grandfather's footsteps by setting up a trust of his own, **Lord Leverhulme's Charitable Trust**, which has now been operating for over 35 years. In 1990/91 the trust made donations of over £424,000 to a wide range of causes, with income derived from investments and from the estate of the 2nd Lord Leverhulme. The largest grant of £100,000 went to Liverpool University – the institution of which Leverhulme is chancellor. Other major grants of £50,000 were given to both the Royal College of Surgeons and the heart disease charity CORDA, £30,000 to the Crosby Hall Education Trust, £25,000 to the Church Urban Fund, and £20,000 to Barrowmore Nursing Home. The trust also funds the Lady Lever Art Gallery in Liverpool to the tune of £30,000 per annum, and Lord Leverhulme's Youth Enterprise Scheme, which sponsors young people in the Wirral and Cheshire. His wife, Lady Leverhulme also has a small trust of her own, the **Ann Leverhulme Charitable Trust**, which made total donations of under £1,000 in 1992/93 mainly to causes in the North West.

Apart from his financial support, Leverhulme is also active on a personal basis with a number of charities. He is a patron of the British Wheelchair Sports Foundation, a council member of King George's Jubilee Trust, a trustee of the National Advertising Benevolent Society, and a vice president of the Animal Health Trust, Liverpool School of Tropical Medicine, and the NSPCC. He is also a trustee of his grandfather's grant-maker, the Leverhulme Trust, although we have not included it's donations as part of the present Viscount's charitable donations. He sits on the present Unilever board as honorary advisory director.

Contact for both Lord Leverhulme's and Ann Leverhulme's Charitable Trusts: The Joint Secretary, Barbinder Trust, Plumtree Court, London, EC4A 4HT. Tel: 0171 583 5000.

SIR JOHN TEMPLETON

about £400,000

PREFERENCE: religion, education, free enterprise, non-profit management

AGE: 82

Wealth: £250m-£500m

TRUST LINKS: Templeton Foundation (US), Templeton Education and Charity Trust

COMPANY LINKS: Templeton Emerging Markets Investment Trust

Sir John Templeton gives the lie to the assertion that one cannot serve both God and Mammon. Having built up a fortune of over a quarter of a billion pounds since the war, and in the process acquiring a reputation as a global investment manager of rare acumen, he established the Templeton Prizes for Progress in Religion in 1972. Templeton's approach to religion has a non-sectarian flavour and the annual prize is awarded to 'the person who has contributed the most to new ideas or methods for widening or deepening man's knowledge of God or love of God'.

More recently, Templeton's philanthropy has extended into other areas. His **John Templeton Foundation**, established in the United States in 1988, had charitable expenditure of $640,000 in 1991/92. The foundation gives 'support primarily for operating programmes initiated and managed by the foundation relating to education, free enterprise, and especially progress in religion.' It also makes 'some contributions to charities that have been previously supported and share these same goals'. In fact, most of the foundation's money in 1991/92 went on 13 grants to such charities. Templeton himself chairs the foundation and his son, Philadelphian surgeon Dr John Templeton, is the president.

A naturalised UK subject, Sir John Templeton has also set up a charity in the UK called the **Templeton Education and Charity Trust**. Registered in 1991, it exists for general charitable purposes, and 'in particular to advance education in business management and to advance religion'. Its income for 1992 was only £3,000, however. But Sir John has made large donations in the UK, and they have followed many of the other benefactions recorded in this book in going to Oxford. The Oxford Centre for Management Studies was renamed Templeton College in 1984 when Sir John gave it $5 million. A challenge grant of a further $3 million followed a few years later.

Now an octagenarian, Bahamas-based Templeton has not abandoned his pursuit of money. His new vehicle, the Templeton Emerging Markets Investment Trust, is seen as an idea whose time has come and Templeton has been able to build on his reputation as the great prospector of the Pacific rim.

Contact for the John Templeton Foundation: Frances Schapperle, Executive Director, PO Box 1040, Bryn Mawr, PA 19010-0918, USA. Tel: 00 1 215 520 0995. For the Templeton Education and Charity Trust: Mr Bickson Anderson, Templeton House, Atholl Crescent, Edinburgh EH3 8HA.

KENNETH HORNE

and family

£359,000

PREFERENCE: welfare, youth,

education, medicine, Northants
AGE: 80
WEALTH: £20m-£35m
TRUST LINKS: Horne Foundation
COMPANY LINKS: sold stake in Robert Horne Group

The Horne family made their fortune from the paper trade with the Northampton based Robert Horne Group, which was set up by Kenneth Horne's father in the twenties. They sold the company to a Dutch firm in 1990 for £154 million, of which they received a major chunk in cash and shares.

In 1981 the Hornes set up a family charitable trust, the **Horne Foundation**, with a sizeable portion of the company shareholding. In the four years following the sale of the family company, this grant-making trust has distributed over £2 million to the non-profit sector. The major gifts have been to finance buildings for local education and youth organisations. These include a major grant of £660,000 to pay for a local comprehensive's sixth form centre, and other donations towards school buildings, young people's hostels and youth clubs. Grants are also occasionally made to national/ international charities dealing with young people and the arts. In 1993, the foundation had a sizeable asset base of nearly £6 million, an income of £400,000, and made donations of £359,000.

Aside from these good works, the Horne family have not been resting on their laurels since acquiring their wealth. Kenneth Horne still maintains a link with the Robert Horne Group as president, and one of his three sons runs a company which provides investment capital for small firms.

Contact: Mrs R M Harwood, Horne Foundation, Weldon House, Vyse Rd, Boughton, Northampton, NN2 8RP. Tel: 01604 821515

DOWAGER MARCHIONESS OF NORMANBY
£333,000

PREFERENCE: welfare, heritage, medicine, North Yorkshire
AGE: 71
WEALTH: less than £20m
TRUST LINKS: Normanby Charitable Trust
COMPANY LINKS: Guinness (family member)

The Dowager Marchioness of Normanby and her late husband, the Marquess, established the **Normanby Charitable Trust** in 1966 with general charitable objects, including supporting two named organisations: National Library for the Blind and the Freud Centenary Fund. In 1991/92 the trust made donations of £333,000 funded by the proceeds of investments with a market value in excess of £6 million, the most valuable of which were 260,000 Guinness shares worth £2.8 million. The largest grants made in the year were £50,000 to the Iris Fund for the Prevention of Blindness, £42,500 to Lythe Parochial Church Council, £25,000 to both Camphill Village Trust-Botton Village and the University of West Indies' Development and Endowment Appeal, £15,000 to Carlton Lodge Youth Activity Centre, and £14,000 to Ripon Cathedral Trust. Smaller gifts went to a variety of homeless, medical, youth and disability organisations, and also to causes around Whitby, North Yorkshire, where the Marchioness resides.

The Guinness shares owned by the Normanby Trust give an indication as to the source of the Dowager Marchioness' wealth. Born Grania

Maeve Rosaura Guinness, she is a member of the Guinness family and a descendant of the 1st Earl of Iveagh. *Business Age* magazine reports that she has now passed on much of her wealth to her son, the new Marquess of Normanby.

Contact: Normanby Charitable Trust, c/o Touche Ross & Co, 10-12 East Parade, Leeds, LS1 2AJ.
Tel: 0113 243 9021.

LORD WEINSTOCK
and family
£333,000

PREFERENCE: Jewish charities, heritage, the arts, welfare
AGE: 70
WEALTH: £100m-£250m
TRUST LINKS: Weinstock Fund
COMPANY LINKS: General Electric Company

Like his contemporary Lord Rayne (qv), Weinstock established a charitable foundation in 1962 in the first flush of business success. He endowed it with shares in his creation GEC, now Britain's largest manufacturing company. Weinstock's first job was as a junior administration officer in the Admiralty and he has since made a large part of his fortune through manufacturing arms as well as a whole range of other electronic or electrical systems.

The **Weinstock Fund** was worth £2.3 million by 1993, which enabled donations of £333,000 to be made. Headline donations went to the Jewish Philanthropic Association for Israel, which received £25,000, and to Jewish Care and the Westminster Abbey Trust, which each got £10,000. A wide selection of other smaller grants were made to charities working in the fields of heritage and the arts, disability, and social welfare. Weinstock's well-known passion for classical music was reflected in grants such as the £7,500 that went to the Monteverdi Choir and Orchestra.

Lord Weinstock no longer sits on the board of his foundation, but his son Simon does. Now past 70, Weinstock has also taken steps to transfer the bulk of his wealth to Simon, who is a director at GEC and tipped as a potential successor to the top job when his father retires in 1996. Together, the Weinstocks hold under two per cent of the share capital of GEC, which itself made charitable donations in 1992/93 of £947,000, compared to pre-tax profits of £863 million.

Weinstock could have become even more wealthy in 1993 when his father-in-law, Sir Michael Sobell, died leaving more than £47 million. Sobell had given Weinstock his first break into the big time back in 1955 when he put him at the head of Radio and Allied (Holdings) Ltd., and Weinstock still carries the Sobell enthusiasm for racing. In his will, however, Sobell left virtually all his fortune to charity: he clearly thought the kids had quite enough.

Contact: Jacqueline Elstone, Weinstock Fund, 1 Stanhope Gate, London W1A 1EH. Tel: 0171 493 8484.

ELTON JOHN

£332,000 NEW

PREFERENCE: AIDS charities, general

AGE: 49

WEALTH: £100m-£250m

TRUST LINKS: Elton John AIDS Foundation, Watside Charities

COMPANY LINKS: various including Watside Charities

When Elton John established the **Elton John AIDS Foundation** in February last year it was the latest in a long line of personal activities to help those suffering from the pernicious illness. He has said that 'I want to do whatever I can to help the fight against this disease' (*Independent*, 12/5/93). In the three years previously he had reportedly donated over half a million pounds to various AIDS organisations, but set up his own charity so that he could have a greater say in how the money is spent. The foundation is to get its income from record royalties, concert proceeds, charity events, and donations from the corporate sector. It received part of the takings from Elton John's two London concerts held in May last year, and also shared the revenue from the charity première of the recent box office smash *Four Weddings and a Funeral*.

In July 1993 he auctioned his vast record collection of 25,000 albums and 23,000 singles, and its sale price of £182,000 went to the Terrence Higgins Trust. And later in the year, when he was awarded £350,000 in damages from the *Sunday Mirror* which had defamed his character, he donated the £75,000 he received immediately to a number of charities.

There is also a rather less public side to Elton John's charitable activities. Part of the extensive empire of small private companies which manage his interests is controlled by a charitable company called **Watside Charities**. This was set up as John Woodside Limited ('Woodside' is the name of Elton John's house in Berkshire) in 1982, and shortly afterwards changed its name to Watside Charities. One of its two current directors is John Reid, Elton John's manager, and it owns all but one of the hundred ordinary shares in two companies, Happenstance and J Bondi Ltd, which are 'engaged in the exploitation of entertainers outside the United Kingdom and Ireland' with Elton as their sole employee. In 1992, Happenstance paid Elton John £8 million. The most recent 1991/92 accounts for Watside Charities state that its principal activity is to perform charitable works, and to this end it made donations of £75,000 to unspecified recipients, which compared with £41,000 in 1990/91. This represented a welcome increase from the total in previous years, which for most of the eighties was either nil or only a few thousand pounds.

Elton Hercules John, born Reginald Kenneth Dwight, has amassed a considerable fortune from a long and highly successful career in the music industry, which has been supplemented by a shrewd financial brain. He has always been a prolific songwriter, and along with his long-time lyricist Bernie Taupin recently signed a record breaking £26 million publishing deal with Time Warner. His business interests include the above-mentioned companies, William A Bong, his own label Rocket Records, and the Big Pig Music publishing company which he jointly owns with Taupin. Elton is involved with many charities, including Nordoff Robbins Music Therapy, and the AIDS organisations Body Positive and London Lighthouse. The known charitable donations figure cited above is comprised of the £182,000 he gave to the Terrence Higgins Trust from selling his record collection, £75,000 from his libel case, and £75,000 from Watside Charities (assuming the 1992/93 grant total was similar to that in 1991/92).

Contact: Elton John AIDS Foundation: Nicola Turnbull, Singes House, 32 Galena Rd, London, W6 0LT, Tel: 0181 741 9933. Watside Charities: Messrs Frere Chomley, 28 Lincoln's Inn Fields, London, WC2A 3HH. Tel: 0171 405 7878.

SIDNEY COROB
£318,000

PREFERENCE: general
WEALTH: £20m-£35m
TRUST LINKS: Sidney and Elizabeth Corob Charitable Trust
COMPANY LINKS: Corob Consolidated

Sidney Corob has made a fortune from his dealings in the London property market, and is currently active as director of various property and investment companies, including Corob Consolidated, of which he is chair.

He has chosen to put a substantial chunk of his wealth to charitable ends through the **Sidney and Elizabeth Corob Charitable Trust**, which he established over twenty years ago amending its deeds in 1988. The trust now has a considerable assets base of over £2.5 million which generated an income of £350,000 in 1990/91. In the year donations of £318,000 were made, but as the recipients of donations were not specified in the trust's accounts it is not possible to specify whether the trust has any preferred areas of support.

Contact: Mrs S Berg, Sidney & Elizabeth Corob Charitable Trust, 62 Grosvenor St, London, W1X 9DA. Tel: 0171 499 4301.

VISCOUNT ROTHERMERE
and family
about £305,000

PREFERENCE: education, medicine, heritage
AGE: 68
WEALTH: over £500m
TRUST LINKS: Rothermere Foundation, Harmsworth Memorial Trust Fund
COMPANY LINKS: Daily Mail and General Trust

Viscount Rothermere is head of the last remaining active national press dynasty, which was started by his grandfather, Alfred Harmsworth, founder of the *Daily Mail*. Through various non-charitable trusts, the family owns three-quarters of the public Daily Mail & General Trust company whose subsidiaries include Associated Newspapers (which publishes the *Daily Mail, Mail on Sunday,* and *Evening Standard*) and Northcliffe Newspapers (which produces various provincial titles). Because of their majority holding, we have listed the charitable donations made by DM&GT as part of the family's own philanthropic activities. In 1992, the company gave £205,000

to various causes, mainly connected to the printing industry or operating local to the company and its subsidiaries. In this vein, Lord Rothermere is also joint vice-president of the trustees of the Printers' Charitable Corporation. The firm's programme of community support is handled by Vyvyan Harmsworth, Rothermere's second cousin and Director of Corporate Affairs.

● MEDIA & PUBLISHING GIVERS

Paul Hamlyn	£2,776,000
Barclay brothers	£1,080,000
Viscount Rothermere	£300,000
Michael Green	£272,000
Richard Desmond	£185,000
Lord Iliffe	£150,000
Earl of Stockton	£123,000
Robert Gavron	£109,000
Charles Saatchi	£100,000
Viscount Cowdray	£52,000
Michael Heseltine	£10,000
Tony Elliott	£9,000

Another, more direct, channel through which the family makes charitable grants is the **Rothermere Foundation**, of which the current Viscount Rothermere was a founding trustee when it was set up by his father in 1956. The foundation was initially endowed with £50,000-worth of ordinary stock in Daily Mail & General Trust, which was then a private company. Its purpose was to support general charitable causes, but also to establish and maintain 'Rothermere Scholarships' to be awarded to graduates of the Memorial University of Newfoundland to enable them to undertake further periods of study in Britain. Rothermere has close links with North America: he studied in the US for a year after Eton, spent 18 months working at a paper mill in Quebec, sits on the board of two Canadian companies, Bouverie Holding and Bouverie Investments, and is a director of the Power Corporation (Canada) and Whittle Communications (USA). At the time of writing, the only accounts we were able to obtain from the Charity Commission were for 1988/89. They show that the foundation commanded a substantial asset base with a market value which then stood at over £6 million, including 120,000 ordinary shares in Daily Mail & General Trust. These generated an income of £194,000 which supported charitable expenditure of £100,000 in the year. The bulk of this went in fellowship grants (£17,500), scholarships (£6,000), and other awards (£53,000, including £33,000 to fund a 'Harmsworth professorship'). Other gifts totalling £23,000 were also made, consisting of £11,000 to Mick Field's Cancer Charity, £7,000 to Dr Johnson's House Trust, £5,000 to Lincolnshire Heritage Trust, and £250 to St Peter's Church Daylesford. In addition an interest free loan of £100,000 was made to the St Bride Restoration Fund Trust.

Part of the family also appear to be associated with the **Harmsworth Memorial Trust Fund**, which relates to the Rothermere Trust Fund and various Harmsworth 'Allotment Fields' and 'Recreation Fields' set up in the 1920s. Its purpose is to provide and maintain a community centre, playing fields and recreation ground for the benefit of the inhabitants of Beneden parish in Kent. The bulk of the trust's 1992/93 income of £42,000 was spent in the furtherance of this aim.

The heir to Viscount Rothermere's vast fortune is his son, Jonathan Harmsworth, who followed in his father's footsteps by attending an American university after leaving school in Britain. For tax reasons, Lord Rothermere himself spends much of his time at homes in Paris and Kyoto, with his new Japanese wife. His previous wife, the renowned socialite Lady Pat 'Bubbles' Rothermere, died in 1992. Rothermere is a life patron of the London School of Journalism.

Contact: Daily Mail & General Trust: Mr Vyvyan Harmsworth, Director of Corporate Affairs, Northcliffe House, 2 Derry St, London, W8 5TT. Tel: 0171 938 6000. Rothermere Foundation: Swepstone Walsh, Ref: GBWW, 9 Lincolns Inn Fields, London, WC2A 3BP. Tel: 0171 404 1499.

CLARK FAMILY
about £300,000

PREFERENCE: Quaker causes, education, welfare, overseas, peace, Somerset
WEALTH: £100m-£250m
TRUST LINKS: J Anthony Clark Charitable Foundation, numerous other Clark trusts
COMPANY LINKS: C & J Clark

One of the largest private companies in the country, C & J Clark Ltd have been making shoes for over 150 years, and they have been based in the town of Street in Somerset all that time. The current managing director of the company, John Clothier, is a direct descendant of the founder. The various scions of the Clark family together control over half of the shares in the company, which in 1991/92 made donations totalling £60,000. Support is restricted to charities close to head office or to company factories, and the preferred areas of support are children and youth, education, recreation, environment and the arts.

C & J Clark established the **Clark Foundation (II)**[1] in 1959. The last figures available for this foundation relate only to 1985, when it held assets of £1.4 million and made donations of some £80,000, mainly for education purposes in the West of England. There is no further information on the foundation's file at the Charity Commission and it is not known whether the charity still operates.

However, there are a bewildering array of other charitable trusts connected with the Clark family, most of which are endowed with shares in C & J Clark. Probably the largest is the **J Anthony Clark Charitable Foundation**[2], set up back in 1970, which had assets of £2.3 million in 1992. The children of J Anthony Clark now make up most of the trustees. Donations totalling £423,000 were made in the year, including £30,000 to the Knightstone Housing Association, £20,000 to Oxfam, £8,000 to Survival International and £6,000 to the Street Theatre Workshop. The trustees of the foundation are David Parkes, Lance Clark, Cyrus Clark, Thomas Clark and Caroline Pym, with the last four appearing to have individual discretion over some donations. A total of £234,000, however, was paid over to the new **J A Clark Charitable Trust**, established in 1992, which has the same trustees.

Other sizeable foundations connected to the family include the **Roger and Sarah Bancroft Clark Charitable Trust**[1] (donations of £42,000 in 1992 to Quaker causes, education and charities in Somerset), the **P T and V O Clothier Charitable Foundation**[2] (donations of £35,000 in 1991/92 to Quaker causes, conservation and welfare), the **Hilda and Alice Clark Charitable Trust**[2] (donations of £27,000 in 1993 mainly to Quaker charities), the **Cathy Pelly Memorial Trust**[2] (£30,000 over five years to peace causes and groups in New Zealand) and the **Joanna Pelly Charitable Trust**[2] (£18,000 in donations in 1992/93, mostly for peace work). This does not exhaust

the Clark family philanthropy, however: we also uncovered a further seven charitable trusts connected to the family which were each making donations of a few thousand pounds a year.

Although it could be argued that we are not comparing like with like in grouping such an extended family under one heading in this book, it is a remarkable instance of giving in depth by a series of relatives further connected by a family firm, C & J Clark, the Religious Society of Friends, and the community of Street in Somerset.

Contact: 1:40 High Street, Street, Somerset BA16 0YA. Tel: 01458 43131. For C & J Clark Ltd: Ian Ritchie, at the above address. 2: c/o Peat Marwick McClintock, 15 Pembroke Road, Clifton, Bristol BS8 3BG.

STEPHEN RUBIN
about £300,000

PREFERENCE: Jewish causes, general
AGE: 57
WEALTH: £250m-£500m
TRUST LINKS: Rubin Foundation
COMPANY LINKS: Pentland Group

Stephen Rubin provides a good example of the difficulties involved in getting big social projects co-sponsored between businesspeople and government. The **Rubin Foundation**, which Stephen Rubin set up in 1986, was due to sponsor a new City Technology College in Barnet and had amassed income over some years for that end. The government, however, failed to live up to its own – much larger – side of the bargain and the project lapsed.

With its sudden embarrassment of wealth the foundation made a huge £333,000 donation in 1990, followed by a further £300,000, to the Jewish Philanthropic Association to aid the settlement in Israel of Jewish refugees from Russia.

The foundation benefits from covenanted donations of over a quarter of a million pounds each year, although the exact source is not specified in recent accounts. The foundation's 1988 accounts did note that a large part of the income came from Robert Stephen Holdings Ltd, a Rubin holding company, and its subsidiary company Pentland Industries. Rubin owns a stake of over 50 per cent in Pentland, the quoted sportswear group that has recently bought the Italian Ellesse brand. Rubin made a killing with Reebok in the eighties and in the early nineties is clearly looking for a repeat performance, first with Adidas and now with Ellesse. It is perhaps still too early to tell whether any of the £390 million Rubin made in 1991 from selling his Reebok stake will find its way into his foundation.

The Pentland Group itself made charitable donations totalling £61,000 in the year to 1991, although we are not sure how much of the company's donations are paid through the foundation. The company's donations policy covers support for the scout movement, the arts (specifically the Philharmonia and the National Theatre), education, the environment and local charities in areas of company presence. Pentland has also sponsored the Young Jewish Care Award.

The Rubin Foundation has similarly supported the Philharmonia in the past, as well as make a large number of small grants to youth, health and welfare causes. Donations in 1992/93 totalled £279,000. Aside from the Jewish Philanthropic Association, big grants of £10,000 were made to L'dor V'dor and to the Foundation for Community Awareness. The foundation's board is dominated by family members, including Rubin himself, and the foundation stresses that funds are either committed in advance or are spent on causes 'dear to members of the family' or associated with Pentland. Unsolicited applications are unwelcome and the foundation is anxious that intending applicants should save the cost.

Rubin once stood as a parliamentary candidate for the Liberal Party, but his political sympathies have shifted if the foundation's accounts are anything to go by: they record donations to the Conservative National Golf Tournament Charitable Trust and to the Thatcher Foundation.

Contact: Rubin Foundation: R Feld, Accountant, 124-130 Seymour Place, London W1H 6AA. Pentland Group plc: Mrs J D Robertson, Pentland Centre, Lakeside Squires Lane, Finchley, London N3 2QL. Tel: 0181 346 2600.

GEORGE MOORE
£291,000

PREFERENCE: young people, general, Yorkshire
AGE: 65
WEALTH: £75m-£100m
TRUST LINKS: George A Moore Foundation
COMPANY LINKS: sold Moore's Furniture

George Moore likes things kept local. He grew up near Wetherby in West Yorkshire, made his fortune in Wetherby, and has lived there since he retired from active business in 1987. When his daughter bought an estate in 1994, it was in Wetherby. And it is hardly surprising that the bulk of grants from the **George A Moore Foundation** are centred on Yorkshire.

Moore first set up the foundation as long ago as 1970, but there has been evidence of heightened activity since the late eighties when Moore gave the foundation its current name. Following a heart attack, he netted some £80 million from the sale of his furniture company in 1987 and has since been able to concentrate on enjoying the pleasures of life, including his Rolls Royce and his foundation.

A total of £291,000 was paid out in donations in 1992/93, including £50,000 each to the Leeds General Infirmary Lifescan Appeal, the Prince's Youth Business Trust, and the York Minster Fund. The Order of St John received £42,000 and the Animal Health Trust £40,000. Many of these charities have also benefited in the past. Other grants went to Drive for Youth, Eaton Hall Product Development, North Yorkshire West Girl Guides Association and the NSPCC Leeds Childrens' Centre. The year before, the foundation had donated a total of £712,000, including an exceptional £500,000 grant to the Duke of Edinburgh Award Scheme. The foundation's trustees are all members of the family and its assets now stand at some £4.7 million.

The George A Moore Foundation holds the unusual distinction among charitable foundations of owning a management consultancy. The foundation's accounts record that in February 1992 the foundation acquired the whole of the issued share capital of the then dormant company, Moore Estates Ltd., which commenced trading during the year as business management consultants. The total income of the foundation and its subsidiary in 1992/93 exceeded the £1 million mark.

Contact: Miss L P Oldham, Administrator, George A Moore Foundation, PO Box 150, Wetherby, West Yorkshire LS22 7HP.

SIR BERNARD ASHLEY
and family
£286,000

PREFERENCE: education
AGE: 68
WEALTH: £100m-£250m
TRUST LINKS: Laura Ashley Foundation
COMPANY LINKS: Laura Ashley Holdings, Ashley Inns

When Laura Ashley, founder with her husband Bernard of the clothing and material chain, died in 1986 it was on the eve of the company's flotation on the stock market. While she thus missed out on appreciating the full fruits of 30 years' hard work, it was not before she had ensured that other people would also benefit from her fortune. Established in 1985, once again with her husband, the **Laura Ashley Foundation** now makes donations worth over £0.25 million a year.

The foundation's money is used in the main to help adults get a 'second chance' at education. Grants are made to individuals 'whose first experience of education was unproductive' or to organisations which run further education courses. Some awards are also made to help promising students in conservation and restoration work, and in music. Grants approved by the foundation in 1993 totalled £286,000.

Sir Bernard Ashley is joined on the foundation's board by his son David. Both have wound down their involvement with the Laura Ashley company in recent years, although Sir

Bernard is still a non-executive director. The Ashleys retain their strong links with Wales, where Sir Bernard has a hotel in Brecon. His other great passion is sailing, and he is a member of the Army Sailing Association.

Contact: Annabel Thompson, Administrator, Laura Ashley Foundation, 33 King Street, London WC2E 8JD. Tel: 0171 497 2503.

JOEL JOFFE
£286,000

PREFERENCE: overseas causes
AGE: 60
WEALTH: less than £20m
TRUST LINKS: J G Joffe Charitable Trust
COMPANY LINKS: past links with Hambro Life/Allied Dunbar

Along with fellow South Africans Sir Mark Weinberg and Sir Sydney Lipworth (qqv), the as yet unknighted Joel Joffe made a substantial sum from his interests in the insurance company Hambro Life, now Allied Dunbar, when it was sold to the BAT multi-national in 1984. And like his erstwhile business colleagues he has set up a trust through which to channel support for charities, in his case the **J G Joffe Charitable Trust**.

He created this trust back in 1968, and in the early 1970s and 1980s added a variety of shares, including 235,000 shares in Hambro Life. The Hambro holding was sold in 1984/85 and fetched £1.2 million. This sum was reinvested elsewhere and has since caused a marked increase in the trust's annual income, which in 1992/93 stood at £326,000.

Unusually for one of the rich people in this book, but fittingly for the previous chair of Oxfam's executive committee, the bulk of Joffe's support is directed at overseas organisations active in the developing world. This is exemplified by grants such as £50,000 to Impact, £26,000 to Action for Development and Disability, £25,000 to the Ashoka Trust, and £12,500 to One World Action. A gift of £50,000 went to the Legal Assistance Trust of Southern Africa, a regular recipient, which reflects Joffe's training as a lawyer – indeed before he left South Africa in the sixties he even represented Nelson Mandela, now the country's president.

Because the trust's funds are fully committed for a number of years, no unsolicited applications will be acknowledged or considered.

Contact: Mr Joel Joffe, J G Joffe Charitable Trust, Bishops Court, 76 Bishops Bridge Road, London, W2 7BE.

SIR TERENCE CONRAN
£276,000

PREFERENCE: art and design
AGE: 62
WEALTH: £50m-£75m
TRUST LINKS: Conran Foundation
COMPANY LINKS: Terence Conran Ltd; ex-chair of Storehouse

At the peak of his wealth, when he was boss of the Storehouse retail group, Sir Terence Conran was considerably richer than he is now. However, this seems to suit him fine because he has said that: 'Personal wealth is something which has been of total disinterest to me. Do I regret having been worth £200 million at one stage and only a quarter of that today? Of course not, a quarter of that is far too much in any case. I'm embarrassed to sit here with money in the bank, I truly am. I'd much rather be using it to do something.' (*Times*, 12/1/91).

It is entirely fitting, therefore, that Conran has chosen to sink a large chunk of his remaining money into the Design Museum, of which he is chair and trustee, and funds through the **Conran Foundation Limited**. This is a charitable company which he set up with his industrial product designer son, Sebastian, to take over the assets of a now defunct charity of the same name. The previous Conran Foundation was created in 1981, and ran the Boilerhouse Project at the Victoria and Albert Museum until 1986 before sponsoring the building of the Design Museum at Butlers Wharf, which opened in 1989.

Sir Terence has always been renowned for his interest in good design, and he set up his foundation to promote the education of the public in this subject. He has since covenanted over £5.9 million to the foundation, which owns the Design Museum's building on Butlers Wharf, worth the best part of £7 million. The foundation has made donations to the value of £2.4 million over the last five years to the Design Museum, and has also deposited £800,000 to guarantee its overdraft. The most recent 1992/93 accounts for the Conran Foundation note an income of £300,000 deeded from Sir Terence, of which £276,000 made its way to the museum. His interests in art and design are also apparent in his position as a council member of the Royal College of Art, and his past role as a trustee of the V&A. He is also a governor of Bryanston School, which he attended as a youth.

Sir Terence will no doubt have celebrated the recent 30th birthday of Habitat with mixed feelings. He founded the revolutionary design and furnishings retail chain back in the swinging sixties, ran its eventual owner, Storehouse plc, with great aplomb during the eighties before resigning as chief executive in 1988 and finally selling his remaining stake in the firm for £24 million. Apart from his involvement with setting up the Design Museum, he has kept himself very busy over the past few years through his various business interests. These comprise: Terence Conran Limited; the Conran Shops in London, Tokyo and Paris; six gourmet London restaurants – Le Pont de la Tour, Quaglino's, The Butlers Wharf Chop-House, Blueprint Cafe, Cantina del Ponte, Bibendum; and also his architectural and design practice, C D Partnership.

Contact: Mr D Gunewardena, Company Secretary, Conran Foundation Ltd, 22 Shad Thames, London, SE1 2YU.
Tel: 0171 378 1161.

MICHAEL GREEN
£272,000

(but see below)

PREFERENCE: Jewish causes, education, training
AGE: 46
WEALTH: £50m-£75m
TRUST LINKS: Carlton Television Trust, Tangent Charitable Trust
COMPANY LINKS: Carlton Communications, Tangent Industries

Michael Green is rapidly becoming one of Britain's new media moguls, largely on the back of the successes of the Carlton Communications group, and his other interests including GMTV, ITN and Reuters. He is widely considered the most powerful man in terrestrial television, especially since Carlton gained control of Central Television last year. Whilst we have not been able to unearth any information on donations made by him directly, his charitable inclinations clearly find expression via two trusts which are linked to his main companies – Carlton and Tangent Industries.

Carlton Communications is the most widely publicised aspect of Michael Green's business interests, and as chair of the company he received a salary of over £630,000 last year. He guided Carlton through a period of rapid expansion during the 1980s, fuelled by acquisitions and mergers, which made it one of the glamour stocks of this boom era. The pinnacle was reached when it won the lucrative London weekday television broadcasting franchise. Although the company then hit problems with its purchase of the US company Technicolor, it has since bounced back with a take-over of Central TV. In May 1993 Carlton established the £500,000-a-year **Carlton Television Trust**, with trustees including Michael Green. The trust focuses its support on youth education projects in the London region, especially organisations serving those who are disadvantaged or have special needs.

Michael Green is much more reticent about his involvement as director and chair of Tangent Industries, a private limited company which he set up in 1968 at the youthful age of 20 with his brother David (qv). This printing and photographic firm was modestly successful, but hit pay-dirt in the late 1970s when it bought a run-down direct mail company whose assets included a hugely under-valued building on London's South Bank which was quickly sold. In recent years, Tangent appears to have become the main vehicle for Michael Green's private investments, and it owns much of his £40 million stake in Carlton. Green holds some very valuable shares in Tangent – in 1992/93 the company purchased 230 of its own shares from him for £750,000, which would value his remaining 7,100 shares at a cool £23 million! In the same year he also received a director's emolument of nearly £120,000.

Tangent Industries recently obtained some very unwelcome publicity when it revealed a gift of £15,000 to the Tory Party in its 1991/92 accounts. However, its more charitable donations, made via the **Tangent Charitable Trust**, have not received the same level of attention. This trust, founded by Michael and David Green (qv) in 1984 with general charitable objects, would now appear to be a main vehicle for Michael's personal philanthropic work. It is administered from the Hanover Square building which also houses Carlton Communications and Tangent Industries. Unfortunately, there are no up-to-date accounts on file at the Charity Commission concerning this trust's expenditure, although their computer database gives an income figure of £272,000 for 1991. The most recent accounts on file show five donations made in 1988 totalling £4,400, the largest being £3,000 to Jewish Youth. Previous records note backing for a project which investigated the effects of redundancy and unemployment. To date, the trust has not responded to requests for further information made by the authors.

Michael Green makes no secret, however, about his personal involvement with charities, and in particular his self-confessed passion for education: 'I'm keen on education. I have very, very few regrets but my lack of a good education is one of them' (*Business Age*, April 1993). In this light, he is non-executive chair of the Open College, a council member at the Royal Holloway and Bedford

New College, and governor of Theale Green School. He is also on the appeal committee for Home-Start.

Contact: Tangent Charitable Trust: Mrs Gwen Jeffrey, c/o Tangent Industries Ltd, 15 St George St, Hanover Square, London, W1R 9DE. Tel: 0171 499 8050.

Carlton Television Trust: Liz Delbarre, Carlton Television, 101 St Martin's Lane, London, WC2N 4AZ. Tel: 0171 615 1641.

GRAHAM KIRKHAM

£260,000

PREFERENCE: general
AGE: 49
WEALTH: £250m-£500m
TRUST LINKS: Graham Kirkham Foundation
COMPANY LINKS: DFS Furniture

Graham Kirkham, plain-speaking son of a Yorkshire miner, hit the headlines in November 1993 when the sale of half his stake in the Doncaster-based DFS Furniture retail chain netted him £130 million. With the remainder of the family shareholding valued at a further £140 million, he has been propelled into the ranks of Britain's top fifty wealthiest people. With typical bluntness, however, he dismisses the normal trappings of the mega-rich as 'an absolute waste of money' (*Observer*, 14/11/93). He is clearly not averse to parting with some of his fortune, and in 1991 set up the **Graham Kirkham Foundation**, which made donations of £260,000 in its first year of operation. The accounts on file at the Charity Commission do not specify the recipients of these gifts, although Kirkham's interests include collecting art.

After leaving school at the age of sixteen, without any O-levels, he took a job as a furniture salesman in a local shop. However, after coveting a carpet-fitter's Jag, he set himself up as a carpet wholesaler, before switching to concentrate on furniture. Years of hard graft have built DFS into Britain's largest specialist retailer of upholstered furniture, with a chain of 24 stores in the north and the midlands. He puts much of his business success down to good relations with his suppliers and employees, and also keeping an eye on his competitors: 'We watched what everyone else was doing, and went in the opposite direction' (*Observer*, 14/11/93). Let's hope he does not follow the same strategy when he goes team chasing – a kind of hunt but without foxes.

This work has not been without its rewards – in recent years Kirkham has been near the top of the private sector pay leagues, and last year alone paid himself £20 million including £7 million in dividends and £5.5m in tax-efficient art and antiques. As for what to do with his recent bonanza, Kirkham confesses that 'I haven't given it a thought' (*Observer*, 14/11/93). How about your foundation Graham?

Contact: Graham Kirkham, Graham Kirkham Foundation, Bentley Moor Lane, Adwick le Street, nr Doncaster, S Yorks, DN6 7BD. Tel: 01302 330880.

ANWAR PERVEZ

£245,000

PREFERENCE: education, scholarships
AGE: 59
WEALTH: £50m-£75m
TRUST LINKS: Bestway Foundation
COMPANY LINKS: Bestway Holdings

● ASIAN GIVING

Swraj Paul	£1,050,000
Shivdasani family	£475,000
Anwar Pervez	£245,000
Hinduja bros	£68,000
Raj Bagri	£21,000
Nat Puri	£10,000

Anwar Pervez is a leading member of the Anglo-Pakistani community, and has made his fortune through the cash-and-carry group Bestway. Pervez started the company in 1976, and it has since grown into a profitable chain of fourteen trade cash and carry depots. The company annually directs around 2.5% of its pre-tax profits to the **Bestway Foundation**, which Pervez also founded. Given his intimate connections with the company – he is both the chair and managing director, and his family owns 58% of the shares – the gifts made by this foundation have been included in the total given for Pervez above.

The foundation had an income of £385,000 in 1992/93, of which £250,000 came from the Bestway company, and it made donations of £245,000 directed mainly at educational charities in the UK and abroad, as well as emergency appeals. Of this total, just over £100,000 went to organisations operating in this country, the largest grants being £60,000 to John Kelly School in Neasden, £10,000 to Age Concern, £6,000 to the National Grocers' Benefit Fund, £5,000 to Central Jaima Masjid, and £2,500 to the Macmillan Nurse Appeal. Most of the remainder went to overseas causes, including £60,000 to the Prime Minister's Relief Fund (Pakistan), £20,000 to the Edhi Int Foundation which undertakes medical and relief work, £12,400 to Lahore University, £10,000 to the Imran Khan Cancer Appeal and £7,300 to the Bosnia Relief Fund. Donations of nearly £23,000 were also made to individuals, mainly for educational purposes. A regular surplus of income over expenditure in recent years has helped the foundation build up a substantial asset base of £1.1 million.

Pervez is also personally involved with education and training as a board member of NW London TEC, where Bestway has its head office. Company connections are also reflected in his involvement with the National Grocers' Benevolent Fund, again as a board member. On a wider front, he was a 25th anniversary patron of the Joint Council for the Welfare of Immigrants.

Contact: Dawn Taylor, Secretary to Bestway Foundation, Bestway (Holdings) Ltd, Abbey Road, Park Royal, London NW10 7BW. Tel: 0181 453 1234.

NOEL LISTER
£232,000

PREFERENCE: young people
AGE: 65
WEALTH: £75m-£100m
TRUST LINKS: Lister Charitable Trust
COMPANY LINKS: sold MFI

Noel Lister has a passion for sailing which informs his charitable activities. Through the **Lister Charitable Trust** he funds the UK Sailing Centre and Cowes Leisure Management College on the Isle of Wight to help youth development, as well as other recreational facilities. Since 1988, the trust has spent £1.5 million to this end. In 1992/93 the trust held assets of £4 million and had an income of £300,000, which supported charitable expenditure of £232,000.

Lister set up his trust in 1981, and by the mid-eighties it had been endowed with 75,000 shares in MFI with a cost value of £101,000. This holding was cashed in when the home furniture company was bought by ASDA group in 1985 for over £600 million. The buyout also helped make Lister a rich man thanks to his personal stake. He had founded MFI with a partner back in the sixties, and the company supplied self-assembly furniture by mail order before selling direct, and leading the trend for out-of-town store locations.

Contact: Mr A C Southon, Lister Charitable Trust, Windyridge, The Close, Totteridge, London, N20 8PT. Tel: 0181 446 7281.

VESTEY family

£226,000

PREFERENCE: general
WEALTH: over £500m
TRUST LINKS: Vestey Foundation
COMPANY LINKS: Western United Investment

The Vesteys can trace their considerable fortune back to nineteenth century Liverpool, when brothers William and Sir Edmund Vestey established Union Cold Storage to enable them to tap into cheap supplies of meat from overseas. This proved a very wise move, and the family has gone on to create a truly global business empire which ranges from South American ranches to British butchers shops, but is still primarily based around producing, processing and transporting meat. The holding company for the Vestey group is Western United Investments, whose principal subsidiaries are Union International and Frederick Leyland & Co. It is still very much a family concern, with descendants of the founders still on the board and still holding the majority of the equity. Times have been somewhat lean recently, but it seems that there will soon be more flesh on the bone as the group returns to profitability.

In 1991 Western United made charitable donations of £226,000, of which a large chunk went to fund the **Vestey Foundation**. This was set up in 1990 and its current trustees are all leading family members: Lord Vestey, his cousin Edmund (grandson of Sir Edmund), Edmund's son Tim, and the Hon Mark Vestey. In 1992 the foundation had an income of £109,000 and made charitable donations of £78,000. The grants were dominated by £60,000 given to the Royal Veterinary College, with smaller gifts including £5,000 to the Royal Opera House, £3,000 to the Prince's Youth Business Trust, £2,500 to Dunn Nutritional Centre, and £2,000 to the City of London Endowment Trust for St Paul's Cathedral.

Edmund Vestey is chair of Western United, and is also president of Essex County Scout Council. His son Tim, has recently completed his MBA at Cranfield and looks likely to play a central role in the company's future, possibly by replacing his father. Edmund's cousin, Lord (Samuel) Vestey is a director of the family firm, and is president of both Gloucestershire Association of Boys' Clubs and the London Meat Trade & Drovers' Benevolent Association.

Contact: Mr J R Cuthbert, Secretary to the Management Committee, Vestey Foundation, 29 Clothfair, London, EC1A 7JX. Tel: 0171 710 1212. Western United Investment Co Ltd: 24-30 West Smithfield, London, EC1A 9DL. Tel: 0171 248 1212.

HENRY HOARE
and family

£224,000

PREFERENCE: disability, education, arts, conservation, welfare

AGE: 62

WEALTH: £35m-£50m

TRUST LINKS: Golden Bottle Trust, Bulldog Trust

COMPANY LINKS: C Hoare & Co.

The Hoare family's charitable works have been going on as long as their business activities. For over three hundred years they have controlled the highly discrete banking partnership C Hoare & Co. And for the same length of time they have been stewards of perhaps the oldest charitable trust in this publication. **Henry Hoare's Charity for the Distribution of Bibles and Religious Books** was established by the will of a previous Henry Hoare way back in 1722, with objects aptly described by its name. Despite its venerable age, this trust is still active and in 1993 had capital of £7,000 providing an income of £850. It still has close links with the family, and the present Henry Hoare is a trustee.

There are, however, a pair of larger and much more youthful grant-making trusts which the family has set up. The **Golden Bottle Trust** and the **Bulldog Trust** derive the bulk of their income from companies closely connected with the Hoares. The Golden Bottle Trust was established in 1985 by C Hoare & Co, from which it has since received more than £1.2 million via covenants and Gift Aid. In 1992 alone it received quarter of a million from the company, which allowed it to make donations amounting to £187,000. The major recipient of this trust's largesse in that year was the Lady Hoare Trust for Physically Disabled Children, which was given six grants totalling £70,000. This charity was set up in the early sixties by Lady Mary Hoare, who at the time was Mayoress of London, and now has the present Henry Hoare as its chair. Its aims are to give 'practical and some financial support to children up to the age of eighteen who have arthritis or limb disabilities.' Other grants made by the Golden Bottle Trust in 1992 included £5,700 to the Royal Opera House Trust, £5,000 to each of the Cambridge Foundation, the National Maritime Museum and the Study Centre Scholarship Fund, and £4,500 to the family's other trust, the Bulldog Trust. Smaller gifts were given to a range of causes, with an emphasis on education, heritage, wildlife and natural history, health, and the arts. Amongst these were a £2,000 grant to the British Butterfly Conservation Society, of which family member Anthony Hoare is director, and £1,500 to the Heythrop Hunt Charitable Trust. Henry Hoare's interests in countryside pursuits are also apparent in his position as vice president of the Game Conservancy Trust.

The Bulldog Trust has particularly close links with one family member, Richard Hoare, and the firm of which he is chair and director, Bulldog Holdings and subsidiaries. It was set up by him in 1983 and has general charitable objects. Through most of the eighties this trust had a relatively modest income and built up a portfolio of shares including a holding of 150,000 shares in Bulldog Securities. In the year 1990/91, however, its income was £230,000, which came mainly from donations from C Hoare & Co, Bulldog Holdings and Bulldog Securities, the Golden Bottle Trust, and £37,500 from Richard Hoare himself. However, most of this income was not distributed in the year, as donations of only £36,000 were made. The main recipient was the Winchester Cathedral Trust which received two donations totalling £23,000, with other large grants going to three schools – Tylehurst School Trust (£5,000) Elstree School (£2,000) and Godstone Prep school (£1,000). The remaining gifts were directed to organisations active in the education, welfare and wildlife sectors.

The main family company, C Hoare & Co, is one of the most exclusive and private banks in the country – as a partnership it does not have to issue annual accounts. Top dog in the company is Henry Hoare, who has been chair since 1988. Apart from their business holdings, the family also owns Luscombe Castle in Devon and some surrounding land.

Contact for both Golden Bottle and Bulldog Trusts: Messrs Hoare Trustees, 37 Fleet St, London, EC4P 4DQ. Tel: 0171 353 4522.

CLIFF RICHARD
£224,000

PREFERENCE: Christian causes, youth, arts, disability, tennis
AGE: 43
WEALTH: £20m-£35m
TRUST LINKS: Cliff Richard Charitable Trust, Cliff Richard Tennis Development Trust
COMPANY LINKS: none

Cliff Richard, the Peter Pan of pop, is renowned for his charitable activities almost as much as his longevity in the entertainment business. The donations he makes through the **Cliff Richard Charitable Trust** have received considerable press attention in recent years, and in 1992/93 these amounted to £120,000. This total is somewhat down on previous years, reflecting a drop in the trust's income from nearly half a million pounds in 1990/91 to £222,000 in 1992/93. In 1990/91 the recipients of the largest gifts were Children of Chernobyl (£80,000), the British Deaf Association and PHAB (£53,000 each), Evangelical Alliance Art Centre (£10,000), and the Genesis Art Trust (£6,000).

This fall in donations through his grant-making trust does not necessarily mean that Cliff is giving less away, because he has recently established the **Cliff Richard Tennis Development Trust**. Given his passion for the sport, it is unsurprising that he should wish to foster its development amongst young school children in order to help ensure that 'due attention is given to the physical education and development of such pupils as well as to the development and occupation of their minds'. The trust also has the wider purpose of providing recreational facilities in the interests of the social welfare of the general public. In its first two years of operation, the trust received income of £244,000, mainly in the form of unspecified donations, but also £32,000 from coaching fees. Its total expenditure for the period has been £153,000, of which two-thirds (£104,000) was spent in 1992/93. The main elements of this total expenditure over the two years have been £69,000 on 'Tennis Trail Venue costs', £25,000 on 'advertising and publicity', £18,000 on 'scholarship fees', £17,000 on 'consultancy fees', and £5,600 on 'entertaining' and 'travel'.

His financial support for the voluntary sector is complemented by personal involvement with a number of charities. Since 1966 he has been a high profile representative of The Evangelical Alliance Relief Fund (or TEAR Fund), an international relief agency which has been a past recipient of donations from his charitable trust. As befits a committed Christian, he is patron of the Crusaders' Union. He is also a patron of AIDS Care Education and Training and the Princess Alice Hospice, and is vice-president of PHAB.

Cliff's remarkable career stretches back over three decades to the first of his thirteen Gold Discs which he received for his famous single *Living Doll*, which won him another Gold Disc in 1986 when he re-recorded it with the Young Ones to aid Comic Relief. It is the length of this success at the top which has been the source of his considerable wealth, especially his highly popular concert tours and frequent Christmas singles.

Contact: Cliff Richard Charitable Trust: Mr W Latham, Harley House, 94 Hare Lane, Claygate, Esher, Surrey, KT10 0RB. Tel: 01372 467752. Cliff Richard Tennis Development Trust: Ms Diane Sanders at same address.

SHEPHERD family

£220,000

PREFERENCE: general, Yorkshire
WEALTH: £250m–£500m
TRUST LINKS: Patricia and Peter Shepherd Charitable Trust, Sylvia and Colin Shepherd Charitable Trust, Patricia and Donald Shepherd Charitable Trust
COMPANY LINKS: Shepherd Building Group

The Shepherd brothers, Colin, Donald and Sir Peter, have headed the family-owned Shepherd Building Group for over 35 years. Back in May 1973 each brother set up a charitable trust with his wife and subsequently endowed it with a block of shares in the company. Donations from the three trusts last year totalled £80,000.

The eldest brother, Sir Peter, retired as chair of the business in 1986 when he was 69. The activities of the **Patricia and Peter Shepherd Charitable Trust** have remained modest, however, with donations in 1992/93 totalling £9,500, out of an income of £21,000 including £3,000 covenanted from Sir Peter. Beneficiaries included the York Company of Merchant Adventurers' Appeal, St Leonard's Hospice in York, the Home Farm Trust and the York Theatre Royal Restoration Fund.

The **Sylvia and Colin Shepherd Charitable Trust** made donations of £13,500 out of an income of £61,000. A large number of small gifts were made, once again mainly to charities in Yorkshire, including the Merchant Adventurers' Appeal, Age Concern York, the Acorn Centre in Harrogate, the Friends of York Cemetery and the National Trust Yorkshire Moors and Dales Appeal. However, grants were also made to the Conservative and Unionist Agents Benevolent Association, VSO and the Iris Fund for the Prevention of Blindness. Colin is the current chair of the family company.

It is, however, the trust established by deputy chair Donald and his wife Patricia that is the largest. Income of £80,000 in 1992/93 financed donations of nearly £57,000, although details of beneficiaries were not provided in the accounts on file at the Charity Commission. Some £47,000 had been donated in the previous year.

The Shepherd Building Group is almost entirely owned by members of the extended Shepherd family. In 1992 it made charitable donations of £140,000, concentrated on Yorkshire, in particular the city of York. The main areas of support are children and youth, social welfare, education, medicine and enterprise and training.

Contact: For the Patricia and Peter Shepherd Charitable Trust: Galtres House, Rawcliffe Lane, York YO3 6NP. For the Sylvia and Colin Shepherd Charitable Trust: 15 St Edwards Close, York YO2 2QB. For the Patricia and Donald Shepherd Charitable Trust: PO Box 10, York YO1 1XU.

For the Shepherd Building Group Ltd:
William James, Group Secretary,
Blue Bridge Lane, York YO1 4AS.
Tel: 01904 653040.

LORD ATTENBOROUGH
£219,000  NEW

PREFERENCE: acting, education, disability, Third Word
AGE: 70
WEALTH: unknown
TRUST LINKS: Richard Attenborough Charitable Trust
COMPANY LINKS: Richard Attenborough Productions Ltd

Lord Richard Attenborough, who received his life peerage in 1993, is perhaps best known for producing and directing three biographical films: the multi-Oscar winning *Gandhi, Cry Freedom,* and *Shadowlands.* He has also recently revived his acting career by appearing in *Jurassic Park* and *Miracle on 34th Street.* He is active in the charity field, especially with organisations linked with the acting profession, education, various forms of disability and projects in less developed countries.

Whilst by no means one of the richest individuals in this book, he directs considerable financial support via the **Richard Attenborough Charitable Trust**. He set up this trust back in 1969, the year after his successful directing debut on *Oh! What a Lovely War.* The donations for the last three years ending 31st March 1992, 1993, and 1994 were respectively £97,000, £138,000 and £219,000, demonstrating his interests as set out above. It is likely that these preferences will continue.

He is president of the Actors' Charitable Trust, the Combined Theatrical Charities Appeals Council,

the Gandhi Foundation, Brighton Festival, Arts for Health, the MD Group of Great Britain and Northern Ireland, and is chair of the trustees of BAFTA. He is also a trustee of Help a London Child, the Prison Charity Shops Trust, the Tate Foundation, the Cinema & Television Benevolent Fund, and the Foundation for Sports and the Arts, and chair of the UK trustees of the Waterford-Kamhlaba School in Swaziland. He is chair of RADA, the Gardner Centre for the Arts at Sussex University, the European Script Fund, and governor of Motability. He is patron of Kingsley Hall and the Richard Attenborough Centre for Disability and the Arts at Leicester University. And he still finds time to act as pro-chancellor of Sussex University and goodwill ambassador for UNICEF.

Lord Attenborough stated that he was not at all keen to appear in this publication.

Contact: Secretary to the Trustees, Richard Attenborough Charitable Trust, Old Friars, Richmond, Surrey, TW9 1NH.

THE QUEEN

£208,000

(but see below)

PREFERENCE: the Church, welfare, general
AGE: 68
WEALTH: £50m-75m (but see below)
TRUST LINKS: Privy Purse Charitable Trust
COMPANY LINKS: n/a

The problem faced by commentators who try to gauge the wealth of the Queen is how to separate her personal wealth from the riches she enjoys as head of state. This has resulted in the figures placed by her name ranging from £5 billion or more down to under £50 million, the last being an estimate of how much she could take with her, as it were, if she left the country tomorrow. The one thing all the commentators agree on is not, as you might think, that she's rich, but that she is strapped for cash at the moment, what with the fire at Windsor Castle and the demands of a growing family, to say nothing of the Inland Revenue.

Trying to gauge how much the Queen gives to charity presents a similar problem. It is well-known in the charity world that occasional donations are forthcoming from Buckingham Palace in order to help a charity launch a major appeal:

recipients can acknowledge the Queen's support publicly – it helps in persuading other donors – but are impressed on not to reveal the amounts donated. The amounts are in fact usually modest, but how much is given in all? The fact that until April 1993 the Queen had paid no tax has not made uncovering the level of her giving any easier, most information on charitable donations being linked to the granting of tax reliefs.

There is, however, a charitable trust connected with the Queen, established as far back as 1987, when the Queen was 60 years of age. Renamed the **Privy Purse Charitable Trust** last year, it originally went by the cryptic name of the January 1987 Charitable Trust. In 1994 the trust held assets of £1,135,000 and made donations totalling £208,000. These were divided between the Church (£103,000); social, benevolent and welfare (£17,000); youth, schools and sports (£67,000); armed services and public utility charities (£5,000); animal charities (£2,000); medical charities (£11,000); and miscellaneous (£3,000). Donations made in the previous year had come to £211,000 in total.

The trust is financed by a combination of income from its investments and from donations, the source of which is not specified in the accounts. The trustees are Major Sir Shane Blewitt, the current Keeper of Her Majesty's Privy Purse, Sir Matthew Farrer, the Queen's solicitor, and John C Parsons, Deputy Keeper of the Privy Purse. The trust benefits from investment income but also sizeable donations. In their 1994 report the trustees note: 'During the year the trust received donations of £261,612.' Whether these donations are from the Queen, or from people charitably disposed to the Queen, is unclear.

Perhaps the Queen's best-known

charitable activity is the annual payment of Maundy money, organised through an office known as the Royal Almonry. In a largely ceremonial affair, the Queen hands out specially-minted coins to a group of suitably deserving subjects, matching her age in number. Rather more lucrative, from charities' point of view, was the Queen's decision to give away the £200,000 offered by the *Sun* newspaper in settlement of a legal action she had brought over the advance publication of the contents of her Christmas broadcast to the nation. Half the money was donated to the Save the Children Fund (of which her daughter, the Princess Royal, is president) and half to the Leonard Cheshire Foundation, which featured in her speech.

The Queen herself is patron or president of over 200 charities, at the last count, and her husband Prince Philip of a further 140. It is up to the fundraisers to make the connections and organise the events to turn this patronage into hard cash. Quantifying the value of a royal patron one charity pointed out that 'the going rate is about a thousand pounds a handshake.' One of Prince Philip's more personal charities is the **Prince Philip Trust Fund for the Royal Borough of Windsor and Maidenhead**, set up to commemorate the Queen's silver jubilee in 1977, with Prince Philip as one of the original trustees. The fund was established with £1,000 from 'charitably disposed persons', but raises its income mainly through donations and special fundraising events. The fund paid out £20,000 in 1992/3 to beneficiaries not specified in the accounts.

There are separate entries in this book for the Queen's two most active children in the charity world, the Princess Royal and Prince Charles, as well as for her daughter-in-law Princess Diana. Prince Andrew also has a small trust which was established ten years ago. By 1994 the **Prince Andrew Charitable Trust** was worth £205,000 and made donations in the year totalling £13,000. Social welfare, youth and medical charities were the principal beneficiaries.

In addition to the Queen's decision to pay tax voluntarily on her private income, the last two years have seen major changes to the royal finances. The cost to the taxpayer has shrunk, with Her Majesty herself carrying the costs of Prince Andrew, Prince Edward, Princess Anne and Princess Margaret, and the doors of Buckingham Palace have been flung open to visitors, at £8 a head. It seems unlikely, however, that the door will open too far on the charitable donations made by the Queen, who must continue to be seen to smile down benignly – and equally – on all her subjects.

Contact: For the Privy Purse Charitable Trust: John C Parsons, Buckingham Palace, London SW1A 1AA. Tel: 0171 930 4832.
For the Prince Andrew Charitable Trust: Capt. Neil Blair RN, at the above address.
For the Prince Philip Trust Fund for the Royal Borough of Windsor and Maidenhead: Mr J E Hancock, 4 Park Street, Windsor SL4 9JS.
Tel: 01753 851133.

ELLIOTT BERNERD

£189,000

PREFERENCE: arts, Jewish charities, health, general
AGE: 49
WEALTH: £75m-£100m
TRUST LINKS: Bernerd Foundation
COMPANY LINKS: Chelsfield

BRITISH SCHOOL OF OSTEOPATHY
1-4 SUFFOLK ST., LONDON. SW1Y 4HG
TEL. 01 930 9254-8

Teaboy turned tycoon Elliott Bernerd, with his sleek black hair and sharp-but-not-too-sharp suits, is the Platonic idea of the successful businessman. Bernerd's business is property, a field he entered on leaving school aged 15 and to which in the intervening years he has contributed three public companies. The latest and largest, Chelsfield, he decided to bring to the market in 1994.

What does the successful businessman do when he knows he is turning 40? He sets up a charitable foundation. Established in 1984, the **Bernerd Foundation** has been shelling out some £200,000 annually in recent years, most of it to the arts and to Jewish causes. Unusually, Bernerd himself is not one of the trustees of the foundation, which is run from the offices of a London solicitor. Despite the fact that Bernerd's grandfather was an early British film magnate, running Gaumont-British, Bernerd himself appears to have limited interest in film, although Chelsfield does own a cinema in Plymouth.

Grants from the Bernerd Foundation totalled £189,000 in 1991/92. The London Philharmonic Trust received £75,000 and the Lubavitch Foundation £33,000: both have been regular beneficiaries in the past, although Bernerd resigned as chair of the Philharmonic's trustees in 1994 and may direct his patronage elsewhere in future. Bernerd gave no reason for standing down, but his move followed a battle between trustees and the management, who wanted the board to put more effort into fundraising. Bernerd, understandably, may have felt that he'd done his bit. Other recipients included the Institute of Family Therapy (£30,000), Help the Aged (£20,000), the Oxford Centre for Postgraduate Hebrew Studies (£10,000) and the Musician's Benevolent Fund (£5,000). That last grant has a particular significance given Bernerd's recent opposition to Arts Council plans to withdraw funding from two of London's three orchestras.

Now with his 50th birthday looming, Bernerd's thoughts show signs of turning from private business to more public matters, and not just at Chelsfield. He was quoted in the *Independent on Sunday* saying: 'Latterly, I have been finding that I enjoy good quality architecture – both the design and the concept. I don't like glass boxes. I am a great fan of [James] Stirling, and it is a tragedy that he died.' Chelsfield in fact gave Stirling one of his last commissions, to replace Wool House in Carlton Gardens.

The successful businessman, after all, needs something that people can remember him by. Bernerd has whacked in sizeable amounts to his foundation every year, giving it a healthy income, but to date it is not endowed. Perhaps the successful flotation of Chelsfield will have a more lasting impact than just signalling the end of the property recession.

Contact: I Montrose, Bernerd Foundation, c/o Goodman Derrick, 90 Fetter Lane, London EC4 1EQ. Tel: 0171 404 0606.

SIR HARRY SOLOMON

£187,000

PREFERENCE: general, medicine
AGE: 57
WEALTH: less than £20m
TRUST LINKS: Solomon Family Charitable Trust
COMPANY LINKS: Hillsdown Hldgs.

Sir Harry Solomon lists 'charitable work' as one of his recreations in *Who's Who in Industry*. He is certainly an active financial supporter of charities through the **Solomon Family Charitable Trust**, which he set up in 1984, along with his wife as trustee. In 1985/86 he made an interest free loan of £950,000 to the trust – £860,000 was repaid the following year during which Solomon gave the trust a further £100,000. The trust's accounts for 1991/92 show assets of £117,000 and 12,500 unvalued shares in Faithwood Investments. Much of its £75,000 income in the year came from Sir Harry, and the trust made donations of £187,000. Unfortunately, the accounts on file at the Charity Commission do not specify the recipients of these grants, although Solomon's involvement as chair of the Help Medicine Appeal Fund for the Royal College of Physicians and trustee of the heart disease charity CORDA may point to some support for other medical causes.

Solomon trained as a solicitor, before setting up the Hillsdown Holdings food company with David Thompson (qv) in 1974. The pair made their fortunes when the company was floated ten years later, after which Thompson left and Solomon remained as chair. During the next five years he oversaw the purchase of Premier Brands, which made a rich man of Paul Judge (qv). In 1993 Solomon stood down from the helm to become a non-executive director of the company, and was replaced by former Tory defence minister Sir John Knott.

Contact: Sir Harry Solomon, Solomon Family Charitable Trust, c/o Hillsdown House, 32 Hampstead High St, London, NW3 1QD.
Tel: 0171 794 0677.

RICHARD DESMOND
£185,000 NEW

PREFERENCE: children, general welfare
AGE: 42
WEALTH: £35m-£50m
TRUST LINKS: Richard Desmond Charitable Trust
COMPANY LINKS: Northern & Shell

Little-known publisher Richard Desmond is increasingly gaining a reputation as a generous donor to charities. Over the past seven years has apparently given and raised several million pounds for worthy causes. Organisations receiving his support include the London Federation of Boys' Clubs, Help the Aged, Ravenswood, Norwood Child Care, Jewish Care, National Asthma Campaign, and the Stroke Association. He is closely involved with the Variety Club of Great Britain, and has donated many Sunshine Coaches for handicapped children, in particular to Norwood Child Care, Ravenswood, the Brickfields Centre, and Grosvenor House School. In 1989, he was made chair of the Newsvendors' Benevolent Institution, and headed their 200th anniversary appeal which raised around £0.75 million. And when the Duke of Edinburgh opened Northern & Shell's new Docklands head office in June last year, Desmond presented him with a cheque for the London Federation of Boys' Clubs.

Some of Desmond's financial support is directed through the **Richard Desmond Charitable Trust**, which he established in 1992. This trust had an income of £95,000 received via Gift Aid in its first year of operation, and made donations totalling £68,000. The accounts on file at the Charity Commission do not name the recipients of gifts made by the trust, but it does have a stated preference for the relief of poverty and sickness, especially amongst young people.

Northern & Shell, Richard Desmond's company, publishes a wide range of over sixty magazine titles including *Penthouse*, which is stocked on the top-shelves at newsagents across the country. It is perhaps best known for its slightly less risqué *OK! Magazine*, which was recently launched as a rival for *Hello!* and has a similar mix of interviews with the stars and pictures of their homes. As Northern & Shell's chair and sole director, Desmond received emoluments of just over £1 million in 1992/93. In that year, the company reported various charitable contributions amounting to just over £117,000, although this understates its support which includes the production of brochures and catalogues for many charities. Northern & Shell is currently celebrating twenty years in business by matching the amounts generated by employee fundraising efforts which will be directed at charities of the staff's choice. Because he is sole director and is beneficially interested in the whole of the issued share capital of the company, the gifts made by Northern & Shell have been included in the figure for Richard Desmond's personal donations cited above.

Contact: Scott Smith, Richard Desmond Charitable Trust, c/o Northern & Shell Tower, City Harbour, London, E14 9GL.

> # WARNING
> **Unsolicited requests for funding often lead to annoyance and are rarely productive. This book should not be used as a mailing list. Inappropriate applications waste time and money and may prejudice chances of future success.**

EARL CADOGAN
and family
£179,000 NEW

PREFERENCE: welfare, education, health, general, London
AGE: 80
WEALTH: £100m-£250m
TRUST LINKS: Earl Cadogan's Charity, Viscount Chelsea's Charity
COMPANY LINKS: Cadogan Estates

Earl Cadogan's Charity is one of the largest aristocratic grant-making trusts in this book, as befits one of the country's more wealthy landowners – the Cadogan family control a large chunk of Chelsea through their company Cadogan Estates. The donations made by Earl Cadogan's Charity are mainly funded by dividends from its holding of 837,500 shares in Chelsea Land, a subsidiary of Cadogan Estates. In 1991/92 these shares helped provide an income of £148,000 which supported payments of £177,000 to a variety of causes. The largest grant of £52,000 went to the Salvation Army, a regular recipient of gifts from the Charity, with other donations directed to Croftinloan Holdings Ltd school appeal (£10,000), King Edward VII's Hospital for Officers (£6,000), and £5,000 to various organisations including North Herts Hospice Care Association, East Chelsea Community Contact, and the Royal British Legion's Poppy Appeal and its Chelsea & Kensington Branch. A grant of £5,000 was also received by the New Masonic Samaritan Fund, which reflects the Earl's past position as Pro Grand Master of the United Grand Lodge of Freemasons from 1969-82.

As well as being a trustee of Earl Cadogan's Charity along with his parents, the Earl's eldest son and heir, Viscount Chelsea, also gives money to charitable causes through his personal eponymous trust. **Viscount Chelsea's Charity** was set up in 1974 with 100,000 Chelsea Land shares, and by the early 1990s was donating over £20,000 per year, with a total of £40,000 given to the Royal Veterinary College's Animal Care Trust and £12,500 to NSPCC in Chelsea. The most recent accounts for 1992/93, however, record grants totalling less than £2,000 despite income of £19,000.

Amongst their other charitable activities, Lord Cadogan is trustee of the British Epilepsy Association, and Viscount Chelsea is chair of the Leukaemia Research Fund.

When contacted, Earl Cadogan stated that he did not wish to be included in this book, because: 'There may be people who like to "boast" of their charity activities but that has always been a matter which I have kept to myself'. He also commented that some of the facts and figures as stated are incorrect, although he did not specify the precise nature of these inaccuracies.

Contact: Earl Cadogan's Charity: Miss J Castle, Secretary to the Trustees, The Cadogan Office, 18 Cadogan Gardens, London, SW3 2RP. Viscount Chelsea's Charity: Messrs May May & Merrimans Solicitors, 12 South Square, Grays Inn, London, WC1R 5HH. Tel: 0171 408 8132.

CORAL SAMUEL

£178,000

PREFERENCE: general
WEALTH: unknown
TRUST LINKS: Coral Samuel Charitable Trust, Basil Samuel Charitable Trust

COMPANY LINKS: past connections with Great Portland Estates

The two Samuel Charitable Trusts are able to donate major sums to charity due to the efforts of the late Basil Samuel, who was co-founder of the property company Great Portland Estates but was always keen to avoid the limelight. Shares in the firm are the source of funding for two major charitable trusts set up by him and his wife, but the 'known charitable donations' figure given above is comprised only of the gifts made by the **Coral Samuel Charitable Trust**.

Coral Samuel set up her eponymous grant-making trust in 1962 with an initial endowment of 50,000 shares in Great Portland. Over the subsequent thirty years the Coral Samuel Charitable Trust has increased its asset base to 1.5 million shares in the company worth over two million pounds. These generated an income of £232,000 in 1991/92 which supported donations of £178,000 to a variety of causes, with the largest grants focused on the arts and medicine. Gifts to cultural charities included £25,000 to Dulwich Picture Gallery, £10,000 to the Natural History Museum Development Trust, £7,000 to the Academy of St Martins in the Fields, £6,500 to the Textile Conservation Society, and £5,000 to each of the Royal College of Music, National Opera Studio and Glyndebourne Opera Festival. Health and medical donations included £25,000 to Hammersmith Hospital's Royal Postgraduate Medical School, and £5,000 to both St Catherine's Hospice in Crawley and the Royal Free Hospital's Breast Cancer Appeal. The Samuel family's connections with horse racing are evident in £25,000 given to the Racing Welfare Charity. Other donations included £10,000 to the Churches College and the

Abbeyfield Society, £7,000 to Brathay Hall Trust, and various gifts to Jewish, youth and disability organisations.

The **Basil Samuel Charitable Trust** holds an even larger tranche of shares in Great Portland, with a current market value of £4.9 million, although at one stage in 1990/91 they were worth nearly twice this amount. The trust was established in 1959 by Basil Samuel, and Coral Samuel is now a trustee. The donations of just under £500,000 in 1991/92 went to a similar mix of causes as those supported by Coral Samuel's trust.

Coral Samuel's solicitors stated that their client was 'most unhappy' to be included in a directory of this type.

Contact for both Basil Samuel and Coral Samuel Charitable Trusts: The Correspondent, Knighton House, 56 Mortimer St, London, W1M 8BD.

WAFIC SAID
£177,000
(but see below)

PREFERENCE: education and health, particularly Arabic and Middle Eastern
AGE: 54
WEALTH: £250m-£500m
TRUST LINKS: Karim Rida Said Foundation
COMPANY LINKS: Said Holdings Limited

By all accounts Wafic Said is one of the richer individuals in this book, thanks to his international investment and trading activities. He is Syrian by birth, was resident in London for a period, but now lives in Monaco. He has a reputation as a contributor of substantial sums to charitable causes, and directs some of this support via the **Karim Rida Said Foundation**.

This foundation was established by Said and his wife Rosemary in 1986 to commemorate his late son Karim, who died in the seventies. It concentrates on educational and health projects in the Middle East with the aim of helping to relieve poverty and suffering, and it also assists Arab students in financial need to study elsewhere in the world, and seeks to promote greater understanding of the Arabic language and culture. By August 1993 the foundation had built up assets of £14.4 million, derived largely from gifts from Said and family interests. This capital produced an income of £536,000 in 1992/93 which helped finance charitable expenditure in that year of £177,000.

The Cambridge Overseas Trust (UK) received £40,000 as part of a ten year commitment made by the foundation to sponsor the 'Karim Rida Said Cambridge Scholarships' which help students from Arab League member states. The American University of Washington DC received £28,000 and the American University of Beirut received £30,000, in both cases for Karim Rida Said scholarships awarded under ten-year schemes. New scholarship schemes administered by Oxford University and the British Council will come into effect with the 1994/95 academic year.

In 1992/93 the foundation also contributed £10,000 to another of its long-term beneficiaries, the Alexandria Project, which enables British students of Arabic to spend a year in Alexandria; £42,000 to Medical Aid for Palestinians as part of a three-year commitment to help upgrade facilities and retrain personnel at Hamsharry Hospital in Sidon, Lebanon; and £23,000 to UNIPAL as half of a two-year commitment to support five teachers of English as a foreign language in the Occupied Territories. More recent commitments include: $103,000 payable over three years to Save the Children Fund to support a revolving book programme for secondary schools and the training of nurse aides in Lebanon; sponsorship of two annual fellowships at the Refugee Studies Programme in Oxford (£30,000); support for VSO for small business training in Jordan (£18,000); and a grant of £56,000 to Oxfam for educational and health projects in Lebanon, Jordan and the Occupied Territories.

Several of the past and present trustees of the foundation are of note. Founding trustee Sir James Craig is an expert on the Middle East, having served as HM Ambassador to Syria and then Saudi Arabia. Another founding trustee was Jonathan Aitken MP, former defence procurement minister, who resigned as a trustee in 1991/92 and was replaced by Sir Charles Powell, who served as Margaret Thatcher's Private Secretary in the eighties.

Although no longer resident in Britain, Wafic Said is still an active supporter of charitable causes in this country through gifts and commitments made outside the framework of his foundation. In recent years these have included: £630,000 to the Prince's Youth Business Trust; £500,000 to the Europaeum Initiative at Oxford University which facilitates the exchange of students, lecturers and ideas between university institutes in various European countries (he and his wife are members of Oxford's Court of Benefactors); £312,000 to the Royal Shakespeare Company (of which he is a governor); over £100,000 to the NSPCC (he and his wife are life patrons); and £100,000 to Somerville College, Oxford. In the US he has also given $1 million to the Texas Heart Institute and $125,000 to St Luke's Episcopal Hospital in Houston. These donations have not been included in the figure given above, however, as they have been made over varying timescales during the past few years.

Contact: The Director, Karim Rida Said Foundation, 49 Park Lane, London, W1Y 3LB. Tel: 0171 491 2822.

MICHAEL STONE
£175,000 NEW

PREFERENCE: medicine, education, animals, children
AGE: 57
WEALTH: £20m-£35m
TRUST LINKS: M J C Stone Charitable Trust
COMPANY LINKS: E D & F Man

Michael Stone has been the chair of E D & F Man, a leading London commodities trading group, since 1983. He made his fortune when a stake in the Man group was acquired in 1987 by the Swiss chocolate company Jacob Suchard, which has since sold this holding. He has diverted a part of his wealth to charitable causes through the **M J C Stone Charitable Trust**.

He established this trust in 1981, and its five current trustees are all members of the Stone family, including Michael Stone and his wife. By 1989/90 the trust had built up assets of over £630,000, and had an income of £214,000 of which over half was covenanted from the Stone family. This income enabled £175,000 of donations to be made in the year, of which the most significant were £100,000 given to St Catherine's Hospice and £25,000 to the Game Conservancy Trust, of which Michael Stone is a former council member. Other sizeable grants included

£10,000 to both the European Business School Development Foundation and Friends of Killhope, and £5,000 to each of the Peter Scott Memorial Appeal, BBC Children in Need Appeal, and Tower Hamlets Environment Trust. The remaining donations were directed to a variety of causes, including medical charities and those operating in the Surrey and Sussex region where the trust was based until its recent move to Gloucestershire.

As befits a firm run by a director of Business in the Community, the E D & F Man group made donations of £166,000 through its own charitable trust. The main recipients were business enterprise schemes in East London, and also mainstream arts and music organisations. Although a contact address is given below, the gifts made by this trust have not been included in the figure for personal donations made by Michael Stone because of his limited shareholding in the company, which is reportedly planning a £400 million flotation on the stock-market.

Contact: Mr M J C Stone, M J C Stone Charitable Trust, Estate Office, Ozleworth Park, Wotton under Edge, Glos, GL12 7QA. Tel: 01453 845591. E D & F Man Ltd Charitable Trust: Mr David Boehm, Trustee, E D & F Man Ltd, Sugar Quay, Lower Thames St, London, EC3R 6DU. Tel: 0171 285 3000.

KESWICK family
£171,000 NEW

PREFERENCE: Hong Kong, education, general
WEALTH: £250m–£500m

TRUST LINKS: Keswick Foundation, Simon Keswick Charitable Trust, Teresa Keswick Charitable Trust
COMPANY LINKS: Jardine Matheson Group

The Keswick family have a wide-ranging influence upon Hong Kong through the Jardine Matheson trading group, which until recently was based in the colony. The company was created back in 1832 by James Matheson and William Jardine, into whose family the Keswicks of Dumfries married during the late 1800s. The family's various direct and indirect holdings in the company, although comprising a minority of its shares, are the basis of their considerable wealth.

The link with the Far East is evident in the activities of the **Keswick Foundation**, which was set up by members of the family in 1979. It has general charitable objects but in particular aims to fund the development of pilot projects filling the gaps in the social services of Hong Kong. The current directors of the foundation include Simon Keswick, his wife Emma, and Margaret Keswick Jencks. By 1990 the foundation had built up assets worth around £5 million, consisting mainly of 2.7 million shares in Jardine Matheson Holdings, the private parent company for the group. These provided the bulk of the £237,000 income for the year, which funded charitable distributions of £165,000, although the beneficiaries were not specified.

Further support for causes in the colony comes from Matheson & Co, part of the Jardine Matheson Group, which gave £130,000 in 1990 with a preference for Hong Kong related organisations such as the Gurkha Welfare Fund. These grants have not, however, been included in the Keswicks' personal donations as the family owns only around 10% of the parent company.

Charitable gifts on a slightly smaller scale are made by two grant-making trusts which are administered from Jardine Matheson's offices in London, and are connected with the three Keswick brothers – Henry, the eldest, Sir Chippindale, and Simon, the youngest . The **Simon Keswick Charitable Trust** was established by its namesake in 1977, who is still a trustee along with his wife. It has general purposes, and in 1992/93 donated just over £1,000 with a bias towards health and disability causes. These gifts were financed by dividends from 20,366 shares in Jardine Matheson Holdings. The **Teresa Keswick Charitable Trust** has a slightly larger asset base, with 55,366 shares in the company which cost £61,000. This trust was created by Teresa Keswick in 1978, and its trustees are now Henry and Sir Chippindale Keswick. In 1992/93 it made a single £5,000 donation to the Edith Bessie Gibson Charitable Trust, which promotes Catholicism.

Henry Keswick is the chair of Jardine Matheson, and various group companies, and is also director of Sun Alliance, Robert Fleming Holdings, the *Telegraph* and Rothmans International. He is a trustee of the National Portrait Gallery, and chair of the Hong Kong Association. His wife, Tessa, is an advisor to Kenneth Clarke, the Chancellor of the Exchequer. Sir Chippindale Keswick is deputy chair of Hambros plc, vice councillor of the Cancer Research Campaign, and honorary treasurer of the Children's Country Holiday Fund. Simon is the younger of the Keswick brothers and past chair of Jardine Matheson Holdings. He is a trustee of the British Museum, and an ordinary governor of the London Hospital Medical College.

Contact: Keswick Foundation: Frere Chomley Bischoff Solicitors, 4 John Carpenter St, London, EC4Y 0NH. Simon and Teresa Keswick Charitable

Trusts both: K H Galloway, Matheson Bank Ltd, Jardine House, 6 Crutched Friars, London, EC3N 2HT. Tel: 0171 528 4000.

FORTE FAMILY
about £169,000

PREFERENCE: education, hotel trade, general
WEALTH: £100m-£250m
TRUST LINKS: Forte Charitable Trust, Lord Forte Foundation, Forte plc Charitable Trust
COMPANY LINKS: Forte

What do you give the man who has everything for his 80th birthday? Lord Forte's children set up a foundation to commemorate his 80th birthday, with the primary objective of encouraging excellence 'by helping talented individuals in the hotel, catering and tourism industry to acquire new professional skills and knowledge'. The **Lord Forte Foundation** is not endowed and its income comes from donations and fundraising events. In 1991/92 it made awards totalling £14,000, but has the capacity to do quite a lot more in the future, having amassed assets of £738,000.

Charles Forte had arrived in London from Italy to set up a milk bar in Regent Street in 1935. Nearly 60 years later, the Forte empire is now worth some £2 billion and covers luxury hotels to roadside restaurants and motorway service areas. Lord Forte's son Rocco took over as chair of the company in 1993.

It is in fact the second generation who seem the most interested in philanthropy. Rocco Forte also set up the **Forte Charitable Trust** in 1982, the year before he became chief executive at Forte plc, and he and his sister, Olga Polizzi, remain trustees. In 1992/3 the trust made donations totalling £10,500, with £5,000 going to the British Home and Hospital for Incurables, £2,000 to Childline and £2,500 to the Centre Charles Peguy. The bulk of the trust's £1.6 million assets were invested in Forte shares. In the past the trust has made donations to a variety of different groups, including those concerned with education, disability and Roman Catholic causes. In a letter on the trust's file at the Charity Commission, the trustees point out that they have raised the level of grants made in 1993/94 to 41 donations totalling £155,500.

In recent years Forte plc has made donations to charities of about £0.5 million annually. Health and medical causes do particularly well. The company also put up £257,000 for the Landau Forte City Technology College in Derby and runs the Forte Community Chest in conjunction with the Conservation Foundation which has helped over 200 small-scale environmental projects from mending church steeples to creating gardens for disabled people.

Contact for the Forte Charitable Trust: George Proctor, 166 High Holborn, London WC1V 6TT. Tel: 0171 836 7744. For the Lord Forte Foundation: Jonathan Edis-Bates, at same address. For Forte plc: Ms A M McBride, charities administrator, at same address.

DAVID LEWIS
and family
£164,000

PREFERENCE: medicine, Jewish causes, children

AGE: 69

WEALTH: £100m-£250m

TRUST LINKS: Lewis Family Charitable Trust

COMPANY LINKS: Lewis Trust Group Ltd

David Lewis and his family are dedicated followers of fashion, with a high street presence via their River Island clothes stores. They are also dedicated donors to charity, with a trust which makes grants of more than one hundred thousand pounds per year.

The **Lewis Family Charitable Trust** was established in 1969 by the Lewis family, with an initial settlement of £14,000 from their private company, the Lewis Trust Group. By 1988, the last year for which accounts are on file at the Charity Commission, the charitable trust's assets had grown to nearly £3 million, its income was £284,000, and the trustees were David and Bernard Lewis. In that year the trust made grants of £164,000, the major recipient being the Lewis National Prosthetics Institute which received £100,000. The other beneficiaries were Jewish and Israeli charities, notably the Medical Aid Committee for Israel which received £43,000, and the Jewish Welfare Board which was given £10,500. This preference is not entirely unexpected given the family's strong connections with Israel, notably their substantial property holdings in the resort of Eilat, which is apparently known locally as 'Lewisville'. The family has also given substantial support in recent years to the Birth Defects Foundation, and various medical research charities.

The story of the Lewis brothers is one of rags to rag-trade. They are sons of an East End greengrocer, and were brought up above his shop. Bernard and David set up their first fashion shop nearby in the 1950s, and on the back of this formed the family company, the Lewis Trust Group. The growth of their company came with the sixties fashion revolution. Through their Chelsea Girl shops, complemented by Concept Man, they brought contemporary fashion trends within reach of everyday people. The chain was later rebadged in the 1980s to become the River Island Clothing Company. The Lewis Trust Group has diversified in recent years into overseas property and travel, and its current directors are all Lewis family members: Bernard, David, Leonard, and Julian.

Contact: The Secretary, Lewis Family Charitable Trust, Chelsea House, West Gate, London, W5 1DR.
Tel: 0181 998 8822.

McALPINE family
about £160,000

PREFERENCE: general, education
WEALTH: £20m-£35m
TRUST LINKS: Robert McAlpine Foundation, McAlpine Educational Endowments
COMPANY LINKS: Sir Robert McAlpine & Sons, Newarthill

The McAlpine family have made a fortune through their involvement with the construction and civil engineering industries, despite the impact of the current recession. The arm of the family headed by Sir Robin McAlpine makes donations via two charities associated with their private building company, Sir Robert McAlpine & Sons. The first is the **Robert McAlpine Foundation**, which was set up by the company in 1963 with three McAlpines, including Sir Robin, amongst the original trustees. The last accounts on file at the Charity Commission show that in 1987 the foundation held assets with a market value of over £5 million. These produced an income of £188,000 which supported grants of £139,000, but the beneficiaries were not specified. The **McAlpine Educational Endowments Limited** is considerably smaller, with capital of £169,000 and a 1993 income of £17,000. This charitable company was created in 1957 by subscribers including Sir Robin, in order to advance education through scholarships at preparatory, public or other independent schools, and at any technical college or university. It had a charitable expenditure of £21,000 in 1993, of which £17,500 went on a 'Schools Scheme' and the recipients of the remainder were not given.

The family member with the highest public profile is not directly connected with either of these grant-makers, although he is a director of Sir Robert McAlpine & Sons. Lord McAlpine of West Green was one of the Conservative Party's main fundraisers during the eighties and was honorary treasurer from 1975-90, and deputy chair between 1979 and 1983. He is a close confidant of former Prime Minister, Lady Thatcher (qv), and is now a director of her non-charitable grant-maker, the Thatcher Foundation. Although there are no trusts registered in his name, Lord McAlpine is connected with a variety of causes. He is active in the arts as vice-president of Friends of the Ashmolean Museum, and director of the Theatre Investment Fund, and is a past trustee of the Royal Opera House and past member of the Friends of the V&A. He is also a trustee of the eponymous charitable trust funded by David and Frederick Barclay (qqv), is president of the Medical College of St Bartholomew's Hospital, is a patron and past president of the British Waterfowl Association, and director of Marwell Preservation Trust.

When contacted, the secretary to the two trusts listed above commented that 'much of the factual information submitted in your draft is out of date and not relevant' although he did not provide more recent data. His main objection, however, was that he wished the entry to be withdrawn, because: 'the McAlpine family has no wish to be included in your, or anyone else's, work of reference on wealth and philanthropy in Britain. The McAlpine family has traditionally adopted the stance of not seeking publicity in respect of its charitable activities, and will continue to pursue this policy.'

Contact: Robert McAlpine Foundation: Secretary to the Trustees, 40 Bernard St, London, WC1N 1LG. Tel: 0171 837 3377. McAlpine Educational Endowments: Mr G L Prain, Company Secretary, at the same address.

EVERARD GOODMAN
£158,000 NEW

PREFERENCE: medicine, youth, education, elderly people, arts, Jewish causes
AGE: 62
WEALTH: £35m-£50m
TRUST LINKS: Everard and Mina Goodman Charitable Foundation; Everard Goodman Foundation
COMPANY LINKS: Tops Estates; Trust of Property Shares

Everard Goodman – another grand old man of the property game, although he spent 25 years in the retail trade – is currently chair and chief executive of Tops Estates plc, and is chair of Trust of Property Shares plc and family investment companies.

For over thirty years he has been an active supporter of charities with some of this support channelled through the **Everard and Mina Goodman Charitable Foundation**, which he set up with his wife in 1962. The foundation's grant total of £19,000 in 1992/93 is markedly lower than recent years' figures of around £50,000. There has been a similar fall in its income, which is derived principally from donations received from the Goodman family. The grants made in the last year went mostly to Jewish causes, including £5,000 to Jewish Care, £2,000 to the Group Relations Educational Trust, just under £2,000 each to Western Marble Arch

Synagogue and the Foundation for Education. There were also a few gifts to non-Jewish organisations, of which the largest was £1,250 to British Red Cross. Since April 1993, however, we were informed that grants totalling £158,000 have been made, including £62,000 to a neo-natal clinic, £25,000 for day care at a youth centre, £21,000 to a medical research appeal, £20,000 to Ravenswood Home for Backward Children, and £10,000 to a home for the elderly, with other grants to medical, arts and educational causes.

There is another charitable trust registered in Goodman's name, the **Everard Goodman Foundation**. He set it up five years ago, with general charitable objects. Its trustees include his son Michael, and it is administered from the offices of one of his property companies in London. At the time of writing, there were no accounts on file at the Charity Commission for the foundation, so it was not possible to assess its size or preferences.

Contact: Everard and Mina Goodman Charitable Foundation: Mr E N Goodman, 5 Bryanston Court, George St, London, W1H 7HA. Tel: 0171 486 4684. Everard Goodman Foundation: Mr E N Goodman, 77 South Audley St, London, W1Y 6EE.
Tel: 0171 486 4684.

BAMFORD family

£155,000

(but see below)

PREFERENCE: Rocester in Staffordshire
WEALTH: £100m-£250m
TRUST LINKS: Bamford Charitable Trust
COMPANY LINKS: JC Bamford Excavators

Many people will have been asked the question: 'Did the earth move for you?' Few will be able to reply, as the Bamfords could, 'Yes, and it made me a millionaire.' The manufacture of hydraulic earth-movers has in fact netted the Bamford family a fortune variously estimated at between £180 million and £200 million.

Joe Bamford set up JC Bamford Excavators in the forties, and the famous JCB digger is named after his initials. Now a tax-exile living principally in Switzerland, Joe Bamford has handed over control of the company to his son Sir Anthony, who was knighted for his services to UK exports. Sir Anthony also chairs the **Bamford Charitable Foundation**, which administers the company's donations budget. The Bamford group does have other major shareholders but it is still dominated by the family and for that reason we have included these grants in the Bamford family total given above.

A total of £155,000 was donated by the Bamford Charitable Foundation in 1992, mainly in small grants of £1,000 or under. Support is given in the areas of community services, health and medicine, education, science and religion, but only appeals originating within a 25-mile radius of the company's location in Rocester are considered. The foundation gives a preference to projects in which a member of staff is involved.

Contact: L Mitchell, Bamford Charitable Trust, c/o JC Bamford Excavators Ltd., Rocester, Uttoxeter, Staffs ST14 5JP. Tel: 01889 590312.

ARNOLD LEE

£155,000

PREFERENCE: Jewish causes, Israel
WEALTH: less than £20m
TRUST LINKS: Arnold Lee Charitable Trust

COMPANY LINKS: none found

Arnold Lee realised his paper fortune in 1987 when he sold his property company to Imry Merchant Developers, and netted himself around £20 million. Some of this has since been directed to good causes through the **Arnold Lee Charitable Trust**. This was set up by Lee in 1962, and over the past ten years its assets have grown considerably from £318,000 in 1982 to over £1.25 million in 1992. The trust made donations amounting to £155,000 in 1991/92, matching its income, and these gifts went predominantly to Jewish causes, or to charities operating in Israel. The major grants were £48,000 to the Jewish Philanthropic Association, £12,500 to Yesodey Hatorah Grammar School, £11,000 to Jewish Care, and grants of £6,000 to each of the Huntingdon Foundation (which promotes Judaism), Beth David Institute Trust and Nightingale Home for Aged Jews.

Contact: Mr A Lee, 47 Orchard Court, Portman Sq, London, W1H 9PD. Tel: 0171 486 8918.

TONY CLEGG
£151,000

PREFERENCE: medicine, education, churches, youth, Yorkshire.
AGE: 56
WEALTH: £50m-£75m
TRUST LINKS: Ronald Anthony Clegg Charitable Foundation
COMPANY LINKS: sold stake in Mountleigh

Serious illness has a profound effect on peoples' lives. Nowhere is this better illustrated than in the case of Tony Clegg. A successfully treated brain tumour precipitated an end to his highly profitable business career, which has since been largely replaced by work with, and substantial support for, non-profit organisations.

In recent years Clegg has been noticeable for his activities in the health sector, especially in the area of cancer research and treatment. Perhaps as a sign of his gratitude, he has employed his considerable entrepreneurial skills as chair of the United Leeds Teaching Hospitals NHS Trust, close to his Wetherby home. He is also a council member of both the Macmillan Nurse Appeal and the Critical Care Trust, as well as chair of the British Society for Clinical Cytology Appeal and the Leeds Special Appeal of the Cancer Relief Macmillan Fund. In 1991/92 he backed up his involvement with the latter two causes with donations of £51,000 and £11,333 respectively, made via his personal charity trust – the **Ronald Anthony Clegg Charitable Foundation**.

The foundation was set up by Clegg in 1988, the year his cancer was diagnosed. In 1991/92 it made gifts totalling £151,000 from covenanted income of £240,000. Clegg does not just support medical organisations – the remaining donations made by the foundation give an indication of his other charitable interests. The largest single grant was £60,000 to the Royal Agricultural College's capital appeal, with a further £2,000 given to Wetherby Agricultural Society. Clegg is also a council member of the Yorkshire Agricultural Society. A number of gifts were made to religious causes and buildings, notably £10,000 towards the restoration of Whixley Church, £1,000 to the Square Chapel Building Trust, and £500 to Stanningley PCC. His interests in youth development are manifested through a £10,000 grant to the Duke of Edinburgh's Award scheme, and his role as trustee and deputy chair of the Prince's Youth

Business Trust. Other donations were made to a variety of charities, especially those in Leeds and Yorkshire, or dealing with health and disabilities. Tony Clegg maintains strong links with his local area – he is a patron of Leeds Riding for the Disabled and the Marrick Priory Appeal, a member of the court of Leeds University, a council member of the Yorkshire branch of the Home Farm Trust, and chair of the appeal committee for the Dales Countryside Museum and Education Centre.

For most of his life Tony Clegg had been a notorious workaholic. He left school at the age of sixteen to help in the two restaurants owned by his parents. After a period of National Service he dived into the Yorkshire textiles industry as manager of Mountain Mills. In 1966 this company merged with the publicly quoted Leigh Mills, and Clegg eventually became managing director. The company went from strength to strength, but by the early 1970s the impact of the textiles recession began to be felt. Clegg's response was completely to redirect the company's efforts into property investment and development, under its new name – Mountleigh. With his uncanny ability to spot undervalued assets, he soon proved as adept in this sector as he had been in textiles. The Mountleigh Group rode on the crest of the burgeoning eighties property market, with Clegg at its helm.

Everything came to an abrupt halt, however, when Clegg was diagnosed as having a brain tumour in 1988. After a successful operation, he initially returned to his position as chair and chief executive of Mountleigh, but in 1989 he retired, selling his stake in the company for £70 million to a pair of American businessmen. Maybe his heart was no longer in it, or perhaps he foresaw the imminent property slump. Either way, he has since avoided any high-pressure business activities, although continues to dabble in property as chair and chief executive of E & F Securities, a private company.

Contact: Mr R E Downhill, Roland Anthony Clegg Charitable Foundation, Berwin Leighton Solicitors, Adelaide House, London Bridge, London EC4R 9HA. Tel: 0171 623 3144.

LORD ILIFFE
and family
£150,000

PREFERENCE: Education, heritage, medicine, Midlands and Berkshire
AGE: 86
WEALTH: £50m-£75m
TRUST LINKS: Iliffe Family Charitable Trust
COMPANY LINKS: Yattendon Investment Trust

The Iliffe family are no strangers to charity – indeed Lord and Lady Iliffe gave their home away in 1978 when they handed their Berkshire property, Basildon Hall, and its collection of 18th century furniture and art, over to the National Trust. In 1991/92 they also gave £21,000 from their charitable trust to the National Trust for Basildon.

The **Iliffe Family Charitable Trust** was set up in 1977, with Robert Iliffe, Lord Iliffe's heir and nephew, as one of the founding trustees. Over the next two years it received £65,000 worth of debentures in the family company Yattendon Investment Trust from Lord Iliffe and Robert Iliffe, and subsequently shares in the Birmingham Post and Coventry Newspapers. By 1992, the trust had built up assets of over £1.1 million through the sale of various shares, which enabled it to make donations of over £150,000 in that year. The trust's grants reflect close family connections with the West Midlands and Berkshire, where they have lived and worked for several generations. Grants to the Midlands included £20,000 to Coventry Cathedral, £10,000 towards the upkeep of Castle Bromwich Hall gardens, £10,000 to the Black Country Museum, £8,000 to the Ironbridge Gorge Museum, and £5,000 each to South Warwickshire Scanner Appeal, Myton Hamlet Hospice, and Birmingham Hippodrome. Lord Iliffe is also a trustee of Shakespeare's Birthplace, and he and Robert Iliffe are ex-members of the council of the University of Warwick. Apart from the £21,000 given to the National Trust, other major gifts directed at the Berkshire area included £20,000 to the Bradfield Foundation, which raises funds for Bradfield College, near Reading. We have been informed that the trustees are not able to respond to unsolicited applications, whether from charitable organisations or individuals.

Through their family owned company, Yattendon Investment Trust, the Iliffes have a wide range of business interests, the longest standing of which is newspaper publishing. The present Lord Iliffe's grandfather set up a printing and publishing business in Coventry in the latter part of the last century and founded what is now the *Coventry Evening Telegraph*. More recently, during the last war, the *Birmingham Post and Mail* was acquired and Lord Iliffe was proprietor of these titles from 1960 to the mid-1970s, before handing over the reins to Robert, who ran them until they were sold to an American publisher in the late 1980s. The Iliffes did not sell all their newspaper interests, however, and continue to produce regional papers in Cambridge, Hertfordshire and Essex, Staffordshire and Derbyshire, and the South West. The focus of Yattendon's energies has taken on a further dimension with the acquisition

in 1992 of Marina Developments. The company is now Britain's largest marina operator – which may not be all plain sailing given the recession's disastrous effects upon the sector.

Contact: Mr J R Antipoff, Iliffe Family Charitable Trust, Barn Close, Yattendon, Newbury, Berks, RG16 0UX.

SIR ANTHONY HOPKINS

£148,000

(but see below)

PREFERENCE: general, arts

AGE: 56

WEALTH: less than £20m

TRUST LINKS: Sir Anthony Hopkins Charitable Foundation

COMPANY LINKS: none

Sir Anthony Hopkins achieved international fame on the back of his Oscar-winning performance as Hannibal 'the Cannibal' Lecter in Jonathan Demme's 1991 film *The Silence of the Lambs*. Always one of our most consummate actors, he has since returned to somewhat less controversial pastures including parts in the Merchant-Ivory period dramas, *Howard's End* and *The Remains of the Day*, and the lead role in Richard Attenborough's (qv) *Shadowlands*. Although by no means as rich as most of the other individuals in this book, his long and successful career has helped provide him with a wealth he estimates at less than £5 million.

All of his charitable donations are made through the **Sir Anthony Hopkins Charitable Foundation**, which he set up in February 1993 with two primary areas of interest in mind. The first is to sponsor students through drama schools, as the majority of drama students do not attract LEA discretionary grants. Working solely with schools affiliated to the Conference of Drama Schools, Sir Anthony offers sponsorship of up to £2,000 per annum for first-time drama students embarking on two or three year courses. His second priority is to support alcoholic and drug rehabilitation projects, and the main thrust in this area so far has been support for the Addictive Diseases Trust, helping to finance a pilot scheme at Downview Prison.

The foundation is jointly administered by Sir Anthony and his wife, Jennifer, who are also its trustees. The Charity Commission's computer database records an income of £148,000 for this foundation in the year 1993/94, although it was not possible to verify the figure or check how much of this was distributed as charitable donations as we were unable to obtain a copy of the accounts.

Contact: Lady Hopkins, Sir Anthony Hopkins Charitable Foundation, c/o 7 High Park Rd, Kew, Richmond, Surrey, TW9 4BL.
Tel: 0171 589 2827.

PETER VARDY
£144,000

PREFERENCE: education in the North East
AGE: 47
WEALTH: £35m–£50m
TRUST LINKS: Vardy Foundation
COMPANY LINKS: Reg Vardy

Peter Vardy is one of the select group of entrepreneurs in this book (see also Sir Philip Harris and Michael Ashcroft)
who have given large-scale support to the government's first wave of flagship City Technology Colleges. In 1990/91 the **Vardy Foundation** gave a donation of £125,000 to the Emmanuel College CTC in Gateshead – the only grant recorded in the foundation's accounts. Peter Vardy set up this trust in 1989 with general charitable objectives, and in the following year lent it £379,000 interest free and endowed it with half a million shares in the public car-sales company Reg Vardy. Peter Vardy is chair of this firm, which operates in the north-east from head offices in Sunderland, and which in 1991 set up a four year covenant to pay an annual sum of £125,000 gross to the foundation to be redirected to the Tyneside CTC.

Vardy's wealth comes from his personal holding of half the Reg Vardy company's shares – worth in excess of £35 million – which seems destined to grow thanks to the firm's recent success in being chosen to be part of Nissan's new chain of car dealers. The firm itself made general charitable donations of £19,000 in 1991/92 in addition to the money paid to the Vardy Foundation, which was mainly directed to local causes in areas of company presence, and in particular education and the arts. Given his close links with the firm, these donations have been included in the personal figure given above for Peter Vardy.

When contacted, Peter Vardy requested that his name and details be left out of this publication.

Contact: Mrs Fiona Laughlin, Secretary to the Trustees, Vardy Foundation, c/o Reg Vardy plc, Houghton House, Warrington Way, Sunderland, Tyne & Wear, SR5 3RJ.
Tel: 0191 549 4949.

PRINCESS DIANA

£141,000

PREFERENCE: health, welfare, young people, general

AGE: 33

WEALTH: under £20m

TRUST LINKS: Princess of Wales Charities Trust

COMPANY LINKS: none

lewis '94.

The Princess of Wales is almost certainly one of the least wealthy individuals in these pages. The level of donations made by the charitable trust registered in her name, however, compares favourably with that of many of the others listed in the book.

The **Princess of Wales Charities Trust**, set up in 1981, had an income of £400,000 by 1991/92, the last year for which we have figures. Donations made in the year totalled £141,000, with most of it spent on medical charities, and the remainder spread between schools, social welfare charities and other causes. The trustees are P D C Jephson and the royal solicitor Sir Matthew Farrer.

Princess Diana's commitment to charity clearly does not end there. She is the patron or president of over 100 charities, including Relate, the National AIDS Trust, Centrepoint Soho, and a clutch of groups in Australia and New Zealand. Having announced at the end of 1993 that she was withdrawing from such an active role in public life, she has recently stepped up her level of involvement again and remains *the* member of the Royal family to have at your charity prèmiere.

Contact: Mr P Jephson, Princess of Wales Charities Trust, Buckingham Palace, SW1A 1AA.

HUGH SYKES

£137,000

PREFERENCE: general, South Yorkshire & Derbyshire

AGE: 61

WEALTH: less than £20m

TRUST LINKS: Hugh & Ruby Sykes Charitable Trust

COMPANY LINKS: Bamford Hall Holdings

Hugh Sykes, and his wife Ruby, are major supporters of charitable causes in the North East through the **Hugh & Ruby Sykes Charitable Trust**. They established this grant-maker in 1988, and by 1991/92 had endowed it with capital reserves in excess of £1.6 million. In that year the trust gave away £137,000 and made interest-free loans of an additional £50,000. The accounts on file at the Charity Commission do not, however, indicate the recipients of these donations, although the trust states that it has supported various organisations in South Yorkshire and Derbyshire, such as the South Yorkshire Foundation and the Peak Park Trust. It has also made grants to various medical causes, including St Luke's Hospice and Westcare, and some national charities such as the Prince's Youth Business Trust and the Westminster Abbey Trust.

Hugh Sykes is personally involved with a number of other causes – he is non-executive director of the Arkwright Society, which aims to preserve Britain's industrial heritage, and he is a trustee of the charitable trust set up by his former business colleague, Sir Philip Harris (qv). He is also chair of the Sheffield Development Corporation, where his business nous should be of considerable value. Sykes has built up his fortune by acquiring companies, improving their performance, and then selling them at a profit. He is still active through his private company, Bamford Hall Holdings, is on the board of a number of other firms, and is non-executive director of Yorkshire Bank.

Contact: Mr H R Sykes, Hugh & Ruby Sykes Charitable Trust, c/o Bamford Hall Holdings, Bamford, Sheffield, S Yorks, S30 2AU. Tel: 01433 651190.

WARBURTON FAMILY

£130,000

PREFERENCE: general
WEALTH: £50m-£75m
TRUST LINKS: none found
COMPANY LINKS: Warburtons

The Warburton family own the majority of the shares in their eponymous private bakeries company, whose best known product is perhaps the Soreen malt loaf. Three of the family are on the firm's board – Ross Warburton, Jonathan Warburton, and Brett Warburton. As managing director, the latter is responsible for day-to-day operations, and Brett is also director of the local Bolton Wanderers football team. The family strives to avoid personal publicity, and as such it is not surprising that we have been unable to trace any charitable trusts registered in their name. The donations of £130,000 made by the Warburton company in 1993/94 can, however, be considered as coming indirectly from them given their strong holdings in it. The firm has a stated preference for appeals local to its operations, and especially projects involving young people, social welfare, education and training, and the environment.

Contact: Mrs Jill Kippax, PR Manager, Warburtons Ltd, Hereford St, Bolton, Lancs, BL1 8JB. Tel: 01204 23351.

WARNING

Unsolicited requests for funding often lead to annoyance and are rarely productive. This book should not be used as a mailing list. Inappropriate applications waste time and money and may prejudice chances of future success.

ROBERT MADGE

see below **NEW**

PREFERENCE: welfare, education, general
AGE: 42
WEALTH: £100m-£250m
TRUST LINKS: Madge Trust
COMPANY LINKS: Madge Networks

Robert Madge has been catapulted into the ranks of Britain's mega-rich thanks to last year's successful US flotation of his computer software and electronics company Madge Networks, which last year also won a Queen's Award for Exports. His three-quarter stake in the firm he set up only eight years ago now has a value of over £200 million.

As a result, the **Madge Trust** is clearly a grant-maker with a very bright future. This charitable trust was established by Robert Madge in December 1992, with the aims of relieving hardship and suffering, furthering the education of children, and supporting general charitable institutions. Although we were not able to obtain copies of any accounts filed for the Madge Trust, the Charity Commission's computerised database gives a figure of £130,000 for the trust's income in 1993. We were informed by Robert Madge's representatives, however, that he has not to date made any donations to the Madge Trust and, to their knowledge, any funds held by this charity have been given by another source.

Contact: Leo Abeles, Madge Trust, L Abeles & Co, Park House, 26 North End Rd, London, NW11 7PT.
Tel: 0181 458 4384.

LINDSAY BURY

£123,000

PREFERENCE: general, West Midlands
AGE: 55
WEALTH: £20m-£35m
TRUST LINKS: Millichope Foundation
COMPANY LINKS: SUMIT Equity Ventures

When Lindsay Bury and Sarah, his wife, set up a foundation in 1981 they named it after their Shropshire house. The **Millichope Foundation** distributed £123,000 to various charitable causes in 1991/92, and an income of £100,000 derived largely from investments with a market value of £1.5 million. The largest shareholdings are in two companies with which Bury is closely linked: 200,000 shares in ACT Group, the public computer company of which he is a non-executive director; and 100,000 shares in Sharp Technology Fund, which he chairs.

The grants made by the Millichope Foundation in 1991/92 were directed at a wide range of organisations. The largest single gifts were £11,000 to WWF UK, the global conservation body of which Lindsay Bury is a trustee, and £5,000 to the National Trust. A popular destination for other donations were arts organisations, including £2,500 to both the English National Opera and the Royal Opera House Trust, and £1,500 to the City of Birmingham Orchestra Endowment Fund. Medical organisations also received a number of gifts, including Shropshire Health Authority (£3,000), Shropshire Nuffield Hospital (£2,500) and Birmingham Hospital Help the Children (£2,000). The remaining donations went to a general selection of charities, many in the West Midlands, and some to help the welfare of young people, such as £3,000 to the NSPCC, £2,000 to Save the Children Fund, and £1,500 to Smethwick Society for Mentally Handicapped Children.

Lindsay Bury has made his money by providing investment capital for other firms. He is still active in this area, through his company SUMIT Equity Ventures, and is linked with many small firms. His biggest success has been ACT, previously Apricot Computers, which he chaired during the seventies and eighties. He is a director of South Staffordshire Water, and a non-executive director of the public Christie Group. He is also chair of the governors at Moor Park School, and a trustee of the Moor Park Foundation.

Contact: Mrs Linda Collins, Millichope Foundation, c/o SUMIT Equity Ventures Ltd, Edmund House, 12 Newhall St, Birmingham, B3 3EJ. Tel: 0121 236 1222.

EARL OF STOCKTON
and family
£123,000

PREFERENCE: education, children, arts
AGE: 50
WEALTH: £75m-£100m
TRUST LINKS: none found
COMPANY LINKS: Macmillans

The second Lord Stockton inherited the title from his grandfather, the former Prime Minister Harold Macmillan. Unusually for one of the titled people in this book, the figure we have given for Stockton's personal charitable donations is comprised of the grants made by a company. His family owns just under

two-thirds of the shares in the Macmillan publishing group, which gave away £123,000 in 1992. The contributions made by the firm are the decision of the current chair, Nicholas Byam Shaw, rather than Lord Stockton personally. This support went primarily to local charities operating in areas of company presence or to appeals with links to the business. There is also a preference for education, children and youth, and arts projects.

Lord Stockton is a past chair of Macmillan Ltd, and is now non-executive president of the firm. On a wider front he is heavily involved with the government's Training & Enterprise Councils initiative, as a member of the Secretary of State's TEC Advisory Group, and chair of both Central London TEC and the London TEC Group. When contacted, he expressed his preference not to appear in this publication, as he wishes to keep his family's and his personal donations private.

Contact: Brian McKenzie, Personnel Manager, Macmillan Ltd, Brunel Rd, Houndmills, Basingstoke, Hants, RG21 2XS. Tel: 01256 29242.

JOHN DOUGLAS
£115,000

PREFERENCE: Christian causes, welfare, disability, heritage
AGE: 63
WEALTH: less than £20m
TRUST LINKS: Salamander Charitable Trust
COMPANY LINKS: Tilbury Douglas

The Douglas family fortune was made in construction, Sir Robert Douglas (qv) having founded the Douglas Group in 1930. In 1991 the company was merged with the Tilbury Group, and members of the Douglas family exchanged their shares for a stake in Tilbury Douglas. John Douglas, Sir Robert's son, became non-executive chair of the combined group. The family has strong links with the West Midlands, where their firm was based before the merger, although John Douglas recently moved to Dorset. He estimates his wealth at around £5-7 million, depending upon the vagaries of the stock market.

John Douglas and his wife, Sheila, formed the **John & Sheila Douglas Charitable Trust** in 1966 with a gift of 62,000 shares in Robert M Douglas Holdings. It remained relatively modest for the next ten years, with donations of around £2,500 to £4,000 per annum. In 1977 this trust was wound up, and its property was transferred to a new charity set up by John and Sheila Douglas, the **Salamander Charitable Trust**.

● GIVING BY WOMEN

Vivien Duffield	£2,800,000
Shirley Porter	£966,000
Margaret Thatcher	£500,000
Dowager Marchioness of Normanby	£333,000
The Queen	£208,000
Coral Samuel	£178,000
Princess Diana	£141,000
Rosemary Bugden	£114,000
Princess Anne	£105,000
Margaret Barbour	£54,000
Viscountess Boyd	£53,000
Eileen Joseph	£23,000

This trust is now considerably larger than its predecessor, having grown in recent years, and currently has nearly 180,000 shares in Tilbury Douglas and other investments worth about £400,000, which in 1992/93 supported donations of about £115,000. The latest available schedule of giving (1990/91) reflects John and Sheila Douglas' deeply held Christian beliefs, with the largest donations directed mainly at religious or church-connected causes: £1,500 to the London Bible College, £1,250 to Christian Impact, and £1,000 to the Church Urban Fund in both the Birmingham and Salisbury dioceses. The remaining grants went to a wide variety of charities, with some emphasis on Christian organisations and those active in the West Midlands.

John Douglas undertakes a number of other charitable activities, and was for about six years a trustee of the TSB Foundation for England and Wales. He is a member of the court of governors of Birmingham University, of which he is a graduate. Along with his wife he was also, for many years, a leader of Sutton Coldfield Crusaders, in the town of his birth.

Contact: Salamander Charitable Trust: Mr J R T Douglas, 8 Market St, Poole, Dorset, BH15 1NF.

ROSEMARY BUGDEN

£114,000

PREFERENCE: arts in the South West

AGE: 61

WEALTH: £35m-£50m

TRUST LINKS: Rosemary Bugden Charitable Trust

COMPANY LINKS: Interlink Express

Instead of taking Norman Tebbit's infamous words to heart, ex-motorcycle courier Richard Gabriel got *off* his bike to start his own express delivery service, backed by his mother Rosemary Bugden. The company, Interlink Express, was founded in the late seventies and grew rapidly thanks to franchising to local agents. Within ten years it was floated, and in 1991 was sold to an Australian company for £50 million, of which Gabriel and Bugden received three-quarters. They stayed on to help run the Bristol-based business as non-executive chair and franchise director respectively.

Although we have not been able to uncover any charitable trusts linked to Gabriel, his mother is an active supporter of the arts in the South West through the **Rosemary Bugden Charitable Trust**. She established this trust the year after Interlink went public, and by 1991/92 it had an income of £100,000 and gave grants totalling £114,000. The bulk of the donations went to arts organisations operating in the Avon area, such as: the Bath Georgian Festival Society (£56,000), the Bath Festival Society (£20,000), the Great Elm Music Festival (£10,000), and the Philharmonia of Bristol (£5,000). One of the few substantial non-arts donations was £2,600 to the Greater Bristol Trust.

Contact: Mr J W Sharpe, Rosemary Bugden Charitable Trust, 30 Queen Charlotte St, Bristol, BS99 7QQ. Tel: 0117 923 0220.

MAURICE HATTER

£114,000

PREFERENCE: medicine, Jewish causes
AGE: 63
WEALTH: £75m-£100m
TRUST LINKS: Hatter (IMO) Foundation
COMPANY LINKS: IMO Precision Controls

The **Hatter (IMO) Foundation** was set up by the IMO Precision Controls company in 1987, but the donations it makes have been included as personal gifts made by Maurice Hatter because he owns all the shares in the firm and was one of the foundation's original trustees. In the two years after its creation, the foundation received £875,000 in covenants but made charitable donations totalling only £10,000 enabling it to build up its capital base. In 1989/90 the foundation started to get into its grant-making stride, giving away over £114,000. This was still considerably lower than its income of £637,000, comprised mainly of a further £0.5 million net from covenants topped up by earnings on investments, which added to the foundation's assets of £1.1m in the bank and $600,000 in State of Israel bonds.

The foundation appears to focus its support on several key areas. The largest grant of £40,000 went to the Special Trustees of University College Hospital, and other medical organisations benefiting included the Special Trustees of Royal Free Hospital which received £1,000. Other major gifts were directed to a number of Jewish causes, notably £32,000 to British ORT and a further £1,500 to its Women's Division, £12,000 to Haifa University, and £10,000 to the Parry Group (which works with mentally handicapped Jews in Essex). Several arts groups were supported, including the Royal Opera House (£3,000) and the Royal Academy Trust (£1,000), as were those dealing with young people and education, such as Prince's Youth Business Trust and Edgeware School which both received £1,000.

Hatter's personal worth has been hit by a recent drop in profits at IMO Precision Controls, which he set up in the late fifties with capital of only

£100 and still totally owns. This electronics components business based in north London now has a multi-million pound turnover, and in 1991/92 paid Maurice Hatter nearly £10 million in dividends on his shares.

Contact: Mr J S Newman, Hatter (IMO) Foundation, Messrs Stoy Hayward, 8 Baker St, London, W1M 1DA.

ANDREW COHEN

£112,000

PREFERENCE: youth, elderly people, general
AGE: 40
WEALTH: £20m-£35m
TRUST LINKS: Andrew Cohen Charitable Trust, Cohen Family Foundation, Betterware Foundation
COMPANY LINKS: Betterware

Along with other members of his family, including his father Stanley (qv), Andrew Cohen recently sold part of his stake in his company, Betterware, receiving £14 million. At the time, Andrew told the *Birmingham Post* that 'various charitable foundations are being set up because each of us has causes we believe very strongly in' (11/6/93). True to his word, in 1994 he founded the **Andrew Cohen Charitable Trust**, of which he is a trustee along with his wife Wendy. This may have received part of the proceeds of the share sale, although it is not yet possible to tell because the trust is so new. It has general charitable purposes, and Andrew Cohen reportedly has a preference for causes working with young people. He is also a founding trustee of the **Cohen Family Foundation** set up by his father in 1992.

Andrew Cohen left school before finishing his A levels to work for a soft furnishings business owned by his father. He progressed rapidly, and when the family bought an unknown company from the receiver he was appointed to run it. He is still chair of the now much more widely recognised Betterware group, which has become a market leader in door-to-door sales of household goods, and whose success led to Cohen being crowned Entrepreneur of the Year 1993. He is also non-executive director of his father's investment company Queensway Securities. Along with others in his family, Andrew Cohen has become a very wealthy individual thanks to his stake in Betterware, and despite recent sales the family still controls nearly half the company.

In 1992 Andrew Cohen and his wife, as founding trustees, established the **Betterware Foundation** into which the group transfers 1% of pre-tax profits to fund charitable donations. Last year, the foundation made grants totalling over £112,000 which went to various organisations helping the young, the elderly and the sick. The recipient of the largest gift was Age Concern, which was given £36,000. In the current year, the main beneficiary is to be the RNIB, which will receive £37,000 from the foundation, and next year the major recipient will be ChildLine. Because of the family's close control of the Betterware company and Andrew Cohen's personal involvement, the gifts made by the company through its foundation have been included in the total figure cited above for his personal charitable donations.

Contact: Mr Julian Lewis, Trustee, Andrew Cohen Charitable Trust, Lynton Place, 5 Stanmore Hill, Stanmore, Middlesex, HA7 3DP. Betterware Foundation: Mrs W P Cohen, at same address. Cohen Family Foundation: see entry for Stanley Cohen (qv).

VINCENT WEIR

£111,000

PREFERENCE: wildlife and
conservation
AGE: 59
WEALTH: £50m-£75m
TRUST LINKS: Vincent Wildlife Trust
COMPANY LINKS: Andrew Weir
& Co.

Over the past forty years, the Hon
Vincent Weir has directed substantial
support to wildlife and conservation
projects. Until recently, a particular
recipient of his largesse had been the
Mammal Society research charity – he
funded three of its staff and provided
office equipment. However, in
December 1993 it was reported that
Weir had put a halt to his support, in
order to establish a new Mammal Trust
with the aim of doing for mammals
what the RSPB has done for birds.

A major conduit for Weir's
charitable donations has been the
Vincent Wildlife Trust, which he set
up in 1975 in order to promote study,
education and research into wildlife
conservation. For a while this trust
operated in tandem with the Vincent
Charitable Trust, which Weir had set
up seven years previously, and which
made gifts for general charitable
purposes. However, in 1986 its assets
of 500,000 shares in the family firm
Andrew Weir & Co, with a book value
of three-quarters of a million pounds,
were transferred to the Vincent
Wildlife Trust. By 1992 this trust had
accumulated assets worth over £8.6
million, and had an income of
£740,000. Of this, over £270,000 was
spent on staff costs and upkeep at four
nature reserves owned by the trust,
and a further £111,000 was distributed
in the form of donations to support
conservation organisations and
wildlife research projects. The largest
grant of £28,000 paid for three pieces

of research being undertaken on hares
and bats at Bristol University, and other
research grants included support for a
survey of water shrews and harvest
mice in East Anglia. Various wildlife
charities received support, including
Plantlife (£17,000), the British Butterfly
Conservation Society (£13,000), the
Herpetological Conservation Trust
(£10,000), and Avon Wildlife Trust
(£3,000). The Mammal Society also
received £10,000, but as noted above
this may be the last gift it receives from
this source.

Vincent Weir has been able to give
so much away thanks to his family's
interests in the insurance and shipping
company Andrew Weir & Co. He ran
the company during the eighties,
having taken over the reins in 1982
upon the untimely death of his elder
brother, Andrew Weir, who had
inherited their father's title of Lord
Inverforth. Vincent retired as chair in
1991, to be replaced by Lord
Runciman, but has not been an
individual shareholder in the
company or a beneficiary under the
various family (non-charitable) trusts
since this date.

There is clearly a strong
philanthropic streak running through
the Weir family, as Vincent Weir's elder
brother, the late Lord Inverforth, also
set up a substantial grant-making trust.
The **Inverforth Charitable Trust**
was created by Inverforth in 1977, and
over the next few years received an
endowment of quarter of a million
shares in Andrew Weir & Co from its
settlor. In 1989/90 the trust received
special dividends to the tune of £2
million from its holding in the family
firm, which has since been invested in
a portfolio of shares. These provided
an income of £155,000 in 1992 which
helped fund donations of £210,000.
The largest gifts were £20,000 to the
Aldeburgh Foundation, a regular
recipient of grants from the trust, and
£15,000 to the National Asthma

Campaign. These substantial gifts commemorate the late Lord Inverforth, who died of asthma in 1982, having previously been the chair of Aldeburgh. The current trustees of the Inverforth Charitable Trust include the founder's wife and his son, who inherited the Inverforth title. At present, the young Lord Inverforth's heir is his uncle, Vincent Weir.

Contact: Vincent Wildlife Trust: Leslie Gorrod, Treasurer, 10 Lovat Lane, London, EC3R 8DT. Tel: 0171 283 2089. Inverforth Charitable Trust: Mr Adam Lee, Secretary and Treasurer, The Farm, Northington, Alresford, Hampshire, SO24 9TH. Tel: 01962 732205.

ANTHONY LOFTUS
and family
£110,000

PREFERENCE: Jewish causes
AGE: 52
WEALTH: £50m–£75m
TRUST LINKS: Loftus Charitable Trust
COMPANY LINKS: Accurist Watches

It is easy to see what makes the Loftus family tick – the keystone of their business empire is the Accurist Watches company. The family interests, which also include extensive property holdings around London's Baker Street, are controlled by the three Loftus brothers: Anthony, Richard, and Andrew. The family patriarch, Liverpudlian Asher Loftus, founded Accurist just after the Second World War following a move to London to work with his brother in the watch trade. The business was soon thriving, and on the back of this success Asher diversified into property in the capital.

Before he died two years ago, Asher helped his three sonsset up the **Loftus Charitable Trust** in 1987. The only accounts on file at the Charity Commission show that by 1990/91 the trust's assets amounted to £843,000, which produced an income of £115,000. Whilst the beneficiaries of the total donations of £110,000 were not specified, the objects of the trust restrict support to causes concerned with the advancement of the Jewish religion, the education and relief of Jewish people, and generally to Jewish charities.

Contact: Jane Hills, Loftus Charitable Trust, 48 George St, London, W1H 5PG. Tel: 0171 486 2969.

ROBERT GAVRON
£109,000

PREFERENCE: arts, health and welfare
AGE: 64
WEALTH: £35m–£50m
TRUST LINKS: Robert Gavron Charitable Trust
COMPANY LINKS: retired from St Ives; Folio Society Ltd

Now that he has more time on his hands, Robert Gavron may further increase his charitable work, at present largely focused upon education, literature and the arts. He ran the highly successful St Ives printing group until last year, when he retired as chair and sold off much of his stake in the company. He retains shares worth £23 million and remains a director and continues to be chair and proprietor of the Folio Society.

At present, a major conduit for his philanthropic activities is the **Robert Gavron Charitable Trust**, which in

1991/92 had assets valued in excess of £4 million generating an income of £120,000. Donations totalling £109,000 were made to a number of causes, with an emphasis on education and the arts. The largest grants went to two bodies with which Gavron has close links: £25,000 to the Institute for Public Policy Research, of which he is a trustee, and £20,000 to the Open College for the Arts, of which he is chair as well as trustee. Another substantial donation of £17,000 was directed to the Campaign for Oxford, the university where Gavron studied for a degree at St Peter's College. He is also a trustee of the Royal Opera House, which received a four figure grant from the trust. The remaining donations went to a mixture of causes, but mainly to arts organisations, and medical and welfare charities. It seems likely that the level of donations made by the trust has increased recently, as we were informed that it now has assets of £6.75 million generating an income of around £300,000 per year.

Gavron's interests in literature and the arts are also reflected in his other voluntary sector activities. He is vice-president of the Poetry Society, a past member of the Literature Panel of the Arts Council, and an ex-council member of the Book Trust. His knowledge of printing, literature, and grant-making also come together in his role as trustee of the Paul Hamlyn Foundation, the major charitable trust established by Paul Hamlyn (qv) on the back of the fortune he made from the Octopus book publishing company. Gavron was also a director and shareholder of this firm up until 1987, when it was sold by Hamlyn.

Contact: Mr R Gavron, Robert Gavron Charitable Trust, The Folio Society Ltd, 44-46 Eagle St, London, WC1R 4AP. Tel: 0171 400 4200.

ARNOLD ZIFF
and family
£109,000 NEW

PREFERENCE: education, Jewish causes, Yorkshire, arts, youth, medicine
AGE: 67
WEALTH: less than £20m
TRUST LINKS: I A Ziff Charitable Foundation
COMPANY LINKS: Stylo, Town Centre Securities

Arnold Ziff is a leading light on the North Yorkshire business scene thanks to his family's interests in the Leeds-based Town Centre Securities property firm and the Bradford-based Stylo public footwear company. He is also a significant supporter of charities in the region through the **I A Ziff Charitable Foundation**, which he set up back in 1964 with an endowment of 61,000 shares in Stylo Shoes Ltd, with himself and his wife as trustees.

By 1992/93 the foundation was in possession of assets with a market value of £941,000, consisting mainly of 165,000 shares in Stylo (worth £206,000) and three-quarters of a million Town Centre Securities shares worth around £1 each. It was also proud owner of a silver salver and twenty 'shoe prints', purpose unknown! The foundation had an income of £187,000, partly from dividends but also from one of Arnold Ziff's discretionary settlements. It made donations of £109,000 in the year, substantially up on the previous year's total of £45,000. The bulk of gifts went to Jewish organisations or causes operating in Yorkshire. The University of Leeds received three grants totalling £51,500, and other Yorkshire oriented donations included £1,700 to Leeds City

Council, and £1,000 to Lord Mayor of Leeds' Charity Appeal. Gifts to Jewish groups included £10,000 to both the Jewish Philanthropic Association and the Ashten Trust, £1,500 to B'nai B'rith Lodge of Leeds and £1,100 to the Leeds Jewish Welfare Board. A number of donations were made to various other causes, including the Prince's Youth Business Trust (£10,000), Israel Philharmonic Orchestra (£3,000), Birthright (£1,200) and the British Heart Foundation (£1,000).

Contact: Mr K N Riley, Secretary to the Trustees, I A Ziff Charitable Foundation, Town Centre House, The Merrion Centre, Leeds, LS2 8LY. Tel: 0113 245 9172.

PRINCESS ANNE

£105,000

PREFERENCE: children, medicine, general
AGE: 44
WEALTH: £20m–£35m
TRUST LINKS: Princess Anne's Charities, June 1974 Charitable Trust
COMPANY LINKS: none

● GIVING BY ROYALTY

Prince Charles	£1,480,000
The Queen	£208,000
Princess Diana	£141,000
Princess Anne	£105,000
Prince Andrew	£13,000

Considerably less wealthy than her brother Charles, the Princess Royal is perhaps the member of the royal family with the strongest natural impulse to charitable work. The deeds of settlement on file at the Charity Commission for the **June 1974 Charitable Trust** have the names of the settlor and the original trustees blanked out, but the first set of accounts for the trust record assets of £40,500 including '£36,783 – amounts settled by HRH The Princess Anne'.

The current trustees of the June 1974 Charitable Trust are the royal solicitor Sir Matthew Farrer, Lt-Col Peter Gibbs and Princess Anne's husband, Lt-Col Timothy Laurence. In 1993 the trust's assets were valued at £223,000 but donations in the year comprised only one grant of £1,000 to the King Edward VII's Hospital for Officers, a regular beneficiary. A note to the trust's 1989 accounts points out: 'The income in this charity is comparatively modest and the trustees accordingly do not normally make distributions each year as they prefer to retain the income until sufficient is in hand to make a worthwhile donation.'

The Princess Royal's main charitable vehicle now appears to be the **Princess Anne's Charities**, established back in 1979. The trustees are the same as for her other trust, but the distributions are considerably larger, totalling £105,000 in 1991/92. The bulk of the money, some £54,000, went to children's charities, with medical and social welfare charities and some other causes cleaning up. Total assets held by the charity in 1989, the last year for which the figure is available, came to £349,000.

Princess Anne is well-known for her unstinting work on behalf of the Save the Children Fund, of which she is president. More recently, she has also played an active role in the development of the Princess Royal's Trust for Carers.

Contact: Lt-Col Peter Gibbs, Princess Anne's Charities, Buckingham Palace, London SW1A 1AA.

NORMAN STOLLER

£103,000

PREFERENCE: North West and general
AGE: 60
WEALTH: less than £20m
TRUST LINKS: Stoller Charitable Trust
COMPANY LINKS: Seton Healthcare Group

Following his 60th birthday Norman Stoller intends to move from executive to non-executive chair of the Oldham-based Seton Healthcare Group, which he took public four years ago for £23 million and which currently has a market capitalisation in excess of £100 million. Charities in the North West have benefited from the flotation thanks to the million shares in the company now held by the **Stoller Charitable Trust,** which was first set up in 1982. Up to the time of going public the trust gave away less than £10,000 annually. Since 1992 the amount donated each year has risen substantially, in line with Seton's progressive dividend policy.

In 1993/94, dividends from the Seton shares generated the bulk of the trust's income, and supported charitable gifts of £103,000. These included £22,000 to create a chair at the University of Salford, £10,000 to fund an educational officer at Oldham Museum, £5,000 to the AIDIS Trust, and £2,000 to the Royal Northern College of Music's Lord Rhodes Room. The remaining grants showed a similar preference for causes in the North West, and for organisations working with children in need, the disabled, the socially disadvantaged, education, and the arts. Another sign of Stoller's close links with the region is his role as founding chair of Oldham TEC.

Contact: Roger Gould, Secretary, Stoller Charitable Trust, c/o Seton Healthcare Group plc, Tubiton House, Oldham, Lancs, OL1 3HS. Tel: 0161 652 2222.

SIR MARK WEINBERG

£103,000 NEW

PREFERENCE: youth, education, Jewish causes
AGE: 62
WEALTH: £50m-£75m
TRUST LINKS: Weinberg Foundation, J Rothschild Assurance Foundation
COMPANY LINKS: J Rothschild Assurance; past connection with Hambro Life/Allied Dunbar

Sir Mark Weinberg is heavily involved with the promotion of corporate community involvement as deputy chair of Business in the Community and co-founder of the Per Cent Club with Lord Laing (qv). He has also directed some of his personal wealth to charitable ends through the **Weinberg Foundation** (previously the M A Weinberg Charitable Trust), which he set up in 1971, with himself, his wife, and his business colleague Sydney Lipworth (qv) as trustees. Although none of these are now listed as trustees, and on paper he has no direct links with the foundation that bears his name, Sir Mark still has a strong say in the distribution of funds as settlor.

In 1992/93 the Weinberg Foundation made donations of £103,000 – considerably more than its income of £38,000 for the year. There has been a similar income shortfall in recent years, apparently met by depleting the foundation's assets, which have shrunk from £888,000 in

1989/90 to their present level of £191,000. The largest gifts were £25,000 to the NSPCC, of which Weinberg was honorary treasurer for the eight years up to 1991, £25,000 to the Jewish Philanthropic Association, £15,000 to the Foundation for Communication, and £5,000 to each of the Richmond Fellowship, Leonora Fund, and the Royal National Theatre Endowment Fund. Smaller grants went to a variety of causes, including education, overseas, medical and Jewish organisations. Sir Mark is also a director of the London School of Economics, where he studied for his masters degree in law.

Weinberg is one of three South African born lawyers who came to Britain in the sixties, and made their fortune in the life assurance business. Along with his long-term partners Joel Joffe (qv) and Sir Sydney Lipworth (qv), he set up Abbey Life in 1961. The trio left the company in 1970 when it was acquired by a large US insurance company, and immediately set up another similar business, Hambro Life, backed by Jocelyn Hambro. The company was a roaring success, and Weinberg and friends became super-rich when it was bought in 1984 by the BAT tobacco conglomerate for over £600 million. After a few years running the company for the new owners, Sir Mark has now left and is in partnership with yet another famous banker – this time Jacob Rothschild, with whom he has established the J Rothschild Assurance company. Weinberg was recently settlor of the **J Rothschild Assurance Foundation**, which was created in December 1993 with an annual income estimated by one its trustees upon registration as £30,000. Because it is so new, we have yet to inspect accounts for this grant-making trust.

Contact: Weinberg Foundation: Ms Maria Torok, 33 Roland Gardens, London, SW7 3PF. Tel: 0171 370 6701. J Rothschild Assurance Foundation: Mr M Cooper-Smith,

J Rothschild House, Dollar St, Cirencester, Glos, GL7 2TQ. Tel: 01285 640302.

SIR MICHAEL BISHOP

£102,000

PREFERENCE: opera, West Midlands
AGE: 52
WEALTH: £35m-£50m
TRUST LINKS: Michael Bishop Foundation
COMPANY LINKS: Airlines of Britain Holdings, Channel 4

High-flyer Sir Michael Bishop is an active supporter of various causes in Birmingham and the West Midlands through the **Michael Bishop Foundation.** He set it up in 1987 with £1 million worth of shares in Airlines of Britain (Holdings), a company of which he is a major shareholder, and made a further gift of shares in 1992. In 1992/93 the foundation had an income of £89,000 and made donations of £102,000. The accounts on file at the Charity Commission give no indication as to the recipients of these grants, but the major beneficiary is understood to be the D'Oyly Carte Opera Trust – the Birmingham based opera company of which Sir Michael has been chair since 1989, and of which his foundation is principal sponsor. The remaining donations tend to be directed at charities operating in the West Midlands area, especially inner-city projects, and seventeen such charitable organisations received grants in 1992/93.

Sir Michael has made his fortune from his involvement with the British Midland airline, which is constantly biting at the heels of British Airways on various domestic and European routes flying out of Heathrow. He joined the company when barely out of his teens, and moved rapidly up the hierarchy and was on the board before he was thirty. He became chair when only 36, following a management buy-out with two partners, and still runs it from Donington Hall near Derby. He is the controlling shareholder of the BBW Partnership Ltd, the parent company of Airlines of Britain Holdings, which in turn is British Midland's holding company. His stake has been valued at around £40 million. Airlines of Britain itself made charitable donations of just under £9,000 in 1993. Sir Michael is an outspoken critic of the regulations which control the airline industry in Europe, and also finds time to perform a function as chair of Channel 4. He is a non-executive director of the travel company Airtours and the industrial conglomerate, Williams Holdings plc.

Contact: Rosemary Mellors, Michael Bishop Foundation, Donington Hall, Castle Donington, Derby, DE74 2SB.

DUKE OF NORTHUMBER-LAND

£100,000

PREFERENCE: heritage, general, North East

AGE: 40

WEALTH: £100m-£250m

TRUST LINKS: Duke of Northumberland's Charity

COMPANY LINKS: none

The **Duke of Northumberland's Charity** is one of the largest aristocratic trusts in this book. It was established in 1979 by the 10th Duke, the current

Duke's father, and for the next ten years was relatively small, with annual income and donations only in the range of £1,000-£3,000. The trust has only really got into its grant-making stride since 1989, when it received an interest-free loan of £2 million from the trustees of the will of the 7th Duke of Northumberland. Its annual income has subsequently shot up and is now in the order of several hundred thousand pounds. The current trustees are the 11th Duke, and his brother and heir Lord Ralph Percy.

The major recipient of the trust's largesse in recent years has been another charity – the Lovaine Trust Company Limited – which received two grants totalling nearly £400,000 between 1989 and 1991. This charity, which is named after one of the Duke's titles (he is Lord Lovaine, Baron of Alnwick) was set up by him in 1989 to preserve the environment and heritage in the London borough of Hounslow. The trust's principal activities are given in its accounts as 'the maintenance and opening of the gardens at Syon Park'. These are the grounds of Syon House, one of the Duke's two stately homes, which is located in Hounslow on the bank of the Thames opposite Kew Gardens. The trust owns the lease of parts of Syon Park, which were transferred to it by the executors of the previous duke's will.

The donations made by the Duke of Northumberland's Charity cover the Lovaine Trust's operating deficit, which in 1991 had an operating income of around £70,000, mainly from ticket sales, but spent £176,000 on wages and upkeep. Apart from the support given for Syon Park, in the year 1990/91 a total of £3,200 was donated by the Duke's trust to a number of other charities, the largest gifts being £1,000 to the Spastics Society, £500 to the Royal Agricultural Benevolent Fund (of which he is vice-president) and £400 to the Newcastle Diocesan Society.

The Duke is also involved with a large number of charities, some of which are situated around Syon House, but most are near his other ancestral pile – Alnwick Castle in Northumberland. In the North East he is president of organisations including Alnwick & District Committee for the Disabled, Northumberland Association of Youth Clubs, Northumberland County Victims Support Scheme, North of England Cancer Research Campaign, Tyne Mariners' Benevolent Association, and he is patron of Northern Counties School for the Deaf, the Northern Buildings Preservation Trust, and the NE Branch of the Mental Health Foundation. The Duke and his family's close links with the region are also apparent in the £100,000 they recently donated to establish the **Percy Family Fund** under the aegis of the Tyne & Wear Foundation, for the benefit of the Alnwick area where they have lived for generations. In London he is a patron of the Hounslow & Feltham Victims' Support Scheme and the Hounslow and Twickenham Branch of Arthritis Care.

The recession has had a strong impact upon estimates of the Duke's wealth, with falling land prices hitting particularly hard – he owns nearly 100,000 acres around Alnwick Castle. Syon House, the only non-royal stately home in Greater London, is still worth the best part of £25 million, however, and his fortune is topped up with a collection of art treasures.

Contact: Duke of Northumberland's Charity, May May & Merrimans, 12 South Square, Gray's Inn, London, WC1R 5HH.

CHARLES SAATCHI

£100,000

PREFERENCE: art
AGE: 50
WEALTH: £75m-£100m
TRUST LINKS: none
COMPANY LINKS: Saatchi & Saatchi Company

Charles is the elder of the Saatchi brothers, the duo who have been credited with helping the Conservatives gain control in the 1979 general election with the famous 'Labour isn't working' poster campaign. The subsequent successes of the Saatchi & Saatchi advertising company, despite recent setbacks, have made the brothers rich men. Maurice is still chair of the firm, and Charles was a director from 1970-93. Charles Saatchi has diverted a substantial portion of his wealth into building up a peerless collection of contemporary art, including works by the best of Britain's young artists. He exhibits a selection at his gallery in north London, which until recently was free to the public. Although he says he does this for the love of art rather than as an investment, the value of his collection has increased substantially over the years and enhanced his worth.

In March 1992 the Tate Gallery announced that Saatchi had donated nine works by British artists worth in the order of £100,000. When asked why he did it, Saatchi's answer was typically direct: 'Because they asked me' (*Independent*, 3/3/92). He does, however, concede that this may lead to further calls upon his generosity: 'People are always upset that I don't donate my entire collection to the country' (*Independent*, 3/3/92).

The Saatchi & Saatchi Company is also a supporter of charities through the 'S' Group Charitable Trust, which in 1991 donated a total of £37,000 to various causes. A regular recipient of grants from the trust is the National Advertising Benevolent Society, which received £7,250 in 1991. However, because neither of the brothers currently hold a large stake in the firm, its donations have not been included in the figure given above for Charles Saatchi.

Contact: Charles Saatchi, c/o Saatchi & Saatchi plc, 80 Charlotte St, London, W1A 1AQ.
Tel: 0171 636 5060.

MICHAEL THORNTON

£100,000

PREFERENCE: community related projects, the Church, young people
AGE: 58
WEALTH: less than £20m
TRUST LINKS: trust with the Charities Aid Foundation
COMPANY LINKS: Thorntons

The flotation of the Thorntons confectionery company on the Stock Exchange in 1988 has left a sweet taste in the mouths of many charities thanks to the philanthropic activities of the family who had set up and run the firm. Like his cousin John (qv), Michael Thornton – deputy chair and company secretary of Thorntons, and grandson of its founder – marked the flotation by setting up an eponymous charitable trust in the same year. This grant-making trust, however, has recently been wound-up as a registered charity and its assets transferred to the Charities Aid Foundation to be held in a fund in Michael Thornton's name.

He has recently added further shares to this charitable trust fund, which to date has made total donations of £350,000 – £100,000 pounds in the last year. Major beneficiaries have included the Prince's Youth Business Trust (£52,500), Shirley Church Restoration Appeal (£50,000), the Prince's Trust (£27,000), Cambridge University (£20,000), the Sir Anthony Wharton Charitable Trust and other trusts supporting rugby football (£20,000), and the International Spinal Research Trust (£15,000). His overall preference is for community related projects, the Church, and organisations promoting the welfare of young people.

Michael Thornton also has a wide range of charitable interests as trustee of the Bishop of Derby's Urban Fund, vice-president of the Arkwright Society, honorary member of the NSPCC Council, member of the management board at the Prince's Trust, chair of the Amber Valley Groundwork Trust, and member of the governing body of both Derby University and Belper School, and chair of the New Derbyshire Children's Hospital Appeal. Additionally, he is a patron of Village AiD (a charity he helped to set up to provide support for Third World villages) and of the Derby Branch of the Normandy Veterans Association.

The public Derbyshire-based confectionery company, Thorntons, donates around £60,000 annually to the community and, in addition gives large quantities of confectionery, mainly in small amounts, to a wide range of charitable organisations. We have not, however, included the value of these gifts in the figure quoted above because the Thornton family controls less than half of the company's shares distributed across around 40 individuals. Of this total, Michael Thornton and his immediate family personally own less than 10%, which puts their wealth at not more than £10 million.

129

Contact: Mrs E Cooke, Secretary to the Deputy Chairman, Thorntons plc, Thornton Park, Somercotes, Derby, DE55 4XJ. Tel: 01773 540550.

PILKINGTON FAMILY

£97,000

PREFERENCE: North West, general
WEALTH: £100m-£250m
TRUST LINKS: Rainford Trust
COMPANY LINKS: Pilkington

The Pilkington family has long had a reputation as a champion of an enlightened approach to relations between business and the community. Glass-maker Pilkington plc, of which the family still owns about 10 per cent, is a founder member of the Per Cent Club and runs an active programme of community support in St Helens, where its major site is located. The company's UK donations came to £256,000 in 1992/93, with a further £532,000 in overseas donations. The recession, however, forced the current company chair, Sir Antony Pilkington, to dispense grief as well as largesse: he has had to lay off over 15 per cent of the workforce in St Helens. Sir Antony chairs the Community of St Helens Trust.

Members of the Pilkington family also have a foundation, the **Rainford Trust**, which although adminstered from company offices has its own separate endowment. In mid-1992, this was worth £2.7 million (but will be worth a lot more now as the value of Pilkington shares, in which a large chunk of the endowment is invested, has rallied strongly). Grants paid totalled £59,000, with much of the support going to health and social welfare charities, particularly those based in St Helens or elsewhere in the

North West. The largest awards went to Age Concern St Helens, Clonter Opera for All, the European Nursing Development Agency, the North West Life Education Trust, and the Koestler Award Trust. There were a large number of grants for £500 or less.

The Rainford Trust also runs its own music award, on which £2,500 was spent in 1991/92, and has provided major support for the Citadel, a community arts centre, Which received £36,000 in the year. The secretary points out that the trust is entirely separate from the company's giving programme, and those interested in the latter should address the company directly.

Contact: George Gaskell, Secretary, Rainford Trust, c/o Pilkington plc, Prescot Road, St Helens WA10 3TT. Tel: 01744 20574.

JOHN BECKWITH

£95,000 NEW

PREFERENCE: education, youth, elderly people, disability, health
AGE: 47
WEALTH: £35m-£50m
TRUST LINKS: John Beckwith Charitable Trust, Heather Beckwith Charitable Settlement
COMPANY LINKS: sold stake in London and Edinburgh Trust

Like his elder brother Peter, John Beckwith made his fortune from the London and Edinburgh Trust property development company, which the brothers had set up in the early seventies and sold with perfect timing at the peak of the market to a Swedish firm. This sale netted John and his brother around £40 million each, and both have subsequently directed a portion of this to charitable causes.

John has been acting as a consultant for London and Edinburgh since 1992. Recently, the brothers have set up a new company Riverside Holdings.

Whilst we have been unable to track any single gift made by John Beckwith of the same magnitude as the £5 million his brother gave to Cambridge University, he has directed some of his fortune to good causes through a personal trust. The **John Beckwith Charitable Trust** was founded in 1987 with an initial cash injection of £50,000, followed by a further £45,000 over the next two years. In 1990/91, the year London and Edinburgh was sold, John Beckwith supplemented the trust's capital fund with an additional £1.2 million. This money generated over £134,000 in interest, of which nearly £77,000 was distributed as donations. The RNIB received over £50,000 of this – not surprising given John Beckwith's role as vice-president of the charity. Other major donations were £5,200 to Youth Clubs UK, £5,000 to the Barts Teenage Cancer Unit, £4,500 to Victim Support, and £1,750 to the Home Farm Trust, with which Beckwith has a connection as a trustee of its Development Trust. Like his brother, John Beckwith also gave a grant to the National Council of YMCAs, although of only £1,000.

Heather Beckwith, John's wife and a trustee of his trust, also has a trust of her own, the **Heather Beckwith Charitable Settlement.** Her husband returns the compliment by serving as one of it's trustees. The trust has no significant asset base, and in 1990 received most of its £21,000 income in the form of unspecified 'donations'. It made grants totalling £17,500 in that year, notably £6,000 to Marathon, £3,000 to the Royal Opera House and £1,400 to the Save the Children Fund.

Contacts: John Beckwith Charitable Trust: John Beckwith, Trustee,

52 Mount St, London W1Y 5RE. Tel: 0171 499 6750. Heather Beckwith Charitable Settlement: Mrs H M Beckwith, Trustee, 6 Lichfield Rd, Kew, Richmond, Surrey TW9 3JR. Tel: 0181 940 4499.

KEVIN McDONALD

£94,000 **NEW**

PREFERENCE: medicine, arts, sports

AGE: 59

WEALTH: £35m-£50m

TRUST LINKS: Kevin McDonald Charitable Trust, Kevin McDonald General Charitable Trust

COMPANY LINKS: Polypipe Group

When you are next sitting on the toilet think of Kevin McDonald, because he has made part of his fortune thanks to the humble loo seat! He is obviously determined not to throw his money down the drain, however, as he has recently set up two charitable trusts.

The first of these trusts, the **Kevin McDonald Charitable Trust**, was established by McDonald in 1989, with an endowment of £1,000 and 62,500 shares in his company Polypipe. The only accounts on file at the Charity Commission show a flurry of activity in the subsequent year, with most of the shares sold for £100,000 in order to finance donations of £94,000. Two substantial grants were made: £50,000 to the London City Ballet and £40,600 to Birthright – the baby medical research charity of which McDonald is a trustee. Only two other donations were made: £3,000 was paid to support a ballet student, and £500 was given to the Liverpool

Ocean Racing Trust. In 1991, a second trust, the **Kevin McDonald General Charitable Trust**, was set up by McDonald with £1,000 and 62,000 shares in his company – the same number as sold by his other trust in the same year. As yet there are no accounts on file for this trust, whose purpose is to support other registered charities.

His money has come from the decidedly unglamorous business of making plastic fittings and pipes for the plumbing and building industries. A former plumber, who made £2 million in 1966 when he sold his first company, McDonald set up Polypipe in 1980. This Doncaster-based group has since scored considerable success with its ability to undercut the competition, and has recently diversified into recycling, double glazing and garden furniture. As both chair and managing director, McDonald has profited from his firm's expansion – in July last year he sold two million of his Polypipe shares for more than £1 each, which still left him with a further 33 million shares. The company itself also made charitable donations totalling £66,000 in 1992/93. Kevin McDonald is also a trustee of the Community Action Trust, which runs the high-profile 'Crimestoppers' telephone line.

When contacted, Kevin McDonald expressed his wish not to appear in this publication.

Contact: for both Kevin McDonald Charitable Trusts: Peter Perrey, Trustee and Trust Solicitor, Churchill House, Hagley St, Halesowen, W Mids, B63 3AX. Tel: 0121 550 3226.

RONALD HOBSON

£92,000

PREFERENCE: arts, forces' welfare, children, health, general
AGE: 69
WEALTH: £250m-£500m
TRUST LINKS: Hobson Charity
COMPANY LINKS: National Parking Corporation

Along with Sir Donald Gosling (qv), Ronald Hobson has made a fortune from car parking through the National Parking Corporation which the pair set up from scratch, starting on bomb sites in post-war London. Hobson is generally credited with the initial idea, and owns a slightly larger part of the company, but has a much lower profile than his business partner – he appears neither in *Who's Who* or *Debrett's People of Today*. Both have chosen to divert some of their wealth to good causes via a grant-making trust, although Hobson's is currently the smaller of the two.

The **Hobson Charity** was set up by Ronald Hobson as a charitable private company in 1985, with the help of Sir Donald, who set up his Gosling Foundation within the space of a few weeks. It does not have a very substantial asset base, with only 18,000 shares in the National Parking Corporation amongst other capital totalling £85,000. In 1991/92 the trust had an income of £89,000 and made donations of £92,000, a slight drop from £125,000 in the previous year. Only eight gifts were made: £25,000 to both Childline and the English National Opera, £11,000 to John Grooms Association for the Disabled, £10,000 each to Barnet Mayor's Appeal for Leukaemia Children and the Promise Appeal, £5,000 to the HMS Norfolk Welfare Fund and the Flag Officer Plymouth's Fund, and £1,000 to the National Playbus Association. Like Sir Donald, Hobson is also a supporter of the White Ensign Association, which received £100,000 from his trust in 1990/91.

From its small beginnings, the National Parking Corporation is now the dominant force in the private sector parking market through its National Car Parks subsidiary. NCP gave £32,000 to charities in 1990/91, targeted upon organisations with which it had pre-existing links. Both the Hobson Charity and Gosling Foundation are administered from the company's head office near Marble Arch, and each businessman is a trustee of the other's trust.

Contact: Mr A E Bromfield, Secretary to the Trustees, Hobson Charities, 21 Bryanston St, Marble Arch, London, W1A 4NH. Tel: 0171 499 7050. National Car Parks: Miss A Pell, Sales and Marketing, at same address.

NIGEL WRAY
£92,000

PREFERENCE: general, medicine
AGE: 46
WEALTH: £20m-£35m
TRUST LINKS: Priory Foundation
COMPANY LINKS: Burford Holdings

Nigel Wray established the **Priory Foundation** in 1986, naming it after his house. The foundation currently holds assets to the value of £1.1 million, much of which is comprised of shareholdings in companies associated with Wray: 30,000 shares in Carlton Communications, 36,000 in Takere and 200,000 in Burford Holdings (see below). In addition, it holds 75,000 shares in Associated Nursing Services and 500,000 shares in the Carlisle Group. In 1993 this capital generated income of £64,000 which helped facilitate donations totalling £92,000, mainly to medical, youth and social welfare organisations. The largest grants were

£10,000 given to the Children's Medical Charity, of which Wray was a non-executive director until recently, £9,000 to London Borough of Barnet social need cases, £7,500 to both the Royal Brompton Hospice and Action on Addiction, £5,500 to a recipient listed as 'MEP', and £5,000 each to ABCD and Birthright.

Wray's wealth comes from his various personal investments, most notably in the property company Burford Holdings which he also chairs. He is chair of the Carlisle Group, and is non-executive director of the merchant bank Singer & Friedlander, where he first started his business career as a trainee. He is also non-executive director of Carlton Communications and the Peoples Phone company, and was a non-executive director of Takere until 18 months ago.

Contact: Mr T W Bunyard, Priory Foundation, Hallewell Bunyard, 6 Highbury Corner, London, N5 1RD. Tel: 0171 609 8495.

SIR DAVID ALLIANCE
£88,000

PREFERENCE: general
AGE: 62
WEALTH: £100m-£250m
TRUST LINKS: Alliance Family Foundation
COMPANY LINKS: Coats Viyella, N Brown Group

Iranian-born Sir David Alliance is chair of the two companies through which he has made his fortune. The better known of the two is the Coats Viyella textiles and clothing company, which Sir David has built up over the years, and in which he holds 4.5 million shares worth around £12 million. The bulk of his wealth, however, is derived from his interests in the N Brown Group, a mail order business based in Manchester. Sir David owns shares worth around £175 million in this firm.

Sir David set up the **Alliance Family Foundation** back in 1968 as a charitable company. In recent years it has donated around £80,000-£100,000 per year, including a grant of £100,000 in 1987 to CORDA, the national heart charity of which Sir David is a patron. In 1992/93 the foundation held listed investments with a market value of £4.6 million, which generated the bulk of its £175,000 income. Charitable gifts of £73,000 were made, and although the recipients were not listed, in previous years grants have gone to a variety of causes. In the last year the foundation has made a grant of £100,000 to a school. On the wider front, Sir David is also a trustee of the Central British Fund for World Jewish Relief.

Apart from the gifts made through his foundation, Sir David also makes donations via the N Brown Group in which he has a major holding. The company gives around £15,000 annually to charitable causes.

Contact: Alliance Family Foundation, c/o 12th Floor, Bank House, Charlotte St, Manchester, M1 4ET. Tel: 0161 728 5100. N Brown Group: Secretary to the Financial Director, 53 Dale St, Manchester, M60 6ES. Tel: 0161 236 8256

ALAN PRINCE

£88,000

PREFERENCE: medicine, general
WEALTH: unknown
TRUST LINKS: Prince Foundation
COMPANY LINKS: sold Sharedrug

Alan Prince set up the **Prince Foundation** in 1988, the same year that he sold his Southampton based chain of retail chemists, Sharedrug, to what is now the Kingfisher Group. This transaction reportedly netted Prince several million pounds, some of which he has clearly decided to divert to good causes.

The 1992/93 accounts for his foundation show assets of nearly £23,000, with charitable donations of £88,000 financed mainly by income derived directly from Alan Prince and his wife. The two major gifts were both to local medical research organisations in Hampshire: £50,000 to the Wessex Cardiac Appeal and £36,000 to the Wessex Neurological Centre Charitable Trust. In the previous year no grants had been made by the foundation.

Contact: Mr D L Morgan, Prince Foundation, c/o Messr Rothman Pantall & Co, 10 Romsey Rd, Eastleigh, Hants, SO50 9AL. Tel: 01703 614555.

TRAVIS family

£88,000

PREFERENCE: Northamptonshire
AGE: 50
WEALTH: £35m-£50m
TRUST LINKS: Constance Travis Charitable Trust
COMPANY LINKS: Travis Perkins

The **Constance Travis Charitable Trust** should benefit from the recent improved results posted by the public Travis Perkins timber merchant and builders' supplies company. The trust's one million shares in the firm produced dividends of £115,000 in 1991/92, a sum which should hopefully rise with increases in profits. It was set up by Constance Travis in 1986 and took over the assets of a now defunct grant-maker, the Travis Charitable Trust, which she had set up two years previously. She is currently a trustee along with her son Anthony Travis, who is chair of Travis Perkins and a major shareholder in the firm which was formed when the family timber business Travis & Arnold was merged with Sandell Perkins in 1989.

The trust held assets valued at around £2 million in 1991/92, including its Travis Perkins shareholding, which provided a total income of £152,000. Of this, just over half (£88,000) was donated to various charitable causes, although the accounts do not specify the recipients. There is, however, a preference for charities operating in Northamptonshire, where the family lives and where Travis Perkins is based.

Contact: Mr E R A Travis, Constance Travis Charitable Trust, Quinton Rising, Quinton, Northants, NN7 2EF.

ALAN BRAZIER

£77,000

PREFERENCE: welfare, youth, conservation, West Midlands
WEALTH: £20m-£35m
TRUST LINKS: Vax Charity Trust Fund
COMPANY LINKS: Quillgold Ltd, Vax

Alan Brazier owes his fortune to falling out of a tree! He was going to train as a vet, but had to miss some crucial exams because of his accident. Instead he became a milkman, and learnt how to deal with customers of all kinds. This was to help him later in life when it came to selling the new Vax vacuum cleaner he had invented in his farm workshop. The product has now become one of the leading brand names in both the commercial and domestic markets. Brazier owns all of Quillgold Ltd, the private holding company for the Vax Appliances, and it is through these closely held firms that he has chosen to channel some support for charities.

The **Vax Charity Trust Fund** was set up by the Quillgold company in 1989 with an initial settlement of £45,000. The original trustees included Alan, Elizabeth and Ian Brazier, who are all directors of the company. The purposes of this trust are the support of employees and ex-employees of Quillgold and Vax, the relief of distress of individuals, the promotion of medical research, the development of young people, animal welfare, environmental conservation, and the support of charitable causes in Hereford and Worcestershire. The trust obtains its income direct from Vax Appliances which in 1991 contributed £100,000 funding seven donations amounting to £77,000. Over half was directed to the Birmingham Royal Blind Institute in a £53,500 grant. Further sizeable donations of £12,500 to the Adventure Wood Project and £9,000 to a recipient identified in the accounts simply as 'Kidderminster' were made. Two other grants went to overseas relief organisations – the Save the Children Fund (£1,000) and the Red Cross Gulf Appeal (£1,000). In previous years, a major recipient has been the Droitwich Canal Trust, which received £23,000 from the trust in 1989.

There is another charity linked with the Vax Appliances firm, the **Birmingham Centenary Vax Marathon Limited**. This charitable company was co-founded by Alan Brazier in 1989, and the 1989/90 accounts state that it is 'engaged in the promotion of marathons', in particular, as its name would suggest, the Birmingham Centenary Marathon. It appears that this was a one-off event sponsored by Vax, as the accounts for 1989/90 show an income of £429,000, including £364,000 from Vax, and an expenditure of £436,000, mainly on holding the marathon. The accounts for the following year, however, show a zero income.

Alan Brazier responded to the draft entry we sent him by commenting that: 'Due to substantial changes in the fortunes of other companies owned within the Quillgold group of companies, we find we are financially embarrassed, and continually being embarrassed on a daily basis for requests for donations which we have to refuse. As this trend is not going to change in the next few years, we do not want our name published, which would mean we will only receive more requests for donations which we are unable to satisfy, and create grief and a waste of money as far as the sponsors of the requests are concerned'.

Contact: Mrs E Brazier, Vax Charity Trust Fund, Quillgold House, Kingswood Rd, Hampton Lovett, Droitwich, Worcs, WR9 0QH. Tel: 01905 795959.

● GIVING BY RETAILERS

David Sainsbury	£11,100,000
Sainsbury brothers	£10,400,000
Shirley & Leslie Porter	£966,000
Philip Harris	£742,000
Stanley Kalms	£604,000
Mohamed al-Fayed	£539,000
Bernard Ashley	£286,000
Terence Conran	£276,000
Anwar Pervez	£245,000
Noel Lister	£232,000
David Lewis	£164,000
Reg Vardy	£143,000

JOHN ASPREY
£76,000

PREFERENCE: not known
AGE: 56
WEALTH: £100m-£250m
TRUST LINKS: none found
COMPANY LINKS: Asprey

John Asprey and family own around half of the shares in the quoted Asprey jewellery retail company which has been associated with the family for over two hundred years. The firm is best known for its chain of exclusive shops, including a Bond Street store which recorded sales of over £1 million per week in 1992, and the group also includes Garrards and Mappin & Webb. The recession has had an adverse effect in recent years, however, and the company's profits have been hit hard.

Given John Asprey's strong holding in the company which bears his family's name, the charitable gifts of £76,000 it made in 1991/92 can be considered as coming indirectly from his own pocket. This money is usually focused upon one charity each year, which is selected by the directors. We have been unable, however, to trace any personal grant-making trusts registered in Asprey's name.

Contact: R J Philpott, Director, Asprey plc, 165-169 New Bond St, London, W1Y 0AR. Tel: 0171 493 6767.

WHITBREAD FAMILY
£76,000

PREFERENCE: medicine, churches, general, Bedfordshire
WEALTH: £100m-£250m
TRUST LINKS: Samuel Whitbread

Charitable Trust, Simon Whitbread Charitable Trust, Humphrey Whitbread's First Charitable Trust
COMPANY LINKS: Whitbread

Having dominated Whitbread brewers ever since it was founded in 1742, the Whitbread family now takes a backseat following the retirement of Sam Whitbread as chair in 1992. The family still retains a major stake in the business, however, and Whitbread plc's reputation as one of the most enlightened companies in the community looks set to continue untarnished. Charitable donations made by the company came to over £0.5 million in 1993, but its total contribution to the charitable sector – including the value of secondments, support-in-kind, etc. – was £1.8 million.

The Whitbreads have long supported charities on a personal basis as well. Sam Whitbread set up a charitable trust in 1965, which was worth over £100,000 by 1993, the bulk of it held in Whitbread shares. The trust's investment income was supplemented by a £3,000 covenanted payment from Sam Whitbread, and donations made in the year came to £15,000. Most of the grants were small, with the emphasis on Bedfordshire and Hertfordshire, and on medical charities. Beneficiaries included the Bedford Hospitals Charity, Beds and Herts Historic Churches Trust, the Bedfordshire Scouts Promise Appeal, and the Bedfordshire branch of Headway.

Sam's father, the late Major Simon Whitbread, had also set up a trust in the early 1960s. With 180,000 Whitbread shares as assets, the trust made donations totalling £45,000 in 1992/93. The larger donations included £5,000 each to Riseley PCC and the Winchester Cathedral Trust, £2,000 to St Luke's Hospital for Clergy, and £1,000 each to Charing Cross and Westminster Medical School and North Bedfordshire Marie Curie Cancer Care. A wide spread of other charities was supported.

Finally, an even older trust connected with the family was set up in 1949. **Humphrey Whitbread's First Charitable Trust** had investments with a market value of £1.6 million by 1991, the last year for which accounts are available. Current trustees include both Humphrey and Sam Whitbread. Donations made in 1990/91 totalled £61,000, with sizeable awards to Cardington PCC, the Historic Churches Preservation Trust, the National Trust, the Salisbury Cathedral Spire Appeal, the Norwich Playhouse Theatre, the Jefferiss Research Wing Trust, the British Red Cross and the Great St Mary's Organ Appeal, among others. A large number of small donations were also made for general charitable purposes.

Contact for the Samuel Whitbread Charitable Trust and the Simon Whitbread Charitable Trust: ECA Martineau, 1 St Peter's Street, Bedford MK40 2PN. For Humphrey Whitbread's First Charitable Trust: Mary Scallan, Secretary, 34 Bryanston Square, London W1H 7LQ. Tel: 0171 402 0052.

JOHN and PETER CLARKE and family
£73,000

PREFERENCE: youth, elderly people, education, medicine
WEALTH: £50m-£75m
TRUST LINKS: none found
COMPANY LINKS: Silentnight Holdings

The public Silentnight bed manufacturing company was the creation of Tom Clarke, who died recently. He had retired from the day-to-day running of the firm in 1987, and the family's controlling stake is now looked after by his sons John, who is deputy chair, and Peter, who is a non-executive director. Whilst we have been unable to identify any grant-making foundations or trusts registered in the Clarkes' name, Silentnight distributed £73,000 of grants in 1992/93 to a variety of local and national charities. It has some preference for organisations working with young people, the elderly and in the medical and education sectors.

Contact: B McKenzie, Group Finance Director, Silentnight Holdings plc, Salterforth, Colne, Lancashire, BB8 5UE. Tel: 01282 812711.

FENWICK family
£73,000 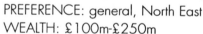 NEW

PREFERENCE: general, North East
WEALTH: £100m-£250m
TRUST LINKS: James Fenwick's Charitable Settlements, John Fenwick's Charitable Settlements
COMPANY LINKS: Fenwick department stores

We have been able to track down six relatively small charitable trusts connected with current members of the Fenwick family, which together made donations totalling around £13,000 in 1992/93. These are all funded by shares in the Fenwick chain of department stores, the family firm based in Newcastle-upon-Tyne. Whilst each of these trusts has its own particular preferences, overall there is a concentration of support in the North East around Newcastle-upon-Tyne, and in the medical, welfare and religious sectors.

Three of the trusts, known collectively as **James Fenwick's Charitable Settlements** were set up in 1963 by the late James Fenwick for his sons John, Peter and Christopher with an initial endowment of seventy ordinary £10 shares in Fenwick Ltd. All are time charities, with general charitable objects for sixty years, beyond which the balance is to be held for the British Red Cross and the NSPCC. Each of them still holds Fenwick shares with a book value of £5,800 although their market value is probably considerably greater. The **J J F Charitable Settlement** was created for John James Fenwick, who is the present chair of Fenwick Limited, director of Ricemans Holdings and also non-executive director of the Northern Rock Building Society. This made donations of £2,000 in 1992/93, the largest gift being £1,000 to the North East Civic Trust, of which he is a trustee. The **P T F Charitable Settlement** was set up for Peter Fenwick who is vice-chair and director of Fenwick Limited as well as director of Ricemans Holdings. It made donations of £4,300 in 1992/93, including gifts of £1,000 to both the Animal Health Trust and Chipping Warden Village Hall Trust. The other trust founded by James Fenwick was the **C M F Charitable Settlement**, created for Christopher Fenwick, a director of the family firm. This trust made donations of £3,700, the largest of which was £500 to the Valence Mary Endowment Fund and £200 to the North of England Cancer Research Campaign.

John Fenwick's Charitable Settlements were founded by John Fenwick (not to be confused with John James Fenwick, the current company chair listed above) for his sons in 1964. Again they are time charities which after sixty years hold their balance in trust for the Church of St Bartholomew at Whittingham near Alnwick. Each was initially endowed with a bundle of preference shares in Fenwick Ltd, which in 1992/93 had a book value of £10,700 but whose market value is no doubt much higher. The **J F F Charitable Settlement** made donations of £1,300 in 1992/93, the biggest to King Edward VII's Hospital in London, and was established for company director James Frederick Fenwick (not the same James Fenwick described above). Mark Fenwick, director of Fenwick Ltd, Ricemans Holdings and EG Music Group, determines the beneficiaries of the **M A F Charitable Settlement**, which also made grants of £1,300, the largest £250 to St Oswald's Hospice. The final trust we have identified is the **J E F Charitable Settlement**, controlled by John Edward Fenwick which gave away only £460 in 1992/93, including £200 to Princess Alice Hospice.

The Fenwick family's wealth comes from their eponymous chain of stores, which was set up over one hundred years ago. The company has weathered the recession relatively well, and has a healthy balance sheet. The company chair, John James (J J) Fenwick is approaching retirement age but still going strong, and in 1993 received a salary of over half a million pounds. He is one of the wealthier individuals in the family, and is a governor of the Royal Grammar School in Newcastle-upon-Tyne, and a past-governor of Moorfields Eye Hospital. Because of the family's strong interests in the company, the charitable donations made by Fenwick Limited could be considered as part of the family's largesse. In 1992 the firm made grants totalling nearly £60,000, with a preference for charities in areas where it has a strong presence. It has also sponsored the Royal Shakespeare

Theatre, of which John James Fenwick is governor, as well as the Northern Symphony Orchestra and the Royal Opera House.

Contact: J J F, P T F and C M F Charitable Settlements: Mrs J Jeffrey, Secretary to the Trustees, Fenwick Ltd, 39 Northumberland St, Newcastle-upon-Tyne, NE99 1AR. Tel: 0191 232 5100. J E F and J F F Charitable Settlements: Mrs S Thompson, at same address. M A F Charitable Settlement: Messrs Dickinson Miller Turnbull, Cross House, Westgate Rd, Newcastle-upon-Tyne, NE16 3AJ.

HINDUJA brothers

£68,000

PREFERENCE: developing countries, youth, religion
WEALTH: over £500m
TRUST LINKS: Hinduja Foundation
COMPANY LINKS: numerous interests in India, the US and the Middle East

Having moved to London from Iran after the 1979 revolution, the Hindujas built up a business empire that now encompasses manufacturing and trading and extends from India to the Middle East to the US. The purchase of Gulf Oil Trading in 1989 marked an acceleration in their activities and their latest ambitions include moving further into telecommunications and banking.

It was also in 1989 that three of the four brothers, Sri, Gopi and Prakash, established the charitable **Hinduja Foundation** in the UK. As well as general charitable purposes, with an emphasis on developing countries, the foundation's objects include the promotion of 'study and research into the social and economic causes of under-development; how nations can achieve higher rates of economic and social development; relations between developing and developed countries and international efforts to aid development'. The foundation seemed well-timed to fill the gap left by the BCCI-related Third World Foundation, and it noted that it would be supporting 'public health, and education in the UK, especially when they are connected with India'.

However, the foundation's largest commitment has been to the Prince's Youth Business Trust, which has received an annual donation of £25,000 from the foundation. In 1992 charitable expenditure totalled £68,000. In addition to the PYBT, grants were made to the Duke of Edinburgh's 7th Commonwealth Study Conference, and to the International Society for Krishna Consciousness (ISKCON). The foundation's report also records expenditure of £28,000 on a project commissioned 'in conjunction with ISKCON to determine the feasibility of developing a community based on the principles of Vedic culture and knowledge and centred around the worship of the Deities'. In the previous year a grant of £30,000 had been made to the Gulf Trust out of total donations of £93,000. The foundation has some £41,000 in assets and is financed through regular donations. The accounts note that a further £250,000 was received in donations in 1993.

Sri, the eldest of the brothers, and Gopi work out of London, based in an office in Haymarket a few doors down from the Charity Commission.

Contact: The Director, Hinduja Foundation, Banton House, 25 Haymarket, London SW1Y 4EN.

GAD and HANS RAUSING

£67,000

(but see below)

PREFERENCE: education
Ages: 71, 68 respectively
WEALTH: over £500m
TRUST LINKS: none found
COMPANY LINKS: Tetra Laval

Swedish brothers Gad and Hans Rausing topped the 1994 *Sunday Times* survey of Britain's rich with a combined wealth in the order of five billion pounds. Their massive wealth has come from one of the simplest of everyday objects, the 'TetraPak' container for milk and fruit juices which was invented by their father, Ruben. The Rausing family controls the private Tetra Laval business through a Liechtenstein foundation and a Dutch holding group. The brothers moved to Britain in the early 1980s to escape the onerous tax regime of their native Sweden and to better access international communications, and they have lived here ever since.

Gad, the elder of the two, donated £400,000 in February 1990 to the Campaign for Oxford, to fund a readership in Ancient Icelandic Literature and Antiquities. Appropriately enough, he is a Doctor of Philosophy himself and is a part time archaeology lecturer in Sweden. He is also reputed to be an avid patron of the arts. This is, however, the only charitable donation we have been able to trace for the Rausing brothers, and there is no trust registered in this country under their name. Because of their major shareholding in the company, the gifts made by Tetra Laval can be considered as coming from their pockets. In 1991 the Kingston-upon-Thames based firm made total charitable grants of £67,000, but has no set policy. Whilst their family still controls Tetra Laval financially, in June 1993 the brothers announced their retirement from business life.

Contact: Peter Wiggs, Manager of Communications Department, Tetra Laval, 31-35 High St, Kingston-upon-Thames, Surrey, KT1 1LF. Tel: 0181 546 2188.

DAVID SAMWORTH
and family
£62,000

PREFERENCE: East Midlands, recreation, medicine, education, agriculture
AGE: 57
WEALTH: £50m-£75m
TRUST LINKS: Cadell-Samworth Foundation, Chetwode Foundation
COMPANY LINKS: Samworth Bros

Walkers Pies and Ginsters Pasties have helped make the Samworth family's bank balance bulge – both are owned by their firm, Samworth Brothers. They have also helped feed two charitable trusts established by the family, which are significant donors in the East Midlands.

The first of these trusts is the **Chetwode Foundation**, which was established in 1973 taking its title from the family's middle name, Chetwode. The trustees currently include David Chetwode Samworth and his wife Rosemary, who are in control of assets of nearly £650,000, mainly in blue chip shares. In the year 1992/93 this trust made grants totalling £31,000, the bulk of which was accounted for by a £25,000 donation to the Sports Aid

Foundation. The foundation also appears to have some preference for causes in the East Midlands, where the family live and their business is located – previous gifts have included £42,000 to the Newark and Nottinghamshire Agricultural Society and £10,000 to Cropwell Butler PCC.

The other family trust is the **Cadell-Samworth Foundation** (also known as the Chetwode Samworth Charitable Trust), which is partly named after Rosemary Samworth's maiden surname, Cadell, and whose current trustees are David and his brother John. This trust has assets of over £1 million which generated an income of £62,000 in 1991/92. It has a preference for charities located in Nottinghamshire and Leicestershire, as well as national medical appeals. Its grants for the year 1991/92, however, largely reflect David Chetwode's major passion – hunting. Of a total of £31,000, the trust directed £15,000 to the British Field Sports Society and £2,000 to the Cottesmore Hunt Trust, the Leicestershire hunt with which he rides as joint master.

The Samworth family has made its money from the meat trade, starting with a market stall in Birmingham run by David's father and grandfather, before progressing into pork wholesale and then processing, with a pie factory built in 1960. After military service and attending Harvard Business School, David Samworth became chair and managing director of the expanding family firm in the mid 1960s, and bought Pork Farms from Garfield Weston (qv), which became the company's new title. After a successful stock market flotation in 1971, the group was taken over by Northern Foods in 1978, and the family received a reported £10 million for their share. They continued in the same vein in 1984 by setting up Samworth Brothers, a private company best known for its pies and

THE BRITISH SCHOOL OF OSTEOPATHY
1-4 SUFFOLK ST., LONDON. SW1Y 4HG
TEL. 01 - 930 9254-8

pasties, which is totally owned by the family. David Samworth is also a non-executive director of another well-known East Midlands food producer – Thorntons, the chocolate company.

Contact: For both the Cadell-Samworth Foundation and the Chetwode Foundation: J G Ellis, Secretary, Samworth Bros, Fields Farm, Cropwell Butler, Notts, NG12 3AP. Tel: 0115 933 5221.

BULMER FAMILY

£60,000 **NEW**

PREFERENCE: Hereford, general
WEALTH: £100m-£250m
TRUST LINKS: Howard Bulmer Charitable Trust, Becket Bulmer Charitable Trust, E F Bulmer Benevolent Fund
COMPANY LINKS: H P Bulmer Holdings

The prize apple in the Bulmers' charity basket dates from the first generation of cider-making Bulmers. Fred, the brother of Percy Bulmer who founded the business in the nineteenth century, set up the **E F Bulmer Benevolent Fund** in 1938 while he chaired the company and endowed it with company shares. Established for the purpose of relieving poverty among needy employees and their dependants, 'the trustees may also make grants to any charitable organisation existing for the relief of poverty if in their opinion there is more money available than is required for the primary object'. With assets now worth about £4.5 million, the chances of other charities getting a look in have clearly increased. Donations totalled £105,000 in 1990.

Fred Bulmer was further remembered, together with Becket Bulmer, in 1986 when the **Becket Bulmer Charitable Trust** was established in their memory by George Bulmer and Sophia Maude. Its objects are the cultural advance of the people of Hereford and Herefordshire, the support of the Hereford Cider Museum Trust, and other charitable purposes. In 1988, the last year for which accounts were on file at the Charity Commission, the trust made grants totalling just over £6,000, all in small awards to local charities and individuals. 'The trustees continue to seek deserving applicants to benefit from the funds available for distribution and to promote the fund to potential recipients.'

The slightly larger **Howard Bulmer Charitable Trust** was set up under the will of the late Howard Bulmer in 1985, who bequeathed it all his ordinary shares in H P Bulmer Holdings. In 1992/93 donations were made from the trust included £2,000 each to University College London and the Motor Neurone Disease Association, £750 to Prader Willi Syndrome and £500 to the Whitney Play Group. By far the largest grant, of over £11,000, went to Alcohol Concern. Cider-drinking is clearly not what it used to be.

The Bulmer family currently own over half of H P Bulmer Holdings, with the largest single stake controlled by Esmond Bulmer, chair of the company and former Tory MP for Kidderminster and for Wyre Forest. The company made donations of £54,000 in 1993, with the support dedicated to local charities, particularly in Hereford, and specific trade-related charities.

Contact: Giles Bulmer, H P Bulmer Holdings Ltd., The Cider Mills, Plough Lane, Hereford HR4 0LE. Tel: 01432 352000. For the Howard Bulmer Charitable Trust: MacFarlanes, Solicitors, 10 Norwich Street, London EC4A 1BD. Tel: 0171 831 9222.

JOHN CLEESE

see below

PREFERENCE: children, ecology, birth control, Tibet

AGE: 54

WEALTH: less than £20m

TRUST LINKS: none

COMPANY LINKS: Waterfall Productions; sold stake in Video Arts

John Marwood Cleese will be forever associated in the British public's mind with the manic Torquay hotelier Basil Fawlty, his comic creation in the classic BBC series Farty Towels (or should that be *Fawlty Towers?*). His wealth does not derive from the series, which earned him relatively little, but instead has come from his subsequent activities in films and business training. In particular, he realised a considerable sum when he sold his stake in the Video Arts company in 1989. This proved a very good year for Cleese due to his interests in *A Fish Called Wanda*, which took a total of $62 million at the US box office alone. He estimates his personal worth at around £6 million.

Like many of the other individuals in this book, John Cleese informed us that over recent years he has received a 'bewildering' number of requests from various charities for assistance. As a result he took the decision to restrict his donations to the following organisations: NSPCC; Families at Risk; Child Psychotherapy Trust; Exploring Parenthood; British Trust for Conservation Volunteers; Friends of the Earth; Greenpeace; Brook Advisory Centres; International Planned Parenthood Federation; Tibet Foundation; and the RIGPA Fellowship. He also helps Charter 88, Amnesty, the British Trust for Brain Injured Children, and the Fullbright Foundation. The latter organisation also reportedly received a £25,000 out of court settlement he obtained in July 1992 from the Sun newspaper, and this sum has been used to provide scholarships for British screenwriters.

These various organisations receive assistance from John Cleese on what he describes as a regular, if occasional basis. Over the past five years he told us that his personal charitable donations have averaged around £60,000 annually, although in the last year were much lower. He intends to pursue his policy of focused support for a small group of non-profit bodies, and so does not wish to receive unsolicited requests for help.

Contact: John Cleese, c/o David Wilkinson Associates, 115 Hazlebury Rd, London, SW6 2LX.

143

ABE JAFFE
and family

£60,000

PREFERENCE: not known
WEALTH: £20m–£35m
TRUST LINKS: none found
COMPANY LINKS: Curfin
Investments

Amongst extensive international business interests, the Jaffe family control the bulk of the shares of Curfin Investments, a private company chaired by Abe Jaffe. Curfin's principal subsidiary is the Currie Motors chain of car dealers which operate in and around Greater London. Whilst we have been unable to uncover any charitable trusts registered in Jaffe's name, Curfin Investments made donations to the tune of £60,000 in 1991/92, with a preference for local charities around the areas where it operates.

Contact: Mrs J Langford, Secretary to the MD, Curfin Investments Ltd, 161 Chertsey Rd, Twickenham, Middlesex, TW1 1EP. Tel: 0181 891 1313.

DEREK FAWCETT

£55,000

PREFERENCE: general, Portsmouth
WEALTH: less than £20m
TRUST LINKS: Fawcett Charitable Trust
COMPANY LINKS: sold holding in Nautech

Derek Fawcett made his fortune a few years ago when he sold his private Portsmouth-based yachting navigation equipment company Nautech to a US electronics firm. Like many entrepreneurs in his position, he ensured that good causes benefited from his new-found wealth through his grant-making trust. He had set up the **Fawcett Charitable Trust** with his wife in 1990 and had soon endowed it with 17,500 Nautech shares worth £1.6 million. Dividends of nearly £0.5 million received in the trust's first six months enabled gifts of £670,000 to be made in 1991/92, its first full year of operation. Although not specified in the accounts, beneficiaries reportedly included Portsmouth Cathedral, a local grammar school, SENSE and Children in Need. In 1992/93 the trust appeared to be consolidating its position, with assets worth £1.5 million, an income of £125,000, and total donations of £55,000 to unspecified recipients.

Contact: Mr S G Campbell, c/o Blake Lapthorn, 8 Landport Terrace, Portsmouth, Hants, PO1 2QW. Tel: 01705 822291.

MARGARET BARBOUR
and family

£54,000

PREFERENCE: North East, health and welfare
AGE: 54
WEALTH: £35m–£50m
TRUST LINKS: Barbour Trust
COMPANY LINKS: J Barbour & Sons

The 'Barbour' waxed jacket celebrated its hundredth birthday in 1994, but it has only really been in the past decade that the brand has achieved fame thanks to the whims of the notoriously fickle fashion industry. When the weather looks inclement, it is definitely the thing to be seen in, amongst both the smart country set and the capital's office workers.

The family who lent their name to the jackets also control the North East based company which makes them – J Barbour & Sons. Margaret Barbour has chaired the firm since her husband died in the early seventies and is also trustee of the **Barbour Trust** which was set up in 1988. The trust's income is derived mainly from an endowment of shares held in the family business, and it is currently accumulating most of its annual income of around £120,000 to consolidate its asset base. However, donations of £54,000 were made in 1991/92 with a strong preference for causes in Tyneside and the North East, typified by grants of £6,000 to the Tyne & Wear Foundation, a regular recipient of gifts, and £5,000 to both Tyneside Housing Aid Centre and South Tyneside Women's Aid. There is also an emphasis on medical research, with donations of £5,000 to the British Heart Foundation and the Heart Call Appeal.

Contact: Mr H J Tavroges, Saville Chambers, 63 Fowler Street, South Shields, Tyne & Wear, NE33 1NS. Tel: 0191 455 3181.

VISCOUNTESS BOYD

£53,000

PREFERENCE: culture & art, heritage, churches, South West

Age: 76

WEALTH: £100m-£250m

TRUST LINKS: Viscountess Boyd Charitable Trust

COMPANY LINKS: Guinness

Patricia, Viscountess Boyd is a member of one of the richest families in Britain and Ireland – the Guinness family. Much of their fortune is tied up in a complex web of non-charitable overseas family trusts, notably the Iveagh Trust. The Viscountess is one of the wealthier individuals in the clan due to her shares in the Iveagh Trust, and for the past ten years has supported various causes through an eponymous charitable trust. She founded the **Viscountess Boyd Charitable Trust** in 1982, and by 1991/92 it held assets with a market value of over £1.1 million including 71,000 Guinness shares worth £383,000. This large capital base generated an income of only £32,000 in the year, which funded donations of £38,000. The bulk of this went in a

£20,000 gift to Oxford University's Bodleian Library, with grants of £2,500 to the Tate Gallery at St Ives and the National Trust, and £1,000 to Friends of the Royal Botanic Gardens and the University of West Indies UK Appeal. The remainder went to a variety of causes, notably churches, medicine and education, and organisations operating in the South West.

Just before the Second World War Lady Patricia Guinness, daughter of the 2nd Earl of Iveagh, married the Conservative MP Alan Lennox-Boyd. Both served on the board of Arthur Guinness & Co for many years, and Lennox-Boyd was made Viscount Boyd in 1960. When he died in 1983, this title passed on to his eldest son, Simon, who is now the Second Viscount Boyd. A year later, the Second Viscount helped establish the **Lennox-Boyd Memorial Trust** in order to commemorate his late father. This trust receives most of its income in the form of donations from other trusts and individuals, many connected with the Guinness family: since its formation it has obtained funds from Viscount Boyd, Mark Lennox-Boyd, Lady Nugent, Prince von Preussen, Viscountess Boyd's Charitable Trust, the Normanby Trust and the Channon Charitable Trust (qqv). The last accounts on file at the Charity Commission show assets of over £300,000 and grants of £36,000. The main objects of the trust are to promote the study and practice of tropical medicine, which it did through grants to various individuals and institutions, as well as to support charities generally such as St John's Ambulance and the Royal Commonwealth Society for the Blind.

The National Trust has also been the beneficiary of the family's largesse: its 1991/92 accounts report the donation of a chalet at Chastleton worth £15,000 by Viscount Boyd amongst the gifts in-kind given by individual benefactors. On a wider front, the Viscount is chair of the Stonham Housing Trust and is involved in overseas aid and development as past chair of Save the Children Fund and past president of the council of British Executive Service Overseas. On the business front, he is director of Iveagh Trustees and a trustee of the Guinness Trust housing association.

Contact: M D Smith, Viscountess Boyd Charitable Trust, Iveagh Trustees Ltd, Iveagh House, 41 Harrington Gardens, London, SW7 4JU. Tel: 0171 373 7261.

LORD CAYZER and family
£53,000

PREFERENCE: general
AGE: 84
WEALTH: £250-£500m
TRUST LINKS: B G S Cayzer Trust
COMPANY LINKS: Caledonia Investments

The fall of shipping giant British and Commonwealth in 1990 marked, perhaps more than any other single event, the end of the eighties and the eighties' style of doing business. But not for the Cayzers. They sold B & C for £427 million in 1987, with enough bank guarantees to ensure the pay-off millions kept rolling in years after the company went down. The cash was reinvested highly profitably, including in an old B & C business, money-broker Exco, which was refloated in 1994. Head of the family Lord Cayzer has consequently become a legend in his own lifetime in the City. Aged 84, he retired from chairing Caledonia Investments, the Cayzers' main vehicle, in 1994.

We have only been able to track down one trust bearing the Cayzer name. The **B G S Cayzer Trust** was set up in 1982 under the will of the late Bernard Cayzer, a former director at Caledonia. Donations totalling £14,500 were made in 1991/92, with the main awards going to the Glyndebourne Festival Society, the Save the Children Fund, the Bulldog Trust (run by another City figure, Richard Hoare, qv), the John Younger Trust, St Paul's Knightsbridge and the Friends of the Royal Botanical Gardens. The grant total does not reflect the real size of the trust which held 40,000 shares in Caledonia Investments, 165,000 cumulative preference shares in the Cayzer Trust Company Ltd. and £112,000 in cash, plus some other investments. The trustees currently comprise Peter Buckley, Caledonia's chief executive, and solicitor Peter Davies.

Caledonia Investments itself made charitable donations totalling £53,000 in 1992/93. The Cayzer family own nearly half the share capital of Caledonia and given Lord Cayzer's chairmanship of the company at the time, we have stretched a point to list this sum as the figure for the family's donations.

Contact: J H Sefton, c/o The Cayzer Trust Co. Ltd., Cayzer House, 1 Thomas More Street, London E1 9AR. Tel: 0171 481 4343.

MARQUESS OF CHOLMONDELEY
and family
£52,000 NEW

PREFERENCE: general, youth, Cheshire, Norfolk
AGE: 33
WEALTH: £100m-£250m
TRUST LINKS: Marquess of Cholmondeley's Charitable Fund, Pennycress Trust

COMPANY LINKS: none

When the sixth Marquess of Cholmondeley died in 1990 he bequeathed his family an estate worth £118 million, most of which went to his heir, David George Philip the present Lord Cholmondeley. He also left behind the **Marquess of Cholmondeley's Charitable Fund**, which he had set up in 1983 to benefit local Cheshire charities. The only accounts we were able to obtain from the Charity Commission for this grant-making trust predate the sixth Marquess' death, and show that in 1988/89 the late Marquess and his wife were trustees, and as such were stewards of assets worth £35,000 together with an unvalued property. In that year, the fund had an income of £4,500 which covered grants of £4,000. The largest single donation of £1,100 went to the NSPCC, and the other gifts were directed at a cross-section of general and welfare causes, including several in Cheshire. The list of donations also included £50 to the campaigning group Peace Through NATO. It is likely that the current Lord Cholmondeley will have become a trustee of this charitable fund since his father's death.

A large part of the Cholmondeley family's charitable work is undertaken by the **Pennycress Trust,** which was set up by Lord Cholmondeley's grandmother, Sybil the Dowager Marchioness of Cholmondeley, in 1970. Upon her death, she bequeathed certain jewellery to the trust, which received £442,000 upon its sale. In addition, Lady Aline Cholmondeley gave to the trust the greater part of her interest in a one-third share of the residue of the Dowager Marchioness' estate, from which the trust received shares to the value of over £0.5 million. As a result, by 1992/93 the trust held assets with a value of just over £1.1 million, which generated an income of £101,000. Donations of £43,000 were made, substantially up on previous years, and were split into a large number of relatively small donations with some preference for local charities in Norfolk and Cheshire. The largest gifts were £1,400 to the Royal Horticultural Society to provide a mobility unit at Wisley Gardens, £1,000 to Mary Hare Grammar School for Deaf Children near Newbury, and £1,000 to the Priory and Parish of St Margaret, King's Lynn, 1991 Appeal. The trust had apparently recently endowed scholarships at the Yehudi Menuhin School and the Royal Academy of Art. The current trustees include Lady Aline Cholmondeley and Mr C G Cholmondeley.

Apart from donations through these two trusts, Lord and Lady Cholmondeley make other gifts on a private basis, which this year have included £5,000 to the AIDS Crisis Trust. There is also a Cholmondeley Award for Poets, set up in 1965 by the late Dowager Marchioness of Cholmondeley, and a Flying Award administered by the RAF.

The Cholmondeley family's wealth is derived from a collection of art treasures, 12,000 acres of land, and two stately homes – Houghton Hall in Norfolk and Cholmondeley Castle in Cheshire. This wealth of around £100-110 million would be hard to realise, however, as the bulk is made up of Heritage Property and works of art, which are mostly exemptable and would be taxed heavily on eventual sale. Lord Cholmondeley suffered a bit of a blow at the end of 1992, however, when his Norfolk property was broken into and an estimated £10 million of paintings and clocks were taken.

Contact for both the Marquess of Cholmondeley's Charitable Fund and the Pennycress Trust: Mr P R Fitzgerald, Fladgate Fielder Solicitors, Heron Place, 3 George St, London, W1M 6AD. Tel: 0171 486 9231.

VISCOUNT COWDRAY
and family
£52,000

PREFERENCE: medicine, disability, general
AGE: 84
WEALTH: over £500m
TRUST LINKS: Hon Charles Pearson Charity Trust, Lady Blakenham's Charity Trust
COMPANY LINKS: Pearson

Viscount Cowdray, octagenarian head of the publishing-to-banking Pearson family, also happens to be one of the country's richest landowners, with estates in Sussex and Scotland. He is still president of Pearson plc, publishers of the *Financial Times*, although the company is now run by his nephew, Viscount Blakenham. Pearson, of which the family owns about one fifth of the shares, is one of the country's largest corporate donors. In 1992 it donated a total of £656,000 to mostly national causes, including education, disability and the arts. The company has established the post of new media librarian at the Bodleian in Oxford with an endowment of £1 million over 10 years.

There are a number of small charities in the Cowdray name connected with Lord Cowdray's estates in Easebourne and Midhurst. In addition, in 1978 a charitable trust was established in the name of the Hon Charles Pearson, Lord Cowdray's younger son. By 1992 it had assets worth £1 million and was making grants of £32,000 a year, although the accounts do not specify the beneficiaries. The trust has general charitable purposes, with a beneficial area covering Great Britain and Northern Ireland, and is managed by the Cowdray Trust Ltd. We have been unable to track down any foundations connected to Lord Cowdray's eldest son and heir, Michael Pearson.

Cowdray's sister, Lady Blakenham, also has a trust, set up in 1973. Her son Viscount Blakenham is one of the trustees. In 1991/92 the trust made donations totalling £20,000 with th emphasis on old people, blind and physically incapacitated people, and on the relief of poverty. The trust also supports holiday homes for disabled people.

Contact for the Hon Charles Pearson Charity Trust: the Secretary, the Cowdray Trust Ltd, Pollen House, 10-12 Cork Street, London W1X 1PD. Tel: 0171 439 9061.
For Lady Blakenham's Charity Trust: Chipping Warden Manor, Nr Banbury, Oxon. For Pearson plc: Anette Lawless, Company Secretary, Millbank Tower, London SW1P 4QZ, Tel: 0171 411 2000.

MICHAEL EVANS
and family
£52,000

PREFERENCE: education
AGE: 59
WEALTH: £50m-£75m
TRUST LINKS: Rhoda Evans Charitable Trust
COMPANY LINKS: Evans of Leeds

The Evans family are major movers in Yorkshire through their public property investment and development company, Evans of Leeds. They prefer to keep out of the limelight, and perhaps as a result we have only been able to track down one charitable trust directly linked to them.

The **Rhoda Evans Charitable Trust** was established in 1980 by Frederick Evans, the family patriarch who built up Evans of Leeds over a period of forty years, but who died in 1992. It remains a fairly small trust, with assets of around £65,000 and total grants of £7,500 in 1990/91. Its objects are the advancement of education of the children of doctors and other health professionals, and the relief of poverty amongst children. To this end, the donations made in 1990/91 comprised of £5,000 to the British Medical Association, four individual grants of £500 each to Rugby School, and £500 to Epsom College.

Evans of Leeds is now controlled by Michael Evans and his three brothers, and the family holds over half of the shares in the group. Given their considerable stake, the donations of £44,000 made by the company in 1991/92 have been included in the figure given above for the family's donations.

Contact: Rhoda Evans Charitable Trust, Messrs S R Dalton & Co, Oxford Row & Gt George St, Leeds, LS1 3BD. Evans of Leeds, Millshaw, Ring Rd, Beeston, Leeds LS11 8EG. Tel: 0113 271 1888.

MARQUESS OF NORTHAMPTON
£52,000

PREFERENCE: general, north London, Northants
AGE: 48
WEALTH: £75m-£100m
TRUST LINKS: Compton Charitable Trust
COMPANY LINKS: none

The **Compton Charitable Trust** is one of the few sizeable trusts in this book to have been set up by a still living wealthy landowner. The 7th

Marquess of Northampton, 'Spenny' Compton, established the trust in the family name in 1980, and it currently has assets of nearly £150,000 controlled by him and his fifth wife Pamela. Grants totalling £52,000 were made in the year 1990/91, the largest of which were £45,000 to the Canonbury Tower Charitable Trust, £4,000 to the Northampton Philharmonic Choir and £1,400 to the Hermetic Research Trust. Other donations were directed to a general selection of charities, notably those operating with young people, the disabled, and in medical research.

In the previous year, a loan of £170,000 was also made to the Canonbury Tower Charitable Trust, of which £100,000 was repaid in 1990/91. The object of this recipient organisation, set up by the Marquess in 1985, is the preservation of the property of the Canonbury Tower in Islington, a part of north London in which his family has large landholdings. There also seems to be some preference towards organisations operating around one of the Compton family's stately homes – Castle Ashby in Northamptonshire.

● GIVING FROM GAMBLING FORTUNES

Moores family	£2,800,000
Barclay twins	£1,080,000
Cyril Stein	£478,000
Robert Sangster	£50,000

The Marquess is no doubt feeling particularly charitable at the moment, having gained legal title to a £50 million treasure trove. In November 1993 a New York state jury declared him to be rightful owner of the 'Sevso treasure', a 14-piece collection of Roman silver Northampton had brought together over the past ten years. The Hungarian and Croatian governments, who both laid claim to the bounty, immediately appealed for a mistrial, but they lost the case. For his part, the practically minded Marquess has stated that he now wishes to sell it. He has always held the view that art is not part of the nation's heritage, as it has always been traded on a worldwide scale. This was bourne out with his 1985 sale of the Renaissance masterpiece *Adoration of the Magi* to the Getty Museum in America for £7.5m. Apart from other valuable family heirlooms, Northampton's fortune stems from the family's land in London and his 10,500 acres around Castle Ashby, and 3,750 at his other home, Compton Wynyates, a Tudor mansion in Warwickshire. He was also a non-executive director of Specialeyes, the quoted spectacles company, until he resigned from its board last year.

Contact: Marquess of Northampton, Compton Charitable Trust, Compton Wynyates, Tysoe, Warwick, CV35 0UD. Tel: 01604 696696.

ROBERT SANGSTER

£50,000

(but see below)

PREFERENCE: general

AGE: 57

WEALTH: £100m-£250m

TRUST LINKS: Sangster Charitable Foundation

COMPANY LINKS: Sangster Group, sold Vernons Pools

In the late eighties, Robert Sangster sold Vernons, the family football pools company previously run by his father, for a reported £90 million. Within a year his private firm, the Sangster Group, had set up the **Sangster Charitable Foundation** with him and his son Guy as trustees, in order to support general charitable causes. As there appear to be no accounts on file at the Charity Commission for this grant-making trust, we were not able to determine whether it has yet made any donations. The Charity Commission's computer database states, however, that the foundation had an income of £50,000 in 1990/91.

In recent years, Sangster has been best known for his activities in the world of horse-racing as an owner of many thoroughbreds and proprietor of multi-million pound stables at Manton House, Wiltshire. His success in the 'sport of kings' contrasts, however, with the mixed fortunes he has encountered on the business front since selling Vernons, and in particular his financial losses due to the collapse of an Irish bloodstock agency and a South African company in which he had invested. The Sangster Group currently has various property interests.

Contact: Mr Sarsfield, Secretary to the Trustees, Sangster Charitable Foundation, Manton House, Manton House Estate, Marlborough, Wilts, SN5 1PN. Tel: 01672 514904.

EDDIE HEALEY
and family
see below

PREFERENCE: general
AGE: 56
WEALTH: £35m-£50m
TRUST LINKS: Stadium Charitable Trust
COMPANY LINKS: Stadium Developments

Eddie Healey is one of the richer individuals in the North East, thanks

to his brush with the DIY trade and more recent involvements with the retail property market. He made his fortune thanks to the family's Status Discount home improvements retail chain, which was sold to MFI for £30 million in 1980 although he was only a minority shareholder. He has since enhanced his worth mainly on the back of the successful Meadowhall shopping centre near Sheffield and his private property company, Stadium Developments.

At the end of 1989 Healey set up the **Stadium Charitable Trust** with general charitable purposes. Although the trust's correspondent estimated its future annual income at £50,000 when applying for registration, in the two subsequent years it appears to have been largely inactive, with no income or expenditure, and the only assets being the £100 with which it was initially settled. The company secretary for Stadium Developments noted that 'Mr Healey has, and continues to be, generous in his donations to charitable causes of his choice through means other than the Charitable Trust to which you refer.'

Contact: Stadium Charitable Trust, Stadium Developments Ltd, Welton Grange, Welton, Brough, North Humberside, HU15 1NB. Tel: 01482 667149.

PAUL JUDGE
£47,000 **NEW**

PREFERENCE: education, general, Worcestershire
AGE: 44
WEALTH: £35m-£50m
TRUST LINKS: Judge Charitable Foundation
COMPANY LINKS: sold stake in Hillsdown Holdings

In 1992 Paul Judge took on perhaps one of the most difficult jobs in Britain – trying to balance the books at Conservative Central Office. The Tory party is obviously hoping that some of their new Director General's money-making talents will rub-off and improve their finances, which were in the red to the tune of £19 million when he took over. It is hard to tell if it is working, as although the Party reported a record surplus of £2 million after his first year, it also admitted liabilities of £17 million. Whilst many would think he would have his hands full dealing with the Tories' finances, he has also found the time to support rather more charitable organisations, and in particular his *alma mater.* If Paul Judge is ever awarded a knighthood it will be hard to determine whether it was for his charitable activities or his work 'for the cause'.

● GIVING BY FOOD FORTUNES

David Thompson	£1,200,000
Dowager Marchioness of Normanby	£333,000
Vestey family	£226,000
Warburton family	£130,000
Michael Thornton	£100,000
Whitbread family	£76,000
David Samworth	£62,000
Bulmer family	£60,000
Viscountess Boyd	£53,000
Paul Judge	£47,000
MacDonald-Buchanan family	£34,000
John Thornton	£25,000

He made his fortune from the largest ever buyout in the UK food industry, when Premier Brands was sold to Hillsdown Holdings in 1989. He had led the team which bought up several Cadbury Schweppes' food subsidiaries, such as Typhoo and Chivers, to create the Premier Brands company in the mid eighties. His investment of £90,000 in the new firm realised £45 million when the company was sold. Judge appears to have redirected much of his energy, and a significant portion of his wealth, to more charitable endeavours. On acquiring his fortune, he promptly gave £8 million to Cambridge University to establish the Judge Institute of Management Studies. As a proportion of wealth, this is one of the most generous donations in this book. He is now chair of the Institute's advisory board, and is a trustee of the Cambridge Foundation, the University's fundraising arm. His interests in education are also manifested in other ways: he is a governor of Bromsgrove School, a council member of the Association of MBAs, and recently served on the Economic and Social Research Council.

On a wider front, in 1992 he set up his own personal charitable trust, the **Judge Charitable Foundation**, to make donations for general charitable purposes. The accounts on file at the Charity Commission for the year 1992/93 show a substantial income of £5.3 million, derived mainly from gifts from Paul Judge and associated tax rebates. Most of this is being held to fund the development of the Judge Institute of Management Studies, but charitable donations of £47,000 were made during the year. These consisted of £30,000 to Worcester Cathedral Trust, £10,000 to the Prince's Trust, and £6,700 to Worcestershire Nature Conservation Trust.

Since the sale of Premier Brands, Judge has broadened his management experience through various business links. He encountered quangos as chair of the promotion body Food from Britain (from 1989-92) and was a government appointed member of the Milk Marketing Board. He also became a non-executive director of three plcs:

WPP, the world's largest marketing services company, and, until recently, of Boddingtons, the brewers, and of Grosvenor Development Capital, an investment trust. Other business interests include positions as chair of two early stage private companies.

Contact: Mr P R Judge, Trustee, Judge Charitable Foundation, Grange Farm, Elmbridge, Worcester WR9 0DA. Tel: 01527 861204.

EARL OF AYLESFORD
and family
£45,000

PREFERENCE: West Midlands, medicine, children, conservation, education
AGE: 76
WEALTH: £35m-£50m
TRUST LINKS: Aylesford Family Charitable Trust
COMPANY LINKS: none

Although perhaps not the most famous or most wealthy members of the British aristocracy, Lord Aylesford and his family appear to be amongst the more generous, supporting mainly charities situated in the West Midlands. A conduit for their gifts is the **Aylesford Family Charitable Trust** which was set up in 1989 by Aylesford's eldest son and heir, Lord Guernsey, who is a trustee along with his wife.

The trust now has a considerable asset base worth £800,000 – consisting mainly of a large portfolio of shares – which generated an income of £132,000 in 1990/91. This supported gifts of £45,000 concentrated mainly around Coventry and in Warwickshire. The largest grant of £15,000 went to the Coventry and Warwickshire Awards Trust, which provides sports facilities for young people in the area, and other local gifts included £5,000 to both Outward Bound Solihull and the Coventry Trust, £3,000 to Spencer's Industrial Arts Trust (which assists Coventry residents in further education), and £1,500 to Warwickshire Farming and Wildlife Advisory Group, and £1,000 to both Coventry Boys' Club and NCH Kingshurst Appeal. Other donations made by the foundation included £6,500 for the Coventry-based national charity Association for Brain-Damaged Children, £1,700 to the NSPCC, and £1,000 to the Atlantic Salmon Conservation Trust. The slight bent towards conservation is unsurprising given that Lord Aylesford lists wildlife preservation as one of his recreations.

The family's wealth comes from their 18th century mansion Packington Hall, which is near Coventry, and its surrounding 4,500 acres of land which incorporates several tenanted farms, a golf course, and a deer park. Aylesford is patron of Warwickshire Boy Scouts Association, and president of the county's cricket club.

Contact: Mr Hugh Bampfield Carslake, Aylesford Family Charitable Trust, c/o Messrs Martineau Johnson (HBC), St Philips House, St Philips Place, Birmingham, B3 2PP. Tel: 0121 200 3300.

PETER
GOLDSTEIN
£42,000

PREFERENCE: Jewish causes, general
AGE: 54
WEALTH: £20m-£35m
TRUST LINKS: Solo Charitable Settlement

COMPANY LINKS: sold Superdrug to Kingfisher

On the same day in 1983 that his brother Ronald (qv) set up a grant-making trust, Peter Goldstein founded the **Solo Charitable Settlement**, with his wife, his brother, and Howard Goldstein as trustees. Over the next few years he put 250,000 Superdrug shares worth £1.3 million into the settlement, which were transformed into 425,000 Woolworth Holdings shares of equivalent value when the company took over the Goldstein brothers' chain of pharmacies. In 1992/93 around one-quarter of this stake was sold for £455,000, leaving 300,000 Kingfisher shares. In that year the trust had an income of £121,000 from assets worth £2.75 million, which supported charitable gifts of £42,000. These donations were directed mainly at various Jewish causes, some of which were also supported by his brother's trust. The biggest gifts were £22,500 to the Jewish Philanthropic Association, £12,750 to the Ashten Trust, £1,300 to the Weizmann Institute and £1,250 to Jewish Care. Other grants were made to a general variety of charities dealing with health, young people and recreation.

Peter Goldstein became rich on paper when the Superdrug chain was bought by Kingfisher in 1987 and he received a combination of cash and shares. He had fostered the company's growth along with his brother for twenty years until the takeover. At present, however, their active business involvements are minimal since the Volume One book stores they bought from Kingfisher ceased trading.

Contact: Mr V Washtell, Solo Charitable Settlement, Touche Ross & Co, Hill House, 1 Little New St, London, EC4A 3TR. Tel: 0171 936 3000.

KEN FOLLETT
£40,000 NEW

PREFERENCE: education and research, welfare, arts
AGE: 43
WEALTH: £20m-£35m
TRUST LINKS: Follett Trust
COMPANY LINKS: none

Ken Follett must have been deeply shocked by the tragic death of Labour leader John Smith in May 1994. Just the night before he died, Smith had been star speaker at the £500-a-head gala dinner organised by Follett to raise funds for the Party's European election campaign. The best-selling thriller writer has a strong commitment to the cause, and has long been an active Labour fundraiser and supporter. He is a trustee of 'Arts for Labour', which campaigns for the arts and provides left-leaning celebrities for Party functions. His wife, Barbara, has advised leading Labour politicians on the image they present to the media, and is also involved with getting more female Labour MPs into the House through the organisation Emily's List UK.

He is an active supporter of various charities through the **Follett Trust** which he founded in 1990, and which seems to have a general preference for educational causes, the arts and welfare. In 1992/93 the trust made donations of £40,000 funded by an income of £43,000 derived via Gift Aid and covenants. The biggest grant of £16,000 went to the Canon Collins Educational Trust, which aids South African students both in their home country and overseas, which also received £10,000 in the previous year. Other donations for education and research included £7,000 to the Institute for Public Policy Research, and £5,000 to Demos – both independent think-tanks. Given

Follett's literary links, it is not surprising that a number of grants were directed at the arts, including £3,600 to support an actress student, £1,000 to the Writers' and Scholars' Educational Trust, £660 to the Poets' and Writers' Inc (USA), £640 to the Central College of Speech and Drama, and £250 to the Royal Court Theatre. Other sizeable gifts went to a variety of charities, including sums of £1,000 to Shelter, the Royal Marsden Cancer Appeal and the World Memorial Fund for Disaster Relief, and £1,500 to One World Action – which received an additional £14,500 in 1991/92.

Ken Follett was born in Cardiff, and started off in the writing trade as a journalist with the South Wales Echo. He was spurred into starting his first novel to try to finance motor repairs. He could now buy a whole garage-full of cars with the proceeds of his books, which are such guaranteed bestsellers that he received £7 million in advance from a US publisher for his next two. He lives in some style in Chelsea, and is a keen bass player in a blues band. He also reportedly gives financial support to a scholarship fund which was set up to commemorate his wife's former husband, Rick Turner, a South African political activist and lecturer who was murdered in the eighties.

Contact: Mr Martin Follett, Follett Trust, 17 Chiscombe Rd, Yatton, Bristol, BS19 4EE.
Tel: 0117 983 8337.

PETER RIGBY
see below

PREFERENCE: youth, hospices
AGE: 49
WEALTH: £50m-£75m
TRUST LINKS: Rigby Foundation
COMPANY LINKS: Specialist Computer Holdings Ltd

Peter Rigby is a self-made multi-millionaire who is not content to rest on his laurels. He has recently put much of his fortune at risk by committing much of it to his company's latest venture – the 'Byte' chain of computer superstores.

If all goes well, Rigby's wealth will continue to grow. This will be good news for charities because he has recently set up a personal charitable trust, the **Rigby Foundation**, through which to channel some donations. Peter Rigby and his wife Patricia established the foundation in 1992 with an initial payment of £75,000. Accounts on file at the Charity Commission for the year 1992/93 indicate that the trust had not yet got into its grant-making stride. It made no charitable donations, and its capital was still comprised only of the initial cash settlement which generated an income of nearly £5,000. We have, however, been informed that within the last year the bulk of the funds which were initially committed to setting up the foundation were donated to a series of charities dealing with young people, including two hospices and two centres which provide support for terminally ill children. The foundation also provides funds and advice for voluntary organisations wishing to purchase computer equipment.

In addition, Rigby supports various charities through his Specialist Computer Holdings company, notably the Duke of Edinburgh's Award Scheme, of which the firm is a founder charter member.

In a letter to us, Peter Rigby commented that 'if there has been a theme to the initial charitable contributions we have made, it has been towards young people, though this may change in the future, where it is our sole intention to support those charities which we feel able to relate to and where we acknowledge that they are in need of help from what is after all, a relatively small charitable scheme, but where we are keen to donate our contributions towards a truly worthwhile cause.'

Peter Rigby has been involved with computers all his working life. He started out with NCR at the age of eighteen before moving to Honeywell, where he became one of the most successful members of their salesforce. He left when still less than thirty and set up his own company, Specialist Computer Holdings in Birmingham. Its first activity was computer recruitment, a highly lucrative sector in the mid-1970s with large numbers of companies chasing a restricted pool of skilled workers. The turning point for the firm, however, was the introduction of IBM's personal computer range in 1982. With Peter Rigby's nose for sales, and Specialist Computer's position as IBM's first UK distributor, the company won several major accounts and continued to grow rapidly during the next decade. Rigby has now directed his energies into transforming computer retail with his Byte chain of superstores, with four opening in 1993 and a further ten planned or under construction by the end of 1994.

Contact: Mr P Rigby, Rigby Foundation, c/o SCH Ltd, James House, Warwick Rd, Birmingham, B11 2LE. Tel: 0121 766 7000

MICHAEL CORNISH
and family
£39,000

PREFERENCE: not known
AGE: 41

WEALTH: £100m-£250m
TRUST LINKS: none found
COMPANY LINKS: Linpac Group

Linpac, the packaging manufacturing group, has grown to be one of the country's largest private companies under Evan Cornish's careful stewardship over the past three decades. Cornish, the company's founder, recently retired and was succeeded as chair by his son, Michael. The family owns a major stake in the business, which in 1990 made total charitable donations of £39,000. We have not been able, however, to find any grant-making trusts registered in the family's name at the Charity Commission.

Contact: R D Coulam, Marketing & Sales Director, Linpac Group Ltd, 1 Charles Street, Louth, Lincs, LN1 0LA. Tel: 01507 600700

BRUCE COHEN
and family
£37,000 NEW

PREFERENCE: general, Jewish causes
AGE: 54
WEALTH: £20m-£35m
TRUST LINKS: Bruce Cohen Charitable Trust and 8 others
COMPANY LINKS: Courts Furnishers

Through a string of nine charitable trusts set up by past and present members of the family, the Cohens support charitable causes to the tune of at least £37,000 thanks to shares in the Courts furnishing company. The family owns a stake worth around £28 million in the Surrey-based retail chain, but their grant-making trusts hold over half a million shares in their own right.

Bruce Cohen is one of the leading family members in his position as managing director of Courts. He founded the **Bruce Cohen Charitable Trust** in 1976, and by 1992/93 had endowed it with a total of 82,000 Courts shares. These generated an income of £8,000 in the year which financed donations of £7,000, mainly to Jewish causes – such as £2,700 to West London Synagogue and £1,000 to the Weizmann Institute – with some support for general welfare and medical charities.

Paul Cohen is chair of Courts, and makes gifts via the **P C Cohen No.2 Charitable Trust**. He endowed it with 10,000 shares in the company in 1977, and his wife and Bruce Cohen were the original trustees. In 1992/93 the trust's 23,000 Courts shares produced dividends of £1,600 which helped fund gifts of £2,000. These went to a variety of organisations, with some emphasis on Jewish organisations, such as Wimbledon and District Synagogue (£600).

Courts director Edwin Cohen is an active supporter of charitable causes via two grant-making trusts registered in his name. The elder of the two is the **E N Cohen 1973 Charitable Trust**, which currently owns over 80,000 shares in the company with a market value of £253,000 in 1992/93. These generated an income of only £5,500 which supported £3,000 of donations to general causes and Jewish groups, including £300 to West London Synagogue. Along with his wife, Sylvia, he also founded the **Sylvia & Edwin Cohen Charitable Foundation** in 1977 with general charitable purposes. By 1991/92 it held 126,000 shares in Courts, which produced an £8,000 income. Gifts of just under £3,000 were made to various organisations, including £500 each to Framlington College and Jesus College Cambridge, and several grants to Jewish causes.

Both Bruce and Clive were also founding trustees of the relatively small **R J Cohen No.2 Charitable Trust**. This was set up in 1972 by Richard Cohen as a time charity which in 1997 will make over its trust fund to the settlor's children. It holds 21,500 Courts Furnishers shares, producing an income of £1,700 in 1992/93 when donations of only £600 were made. Bruce Cohen was also an original trustee of the **E G Cohen Charitable Trust**, established by Edmund Cohen in 1977 with 10,000 Courts shares. This stake has since grown to 37,000 shares with a 1992/93 market value given as £118,000. The income of £2,400 generated from these shares helped the trust make grants of £2,800 to a number of general and Jewish causes, such as £1,300 to Thames Valley Friends of Ravenswood and £550 to Liberal Jewish Synagogue. Edmund's wife, Daphne Cohen – who was a founding trustee of his trust – has also created a grant-making trust. The **Mrs Daphne Cohen Charitable Trust** was set up in 1986 with her husband as one of its trustees. It owns 24,000 Courts shares with a 1992/93 market value of £77,000, the dividends on which supported charitable gifts of £1,500 in the year to various general causes.

The final two trusts we have uncovered were established by members of the family who have since passed away. When Henry Cohen died in 1988 he bequeathed 71,000 Courts shares worth £150,000 to a trust he had set up in 1977 with Edmund Cohen (see above) as a founding trustee. The **H M Cohen Charitable Foundation** now holds a total of 196,000 shares in the family firm, which in 1992/93 provided an income of £13,000. In the year grants of nearly £16,000 were made, including £3,500 to the West India Committee, £3,000 to Sports Aid Foundation, and £750 to the Furnishing Trades Benevolent

Association. Other causes receiving support included Jewish and medical organisations. Alfred Cohen also died in 1988 and left 90,000 Courts shares to his grant-making trust the **A S Cohen Charitable Foundation**, of which the chair of Courts, Paul Cohen, was an original trustee. In 1992/93 this foundation held Courts shares with a stated market value of £381,000, generating an income of £14,000. Most of this was left undistributed, as grants of only £1,700 were made to medical, welfare and Jewish causes. *Contact: Bruce Cohen Charitable Trust: Mrs L Cohen, Trustee, 28 Abbotsbury Rd, London, W14 8EX. Tel: 0181 640 3322. Mrs Daphne Cohen Charitable Trust: Mr E G Cohen, 15 Somerset Rd, Wimbledon, London, SW19 5JZ. P C Cohen No.2 Charitable Trust, H M Cohen Charitable Foundation, A S Cohen Charitable Foundation: all c/o Courts Furnishers Ltd, The Grange, 1 Central Rd, Morden, Surrey, SM4 5RX. All others c/o Coopers & Lybrand, 9 Greyfriars Rd, Reading, Berks, RG1 1JG.*

SIR GEOFFREY LEIGH
and family
£35,000

PREFERENCE: disability, heritage, Jewish causes, general
AGE: 61
WEALTH: £20m-£35m
TRUST LINKS: Sir Geoffrey Leigh Charitable Trust
COMPANY LINKS: Allied London Properties

Property millionaire Sir Geoffrey Leigh moves in high circles within the Conservative Party, and helps raise funds for the cause. He is one of the handful of entrepreneurs in this book to be intimately involved with the government's City Technology College initiative, as council member of the CTC Trust and sponsor of the eponymous Leigh CTC in Dartford of which he is also chair of governors. He has close links with former PM Lady Thatcher (qv) and acts as one of the directors of the non-charitable grant-maker the Thatcher Foundation. Although he attended the University of Michigan, Sir Geoffrey is heavily involved with Lady Thatcher's *alma mater* as member of the Chancellor's Court of Benefactors at Oxford University and founder of the Margaret Thatcher Centre at Somerville College – as well as being a member of the appeal run by the college from which she graduated. This connection is also apparent in the 1991/92 accounts for the **Sir Geoffrey Leigh Charitable Trust**, which lists a grant of just over £4,000 to the Margaret Thatcher Charitable Trust.

Sir Geoffrey set up his charitable trust just over twenty years ago with himself and his late wife as the original trustees. By 1991/92 it held over half a million shares with a market value of £278,000 in Allied London Properties, the company he chairs. These generated an income of £24,000 for the year, which helped fund donations of £35,000. Apart from the grant to the Margaret Thatcher Charitable Trust, other sizeable gifts included £10,000 to MENCAP, £4,000 to English Heritage, and £3,000 for research at the London School of Economics. There were also various donations to Jewish causes with the Jewish Education Development Trust, the Weizmann Institute Foundation, and the Jewish Federation of Palm Beach County each receiving just over £1,000. A few other Stateside grants were made, such as £570 to Palm Beach Community Chest United Way and £290 to the American Cancer Society. The remaining beneficiaries operated in a variety of sectors, including medical care and the welfare of children and the disabled.

He is also involved on a personal basis with a large number of voluntary organisations. In the field of culture, he is member of the London Historic House Museum Trust and the Royal Fine Art Commission's Art and Architectural Education Trust, and was a founder sponsor of Friends of the British Library. He has interests in education and youth development as member of the American University of Washington's international advisory board, the advisory council of the Prince's Youth Business Trust, and the financial development board of the NSPCC. Other activities include positions on the governing council of Business in the Community and the City appeal committee of Royal Marsden Hospital, as well as a dual role as treasurer and trustee of Action on Addiction.

The Leigh family's wealth is derived mainly from their £18 million holding of around one-fifth of the public Allied London Property Group, which is chaired by Sir Geoffrey. Last year they also sold a tranche of their shares in the company for £9.3 million. Sir Geoffrey is also chair of another firm, Sterling Homes.

Contact: Sir Geoffrey Leigh, Sir Geoffrey Leigh Charitable Trust, 26 Manchester Square, London, W1A 2HU.

RONALD GOLDSTEIN

£34,000

PREFERENCE: Jewish causes
AGE: 57
WEALTH: £20m-£35m
TRUST LINKS: Ramar Charitable Settlement
COMPANY LINKS: sold Superdrug to Kingfisher

Ronald Goldstein and his brother Peter (qv) set up their first toiletries store in the mid-sixties, and their business expanded rapidly over the ensuing decades to become the 300-shop Superdrug chain. In 1987 they sold this successful enterprise to the Kingfisher Group, for a combination of cash and nearly 16 million shares in Kingfisher which they shared equally. Ronald Goldstein keeps an eye on his Kingfisher stake as non-executive director of the group.

Goldstein supports charities through the **Ramar Charitable Settlement**, which he established in 1983 with himself, his wife and his brother as co-trustees. Within two years he had endowed it with 100,000 Superdrug shares worth a quarter of a million pounds, which comprised all its capital. In 1987/88, the year Superdrug was sold, the trust's accounts shows a switch to 170,000 shares in Woolworth Holdings with a market value of £456,000, which became Kingfisher shares when the group was renamed the following year. The 1992/93 accounts note the sale of 100,000 of these Kingfisher shares for a fraction under £0.5 million, which was then invested in Treasury stocks and loans. Along with the remaining Kingfisher stake, the settlement had assets with a market value of £911,000 providing an income of £64,000. In the year, donations of £34,000 were made, somewhat lower than the £234,000 total in 1991/92. The recipients were predominantly Jewish causes, the largest grants were £13,000 to the Ashten Trust, £7,500 to the Friends of the Hebrew University, £4,200 to the Ravenswood Foundation, and £1,000 to the Corinne Burton Trust.

Contact: Mr V Washtell, Ramar Charitable Settlement, Touche Ross & Co, Hill House, 1 Little New St, London, EC4A 3TR. Tel: 0171 936 3000.

MacDONALD-BUCHANAN family

£34,000 NEW

PREFERENCE: education, racing charities, Northamptonshire, Scotland

Ages: 69, 62 respectively
WEALTH: £35m-£50m
TRUST LINKS: MacDonald-Buchanan Charitable Trust, Orrin Charitable Trust
COMPANY LINKS: Distillers (prior to takeover)

The MacDonald-Buchanan family owes its fortune to the national fondness for a 'wee dram', which was tapped by the whisky business they founded, Distillers. Brothers John and James inherited most of their wealth in the form of art treasures and land in 1987, upon the death of their mother, Catherine, who was the only child of the company's founder James Buchanan. She was also the originator of the family's major known conduit for charitable donations, the **MacDonald-Buchanan Charitable Trust**.

Established by the Hon Catherine MacDonald-Buchanan in 1964, with John and James amongst the founding trustees, this trust is in fact an amalgamation of two previous eponymous trusts which together held 100,000 shares in the Distillers company. By 1991/92, this holding had been diversified into a nice portfolio of blue chip shares, and the trust's asset base had grown in value to nearly £2 million providing an income of £162,000. Over one hundred grants were made in the year by this trust, amounting to £183,000. The largest of these was a gift of £50,000 to the Jockey Club Charitable Trust, which together with a £5,000 grant to the Horseracing Museum and other racing charities, bear witness to John's passion for racing and his past role as chair of the Jockey Club. Other grants were made to the causes active in areas close to John's home in Northamptonshire, and James' house in Scotland – examples include £5,000 to both Northants Grammar School and Northants County Scout Appeal, and £6,000 to the Highland Hospice. A number of donations were also directed to armed forces' charities, the largest being £10,500 to the Scots Guards Charitable Fund. There was also support for young people and education, most notably in the form of £10,500 to fund 'MacDonald Buchanan Bursaries and Scholarships.'

The MacDonald-Buchanan Charitable Trust also made two sizeable donations to a pair of other grant-makers with which its trustees have close links – the **Orrin Charitable Trust** which received £12,500, and the **Saranda Charitable Trust** which received £10,000. The first of these was established in 1977 by James MacDonald-Buchanan with some shares in Associated TV and Shell Transport. By 1988/89, the last year for which accounts are available at the Charity Commission, the Orrin Trust had assets of £257,000, an income of £33,000, and made grants totalling £12,000. The recipients of these donations were similar in nature to those of the MacDonald-Buchanan Trust, with an emphasis on racing charities, health and hospices, religion, and Scottish charities. The bigger gifts included £2,000 to the Queen Elizabeth Foundation for the Disabled, and £1,000 each to the National Horseracing Museum, Highland Hospice, St James and St Annes Episcopalian Churches, Salisbury Cathedral Spire Appeal, and the Mayflower Centre. The trust's entry in CAF's *Directory of Grant-*

Making Trusts gives more up to date information for 1991, when the trust made donations of £34,000.

The second of these trusts, the Saranda Charitable Trust, was set up in 1990 by Jean Humphries, who is also a founding trustee of the MacDonald-Buchanan Charitable Trust. The accounts for the period up to April in the same year note assets of £267,000, and an income of £31,000. Thirteen donations totalling £6,500 had already been made to a range of national and international charities, although the largest grant was £1,000 given to St Mary's Church, Tarrant Gunville.

Contact: MacDonald-Buchanan Charitable Trust: Secretary to the Trustees, Kleinwort Benson Trustees Ltd, 10 Fenchurch St, London, EC3M 3LB. Tel: 0171 956 6600. Orrin Charitable Trust: the Secretary, c/o Hedley Foundation, 9 Dowgate Hill, London, EC4R 2SY. Tel: 0171 489 8076. The Saranda Charitable Trust: Mr R J A Furneaux, Richmond Park House, 15 Pembroke Rd, Clifton, Bristol, BS8 3BG. Tel: 0117 973 2291.

PETER GABRIEL
£33,000

PREFERENCE: not known
AGE: 44
WEALTH: less than £20m
TRUST LINKS: none found
COMPANY LINKS: Peter Gabriel Limited, Real World

Peter Gabriel seemingly devotes as much time furthering the cause of world music through his Real World record company as he does advancing his own recordings. As a result, since leaving Genesis to pursue a solo career in the seventies he has not accumulated wealth on the same scale as his erstwhile colleague, the band's drummer and current lead vocalist, Phil Collins (qv). The success of Gabriel's two recent albums, *So* and *Us*, and singles such as *Sledgehammer* and *Kiss that Frog* with their superbly animated videos, has enabled him to maintain his artistic integrity whilst scouring the globe for new and exciting artists to record. He is also involved with the burgeoning world of multi-media technology and recently released a trail-blazing interactive CD-ROM of his music and videos.

Whilst we have been unable to trace any grant-making trusts registered in his name, Peter Gabriel gives support to charities through his private company, **Peter Gabriel Limited**. In 1992 it recorded donations to unspecified recipients of nearly £33,000, slightly down on the previous year's total of £55,000. The most recent accounts also show that Gabriel received dividend payments of £1 million from his company, but was paid no emoluments. In the previous year he received slightly higher dividends of just under £1.5 million, but this was nowhere near the erroneous figure ten times greater which was widely reported in the national press last year.

Contact: Peter Gabriel, c/o Peter Gabriel Ltd, Baker Tilly, Neville House, 55 Eden St, Kingston-upon-Thames, Surrey, KT1 1BN. Tel: 0181 541 0144.

WARNING
Unsolicited requests for funding often lead to annoyance and are rarely productive. This book should not be used as a mailing list. Inappropriate applications waste time and money and may prejudice chances of future success.

TONY BRAMALL

£31,000

PREFERENCE: medicine, welfare, Yorkshire
WEALTH: £35m-£50m
AGE: 58
TRUST LINKS: Tony Bramall Charitable Trust
COMPANY LINKS: Sanderson Bramall; sold stake in C D Bramall

In 1987 Tony Bramall sold the family motor retailing business C D Bramall to the car rental company Avis Europe, netting £45 million for the family's stake. He soon put some of this fortune to very good use by creating the **Tony Bramall Charitable Trust** with an endowment of shares in Cilva Holdings plc worth £600,000. In 1991/92 this substantial asset base generated an income of £72,000, although in that year only £550 was given away. In the following year, however, nearly half of the trust's £66,000 income was used to provide donations in excess of £30,000, most of which went in a gift of £25,000 to St Michael's Hospice in Harrogate, to help fund its relocation. A further £5,000 was paid to an evening in aid of the Yorkshire Children's Hospice, the Dales Countryside Museum, and the Georgian Theatre Trust. A handful of smaller donations were made to national and Yorkshire based medical and disability charities.

The trust is administered from the headquarters of Bramall's new business venture, Sanderson Bramall, which is based near Harrogate. This is another chain of car dealerships which he has built up over the past few years since selling his previous firm. Bramall has a holding of around one-third of the shares in this new company, with a value of around £18 million, and looks well on his way to making a second fortune from motor sales. It also maintains the family's links with the trade which stretch back to when his father first set up shop.

Contact: Mr J R Illingworth, Secretary to the Trustees, Tony Bramall Charitable Trust, Harlow Court, Otley Rd, Beckwithshaw, Harrogate, W Yorks, HG3 1PU. Tel: 01423 569961.

TOPHAM BRINTON and family

£31,000

PREFERENCE: Kidderminster
AGE: 54
WEALTH: £20m-£35m
TRUST LINKS: none found
COMPANY LINKS: Brintons Carpets

The private Brintons carpet company has been controlled by the Brinton family since it was established over two hundred years ago, and Michael Brinton is currently chair having taken over from his elder brother, Topham. Whilst we have been unable to trace any grant-making trusts registered in their name, they do support good causes indirectly via their company. In 1990/91 it made charitable donations of £31,000 with a preference for local causes in areas where the firm operates, and had a total community contributions figure in the order of £50,000. Topham Brinton is involved with business and enterprise development in the West Midlands as vice-chair of the CBI in the region, as well as acting as chair of the West Midlands Enterprise Development Agency and CENTEC.

Contact: Mrs Barbara Turner, Welfare Officer, Brintons Ltd, Exchange St, Kidderminster, DY10 1AG. Tel: 01562 820000.

SIR ROBERT DOUGLAS

£30,000 **NEW**

PREFERENCE: Christian causes, medicine, West Midlands

WEALTH: less than £20m

TRUST LINKS: R M Douglas Charitable Trust, Sir Robert Douglas Training Fund

COMPANY LINKS: Tilbury Douglas

Sir Robert Douglas helped found his family's fortune when he set up the Douglas Group of construction companies over fifty years ago. When it merged with the Tilbury Group, the whole family received a reported £35 million worth of shares in the new Tilbury Douglas company, in return for their stake in the family firm. Both Sir Robert and his son John (qv) make charitable donations through grant-making trusts.

Sir Robert set up the **R M Douglas Charitable Trust** in 1966, with 100,000 shares in the family firm, and is still a trustee with his son. This trust has general charitable purposes, and in particular provides assistance for ex-employees of the company and their dependents. It also has a preference for charities in Staffordshire, where Sir Robert lives. By 1991/92, the trust had assets worth over £215,000 as well as 103,000 Tilbury Douglas shares. The proceeds of these investments provided an income of £24,000 in the year, which helped cover charitable donations of £22,000 and payments to former company employees of £8,000. The largest grants were restricted to Staffordshire, and the Dunstall area in particular, and showed a preference for churches and medical causes. Donations to the former included £5,000 to St Mary's Church in Dunstall and £1,000 to the vicar of Dunstall, £1,500 to Lichfield Cathedral, and £1,000 to St James' Church Restoration Appeal. Medical gifts included £5,000 to Burton Graduate Medical Centre, of which Sir Robert is president, £1,000 to St Giles Hospice, and £500 to Stafford Hospital Scanner Appeal. Other donations tended to be relatively small, and went to a range of general national charities, with some in the Midlands.

● BIGGEST DONORS TO CHRISTIAN CAUSES

Kirby & Maurice Laing	*£3,600,000*
Tim Sainsbury	*£3,600,000*
Bob Edmiston	*£3,000,000*
Wates family	*£1,450,000*
Julian Hodge	*£1,000,000*
O'Hea family	*£439,000*
John Templeton	*£400,000*
Cliff Richard	*£300,000*
The Queen	*£208,000*
John Douglas	*£115,000*
Robert Douglas	*£30,000*

Sir Robert is also actively involved with the **Sir Robert Douglas Training Fund**, a relatively small trust set up by him and a number of other employees of the family firm in 1981 to mark the fiftieth anniversary of the founding of the Douglas Group of construction companies. It owns 7,300 shares in Tilbury Douglas and the most recent accounts show payments totalling £2,000 for prizes and books to construction industry trainees. The Tilbury Douglas company itself made charitable donations of around £3,000 in 1991.

When contacted, Sir Robert requested not to appear in this publication.

Contact: R M Douglas Charitable Trust: Sir Robert Douglas, Dunstall Hall, Barton under Needwood, nr Burton-on-Trent, Staffs, DE13 8BE. Sir Robert Douglas Training Fund: Mrs J M Latchwood, 295 George Rd, Erdington, Birmingham, B23 7RZ.

JAMES HARTNETT

£30,000

PREFERENCE: mental health
WEALTH: £20m-£35m
TRUST LINKS: Hartnett Charitable Trust
COMPANY LINKS: Eurotherm International

James Hartnett, the founder of Eurotherm International plc, in 1978 diverted part of his valuable holding of shares in the electronics equipment company into the **Hartnett Charitable Trust**. He established this grant-making trust with an initial endowment of 55,000 shares, and it now holds 157,500 shares in Eurotherm with a current listing value of around £4 each. Over the past five years the trust has donated around £30,000 per annum. Examples of grants made over the period include £50,000 to the Prince's Trust, £30,000 to King's College School of Medicine, £19,000 to the Royal Postgraduate Medical School, and £5,000 to the Armenian Earthquake Appeal.

In March 1990 Hartnett gave a further 300,000 shares from his personal holding in Eurotherm directly to the Royal Postgraduate Medical School at Hammersmith. This was to be used to help fund research into mental health under the aegis of Richard Frackowiak who was appointed to the chair set up for that purpose. The shares have since been sold by the Royal Postgraduate Medical School, realising in excess of £2 million.

Contact: Mr J A Hartnett, Hartnett Charitable Trust, Belmoredean, Maplehurst Rd, West Grinstead, nr. Horsham, West Sussex, RH13 6RN.

JULIAN RICHER

£29,000

PREFERENCE: welfare, environment
AGE: 35
WEALTH: less than £20m
TRUST LINKS: see below
COMPANY LINKS: Richer Sounds

The very aptly-named Julian Richer has made his money by helping people spend less of theirs! He runs and owns Richer Sounds, which is renowned in the world of hi-fi for selling audio components and systems at bargain prices. The public firm also merits an entry in the *Guinness Book of Records* because its original store near London Bridge has the highest figure for retail sales per square foot in the world.

In 1991/92 Richer Sounds made gifts totalling £29,000 with a preference for social welfare, environmental and heritage causes, and the company states in its brochures that it gives one-fifth of profits to employees and charities. Julian Richer is also involved with the Persula Foundation, a charitable company which was only established in March this year. In association with the Homeless Network, the Persula Foundation has recently funded 'On the Right Track', an innovative computer terminal system which provides information for the homeless. This is being piloted at Charing Cross railway station in London, before hopefully spreading across the whole of the capital. Because it is so new, however, we have no other information on the foundation's activities or possible size.

Julian Richer has been a director of the Persula foundation along with other Richer Sounds company executives, but is neither a director or trustee at the present time.

Contact: Richer Sounds plc, Richer House, 202 Long Lane, London, SE1 4QB. Tel: 0171 407 5525.

JOHN BLOOR

£28,000

PREFERENCE: not known
AGE: 49
WEALTH: £75m-£100m
TRUST LINKS: none found
COMPANY LINKS: Bloor Holdings

John Bloor single-handedly saved a part of British motorcycling history when he bought the Triumph marque from its liquidators in 1983. He has since pumped money into Triumph from his successful Bloor Holdings building group, which enabled it to develop a competitive range of new models. John Bloor owns 95% of Bloor Holdings, and although we have not found any charitable trusts registered in his name, the company made grants to charities totalling £28,000 in 1990/91.

Contact: D Mehta, Financial Director, Bloor Holdings, Ashby Rd, Measham, Burton-on-Trent, Staffs, DE12 7JP. Tel: 01530 270100.

MARQUESS OF TAVISTOCK
and family

£26,000 NEW

PREFERENCE: welfare, medicine, Bedfordshire

AGE: 54
WEALTH: £100m-£250m
TRUST LINKS: Woburn 1986 Charitable Trust, Woburn Trust
COMPANY LINKS: Berkeley Development Capital, Berkeley Grovett & Co

The Marquess of Tavistock is the son and heir of the Duke of Bedford, who has lived in tax-efficient in Monte Carlo for the past twenty years. The family's Bedford Estates holds a considerable fortune in art and land, including their much-visited stately home, Woburn Abbey in Bedfordshire. Their holdings in the central London area of Bloomsbury are highlighted by place names such as Bedford Square, Tavistock Square and Russell Square, the latter being the family name. We have been able to trace two charitable trusts established by members of the family.

The **Woburn 1986 Charitable Trust** was created in 1986 by Lord Howland, who is Tavistock's son and heir, and both father and son were founding trustees. It has general charitable aims, including the relief of poverty of retired Bedford Estates' employees living near Woburn. The only accounts on file at the Charity Commission for this trust show that in 1988 it held assets to the value of three quarters of a million pounds, half in cash and the remainder in property, which produced an income of £37,000. During the year the trust spent around £20,000 on property repairs and insurance, presumably on accommodation for ex-employees, and made unspecified charitable donations totalling £6,000. The accounts also note that the trust had submitted a planning application to construct a twenty unit home for the elderly in Woburn.

Tavistock's grandfather, the 12th Duke of Bedford, set up the **Woburn Trust** (also known as the 12th Duke of Bedford Settlement of 11 June 1946) just after the war with a bundle of shares worth around £10,000. Since his death in the early fifties, this charitable trust has grown considerably in size and in 1989/90 held assets worth £372,000. These provided an income of £16,000 which helped support grants of £20,000. The family's close links with the sport of horse-racing (the Marquess is director of United Racecourse and Lord Howland is a partner in Bloomsbury Stud) are evident in some of the donations made. The largest gift of £10,000 was directed at the British Horse Society Development Fund, and other similar grants included £1,000 to Mark Davies Injured Riders Club and £500 to the New Chasers Charitable Trust. The remaining donations were directed at a variety of causes, with some emphasis on medical organisations, such as £5,000 to Trustees for Former United Birmingham Hospitals and £1,000 to Llandrindod Wells Hospital Appeal, and charities operating in Bedfordshire.

This preference for medical causes is reflected in Tavistock's position as trustee of the National Hospital for Neurology and Neurosurgery Development Foundation. He is also honorary trustee, and past chair, of the Kennedy Memorial Trust. On the business front, the Marquess is a director of Berkeley Grovett & Co and United Racecourse Holdings, and was a director of Trafalgar House from 1977-91.

Contact: Woburn 1986 Charitable Trust: J C Wright, Bedford Estates, Bedford Office, Woburn, Milton Keynes, MK17 9PQ. Tel: 01525 290666. Woburn Trust: Lord Hugh Russell, The Bell House, Dolau, Llandridnod Wells, Powys, LD1 5UN. Tel: 01547 81615.

NIGEL MANSELL

£25,000

(but see below)

PREFERENCE: hospitals, children, education
AGE: 40
WEALTH: £35m-£50m
TRUST LINKS: none found
COMPANY LINKS: none

The recent spate of unfortunate deaths in the Grand Prix world has served to highlight the considerable risks taken by Nigel Mansell to earn his fortune. Having at long last won the Formula One World Drivers' Championship in 1992, he was lured to the rich pastures of Indy-car racing in the US by the Newman-Haas racing team, co-owned by the film star Paul Newman. Mansell promptly became champion of this series in his rookie year, which did not harm his earning potential. Following the death of his erstwhile rival, Ayrton Senna, in 1994, Nigel Mansell was tempted back to race for the Williams Formula One team on a part-time basis when race dates do not clash with his prior Indy-car commitments.

Mansell has something of a reputation as a generous, but relatively low-key supporter of causes such as hospitals, schools and children's charities. Accordingly, we have not been able to trace any grant-making trusts registered in his name, but he reportedly made a £25,000 gift to a children's ward at Poole General Hospital in 1990.

Contact: Nigel Mansell, c/o Sue Membery, The Old Smithy, Sealeys Farm, Church Rd, West Huntspill, Somerset.

ALAN PASCOE
£25,000 **NEW**

PREFERENCE: athletics, medicine, disability, general
AGE: 47
WEALTH: less than £20m
TRUST LINKS: Alan Pascoe Charitable Trust
COMPANY LINKS: Alan Pascoe Associates

In the mid-seventies, when Alan Pascoe was one of our top 400 metres hurdlers, there was no real money to be made out of competing at the highest levels in the still amateur pursuit of athletics. Instead, since his retirement from the sport in 1978, he has generated a fortune of at least £2 million from his sponsorship and marketing company, Alan Pascoe Associates.

Pascoe has clearly not forgotten his roots, as he is a supporter of various athletics organisations through the **Alan Pascoe Charitable Trust** which he set up in 1986 with general charitable purposes and an original endowment of 300 ordinary shares in his firm. By 1992, the trust had built up a substantial asset base worth over £400,000 along with some 34,000 unvalued shares in the public Aegis Group. This capital generated a £42,000 income in the year, of which £25,000 was distributed via charitable grants. The majority went to various sports-related bodies, including £3,000 to the Team Solent Young Athlete Fund (a regular recipient), £3,000 to the British Olympic Appeal, £1,500 to the Paralympic Appeal, £1,300 to the Lord's Taverners, and £250 to the Ron Pickering Memorial Fund. A total of £1,300 was also directed to the Cameron Sharp Appeal, which aids the former Scottish sprinter who was paralysed in an accident. The remaining donations benefited a variety of causes, notably those active in the field of medical care, such as £3,000 to the Evelina Children's Appeal at Guy's Hospital, and £2,000 to both the Portsmouth Renal Unit Amenities Fund and Great Ormond Street Hospital. Other major gifts included £2,500 to Childline and £2,000 to 'V & J Trister Care A/C'.

Contact: Mr E P S Leask, Alan Pascoe Charitable Trust, 2nd Floor, The Old Treasury, 7 Kings Road, Portsmouth, Hants, PO5 4DJ.
Tel: 01705 875187.

JOHN THORNTON

£25,000 NEW

PREFERENCE: general, education, recreation, art, animal welfare
AGE: 50
WEALTH: less than £20m
TRUST LINKS: John Thornton Charitable Trust, Mandy Thornton Memorial Trust
COMPANY LINKS: Thorntons

In 1988, the year the family confectionery business Thorntons was floated on the stock exchange, John Thornton – company chair and grandson of its founder – created an eponymous trust with a block of shares in the company. The **John Thornton Charitable Trust** now holds around 100,000 Thorntons shares, which produced an income of nearly £7,000 in 1992/93. A single donation of £1,000 was made to the National AIDS Trust, and in the previous year a pair of £2,000 grants had been made to the RNIB Looking Glass Appeal and Derby Cathedral Organ Appeal. This trust was established to support general charitable causes, and specifically the provision of recreational facilities for the welfare of the general public.

A further 50,000 Thorntons shares comprise the asset base of the **Mandy Thornton Memorial Trust**. This is a more recent grant-maker which John Thornton set up in 1992 with general charitable aims, but in particular to promote education and appreciation of the arts, and to relieve the suffering of animals in need of care and attention. In its first year of operation, however, the trust appeared to be consolidating its position, as it had an income of just over £2,000 but made no charitable gifts. Apart from his activities through these two trusts, John Thornton makes other gifts, and we were advised that his total charitable donations last year came to around £25,000.

Each year the Thorntons confectionery company, which is based in Derbyshire, donates about £60,000 as well as gifts of its products, to various community causes. We have not, however, included the value of this support in the figure for John Thornton's personal gifts because the Thornton family controls less than half of the company's shares divided between about forty individuals. Of this total, John Thornton and his children personally own less than 10%, which puts their wealth at not more than £10 million. John's cousin, Michael Thornton (qv) is deputy chair and company secretary of Thorntons, and is also an active supporter of various charitable causes.

Contact: John Thornton Charitable Trust and Mandy Thornton Memorial Trust: Mr C J Thornton, Thorntons plc, Thornton Park, Somercotes, Derby, DE55 4XJ.
Tel: 01773 540550.

WILLIAM and FRANK BRAKE

£23,000 NEW

PREFERENCE: general
Ages: 62, 60 respectively
WEALTH: £100m-£250m
TRUST LINKS: William Brake Charitable Trust, Frank Brake Charitable Trust
COMPANY LINKS: Brake Bros

Brothers William and Frank Brake set up a pair of near identical charitable trusts on the same day in 1984, amended the deeds of settlement on the same day in May 1993, and appointed the same two trustees. The trusts differ not only in their names, but also in their size, as one appears to have a bigger asset base. The **William Brake Charitable Trust** is currently the larger of the two and was established in 1993 with 145,000 shares in the food company Brake Bros. The **Frank Brake Charitable Trust** received 45,000 Brake Bros shares from Frank Brake also in 1993. Because their deeds were altered only last year, there are as yet no accounts on file at the Charity Commission for either of these trusts, so it is not possible to give an indication either of preferred causes or their size. They were established to support general charitable organisations.

The Brake Bros frozen food firm was set up by William, Frank, and their late brother Peter, over 35 years ago. It has since grown via a 1986 stock market flotation into a major operator in the field, with a value of more than one-quarter of a billion pounds. William is chair of the business and Frank is managing director, and both hold a substantial stake. The company itself made charitable contributions to the value of £23,000 in 1991, which we have listed as part of the brothers' personal donations given their significant holding.

The solicitors for Frank and William Brake stated that they would prefer that no entry be made for either of them.

Contact for both Frank Brake and William Brake Charitable Trusts: Mr B Rylands, Gill Turner & Tucker, Colman House, King St, Maidstone, Kent, ME14 1JE. Tel: 01622 759051.

LADY EILEEN JOSEPH
£23,000
PREFERENCE: general

AGE: 70
WEALTH: £20m-£35m
TRUST LINKS: Lady Eileen Joseph Charitable Foundation
COMPANY LINKS: none

Lady Eileen Joseph inherited a considerable fortune in 1982 from her husband, the late Sir Maxwell Joseph, who was responsible for creating the Grand Metropolitan foods and leisure group. An astute business-woman herself, she has since enhanced her worth through stock investments in the hotels industry. She has also set up the **Lady Eileen Joseph Charitable Foundation** through which to make donations for general charitable purposes.

There is, however, relatively little information available concerning the activities of this grant-making trust, which was established in 1987. The Charity Commission gives a figure of £234,000 for the trust's 1991/92 income, but there are no accounts on file. Data from CAF's *Directory of Grant-Making Trusts* indicates that in the previous year the foundation had assets of just over half a million pounds, an income of £180,000 and made donations of £23,000. Due to this lack of data it is not possible to determine whether the foundation has any preferred causes or areas of support.

Contact: Mr A A Davis, Trustee, Lady Eileen Joseph Charitable Foundation, Stoy Hayward, 8 Baker St, London, W1M 1DA. Tel: 0171 486 5888.

SIR JOHN GIELGUD
£22,000 **NEW**
PREFERENCE: arts, animal welfare, general
AGE: 90

WEALTH: unknown

TRUST LINKS: Sir John Gielgud Charitable Trust

COMPANY LINKS: none

Sir John Gielgud, the grand old man of British theatre and film, has notched up countless performances ranging from Shakespeare and the classics, through *Brideshead Revisited*, to his Oscar-winning performance as Dudley Moore's disdainful butler in *Arthur*. As a result, he is one of the most famous actors in the country, but has never been unwilling to take a risk or two with his career. Considerably less is known about his charitable activities, although appropriately enough he is president of the Shakespeare Reading Society, and a past president of RADA. We have, however, uncovered the **Sir John Gielgud Charitable Trust** through which he makes donations to various causes.

He created the trust in 1988, and funds it with regular payments via covenants and Gift Aid. In 1992 the trust had an income of £32,000 from donations and associated tax rebates, and gave away £22,000 to a variety of causes. A number of gifts went to supporting the arts, through grants to both individuals and organisations – including sponsorships of around £1,000 each to a pair of art students, and grants of £570 to New York Public Library for the Performing Arts, £280 to the Theatre Development Foundation, and £200 to Soho Theatre Company. A number of other gifts were directed at animal welfare groups, the largest being £1,000 to Lynx, over £500 to the International Fund for Animal Welfare, and other beneficiaries included Animal Vigilantes, Chicken's Lib, and Political Animal Lobby. The remaining donations were received by a wide selection of organisations active in overseas development, conservation and medical research, and with the young, the elderly and the disabled.

Sir John's solicitors stated that he did not wish to appear in this publication as he seeks neither publicity for his gifts nor unsolicited applications for money.

Contact: A D Chambers, Sir John Gielgud Charitable Trust, KPMG Peat Marwick, PO Box 486, 1 Puddle Dock, Blackfriars, London, EC4V 3PD. Tel: 0171 236 8000.

JOHN APTHORP

£21,000

PREFERENCE: education, arts, wildlife, disability, North London, Hertfordshire.

AGE: 58

WEALTH: £50m-£75m

TRUST LINKS: John Apthorp Charitable Trust; Milly Apthorp Charitable Trust

COMPANY LINKS: Wizard and Majestic wine; sold stake in Bejam

John Apthorp clearly believes charity begins at home – he personally supports a number of organisations operating local to his Radlett home. So, apparently, did his late mother, who largely as a result of her son's business acumen was able to establish a major grant-making trust which gives over £500,000 a year to the Barnet area.

John Apthorp was the driving force behind one of the high-street success stories of the 1980s – the Bejam frozen food chain. He built up the company over a period of 21 years, and eventually floated it on the stock market. Now the famous Bejam name is nowhere to be seen, having been subsumed within the identity of a former rival. In the late 1980s the company was faced with a takeover bid from one of its smaller competitors which looked unlikely to succeed, especially as the Apthorp family held nearly one-third of Bejam's equity. After a somewhat acrimonious battle, however, Iceland Frozen Foods managed to gain control of their target in 1989 and have since rebadged the former Bejam outlets.

This takeover forced John Apthorp into premature retirement, but he did not leave empty-handed – the family shares fetched £70 million. Some of this wealth has since been diverted to a number of good causes through two main channels. In the year he left Bejam, Apthorp gave away nearly £140,000 via his personal trust, the **John Apthorp Charitable Trust,** including gifts of £103,000 to the Edge Grove preparatory school in Hertfordshire and £25,000 to the Game Conservancy Trust. For the past few years the trust's income has been around £65-80,000, but the amounts given have fluctuated considerably. In 1991/92 grants totalling £76,000 were made, including £50,000 to the building fund at Glyndebourne, and £15,000 to the Beds & Herts Pastoral Foundation. In 1992/3, however, the amount donated dropped to £21,000, leaving nearly £55,000 of the income unallocated. Only five donations were made, the largest being £8,346 to the Hearing Research Trust, a further £8,000 to Edge Grove school, and £3,500 to Talking Newspaper.

John Apthorp is also one of the two current trustees of the **Milly Apthorp Charitable Trust**, which was established by his mother Mildred in 1982, the year before he set up his own trust. By 1986 she had endowed it with over 2 million shares in her son's company Bejam. In the year of its takeover by Iceland, the shares were sold for £3.1 million. Milly Apthorp died later that year, leaving her trust a further £4.8 million. It trust now has assets of nearly £8.6 million which generate an annual income of just under £900,000. In the past few years it has been rapidly switching its capital from Treasury Deposits to property, acquiring a £2.5 million portfolio of freehold offices and retail units. At present, the trust spends its income in two ways. Nearly two-thirds is administered by the London Borough of Barnet, and is given to charitable activities in that area, especially those dealing with the young, the elderly, and the disabled.

The remainder is distributed directly by the trustees as grants to charities. Past donations have included a £210,000 donation for cancer-treating equipment at the Royal Free Hospital and a £200,000 donation towards the refurbishment of Apthorp Lodge, a home for the elderly in Barnet. In 1992/93 the major grants were £150,000 to the Whitefield Youth and Community Centre in Barnet (which is to receive a total of £500,000), and £65,700 to fund two 'Milly Apthorp Surgical Research Fellowships' for the RAFT plastic surgery charity based at Mount Vernon Hospital (which is to receive a total of £328,500).

Recently, Apthorp has switched his business focus from food to drink. He is the chair of Wizard, the private wine warehouse company based in Hertfordshire, which has recently acquired the Majestic chain. He is also a backer of International Data and Communication, which supplies business information and listings.

Contacts: John Apthorp Charitable Trust: Lawrence S Fenton, c/o Stoy Hayward, 54 Baker St, London W1M 1DA. Tel: 0171 486 5888. For the Milly Apthorp Charitable Trust contact Mr L S Fenton, at the address given above, or for Barnet: Grants Unit, Chief Executive's Dept, London Borough of Barnet, Town Hall, Hendon, London NW4 4BG. Tel: 0181 202 8282 ext. 2092.

RAJ BAGRI
£21,000 **NEW**

PREFERENCE: see below
AGE: 63
WEALTH: £50m-£75m
TRUST LINKS: Bagri Foundation
COMPANY LINKS: Metdist, Minmetco

Raj Bagri is one of the few Asian entrepreneurs to feature in our listing of wealthy givers, which is mainly reflective of their lack of proper representation amongst the ranks of the rich in this country. He has, however, established an eponymous charitable foundation with a substantial six-figure income.

Bagri himself claims that he does not know how much money he has actually got, and anyway argues that: 'what my worth is is not of major concern to anybody. I'd rather be known by how good or bad I am' (*Independent on Sunday*, 20/12/92). He put some of his money where his mouth is in 1990, when he set up the **Bagri Foundation**, in order to support charities both in Britain and overseas. The foundation was established as a private limited company, and its present directors include Raj Bagri, his wife Usha, and his son Apurv. It clearly has close connections with Bagri's company Metdist, as it is administered from the same Cannon Street offices and the bulk of its income is classified as 'subscriptions – corporate', presumably from Bagri's company. However, as the Bagri family totally controls the Metdist group, this money is indirectly coming out of their own pockets.

Over the past few years, the foundation has received £1.25 million in the form of corporate subscriptions, and now has assets of nearly £1.7 million, including a £375,000 loan. Given its substantial recent income, the Bagri Foundation has made relatively little in the way of charitable donations. In 1990/91 grants totalled £63,000, in the next year they dropped to only £20,500 – and in neither year's accounts were the recipients of these donations specified. Given Bagri's close links with his home country – he is vice-chair of the Indian Institute of Culture and chair of the Indian Chamber of Commerce in the UK – it would not be surprising if he directed the bulk of his foundation's grants to Indian causes. It appears that the foundation is building up an asset base to generate a long-term source of income for its philanthropic activities. It is hard to be sure, however, because there are no accounts on file at the Charity Commission, and those submitted to Companies' House contain fairly minimal information.

Although he disagrees with many of the estimates of his worth, Bagri is a very wealthy man by any standards thanks to the international metal market. Now a naturalised British citizen, he was born in India and started out as a filing clerk in a local metal company, Metal Distributors. He rapidly worked his way up the company hierarchy, and by 1959 was in charge of establishing its London office. In 1970, in order to join the 'ring' of the London Metal Exchange, he set up his own company, Metdist. Ten years later he made the break from the Indian company, and also diversified into the manufacture of metal products by founding another company, Minmetco. The Metdist group is now one of the largest privately held businesses in the UK. Bagri has recently reached the pinnacle of his profession – at the end of 1992 he was chosen as the new head of the London Metal Exchange. No doubt because of the extra work this entails, he now leaves the day-to-day running of Metdist to his son, Apurv.

Contact: Mr J M Brito, Chief Financial Officer, The Bagri Foundation, 80 Cannon St, London EC4N 6EJ. Tel: 0171 606 8321 ext. 233.

PHILIP BAXENDALE

£21,000

PREFERENCE: health, Hampshire
AGE: 67
WEALTH: less than £20m
TRUST LINKS: Philip Baxendale Charitable Trust
COMPANY LINKS: Baxi Partnership

Philip Baxendale is considerably less wealthy than he might have been. In 1983 he sold his stake in the private family company, Richard Baxendale and Sons, at a knock-down price to the workforce, creating the Baxi Partnership. He has since missed out on increased profits and share prices which could have netted him nearly £300 million, and his only link with the company is his role as president.

He has recently moved from Lancashire, where Baxi is based, to the New Forest. This is reflected in some of the charitable donations he makes through the **Philip Baxendale Charitable Trust**, which he set up 1972. In 1992/93 he supported various Hampshire based causes such as the Wessex Cancer Trust (£2,000), Southampton Breast Cancer Fund (£1,000) and Lymington Hospital League of Friends (£500). There was further support of medical causes through donations of £1,000 to the British Heart Foundation and the League of Friends of MacMillan Nurses. A few other donations went to overseas causes such as the IT Development Group (£1,000) and Population Concern (£1,000), although the largest single donation of £5,000 went to the Partnership Trust.

Baxendale is also trustee of the **Richard Baxendale Charitable Trust**, which was named after its founder. This trust was initially endowed with a number of shares in Richard Baxendale and Sons, and now has assets in stocks and bonds worth £174,000. These funded donations of £16,000 in 1993 which are directed to a variety of general charitable causes as expressed by the late settlor to the trustees. The largest grants were £3,000 to the Family Holiday Organisation, £2,000 to both BLESMA and the University of Buckingham, and £1,000 each to Army Benevolent Fund, the Methodist Church Central Board of Finance, International Donkey Protection, and the Blue Cross. The gifts made by this trust have not been included in the calculations of Philip Baxendale's total known donations, however, because he makes no direct financial input. Neither trust wishes to receive unsolicited applications from individuals or charitable organisations.

Contact: For both Philip Baxendale Charitable Trust and Richard Baxendale Charitable Trust: Miss Olive Watson, 34 Margaret Rd, Penwortham, Preston, PR1 9QT. Tel: 01772 36201.

ERIC CLAPTON
£21,000 NEW

PREFERENCE: youth, drug & alcohol abuse, disability, welfare
AGE: 49
WEALTH: £20m-£35m
TRUST LINKS: Eric Clapton's Charitable Trust
COMPANY LINKS: Marshbrook Ltd

Eric Clapton's guitar playing skills are legendary, and since his early days with the Yardbirds and John Mayall's Bluesbreakers to his latterday collaborations with the likes of Tina Turner and Phil Collins, he has always been regarded as one of Britain's leading axe-wielders. He now

appears to be benefiting from his three decades in the music business – in 1992 he received £7.3 million from his private company, Marshbrook, following emoluments of £3.9 million and £5.1 million in the previous two years.

Some of this increasing fortune may find its way into **Eric Clapton's Charitable Trust**, which he founded in 1984. This grant-maker was set up for the general relief of poverty and to advance education, but in particular to fund projects which help young people in need, the rehabilitation of drug abusers and alcoholics, or deal with disability or mental health. In 1991/92 Clapton made donations totalling £21,000 from this trust, which he funds annually by covenanted payments. Most of this went in a gift of just under £20,500 to Chemical Dependency, with the only other donation being £500 to the RNLI. In previous years the total amount donated by the trust was considerably lower, although in 1990/91 £5,000 was given to the Cancer Help Fund.

We were informed by his representative that Eric Clapton did not wish to be included in this book and that he does not welcome unsolicited appeals of any kind.

Contact: Mr J E Hamilton, Eric Clapton's Charitable Trust, Messrs Ernst & Young, Becket House, 1 Lambeth Palace Rd, London, SE1 7EU. Tel: 0171 931 4832

ROBERT SPERRING
see below

PREFERENCE: general, biological research
WEALTH: less than £20m
TRUST LINKS: Sperring Foundation
COMPANY LINKS: sold Sperrings

Robert Sperring made an estimated £20 million when he sold his eponymous chain of newsagents and convenience stores and went into retirement. A part of this money has found its way into the **Sperring Foundation**, which he established in 1988. Set up with general charitable purposes, the only donation that appears to have been made by the foundation was a payment in 1989/90 of £20,000 to the UK Associates of the Bermuda Biological Association. Bob Sperring is a trustee of this registered charity, which will receive a further £10,000 from his foundation. The most recent accounts on file at the Charity Commission, for the year 1990/91, show that the Sperring Foundation made no charitable gifts in the year, although it received £10,500 income from its founder via covenants and had cash reserves of £25,000.

Contact: Sperring Foundation, c/o Messr Rothman Pantall & Co, 10 Romsey Rd, Eastleigh, Hants, SO50 9AL. Tel: 01703 614555.

STEVE MORGAN

£18,000

(but see below)

PREFERENCE: general
AGE: 41
WEALTH: £100m-£250m
TRUST LINKS: none found
COMPANY LINKS: Redrow Group

Steve Morgan has built up a cash and shares fortune worth over two hundred million pounds thanks to the steady growth of his Redrow homes construction company. Until recently he owned virtually all of the shares in the group, but floated around half his stake in spring this year. He remains relatively unfazed by his new-found wealth, as he told the *Guardian*: 'I don't think the money will change me. I haven't been short of a bob or two for the past few years and, after all, you can drive only one car or wear one suit at a time' (3/2/94).

We have been unable to find any grant-making trusts registered in Morgan's name, but given his strong holding in Redrow the support given by the company to charitable causes can be taken as emanating indirectly from him. The *Guide to Company Giving* states that in 1990/91 the Redrow Group made donations of £7,500 to a number of national and local causes chosen by regional managers. Morgan reportedly offered a £10,000 reward for information relating to the abduction and murder of the young James Bulger in Liverpool.

When contacted, Steve Morgan noted that the figures given above for Redrow's charitable activities are 'very much understated'. He also stated that 'My preference is for such charitable donations to be made privately and quietly, both from a corporate and personal viewpoint', and that over the past twelve months donations have been considerably ahead of the sums we have quoted above.

Contact: Debby Goodband, PR & Marketing Manager, Redrow Group, Redrow House, St David's Park, Ewloe, Clwyd, CH5 3PW. Tel: 01244 520044.

EARL OF BRADFORD

£17,000 NEW

PREFERENCE: West Midlands, general
AGE: 46

WEALTH: £20m-£35m

TRUST LINKS: Seventh Earl of Bradford's 1981 Charitable Trust; Seventh Earl of Bradford and Countess of Bradford's Castle Bromwich Parochial Charity

COMPANY LINKS: none

The Earl of Bradford is an active supporter of charities, mainly in the West Midlands area, through two charitable trusts registered in his name. The larger of the two is the **Seventh Earl of Bradford's 1981 Charitable Trust** which in 1990/91 made donations of £12,000 supported by assets of over a quarter of a million pounds. This trust was set up with general charitable objects, to support ex-employees of the Bradford Estate, and to relieve the poverty of people living on the Earl's land. The largest donations made in the year were £3,600 to United Non-Ecclesiastical Charities at Tong, and £1,000 to the Nordoff Robbins Music Therapy Centre. A number of smaller gifts were made to a variety of causes local to Lord Bradford's home in Shropshire, such as £800 for roof repairs at Weston-under-Lizard Church and £750 to East Shropshire Support Group for Compton Hospice. The remaining grants were directed to a variety of national charities, including grants of £750 to Action Research, the Samaritans, RNLI and the Tidy Britain Group.

The other grant-maker established by Bradford is the **Seventh Earl of Bradford and Countess of Bradford's Castle Bromwich Parochial Charity**, which in 1989/90 reported assets of just under £100,000 and made just two donations of £2,500 each to Castle Bromwich Hall Gardens Trust, of which the Earl is a trustee, and St Mary & St Margaret Church at Castle Bromwich. The objects of this trust restrict it to supporting charitable bodies operating in the Castle Bromwich area, and the only recipients of grants made have been the two causes listed above.

Amongst his other charitable activities, the Earl is patron of the Foundation for Conductive Education, which is based at Birmingham University, and was president of its 'Stepping Stones' appeal until this year. He is also chair of Wrekin Heritage Association, president of Telford and District Victims' Support Scheme, Newport Branch RNLI and Wolverhampton Friends of the Samaritans, and vice-president of Re-solv – the campaign against drug abuse. He is a trustee of the Weston Park Foundation and a member of the appeal committee for the Institute of Orthopaedics at Oswestry.

Lord Bradford's wealth is derived from an extensive art collection, worth in the region of £10 million, and the 13,000 Shropshire acres owned by the family. His fortune took a bit of a knock, however, after the collapse, four years ago, of a heritage company of which he was a shareholder. He may console himself with a gourmet meal at Porters' Restaurant in Covent Garden, which he owns. Until April this year, Bradford was chair of the private Beacon Broadcasting and Communications company.

Contact: Seventh Earl of Bradford's 1981 Charitable Trust: Mrs J Woodward, Bradford Estate Office, Weston-under-Lizard, Shifnal, Salop, TF11 8JU. Tel: 01952 76203; Seventh Earl of Bradford and Countess of Bradford's Castle Bromwich Parochial Charity: Earl of Bradford, Woodlands House, Mill Lane, Weston-under-Lizard, Shifnal, Salop, TF11 8PX. Tel: 01952 76201.

DAME BARBARA CARTLAND

£16,000 NEW

PREFERENCE: medicine, education, religion, Hertfordshire

AGE: 92

WEALTH: less than £20m

TRUST LINKS: Barbara Cartland Trust, Barbara Cartland-Onslow Romany Fund

COMPANY LINKS: none

Dame Barbara Cartland herself would probably balk at entry in this book on grounds of her wealth, as she argues that she is worth considerably less than most people have estimated. However, being the world's best-selling living authoress cannot be entirely without its rewards, and Dame Barbara is included on the grounds of her charitable activities as much as her wealth.

She gives financial support to various causes through the **Barbara Cartland Trust**, which she created in 1987 and funds directly by gifts and covenants. In 1991/92 the trust made donations amounting to £16,000, slightly up on previous years during most of which the annual grant total was only around £3,000. Most of this sum was directed to St John's Ambulance in a £13,000 gift – Dame Barbara has close links with the Hertfordshire arm of this organisation as chair of the county's St John Council and deputy president of the St John Ambulance Brigade for the area. Other donations ranged in size from £10 to the £1,000 given to Hatfield Polytechnic (which is now the University of Hertfordshire), and were directed to a range of charitable activities, including several donations to individuals who are regular recipients. Several donations were made to religious causes, possibly as a form of repayment, because Barbara Cartland has been quoted as saying, 'I pray to God before starting a novel and he gives me the plot' (*Times*, 19/1/91).

There is another charity registered in Cartland's name: the **Barbara Cartland-Onslow Romany Fund**. She set this up back in 1962 for the relief of poverty and the advancement of education of Romanies. The most up-to-date information on file at the Charity Commission dates back to 1974/75, during which the fund had an income of only £12 per month. Dame Barbara's concern for the plight of gypsy travellers extends to setting

THE BRITISH SCHOOL OF OSTEOPATHY
1-4 SUFFOLK ST., LONDON. SW1Y 4HG
TEL. 01 - 930 9254-8

up a private site for them on her land, which the occupants have apparently dubbed 'Barbaraville'.

On a wider front, Cartland has claimed credit for John Major's recent 'back to basics' campaign, having had the Prime Minister and his wife round for lunch shortly before he launched his crusade. Indeed, as long ago as 1991, Dame Barbara was quoted as saying, 'All the prime ministers...they all want to go back to morality. We've got to have it for everybody' (*Times*, 19/1/91). For his part, John Major himself has not said where he got the idea from.

Contact: Barbara Cartland Trust: Mr C J N Longmore, Longmores, 24 Castle St, Hertford, Herts, SG14 1HP. Tel: 01992 586781. Barbara Cartland-Onslow Romany Fund: Dame Barbara Cartland, Camfield Place, Hatfield, Herts.

LADY WILLOUGHBY DE ERESBY

£16,000

PREFERENCE: general, Lincolnshire, Scotland
AGE: 59
WEALTH: less than £20m
TRUST LINKS: Ancaster Trust
COMPANY LINKS: none

Lady Nancy is the 27th family member to become Baroness Willoughby de Eresby, a title which stretches all the way back to the fourteenth century, and is one of the few hereditary female titles in the House of Lords. Although she does not own the family's Lincolnshire estate around Grimsthorpe Castle, she was given land in Scotland with a value of around £15 million by her father, the Earl of Ancaster, whose title vanished upon his death in 1983 because of the lack of a surviving male heir. In one sense, however, the name lives on thanks to the **Ancaster Trust,** which was established in 1965 by his wife, Nancy Countess Ancaster, with a cash endowment of £50,000.

Lady Willoughby de Eresby became a trustee of the Ancaster Trust soon after her mother died in 1975, and in 1977 transferred to it the £10,000 worth of assets which had previously formed the capital of her own grant-maker, the Willoughby Trust. The Willoughby Trust has since been removed from the Register of Charities, and Lady Willoughby de Eresby now appears to satisfy part of her desire to give through the Ancaster Trust. In 1987/88, the last year for which accounts were on file at the Charity Commission, it made donations to balance its £15,000 income and had assets with a value of £168,000.

The grants went to a wide variety of charitable causes, with the largest being five gifts of £1,000 to the Children's Family Trust, the Trustees of the British Museum Palestinian Project, King Edward VII's Hospital for Officers, the Rutland Historic Churches Preservation Trust, and St Barnabas' Hospice Trust. The remaining donations were directed mainly at health and welfare charities, and causes active in the areas of Lincolnshire and Scotland where the family has landholdings. More recent information on the activities of this trust is available in CAF's *Directory of Grant-Making Trusts*, which records a growth in the value of assets to £450,000 but donations still at the £16,000 level.

Lady Willoughby is also one of the joint hereditary Lord Great Chamberlains of England, a title she shares with the descendants of the Earl of Lincoln and the Marquess of Chomondeley (qv). This title requires the holders to be involved in a formal role at certain State occasions, including being the Coronation staff-bearer.

Contact: Mr S G Kemp, Ancaster Trust, Sayers Butterworth, 18 Bentinck St, London, W1M 5RL. Tel: 0171 935 8504.

JACQUES MURRAY

£15,000

PREFERENCE: medicine, education, West Yorkshire

AGE: 74

WEALTH: £75m–£100m

TRUST LINKS: none found

COMPANY LINKS: Nu-Swift

Jacques Murray first took a stake in the fire protection company Nu-Swift back in 1982 using part of the fortune he had generated from petrol retailing in his native France. His holding has subsequently grown and he now owns the majority of the shares. Last year Murray reportedly decided to take the group private by purchasing the 23% owned by Michael Ashcroft's (qv) ADT group and the remaining 11% he did not hold. Given his close control of the company, the donations of around £15,000 made by Nu-Swift in 1990/91 can be considered as coming indirectly from Murray himself. These were directed at charities local to the firm's sites, and the main areas of support have been cancer research causes and schools. We have, however, been unable to find any charitable trusts registered in Jacques Murray's name.

Contact: Secretary to the Chairman, Nu-Swift, Wistons Lane, Elland, West Yorkshire, HX5 9DS. Tel: 01422 372852.

EARL OF DERBY

£14,000 **NEW**

PREFERENCE: North West, welfare, youth, elderly people, education, medicine

AGE: 75

WEALTH: £50m–£75m

TRUST LINKS: Earl of Derby's Charitable Trust

COMPANY LINKS: none

Edward John Stanley, the current Earl of Derby, has very close links with the North West of England, where the Stanley family estate encompasses over 27,000 acres around Knowsley Hall in Lancashire. He is an active supporter of charities in the region through the **Earl of Derby's Charitable Trust**, which he set up with a cash endowment of £100,000 in 1984. By the year 1991/92, the trustees had invested this money in a tidy bundle of blue chip shares worth over £150,000. The dividends on these investments provided an income of just over £13,000, all of which was distributed via donations amounting to £14,000.

The trust is restricted by its objects to supporting charities which operate for the benefit of inhabitants in the North West, and it does so through a relatively large number of small gifts. Around one-third of the sum given in 1991/92 was allocated through recurrent annual donations. These benefited a wide variety of causes but primarily education, youth, the elderly, the disabled, ill-health, and racing welfare charities. The rest of the income was distributed as one-off gifts, the largest of which were grants of £500 given to the Equine Fertility Centre at Newmarket, the Lung Cancer Fund, and Alder Hey Children's Hospital, and donations of

179

£400 to Anfield Technology Appeal, Bootle and Warrington YMCAs, and the Knowsley Dance Company. Apart from the money given to organisations connected with horse racing, all of the trust's grants went to supporting charities in the North West. The Earl's charitable activities are supplemented by his positions as president of Henshaw's Society for the Blind, and vice-president of the National Playing Fields Association and St Ann's Hospice in Manchester. He is also an elected patron of the NSPCC.

Lord Derby's name is synonymous with the annual flat race held at Epsom, which was started by one of his predecessors over two centuries ago. A love of horse-racing still runs thick in the 18th Earl's blood, who was one of the syndicate that raced Shergar, the ill-fated champion horse. His wider sporting interests are reflected in his position as president of both the Rugby Football League and the Professional Golfers' Association. His fortune stems from the family's landholdings and a considerable collection of art.

Contact: Mr M S Moon, Trustee, Earl of Derby's Charitable Trust, 1 Fir Tree Lane, Littleton, Chester, CH3 7DN. Tel: 01244 336607.

DAVID WILSON

£14,000

PREFERENCE: general
AGE: 52
WEALTH: £100m–£250m
TRUST LINKS: none found
COMPANY LINKS: Wilson Bowden

Despite selling-off a portion of his holding for nearly £12 million last summer, David Wilson and his family still own just under half of the shares in the highly regarded Wilson Bowden homes construction company. The firm, of which Wilson is chair and chief executive, has survived the recession in good shape as it concentrates on the Midlands and the North East, and so remained unaffected by the property slump in the South East. In 1991, this Leicestershire-based business donated £14,000 to a range of local and national causes and we have bent our rules a bit to list this in the figure for Wilson's giving above. We have been unable to uncover any charitable trusts registered in David Wilson's name at the Charity Commission.

Contact: K McEwan, Corporate Director, Wilson Bowden plc, 207 Leicester Rd, Ibstock, Leics, LE67 6HP. Tel: 01530 60777.

PHIL COLLINS

£12,000 **NEW**

(but see below)

PREFERENCE: not known
AGE: 43
WEALTH: £50m–£75m
TRUST LINKS: none found
COMPANY LINKS: Philip Collins Ltd

Pop-star Phil Collins must be amazed by the serious amounts of money he has made from the solo projects he undertakes in parallel to his work with Genesis. His 1981 record *Face Value* was the first in an increasingly successful string of solo albums, and he is now a best-selling international star in his own right. This has been reflected in the accounts of his eponymous private company, which between 1989 and 1992 paid him nearly £45 million including pension contributions. Along with other members of Genesis, he has business interests including The Farm recording studio.

Collins has the reputation of being an active and generous supporter of charities, and has been a high profile trustee of the Prince's Trust since 1983. We have, however, been unable to trace any grant-making trusts registered in his name. His company – **Philip Collins Limited** – declared charitable donations of just over £12,000 in 1992, the recipients of which were not specified.

We were informed by his representative that Phil Collins did not wish to appear in this publication, and that the above entry 'does not show a true reflection of what Mr Collins does to help individuals and charities, as the majority of the money he donates comes from his personal account and not via the Charity Aid Foundation [sic] which can only be used for registered charities.'

Contact: Phil Collins, Philip Collins Ltd, 30 St Ives St, London, SW3 2ND.

NICK FALDO

£12,000

PREFERENCE: health, welfare

AGE: 36

WEALTH: £20m-£35m

TRUST LINKS: Nick Faldo Charitable Trust

COMPANY LINKS: Nick Faldo Ltd

Given his recent track record on the golf course Nick Faldo's wealth looks certain to increase further in the future. He is generally reckoned to be Britain's second richest sportsman, after Nigel Mansell (qv), and has won more major golf championships than you could shake a stick at – including three British Opens and two US Masters. Not only has he collected several million pounds in prize money over the past decade, he has also made growing amounts from equipment and clothing contracts and sponsorships, which invariably incorporate a lucrative success clause. Although he professes ignorance as to his total worth, he is easily able to run a Porsche with the personalised number plate NAF 911 (his initials and the model of the car).

Apart from being welcomed by his bank manager, his continued success is also good news for charities, as Faldo has recently established an eponymous grant-making trust. The

Nick Faldo Charitable Trust was created at the start of 1990 by Faldo's personal company, Nick Faldo (International) Ltd, with him and his present wife as trustees. In its first full year of existence, this trust donated £58,000 to four charities. Fittingly, the recipient of the largest grant of £24,500 was the Sportsman Aid Society, with other donations going to Little Ones (£19,000), the Cystic Fibrosis Research Trust (£10,000) and the Muscular Dystrophy Group (£4,500). In the following year, 1991/ 92, the amount distributed had fallen to £15,000, with a grant of £5,000 to the National Playing Fields Association, gifts of £4,250 to the NSPCC, of which Faldo is a life patron, and to Oxfam, £1,000 to St Thomas' Hospital's Give Tommy a Hand Appeal, and a further £150 to the Cystic Fibrosis Research Trust. The trust currently has only a relatively small asset base, and relies upon donated income, presumably from Faldo himself, to support its donations. The most recent 1992/93 accounts for the trust report an income of £45,000 and charitable gifts of £12,000 to unspecified beneficiaries.

We were informed by a representative of the International Management Group that Nick Faldo did not wish to be included in this book, as he prefers to keep his charitable donations private.

Contact: Jonathan Dudman, Nick Faldo Charitable Trust, International Management Group, Pier House, Strand on the Green, Chiswick, London, W4 3NN.
Tel: 0181 994 1444.

GEORGE HARRISON

£12,000

PREFERENCE: children, medicine, environment
AGE: 51
WEALTH: £20m-£35m
TRUST LINKS: Material World Charitable Foundation Ltd
COMPANY LINKS: Harrisongs; recently sold stake in Handmade Films

George Harrison, best known as one of the 'Fab Four' but also a best-selling solo artist, directs some of his financial support for charities through the **Material World Charitable**

Foundation Limited. This was named after, and apparently funded by, Harrison's successful 1973 album *Living in the Material World*. The foundation was set up as a company with exclusively charitable objects in December of the same year, and took over the assets of a near identically named trust which had been set up previously by Harrison (and which was to have been the 'George Harrison Charitable Foundation' until its deed of settlement was amended by hand by George Harrison). Both Harrison and his wife, Olivia, are currently directors of the foundation.

The Material World Foundation has been involved with some interesting projects during its lifetime. During its first full year in existence it organised and sponsored a British tour by Ravi Shankar, the virtuoso Indian sitar player whose pupils have included George Harrison. The reasons given for this support were to encourage interest in Indian classical music and promote racial harmony and understanding. In the same year the foundation also became sole shareholder of Oops Publishing, a music publishing company which subsequently entered into an agreement to covenant its entire annual distributable income to the foundation. In 1976, the foundation started negotiations to purchase a mansion house in Letchmore Heath, Hertfordshire, so it could be used by the International Society for Krishna Consciousness. The house, now known as Bhaktivedanta Manor, hit the headlines early in 1994 when the local district council tried to bar pilgrims from visiting because of their impact on the surrounding village.

More recently, the foundation appears to have shifted its focus to more mainstream causes. George Harrison explained his rationale to the *Sunday Times*: 'I did it so I could fund the people who contact me. I've limited its sphere of operation to children's charities and all the money is given away every year' (1/7/90).

In the past few years the group which comprises the foundation and its Oops Publishing subsidiary has recorded an annual income of around £50,000-150,000. However, the bulk of this is used to pay unspecified 'operating charges' for the group, so the group's operating profits are considerably lower, as is the amount available for the foundation to direct to charitable causes. In 1992 the foundation had a disposable income of around £15,000 and made charitable grants totalling £11,500 to nine non-profit organisations – including Liverpool Institute for Performing Arts (£5,000), Oxfam (£2,500), and Feed the Children (£1,000). In previous years, large gifts have included £10,000 to Fairground Heritage, £5,500 to the Handicapped Children's Trust, £5,250 to the addiction charity SHARP, £5,000 to Save the Children, £3,000 to Friends of the Earth, and £2,000 to both the Jubilee Campaign and to Olivia Harrison's Romanian Angel Appeal (see below). The total grant level has fluctuated recently: it was around £6,000 in 1988 and 1989, rose to £31,000 in 1990, before dropping to £14,000 in 1991 and falling again in 1992.

Although he normally likes to keep a low profile, when George Harrison does surface it is often in connection with one of his favoured causes. Before the 1992 general election he performed his first British concert for twenty years at the Royal Albert Hall in order to benefit the alternative, and ultimately unsuccessful, candidates put up by the Natural Law Party. It is unlikely that this concert raised quite as much as the famous *Concerts for Bangladesh* – two all-star performances at Madison Square Gardens in New York which Harrison organised to raise money for the victims of famine and civil war. The most recent accounts reportedly show that a total of £7 million has been given to UNICEF from the proceeds of this event.

In July 1990 Harrison did the press rounds to promote a compilation album *Nobody's Child* which he had helped organise to benefit the Romanian Angel Appeal set up by his wife to aid the children of Romania. He had contributed a song to the album with the Travelling Wilburys, whose members include Mark Knopfler (qv), and also gave a donation via the Material World Foundation (see above). His motivation was simple: 'If you can't help your own wife to do something then it's a pretty bad state of affairs, isn't it?' (*Sunday Times*, 1/7/90).

Contact: Lucy Rigo, Company Secretary, Material World Charitable Foundation Ltd, 26 Cadogan Sq, London, SW1X 0JP.
Tel: 0171 581 1265

LORD MARGADALE
£12,000 **NEW**

(but see below)

PREFERENCE: Wiltshire, Western Isles of Scotland, elderly people, welfare
AGE: 88
WEALTH: £35m-£50m
TRUST LINKS: Lord Margadale Charitable Trust, Lady Margadale Charitable Trust
COMPANY LINKS: none

John Granville Morrison was given the hereditary title Lord Margadale of Islay in the early sixties, after two decades as Conservative MP for Salisbury. In his time, he was one of the richest MPs in the house, having inherited his wealth from the family textiles business, including £500,000 on his twenty-first birthday – a considerable fortune now, but even more impressive in 1927! His sons have been keen to follow in his footsteps – one, Sir Charles, was MP for Devizes from 1964-1992, and another, Sir Peter, was a junior minister in the Department of Trade and parliamentary private secretary to Margaret Thatcher before she was deposed.

Margadale has substantial landholdings in Wiltshire, around Fonthill House, and on the island of Islay, the malt-whisky connoisseur's paradise off the western coast of Scotland. He gives support to organisations operating close to these two estates via the **Lord Margadale Charitable Trust**, which he set up in 1977. Unfortunately, no up-to-date information is available for this trust, as the only accounts on file at the Charity Commission are for 1982. However, CAF's *Directory of Grant-Making Trusts* reports that in 1992 the trust had assets of over £110,000 and an income of £12,000. On the same date that Lord Margadale established his trust, his wife set up the **Lady Margadale Charitable Trust**, whose last accounts on file record donations of only £35. No information is available on its preferred areas of support, and it was established with general charitable purposes.

Contact: The Secretary, Margadale Charitable Trusts, Fronthill House, Tisbury, Wilts, SP3 5SA.
Tel: 01747 870202

JACKIE STEWART
see below

PREFERENCE: see below
AGE: 54

WEALTH: £20m-£35m
TRUST LINKS: Grand Prix Mechanics Charitable Trust
COMPANY LINKS: Ford, Rolex, Moët et Chandon, Aston Martin

Jackie Stewart, still one of the most successful racing drivers of all time, retired at the peak of his powers in 1973. Since leaving the sport he has certainly moved into top gear as far as making money is concerned. He has contracts with the Ford Motor Company – test-driving their newest models and ironing out any problems before they hit the open market – and also with Rolex, Moët et Chandon, of which he is a director, and Aston Martin. He still maintains an involvement with motorsport through his son's racing team, Paul Stewart Racing, and has other business interests which include an electronics firm, a film production company run by another son, and the Jackie Stewart Shooting School at Gleneagles.

Jackie Stewart created the **Grand Prix Mechanics Charitable Trust** in 1987 because he had become increasingly concerned about the financial hardship which could result from the death or injury of a Grand Prix mechanic in the performance of his/her duties during Formula 1 events or related testing sessions. The trust aims to provide financial help to such individuals and their families, the form of which could be to provide recurrent assistance to help with living expenses, to enable young children to complete their education, or to make outright grants where a mechanic, for example, is permanently disabled and needs to make alterations to their home.

Through various fundraising events the trust now has funds of £650,000 which have been invested to provide both income and capital growth. The trust has an ongoing commitment to provide medical repatriation insurance and accident cover for the mechanics at all of the Grands Prix held each year, and to this end spends around £12,000 annually. In previous years the trust has also made a small number of donations to charities, the largest of which were a pair of £5,000 gifts made in 1989/90 to the College of Occupational Therapists and Springfield Boys' Club. As president of this boys' club – which is heavily supported by the motor-racing fraternity – Jackie Stewart plays an important part in raising funds to enable the continuation of its valuable work helping disadvantaged youngsters in East London.

Contact: The Secretary to the Trustees, Grand Prix Mechanics Charitable Trust, 1 Hanover Square, London, W1A 4SR. Tel: 0171 493 4040.

JAMIE BOOT
and family
£11,000

PREFERENCE: not known
AGE: 41
WEALTH: £20m-£35m
TRUST LINKS: none found
COMPANY LINKS: Henry Boot & Sons

The Boot family, who have no connection with the famous Boots chemists chain, have made their fortune through their construction engineering company, Henry Boot & Sons. This Sheffield-based firm is controlled by the family, with Jamie Boot as its managing director and David Henry Boot as non-executive chair. We have not been able to trace any charitable trusts registered in their name, although the donations made by their company amounted to just over £11,000 in 1991.

Contact: Mr E J Boot, Managing Director, Henry Boot & Sons plc, Banner Cross Hall, Ecclesall Rd South, Sheffield, S11 9PD. Tel: 0114 255 5444.

VISCOUNT INGLEBY
and family
£11,000 **NEW**

PREFERENCE: Christian causes
AGE: 68
WEALTH: less than £20m
TRUST LINKS: Ingleby Charitable Trust
COMPANY LINKS: none

Viscount Ingleby, Martin Raymond Peake, is a major landowner in North Yorkshire around Snilesworth, the family home. He is a supporter of various Christian organisations through his trust, the **Ingleby Charitable Trust**, which he set up in the early eighties. In 1990/91 the trust had assets of £110,000 which generated an income of £9,000. This facilitated nine donations totalling £10,500 which were directed almost exclusively to religious causes. The largest grant was £2,500 to the Timothy Trust, and the other eight gifts were all for £1,000 and went to organisations including Christian Responsibility in Public Affairs, Scripture Union, the Evangelical Alliance, and the Billy Graham Evangelical Association.

Lord Ingleby stated that he would much prefer to be excluded from this book, and commented that: 'the causes which I support I support each year; and the income is fully committed and there is therefore no point in anyone applying to me for gifts from my charitable trust.'

Contact: Viscount Ingleby, Ingleby Charitable Trust, Snilesworth, Northallerton, North Yorkshire, DL6 3QD. Tel: 01609 83214.

MARK LENNOX-BOYD
£11,000
(but see below)

PREFERENCE: education, medicine
AGE: 51
WEALTH: £100m-£250m
TRUST LINKS: Gresgarth Charitable Trust (ceased to exist)
COMPANY LINKS: Guinness

Mark Lennox-Boyd MP, Minister for Overseas Development, followed his father's footsteps into the House of Commons. As a government spokesman, he has been at the centre of recent press attention on the Overseas Development Administration's involvement with the Pergau dam project in Malaysia and its links with UK arms sales. It is perhaps a less well-known fact that he is also one of the richest members in the House, thanks to his links to the Guinness family fortune. He is son of Viscountess Boyd (qv) and the late Viscount Boyd – that is, Alan Lennox-Boyd MP who was a member of Churchill's postwar parliamentary team – and his eldest brother is the current Viscount Boyd. Lennox-Boyd's personal wealth comes from his bundle of shares in Iveagh Trust, a private company which handles the income from the family's various non-charitable trusts.

Until recently, Mark Lennox-Boyd made donations to charities through the **Gresgarth Charitable Trust**, which he had founded in 1982 and named after his home, Gresgarth Hall. In the last accounts on file at the Charity Commission for 1989/90, the trust had assets of £16,000 and a covenanted income of £6,000. In the year it made seven grants totalling £11,000, the largest of which were £7,000 to the Campaign for Oxford Trust Fund, which raises funds for the university Lennox-Boyd attended (he went to Christ Church College), £2,000 to St Mary's Save the Baby Fund and £1,000 to the Ross McWhirter Foundation. The Charity Commission's records state that this trust was removed from their register in February 1991, so whilst it is probable that Lennox-Boyd's philanthropic actions continue, they must find their outlet through a different channel.

Contact: Mark Lennox-Boyd MP, c/o House of Commons, London, SW1A 0AA.

COLIN FRIZZELL
and family
£10,000 NEW

PREFERENCE: medicine, Berkshire
AGE: 55
WEALTH: less than £20m
TRUST LINKS: Anna and Colin Frizzell Charitable Trust
COMPANY LINKS: sold shareholding in Frizzell Group

The Frizzell family made their fortune from the company that bears their name. They sold their valuable stake in the Frizzell Group insurance company in 1992, netting £27 million which was divided between about twenty Frizzell relatives, spanning three generations. Colin Frizzell and his wife Anna received a share of the proceeds, and he has continued to chair the company.

Prior to the sale, Colin Frizzell had diverted 50,000 of his own shares in the firm into the charitable trust he set up in 1977, the **Anna and Colin Frizzell Charitable Trust**, of which

● GIVING BY POLITICIANS

Tim Sainsbury	£3,600,000
James Goldsmith	£2,500,000
Shirley Porter	£966,000
Margaret Thatcher	£500,000
Mark Lennox-Boyd	£11,000
Michael Heseltine	£10,000
Paul Channon	£8,000
Edward Heath	£6,000

he and his wife are trustees. The summary one-page accounts which are on file at the Charity Commission do not specify the current nature of the trust's assets, but do indicate an income of £9,000 in 1989/90 which enabled donations of £10,000 to be made. Most of the thirteen grants made were directed to medical causes, including gifts of £1,500 to Cancer Relief MacMillan Fund, £1,200 to Conway Seymour Leukaemia Fund, £1,000 to Wexham Gastrointestinal Trust, and £800 to the Skin Treatment and Research Trust. Other gifts were focused on Berkshire, where Frizzell and family currently reside, including £1,000 each to Thames Valley Hospice and Holyport Memorial Hall, £750 to West Berkshire Hospital, and £500 to Holyport Preservation Trust. Previous gifts made by the trust include £2,000 given to the Joseph Levy Charitable Foundation – a grant-making trust connected with another member of Britain's rich, Peter Levy (qv).

A further grant-maker listed under the name of Frizzell at the Charity Commission is the **Frizzell Foundation**. However, whilst Anna

Frizzell was one of its trustees for a period, this foundation derived the majority of its income from the Frizzell Group, and so is more properly considered as a company trust rather than a personal one. Given that the Frizzell family has now severed their financial links with the company, the donations made by this trust have not been included in the figure cited above. Furthermore, this foundation, which directed its support to the advancement of the education of elderly and retired people, is currently being wound down, and has directed the last of its reserves to a few significant projects in 1993.

After seeing a copy of this entry, Colin Frizzell stated that he did not wish to appear in this publication, and that 'we are not keen to encourage unsolicited appeals since the comparatively small funds that we are able to distribute are in all cases earmarked and totally utilised.'

Contact: Colin Frizzell, Anna and Colin Frizzell Charitable Trust, Chuffs House, Maidenhead, Berks, SL6 2NA.

EARL OF HAREWOOD

£10,000

PREFERENCE: arts, north England
AGE: 71
WEALTH: £20m-£35m
TRUST LINKS: Lord Harewood's Charitable Settlement
COMPANY LINKS: none

Every time you go to the cinema you see Lord Harewood's name, although you probably don't realise it. As president of the British Board of Film Classification his is the signature you see on the certificate which is shown directly before the start of each movie.

His name is also associated with, **Lord Harewood's Charitable Settlement**, which he founded in the mid sixties and into which he put capital and stocks worth £23,000 in 1976. The last accounts on file for this trust at the Charity Commission date back to 1977, when the trust made donations of just under £2,000, of which £1,000 went to the English National Opera. The entry for the trust in the CAF *Directory of Grant-Making Trusts* states that by 1989 its assets had grown to £278,000 and it made grants of £10,000. Although set up with general charitable purposes, the trust has a stated preference towards music and arts organisations in the north of England. This reflects Harewood's close links in the past with a number of operas and arts festivals, such as the ENO, of which he was chair until recently.

George Henry Hubert Lascalles, the Queen's cousin, inherited the title of the 7th Earl of Harewood in the sixties, along with a vast estate around Harewood House near Leeds. Although much of this land went to pay-off death duties, a few thousand acres still remain. The family wealth has a rather unfortunate origin, as it was built largely upon the profits of the slave trade in the West Indies.

In response to sending a draft copy of the above entry, we were informed that: 'There have been so many changes here at Harewood that the entry you have put is completely inaccurate, although the charitable donations and the information relating to that is indeed correct'. The wish was expressed that the entry should not be included.

Contact: Lord Harewood's Charitable Settlement, The Estate Office, Harewood, Leeds, LS17 9LQ.

MICHAEL HESELTINE

£10,000

PREFERENCE: arts, homeless people, children, medicine, Oxfordshire

AGE: 61

WEALTH: £50m-£75m

TRUST LINKS: Michael Heseltine Charitable Trust

COMPANY LINKS: Haymarket Publishing

Michael Heseltine MP is generally regarded to be one of the richest members of the current government, thanks to his links with the successful Haymarket publishing group. As befits this status, since the mid seventies he has made donations, albeit on a relatively modest scale, through the **Michael Heseltine Charitable Trust**. In 1990/91 this trust had an income of £14,000, of which £6,000 came from Heseltine via deeds of covenant, and it distributed grants totalling just over £10,000. The largest single grants were £1,900 directed to the Ashmolean Museum Appeal – with which he is connected via his wife Anne, who sits on its Task Force – and £1,500 to Shelter. Heseltine would no doubt be able to enlighten fellow Tory MP Charles Hendry, who complained in 1994 about the campaigning activities undertaken by the homeless people's charity, which is supported by Heseltine along with many other Members of Parliament. The remaining donations showed a preference for causes in Oxfordshire, children and education, the arts, and medical charities. They included gifts of between £500-£600 for the Radcliffe Medical Foundation, Katharine House Hospice in Oxfordshire, Friends of the British Library, and Friends of the Tate Gallery.

Michael and Anne Heseltine are also trustees of three eponymous charitable trusts set up in July 1991 by their children, Annabel, Alexandra and Rupert. Each of these trusts has general charitable purposes, but has a relatively limited income used to support causes with which the children are associated. An indication of their restricted resources is given by the accounts on file at the Charity Commission for the **Alexandra Heseltine Charitable Trust** which was settled by the Heseltine's recently married daughter, Alexandra Williams. In the period up to April 1993 this trust received two cash injections of £1,333 and made donations totalling £750 to seven organisations, including the Ashmolean Museum and the Tate Gallery. Annabel and Rupert's trusts are likely to be of a similarly small size.

Always thought of as a possible Conservative Party leader, the President of the Board of Trade has had an eventful past few years, having been at the eye of the storm that followed his announcement of NCB's pit closure programme and suffering a heart attack whilst abroad in Venice, which kept him off the political scene for a while. His business interests have been progressing somewhat more smoothly, with the private Haymarket publishing group continuing to thrive on the back of a portfolio of quality titles. The precise value of Heseltine's wealth is difficult to quantify, however, because although he founded Haymarket in the sixties, he has no direct shareholdings in it. He owns Thenford House, an impressive Palladian mansion in Oxfordshire with a substantial country estate.

Contact: Mr M Heseltine MP, Michael Heseltine Charitable Trust, Thenford House, nr Banbury, Oxon, OX17 2BX.

DAVID HOCKNEY

see below **NEW**

PREFERENCE: Bradford and North East, arts, general

AGE: 57

WEALTH: unknown

TRUST LINKS: David Hockney Foundation

COMPANY LINKS: none

David Hockney is one of the most distinctive and successful modern British artists, and he is constantly making use of new technologies and techniques to express himself. He now lives in California, but maintains close ties with Bradford, where he was born, attended the local Grammar School, and studied his profession at Bradford School of Art before going on to the RCA.

These strong links are apparent in the financial support he has given to various causes in and around Bradford through the **David Hockney Foundation**. This has made donations of nearly £100,000 over the past seven years funded by the proceeds of Hockney's creative talents. Upon creating this grant-making trust in 1987 he gave it two gouache drawings – *Punchinello with Block* and *Eiffel Tower, Satie's Room & Cage*. The foundation has general charitable purposes, with particular emphasis on the relief of poverty and distress amongst the unemployed, the advancement of education in the arts, the provision of recreation and leisure facilities, the conservation of buildings of public or historical interest, the advancement of religion, and charitable support of inhabitants of a particular locality.

The two drawings were sold in 1987/88, and the £12,000 they raised paid for donations of just under £7,000 made to the National Museum of Photography Films and Television in Bradford to help fund its 'Bradford Challenge' competition. In the following year, the foundation received a further work of art from David Hockney, a painting *Montcalm Interior at 7 o'clock 1988*, which was sold for £116,000. A large chunk of the proceeds went to Bradford Grammar School, which received £75,000 to help pay for its theatre refurbishment. In 1989/90 gifts totalling £10,000 were made to the

Freehand Theatre Group to renovate its touring van (£5,000), to fund art prizes at Bradford Grammar School (£3,000), to Gay Switchboard Bradford (£1,000) and to the Charleston Trust (£1,000). The most recent accounts for the foundation show that in 1990/91 it did not make any donations, although it had an income of £3,400 and cash assets of £39,000. Perhaps it is awaiting a further gift from its settlor to finance future grants.

Hockney also has links with another person whose family graces these pages – the late Sir John Moores of Littlewoods pools fame. In 1967, David Hockney won first prize in the John Moores Exhibition at Liverpool, which was funded by the great philanthropist.

When contacted, the foundation's accountant commented that: 'As there are very few funds in the Foundation and there are no proposals at the present time for transferring further funds [the] Trustees would be obliged if no record of the Foundation is included in your publication. The problem arises that as soon as any publicity or information is given about this Foundation we are inundated with requests and we are unable to deal with them.'

Contact: Mr P Hockney, Messrs Paul Hockney Chartered Accountants, The Old Bath House, Manor Lane, Shipley, W Yorks, BD18 3EA.
Tel: 01274 582233.

LIONEL PICKERING

see below NEW

PREFERENCE: general in Derbyshire
AGE: 62
WEALTH: less than £20m

TRUST LINKS: Pickering Foundation
COMPANY LINKS: sold Derbyshire Trader newspaper

Lionel Pickering has a deep love for the city of Derby, and nowhere is this more apparent than in the reported £12 million he has lavished on Derby County Football Club in a bid to help the team achieve Premiership status. Thus far, however, success has not been forthcoming, although Pickering does not regret his investment which rescued the club from the grasp of Robert Maxwell, and which he believes has brought enjoyment to many local people.

He has been able to afford this multi-million pound backing thanks to his successful business career as a local newspaper publisher in the East Midlands. He started in the trade as a cub sports reporter, and after National Service continued his journalistic career in Australia, before returning to England to set up a free newspaper. This was to be the cornerstone of the *Derbyshire Trader* empire of ten titles, with a combined weekly distribution of ten million copies, which Pickering sold in 1989 for £25 million. He justifies diverting much of this considerable fortune to Derby County by explaining: 'The money is there to be spent. You only live once. I don't want my sons to have too much money. I don't think it would be good for them.' (*Guardian*, 2/3/93).

These sentiments are also echoed in the **Pickering Foundation**, which he set up with his wife the year before he sold his newspapers. The aims of this foundation are to benefit the poor and needy inhabitants of Derbyshire. There are, however, no subsequent accounts on file at the Charity Commission for the foundation, so it is not possible to give any indication of its size or scope. We were informed that it was set up for a specific purpose and is not active at present, so it would be inadvisable to approach it with requests for funding.

Contact: Mr I D Spring, Pickering Foundation, Priory House, Sydenham Rd, Guildford, Surrey, GU1 3RX. Tel: 01483 38881.

NAT PURI
£9,500

PREFERENCE: general, Nottinghamshire, India
AGE: 54
WEALTH: £50m-£75m
TRUST LINKS: Puri Foundation
COMPANY LINKS: Melton Medes

Indian-born Nathu Ram Puri arrived in Britain in 1966 with only a few hundred pounds in his pocket. He is now worth much, much more thanks to his success in the business world. He was initially taken on as a trainee engineer with construction company F G Skerritt, and rapidly moved up the hierarchy to contracts manager. He left in the mid-seventies to set up business on his own as a consultant engineer, which proved a great success. So much so that he was later able to purchase his ex-employer for £200,000 when it ran into financial problems. He subsumed it within his holding company, Melton Medes, which he had set up simultaneously and of which he still owns 90%. He has since continued along the same lines with further acquisitions, and the Nottingham-based Melton Medes group now encompasses engineering, property, plastics, paper and textiles. In 1988 Puri even made an ultimately unsuccessful £250 million bid for the Rover cars group, which was recently purchased from British Aerospace by BMW.

Puri looks set to be a major supporter of charities through the **Puri Foundation**, which he established in 1988. This grant-making trust lists several key objectives including the provision of financial assistance to those in need, especially citizens of Mullan Pur and other residents in India, people of Nottinghamshire, and employees or former employees of Melton Medes. It also aims to fund extra equipment at schools, provide recreation and leisure facilities, and support training programmes for the young unemployed of Nottingham, as well as making donations for general charitable purposes. Over the past five years the foundation has received over £1.5 million via covenants and Gift Aid, presumably either from Puri himself or from Melton Medes. It has so far made total charitable gifts of £160,000 to causes which are not specified in the accounts filed at the Charity Commission, although the foundation has committed itself to meet the cost of approximately £250,000 for a new Hindu Temple and community centre in Nottingham. The most recent accounts for 1992/93 show it had a total income of £255,000, most of which came from covenants and Gift Aid, but donations totalled only £9,500, somewhat down on previous years' levels of £24-65,000.

Puri's other charitable works include his position as director of Prince's Youth Business Trust Nottingham, and of Nottingham Development Enterprise. He is also a great lover of cricket, and reportedly gave £60,000 to Notts County Cricket Club for a new press stand.

Contact: Mr N R Puri, Puri Foundation, Environment House, 6 Union Rd, Nottingham, NG3 1FH. Tel: 0115 958 2277.

TONY ELLIOTT
£9,000 NEW

PREFERENCE: arts, education

AGE: 47
WEALTH: less than £20m
TRUST LINKS: Time Out Trust
COMPANY LINKS: Time Out

Tony Elliot wholly owns the private firm that produces *Time Out* the London listings publication. He started it back in 1968 with £70 from the money he received for his twenty-first birthday. Whilst we have been unable to trace any charitable trusts registered in Elliot's name, his company makes donations through the **Time Out Trust,** of which he is trustee.

The Time Out Trust was established as a charitable company in 1989, by transforming the memorandum and articles of a previous company, Lakewatch Limited, set up a year earlier. Over the past four years the trust has received an annual net income of £25,000 through covenants and Gift Aid from Time Out Magazines, and has made total donations of £43,000. In the year 1992/93 it held assets of £56,000, had an income of £27,000, and made grants of £9,000. These consisted of £5,000 to Vie Marshal, £1,600 to Beatrix Wood, £1,000 to Salon des Artes, £500 to Final Draft Films, and £250 to both Shakespeare's Globe and Munnakatemba Productions. In previous years gifts were directed primarily at education and the arts, with the Young Unknowns Gallery receiving a total of £10,000, the University of London £8,000, Royal College of Art £6,500, the Diorama Arts Trust £3,500, Second Stride £3,000, and the National Film and Television School £2,000.

Contact: Mr K Ellis, Company Secretary and Director, Time Out Trust, Universal House, 251 Tottenham Court Rd, London, W1P 0AB. Tel: 0171 813 3000.

BRYAN ROBSON

£9,000

PREFERENCE: medicine, children
AGE: 37
WEALTH: less than £20m
TRUST LINKS: none
COMPANY LINKS: none

Although by no means the richest sportsman in this book, star footballer Bryan Robson has reportedly accumulated a few million pounds from his long playing career, including the past thirteen years with current Premier League and FA Cup champions Manchester United. He has recently left the club to face the new role of player-manager at Middlesborough, but will no doubt be keen to retain his strong ties with the North West.

In 1991 he set up the **Bryan Robson Scanner Appeal**, a charitable company whose object is given as 'the relief of sickness by the provision of a Magnetic Resonance Imager at the Royal Manchester Children's Hospital.' This appeal, which works in conjunction with the Wallness Children's Project, aimed to raise £1.5 million for the provision of the scanner, although its advisor stated in a letter to the Charity Commission that 'the machine will largely be funded by Mr Robson.' Bryan Robson is chair of the appeal whose 1991/92 accounts state that he gave £9,000 from his testimonial to start the appeal which by May 1992 had reached the £1 million mark. In the year, activities which had contributed funds included a 'Dream Auction' which raised £46,000, a golf day at Withington Golf Club (£14,000), a Sportsmen's Dinner at Old Trafford (£8,000), and the rather exotic sounding 'Foo Foo's All Male

Review at the Apollo Theatre'. Robson is also involved with a number of other charities, including Wallness Hurdles and Adventure Farm.

Contact: Bryan Robson, c/o Middlesborough FC, Ayresome Park, Middlesborough, Cleveland, TS1 4PB. Bryan Robson Scanner Appeal, Mr D T Wilkinson, BDO Binder Hamlyn, 1 Norfolk St, Manchester, M60 8BH. Tel: 0161 831 7121.

PAUL CHANNON

£8,000 NEW

PREFERENCE: arts, education, welfare
AGE: 58
WEALTH: £100m-£250m
TRUST LINKS: Channon Charitable Trust
COMPANY LINKS: Guinness

The source of this Member of Parliament's wealth is not immediately apparent until you know that his full name is Henry Paul Guinness Channon. As such he is part of one of the richest families this side of the Atlantic, with links to the Guinness brewing and property fortune as grandson of the second Earl of Iveagh and director of Iveagh Trust. He is also nephew of Viscountess Boyd (qv) and cousin to her sons, the present Viscount Boyd and Mark Lennox-Boyd MP (qqv).

Like his MP cousin, Paul Channon followed his father into politics, in his case inheriting the Southend West seat of the late Sir Henry 'Chips' Channon. In the late sixties he also received a valuable bundle of shares in the Guinness company previously held by his mother. It looks like some of these found their way to the **Channon Charitable Trust**, which holds 7,500 Guinness shares with a market value of at least £40,000. Paul Channon established this trust in 1982, with himself, his wife and the Iveagh Trustees as co-trustees. By 1991/92 it held capital with a value of £83,000 which provided an income of nearly £4,000. The £8,000 donated by the trust in 1991/92 is up on previous years, when the annual grant total was in the order of £1,000-£4,000. The gifts made most recently by the trust were focused on arts and cultural organisations, the largest being £1,600 to Glyndebourne, £1,200 to the Royal Academy Trust, and £1,000 to both the Bankside Gallery and the British Museum. Other donations went to a variety of causes, such as the Queen's Gate School (£1,000), various memorial funds (such as £150 to the Ian Gow Memorial Fund), welfare charities and churches/cathedrals.

Contact: Channon Charitable Trust, Iveagh Trustees Ltd, Iveagh House, 41 Harrington Gdns, London, SW7 4JU. Tel: 0171 373 7261.

STING (GORDON SUMNER)

see below

PREFERENCE: rainforest conservation
AGE: 42
WEALTH: £35m-£50m
TRUST LINKS: Rainforest Foundation, Outlandos Trust
COMPANY LINKS: Steerpike

Always considered one of our more cerebral pop stars, with literary lyrics and music influenced by jazz and folk, Sting has a high profile involvement with several causes. He is a frequent performer at charity concerts, playing at the Live Aid and Kurd Aid concerts, as well as on Amnesty International's global tour. He is best known, however, for his efforts to protect the natural environment through the **Rainforest Foundation**, which has apparently raised more than £2 million over the past five years through its activities in this country and in the US, France, and Germany.

There are two branches of the Rainforest Foundation registered as charities in Britain – the Rainforest Foundation (UK) and the Rainforest Foundation International. Both had Sting and his present wife, Trudie Styler, as founding trustees when they were set up in 1989. These foundations state that their principal activity is 'to preserve the rainforests of Brazil for the benefit of the inhabitants and for the World environment in general. This includes education of the general public in conservation and balance of natural resources, and provision of medical and education services to the inhabitants of the rainforests'. The powers of the international arm of the foundation also include the ability to demarcate the Megkroguoti, Gorototire and Bau Indigenous Areas and the Xingu National Park in Brazil, which cover a total area of 180,000 square kilometres.

The accounts on file at the Charity Commission show that in 1989/90 the Rainforest Foundation International had an income of £470,000 derived mainly from donations, of which £180,000 went on Brazilian projects costs. This direct charitable expenditure was exceeded by fundraising and administrative expenses which totalled just under £200,000, including £79,000 on consultancy and professional fees, and £46,000 on travel – presumably for the world promotion tour undertaken that year by Sting and Chief Raoni Metyktire of the Kayapo rainforest indians. The accounts for

the UK branch of the charity show that in the same year it raised £194,000, made charitable grants of £53,000 but incurred other expenses of £100,000. In 1990/91 it had an income of £114,000, and the £60,000 expenditure on Brazilian projects equalled the fundraising and administrative expenses.

The Rainforest Foundation is still going strong, despite its well publicised falling-out with Chief Raoni after his tribe sold £6 million worth of mahogany to Europe. In April this year, Trudie Styler organised a fundraising concert in New York at which Elton John (qv) and Pavarotti both performed. This $1,000-a-head function benefited the foundation to the tune of $1.1 million.

There is also another charity linked to Sting, which dates back to his days with the Police, one of the most successful pop groups of the early eighties. The **Outlandos Trust**, founded in 1980, takes its name from the group's first album *Outlandos d'Amour*, and in 1982 the three band members – Andy Summers, Stuart Copeland, and Gordon Sumner (Sting's real name) – were appointed trustees alongside their manager, Miles Copeland, and Anthony Steen MP. It was originally endowed with 100 shares in Angloforce Limited, a private company which has provided the trust with regular income via covenants. The trust states that it was formed 'to further the development of musical education amongst the underprivileged youth in Britain.' The last accounts on file at the Charity Commission date back to 1985, at which time the trust held assets of £60,000, had an income of £9,000, and made unspecified charitable donations of £8,000. Following the group's dissolution in the mid-eighties, it is not clear whether Sting is still a trustee of the Outlandos Trust, but we have found no evidence to the contrary.

Since leaving the Police, Sting has

embarked upon a successful solo career. He was initially aided by leading lights of the American jazz scene including the remarkable saxophonist Branford Marsalis. The title of his most recent album, *Ten Summoner's Tales*, is a twin reference to his own surname and a work by Chaucer. Sting's business interests appear to be controlled though two main companies – Steerpike, which handles his career as a solo performer, and Roxanne Music, which controls earnings from the sales of works by the Police and is jointly owned by the three former band members. In addition to his musical activities, Sting has been making his mark as an actor, including the films *Quadrophenia*, *Brimstone & Treacle*, *Dune* and *Stormy Monday*. In recent years he also reportedly donated a saxophone to Mother Teresa to be auctioned for the homeless.

Contact: Lynne Brooke, Outlandos Trust, 80/83 Long Lane, Barbican, London, EC1A 9ET; or c/o Markham & Froggatt Ltd, Theatrical Agent, 3 Windmill St, London, W1P 1HF.

LADY JULIET DE CHAIR

£7,000 NEW

PREFERENCE: children, medicine, arts
AGE: 64
WEALTH: £20m-£35m
TRUST LINKS: Lady Juliet de Chair's Charitable Trust
COMPANY LINKS: none

Lady Juliet de Chair inherited the substantial Fitzwilliam family fortune in 1979 after control had passed from her late father, the 8th Earl Fitzwilliam – who died in a 1948 flying accident – through the hands of two cousins who successively inherited his family title as he had left no male heir.

In 1980 Lady Juliet established her own grant-maker, with the title of **Lady Juliet de Chair's Charitable Trust**. Over the next decade she endowed it with various assets, and by 1992/93 the trust had built up investments with a market value of around £150,000. These produced an income of £6,500 which supported donations of the same amount. Many of the gifts were directed at causes connected with young people, such as Leonora Children's Cancer Fund (£1,000), NSPCC (£800), and Chernobyl Children (£500). Several arts organisations received support, with gifts of £500 to the Shakespeare Globe Trust and the Tate Gallery Foundation. Other grants went to a variety of charities, including those operating in the medical and welfare sectors. Lady de Chair is still a trustee, along with the Fitzwilliam Trust Corp. Ltd.

In response to the draft entry we sent, we were informed by the trust's solicitors that 'Lady de Chair has no interest in having this entry included in your publication...Lady de Chair does not agree that the contents of your suggested entry in this publication are totally accurate.'

Contact: Lady Juliet de Chair's Charitable Trust, 10 New Square, Lincoln's Inn, London, WC2A 3DQ.

ALAN LEWIS

£7,000

PREFERENCE: Christian causes
AGE: 56
WEALTH: £100m-£250m
TRUST LINKS: none found
COMPANY LINKS: Illingworth Morris Ltd

Karate black-belt Alan Lewis packs a punch in the textiles world as chair and chief executive of Illingworth

Morris, which produces billiard table baize and the felt for tennis balls. Frustrated by the City's short-term investment approach, he took the previously quoted company back into private ownership five years ago, although may float it again if the time is right. He has strong Christian beliefs which no doubt inform his charitable activities, and he works with several organisations including the Acorn Christian Healing Trust. Whilst we have not been able to uncover any charitable trusts registered in his name, the donations of £7,000 made by his company in 1989/90 can be considered as coming indirectly from Alan Lewis.

When contacted, the company requested that this entry be removed from this book as it is 'not correct in content and the publication of this information is strictly contrary to the wishes of the Company'.

Contact: M Bradley, Company Secretary, Illingworth Morris, PO Box No.122, Fairweather Green, Thornton Rd, Bradford, W Yorks, BD8 0HZ. Tel: 01274 542255.

THOMSON family
£7,000

PREFERENCE: Dundee, printing-related
WEALTH: £250m-£500m
TRUST LINKS: none found
COMPANY LINKS: D C Thomson & Co

A multitude of Thomson family members hold shares in the D C Thomson publishing business which is based in Dundee. Whilst their individual holdings are relatively small, in combination they comprise around two-thirds of the company's capital. The executive chair of the company is Brian Thomson, with Derek Thomson as deputy chair and managing director. The only information we have for the firm's charitable donations indicate that it gave away around £7,000 in 1988/89, mainly to local Dundee organisations and to appeals related to the printing industry. We have been unable to find any charities registered in the family's name at the Charity Commission, although some may well exist in Scotland, which falls outside the Commission's geographical remit.

Contact: A McDougall, Company Secretary, D C Thomson & Co Ltd, Albert Square, Dundee, DD1 9QJ. Tel: 01382 23131.

PETER JONES
£6,500 **NEW**

PREFERENCE: North West, welfare, general
AGE: 59
WEALTH: £50m-£75m
TRUST LINKS: Emerson Foundation
COMPANY LINKS: Emerson Developments (Holdings)

When it came to christening both his company and his charitable trust, Peter Jones used his middle name, Emerson. The **Emerson Foundation** was established by Jones and his wife in 1990 with an initial settlement of £1,000, and has since received funding from his private company, Emerson Developments (Holdings). In 1992/93 the foundation held assets of £13,000, had an income of £10,000 from a source described as 'SMHA Directors fees', and made charitable gifts of £6,500. These donations were directed mainly at causes in the north west, although some national charities were supported, with an apparent preference for medical and arts organisations and youth welfare. The largest grants were £2,000 to Douglas Haig Memorial Homes, £1,000 to NCH Greater Manchester Appeal, and £500 to Clouter Farm Music Trust. Major gifts in previous years included £10,000 to the Church of St Edward and £2,000 to Manchester YMCA.

Peter Jones has made his fortune from the building trade, and particularly from developments in the NorthWest of England. The Emerson Developments company, based in Alderley Edge, Cheshire, is still turning in a healthy profit, despite the property recession, and is totally owned by Jones, his wife and various non-charitable family trusts.

After seeing a copy of the above entry, Peter Jones requested not to appear in this publication as, 'Emerson Developments (Holdings) Limited is a private company and The Emerson Foundation is a private trust.'

Contact: Mr P E Jones, Emerson Foundation, Emerson Group, Emerson House, Heyes Lane, Alderley Edge, Cheshire, SK9 7LF. Tel: 01625 584531.

EARL OF HALIFAX
and family
£6,000

PREFERENCE: heritage, churches, Yorkshire, welfare
AGE: 50
WEALTH: £35m-£50m
TRUST LINKS: Halifax Charitable Trust
COMPANY LINKS: none

Along with his late father, Lord Halifax set up the **Halifax Charitable Trust** in 1973 to support general charitable

purpose. By 1992/93 it had built up assets of £130,000 including £35,000 from the settlors, mainly from the deceased second Earl. This capital generated income of £10,500, of which £6,000 was distributed as donations, somewhat lower than the £11,000 in the previous year. The bulk went in two grants totalling £3,500 to the York Minster Fund, the cathedral at which Lord Halifax is high steward. The remaining gifts were directed mainly at causes in Yorkshire, especially to local churches and parochial church councils, and to charities working in welfare and with the disabled. The trustees do not currently include Lord Halifax, but they do include his wife, Lady Camilla.

The family's wealth comes from their 18,000 acres in Yorkshire around the family seat, Garrowby, as well as art treasures which include a Titian and a Stubbs. Lord Halifax also has some connections with the world of business, as director of Hambros Bank and Yorkshire Post Newspapers.

Lord Halifax requested not to appear in this publication, and commented that 'a lot of what you have written is inaccurate', although he did not specify any of these errors.

Contact: Mr J Spofforth, Halifax Charitable Trust, Morgan Brown & Spofforth, 16/18 New Bridge Street, London, EC4V 6AU. Tel: 0171 353 3895.

SIR EDWARD HEATH
£6,000

PREFERENCE: education, Christian causes, youth
AGE: 77
WEALTH: less than £20m
TRUST LINKS: Edward Heath Charitable Trust
COMPANY LINKS: none

Sir Edward Heath MP founded his grant-making trust in 1972 whilst he was Prime Minister. The **Edward Heath Charitable Trust** was set up with £30,000 derived from prizes he was awarded by the Freiherr Von Stein Foundation in Germany and the Edward J Meenan Foundation in the USA.

In the year 1990/91, the trust made charitable donations of £36,000 funded by an income for the year of £44,000. Of this amount, £30,000 was derived from Coca Cola GB as part of a five year covenant totalling £150,000 to pay for the 'Edward Heath Fellowship' on the franchising system at Nuffield College Oxford. This money has not been included in the figure for Sir Edward's personal gifts cited above, which is comprised of the remaining grants made by his trust. These came to just under £6,000, and were dominated by £2,600 to Balliol College Oxford – Heath's *alma mater* – as first payment towards a total of £24,000 that the trustees have committed to create the 'Edward Heath Fund' at the college. Other gifts included support for various Christian groups, such as £250 to Christians for Europe College Project, and charities working with the young, such as £250 to London Taxi Drivers' Fund for Underprivileged Children. There was also some preference towards causes in Sir Edward's constituency (Old Bexley and Sidcup), and the city of Salisbury where he lives.

Sir Edward was Prime Minister for the four years up to 1974, when Harold Wilson's Labour Party regained power. He was deposed as leader of the Tory Party only a year later by Margaret Thatcher, and has since offered a sometimes critical appraisal of his party's performance from the back benches. He is renowned for his love of yachting and music, and is currently president of the European Community Youth Orchestra, vice-president of the Bach Choir and an honorary member of the LSO.

Contact: R D Karran, Trustee Manager, Edward Heath Charitable Trust, Smith & Williamson, No.1 Riding House Street, London, W1A 3AS. Tel: 0171 637 5377.

MICHAEL HELLER

£6,000 **NEW**

(but see below)

PREFERENCE: education, Jewish causes
AGE: 57
WEALTH: £20m-£35m
TRUST LINKS: Michael and Morven Heller Charitable Foundation, Simon Heller Charitable Settlement
COMPANY LINKS: London and Associated Investment Trust, Electronic Data Processing

The Heller family fortune has its origins in the food business, but Michael Heller now has valuable holdings in a listed property company, London and Associated Investment Trust, and a listed software firm, Electronic Data Processing. He also has close connections with two Heller family grant-making trusts which we are informed have combined gross assets worth about £5 million.

Heller used 400,000 of his shares in the Electronic Data Processing company to establish the **Michael and Morven Heller Charitable Foundation** in 1988. The accounts on file at the Charity Commission for 1990/91 do not give any details of the foundation's current assets, but its £19,000 income was probably derived from this shareholding, as in the previous year. Less than one-third of this income was distributed, with charitable grants amounting to £6,000. These were directed predominantly at Jewish causes, with donations of £1,000 to both the Israel Diaspora Trust and the Group Relations Education Trust, and £500 each to Hampstead Synagogue Cultural Fund and Kisharon Day School. Other grants went to various charities, with some emphasis on medical causes such as Birthright, which received £500. Heller is also a director of the right-wing think-tank, the Centre for Policy Studies.

In addition, he is closely connected with the **Simon Heller Charitable Settlement**, which was founded by his late father Simon Heller back in 1972 with general charitable purposes. It was initially endowed with 230,000 shares in a private company S & K Holdings, and the original trustees were Simon Heller and the Yorkshire Novelty Company, whose signatory was its director, Michael Heller. The latter is still the trust's correspondent at the same address as his own foundation. It is not possible to state the current nature or size of the settlement's activities, however, as we were unable to obtain accounts from the Charity Commission.

We were informed by the family's solicitors that the policy of the trustees of both charitable trusts is to fund educational activities and institutions. They also stated that the grants we have cited for the Michael and Morven Heller Charitable Foundation represent 'only a small proportion of the charitable contributions' made by both trusts.

Contact for both Michael and Morven Heller Charitable Foundation and Simon Heller Charitable Settlement:

Mr M A Heller, 30-34 New Bridge St, London, EC4V 6LT, or c/o Mr M H Elliott, Benson Burdekin, 32 Wilkinson St, Sheffield, S10 2GB.

KEVIN KEEGAN
£6,000 **NEW**
(but see below)

PREFERENCE: children, medicine
AGE: 43
WEALTH: less than £20m
TRUST LINKS: Kevin Keegan Charitable Trust
COMPANY LINKS: Newcastle United FC

Kevin Keegan set up the **Kevin Keegan Charitable Trust** in 1981, whilst playing for Southampton Football Club, and over the next few years put several thousand pounds into it via covenants from his personal company KK Limited. The trust has made a relatively restricted number of gifts, including £2,500 in 1982 to the Association of Friends of Westwood House, £5,750 in 1984 to provide a minibus for underprivileged children in Newcastle-upon-Tyne, and most recently £6,200 in 1989 to Steve Mills Leukaemia Fund. Since 1989/90, however, the trust seems to have been lying dormant, with no assets, income or expenditure.

Kevin Keegan started in professional football with Scunthorpe United the year England won the World Cup, but has been considerably more successful over the ensuing decades than our national team. He spent most of the seventies playing for Liverpool FC, during which the team were twice League Champions and won the FA Cup, the UEFA Cup, and in 1977 the European Cup. After a stint playing for Hamburg and being twice

WARNING
Unsolicited requests for funding often lead to annoyance and are rarely productive. This book should not be used as a mailing list. Inappropriate applications waste time and money and may prejudice chances of future success.

selected European Footballer of the Year, he returned to this country to play for Southampton and then Newcastle United, before quitting the game in 1984. With his obvious talents, and one of the best bubble perms in an era of classic 'footballer haircuts', during his playing career Keegan attracted considerable personal sponsorships and endorsements which helped make him a multi-millionaire.

He returned to Newcastle in 1992 as manager, and immediately brought the club back into the top flight. In 1993/94, the team finished third in its first season in the Premier League, partly thanks to the efforts of super-striker Andy Cole and the renaissance of Peter Beardsley. Keegan's managerial success has been rapidly rewarded – in May 1994 he signed an unprecedented ten year contract with his club under which he will become 'Director of Coaching and Football' and will reportedly receive over £300,000 per year with performance related bonuses.

Contact: Kevin Keegan Charitable Trust, Messrs Burnett Swayne & Co, Charter Court, Third Avenue, Southampton, SO3 6TF. Tel: 01703 702345.

STUART LYONS
£6,000 NEW

PREFERENCE: general
AGE: 51
WEALTH: less than £20m
TRUST LINKS: Stuart & Ellen Lyons Charitable Trust
COMPANY LINKS: Royal Doulton

Although not as rich as many other West Midlands entrepreneurs, with a wealth he estimates at less than £5 million, Stuart Lyons is a major mover in the Staffordshire area as chief executive of Royal Doulton, the ceramics company recently demerged from the Pearson conglomerate. Given this connection, it is not unsurprising that he was founder of the Sir Henry Doulton School of Sculpture, of which he is still a trustee. He is also a past director of Staffordshire TEC, chair of Staffs Development Association, a council member of Keele University, and a governor of Staffordshire University.

Lyons gives some financial support for charities in the county through the **Stuart & Ellen Lyons Charitable Trust**, which he created in 1983 with his wife, Ellen. The trust was initially endowed with 40,000 shares in the public UDS Group, of which Lyons was then managing director. As he left the company later in the year this holding was sold and fetched £53,000. By 1992/93 the trust had assets with a value of £104,000, mainly in investment funds, which provided an income of £13,000. In the year, donations totalling nearly £6,000 were made, the largest being £2,500 to the Reform Foundation Trust, and £1,000 each to the Royal Academy Trust and the National Playing Fields Association's Action for Play Appeal. Other gifts were directed to Jewish organisations and causes active in Staffordshire and London.

Contact: Mr S R Lyons CBE, Stuart and Ellen Lyons Charitable Trust, Minton House, London Road, Stoke-on-Trent, Staffs, ST4 7QD.

● SPORTS GIVERS

Alan Pascoe	£25,000
Nigel Mansell	£25,000
Nick Faldo	£12,000
Bryan Robson	£9,000
Kevin Keegan	£6,000
Paul Gascoigne	£1,500

DUKE OF MARLBOROUGH

£6,000

PREFERENCE: heritage, medicine, community

AGE: 68

WEALTH: £35m–£50m

TRUST LINKS: Duke of Marlborough's Charitable Settlement; Blenheim Foundation

COMPANY LINKS: Martini & Rossi

John Spencer-Churchill, the 11th Duke of Marlborough, has been having family troubles. His erstwhile heir, the Marquess of Blandford, received considerable press attention over the past few years concerning his erratic lifestyle, not least when he was arrested last year and subsequently entered a drug rehabilitation clinic. This has clearly given the Duke some cause for concern, and the trustees of his estate have recently been moved to take measures to prevent Blandford from gaining full control of his inheritance. In his defence, Jamie Blandford argues that he is successfully undergoing treatment for his drug problem, and will soon be in a fit state to be a worthy heir. The High Court has recently ruled, however, that a new non-charitable trust can be created that will prevent Blandford from controlling the Blenheim Estate, but enable him to inherit his father's Dukedom and live in Blenheim's private apartments.

There is a considerable inheritance at stake, centring on the family's magnificent English Baroque palace at Blenheim, just north of Oxford, with gardens designed by 'Capability' Brown. The estate was a gift from the nation to the first Duke after he famously defeated the French army at the battle of Blenheim in 1704. The present Duke has a keen business brain, and the palace reportedly has a turnover of around £10 million per year due to its considerable success as a tourist attraction. He has also set up a charity, the Blenheim Foundation, to help preserve the palace and its surrounding gardens for the public benefit, and in 1992/93 this foundation spent £73,000 to this end, funded by investments worth nearly £3 million. The trustees, who include the financial expert Sir Mark Weinberg (qv), state clearly in the foundation's accounts that none its income may be used on any part of Blenheim that is occupied personally by the Duke or is not regularly open to the public.

There is another conduit for the family's philanthropy – the **Duke of Marlborough's Charitable Settlement,** which was set up by the present Duke's father in 1968. The objects of this trust are to help 'persons who are necessitous', and in particular past or present employees of the 10th Duke. The current Duke has made additions to the trust's assets, which now stand at almost £163,000. In 1991/92 payments totalling £1,300 were made to a couple of former employees of the 10th Duke, along with charitable donations of nearly £5,000. The recipient of the largest grant of £1,000 was the Stonefield Community Trust, and the Katherine House Hospice received £580. Other donations were made to a variety of national and Oxfordshire charities, notably in the medical sector, but including £2,500 to the Queen Elizabeth Gate Appeal, and £250 to the Desert Orchid Farriers Appeal Fund. Another older family-linked trust, the **Duke of Marlborough's Fund for Empire Knowledge**, is also registered at the Charity Commission, but does not appear to be active.

The Duke is very active in the charity sector, particularly around the family home. He is chair of

Oxfordshire Association of Boys' Clubs and patron of the county's British Red Cross Society branch. He holds various charity events at Blenheim, which in 1994 included a cricket match in aid of Oxford Association of Young People and a concert /tattoo for the Soldiers' Sailors' and Airmen's Family Association – of whose Oxford branch he is chair. On a wider scale, he is deputy president of the National Association of Boys' Clubs, and chair of the Southern region of the Sports Aid Foundation. He is also closely involved with the Winston Churchill Memorial Trust, the ex-premier who was born at Blenheim.

Apart from running the Blenheim Estate, the Duke of Marlborough is chair of the drinks company Martini & Rossi. In 1991 this firm made donations of around £28,000 which went mainly to trade charities such as the Licensed Victuallers. It also annually gives around £10,000 worth of its products for use in tombolas and raffles. He has also been chair of the private company London Paperweights since the mid 1970s, and is president of Oxford United FC.

Contact: Duke of Marlborough's Charitable Settlement: J P Arnold, Withers Solicitors, 12 Gough Square, London, EC4A 3DE.

DUKE OF NORFOLK

£5,000 **NEW**

PREFERENCE: Sussex, general
AGE: 78
WEALTH: less than £20m
TRUST LINKS: Miles Duke of Norfolk and Edward Earl of Arundel Charitable Trust
COMPANY LINKS: none

Miles, the 17th Duke of Norfolk inherited his title and took control of its associated landholdings in 1975 when his cousin died. He now resides at the family seat, Arundel Castle in West Sussex, but does not own the property which is instead held as a permanent endowment by the **Arundel Castle Trustees Limited**, a charitable company whose principal activity is opening the castle and its grounds to the general public. Lord Norfolk is chair of the company's board of directors, whose members also include his son and heir, the Earl of Arundel. It has assets worth nearly £4 million, but this does not include the value of Arundel Castle because 'the directors feel unable to value the property due to its unique nature.' In 1992, two-thirds of its £640,000 income was derived from payments made by the 156,000 visitors to the castle on the 183 days it was open to the public. Of this, over half a million pounds was directed towards castle expenses, but the company also made charitable grants totalling £19,000. These benefited several regular recipients: £7,350 to Fitzalan Chapel (the family name), £6,000 to the Cricket Foundation, £4,500 to causes in Sussex via the Arundel Castle Fund For Sussex Charities – a grant-making trust set up by the previous Duke's wife, Lavinia Duchess of Norfolk – and £1,000 in other unspecified donations.

The Duke of Norfolk offers personal support to charitable causes through the **Miles Duke of Norfolk and Edward Earl of Arundel Charitable Trust** which he set up along with his son in 1979, and both are trustees along with the Duke's wife, Anne Duchess of Norfolk. In 1990/91 the trust held assets worth £68,000 including £20,000 capital received from the settlors during the year. This provided an income of nearly £10,000 and just over half of this was used for charitable purposes.

The largest grants were £2,000 to Arundel Cathedral Organ Appeal and £1,000 to the Red Cross Romanian Children's Appeal. Other donations were made to general causes and charities operating in West Sussex.

Norfolk is a patron of around twenty charities, including the Handicapped Children's Pilgrimage & Hosanna House Trust. He is also vice-president of Help the Aged, joint chair of Help the Hospices, and both vice-president and joint honorary treasurer of St Dunstans which helps blinded ex-service men and women. On a more general front he is father-in-law to television presenter David Frost – who married his daughter, Lady Carina, in 1983.

Contact: Miles Duke of Norfolk and Edward Earl of Arundel Charitable Trust: D G Mewis, Arundel Services Ltd, Duke of Norfolk's Estate Office, Arundel, West Sussex, BN18 1YZ. Tel: 01903 883400. Arundel Castle Trustees Ltd: Mrs Eileen Wallace, Secretary, Arundel Castle, Arundel, West Sussex.

JOHN NIKE
see below NEW

PREFERENCE: recreation
WEALTH: less than £20m
TRUST LINKS: John Nike Trust
COMPANY LINKS: Nike Land Securities Ltd

John Nike hit the sports pages earlier this year when he was fined £500 by the British Ice Hockey Association for contravening its rules in a dispute with a referee. As the millionaire owner of the Bracknell Bees ice hockey team, Nike should easily be able to pay this penalty.

He merits an entry in this book on the grounds of the **John Nike Trust** which was set up by his Bracknell

based company, Nike Land Securities, with an initial settlement of £100,000 and with the local district council as trustee. The purpose of this trust is to improve public sporting and recreational facilities in Bracknell. It is not possible to determine how much has been spent to this end, however, as there are no accounts on file for this trust at the Charity Commission, which gives a figure of just under £4,500 for the trust's income in 1990/91.

Contact: John Nike Trust, Chief Executive (ref: HS/25.35), Bracknell Forest Borough Council, Easthampstead House, Town Square, Bracknell, Berks, RG12 1AQ. Tel: 01344 424642.

MARK KNOPFLER
£4,000 NEW

PREFERENCE: children, medicine, Jewish causes
AGE: 44
WEALTH: £50m-£75m
TRUST LINKS: Mark Knopfler Charitable Trust
COMPANY LINKS: none

Mark Knopfler could be called the 'mild man of rock'. Despite international fame as lead man for the pop group Dire Straits, he seems determined not to follow the indulgent sex'n'drugs lifestyle of many of his peers. Instead, this modest former English teacher is married, and even gave up his passion for fast cars when parenthood beckoned.

His charitable donations are mainly made to organisations concerned with children and their medical needs. This preference is reflected in his patronage of the Teenage Cancer Trust and the grants made by the **Mark Knopfler**

Charitable Trust. The trust was set up in 1988, and amongst its general charitable objects it specifically mentions the 'relief of need and education of children in any part of the world.' In 1991/92 the trust received income of over £26,000, although it made donations of only £3,700 in that year. Three gifts of £1,000 were made to the Loni Safer Appeal, the Hafetz Haim Orphanage, and Southmead Hospital's H Ward Fund. The other grants were for £200 or £100 and directed to medical, youth and educational charities, including the Canon Collins Education Trust and the National AIDS Trust. The trust carried forward a substantial surplus of over £95,000. We were informed, however, that Mark Knopfler 'courts no publicity of any nature and any entry [in this book] could be seen as a retrospective step to his charitable donations.'

The blend of adult-oriented rock offered by Dire Straits has brought the band world-wide success. Their 1985 album, *Brothers in Arms,* was one of the best selling records of all time, reaching number one in 24 countries, and was credited with establishing the compact disc as a viable medium. Their international tours are legendary: the last one took three years, during which they played to seven million people, with ticket sales in excess of £70 million. Knopfler has also recently got involved with the Travelling Wilburys, the members of which read like a who's who of contemporary music, including George Harrison (qv), Jeff Lynn, and the late Roy Orbison. Another of Knopfler's side-projects is his band, the Notting Hillbillies, which in July 1993 played at a concert in support of the Swan Hunter shipyard workers.

Contact: Mark Knopfler Charitable Trust, Harris & Trotter Accountants, 8-10 Bulstrode St, London, W1M 6AH. Tel: 0171 487 4393.

● GIVING BY POP STARS

Paul McCartney	£1,104,000
George Michael	£428,000
Elton John	£330,000
Cliff Richard	£224,000
Peter Gabriel	£33,000
Eric Clapton	£21,000
Phil Collins	£12,000
George Harrison	£12,000
Mark Knopfler	£4,000

SIR NICHOLAS BACON
and family
£3,000

PREFERENCE: general, Norfolk
AGE: 40
WEALTH: £35m-£50m
TRUST LINKS: Bacon Charitable Trust
COMPANY LINKS: none

Sir Nicholas Bacon, the Premier Baronet of England, is a practising barrister in London. He was a founding trustee of the **Bacon Charitable Trust**, which was set up by his mother Priscilla Dora Lady Bacon, in 1987. This trust is still relatively modest in size, with assets worth just over £50,000 generating an income of £11,000 in 1992/93. Of this total, £3,000 was distributed as charitable donations in the year, and was directed at various causes, but particularly those in Norfolk. These included two gifts totalling £1,250 to parochial church councils in the area around the Bacon family seat, Raveningham Hall.

The family's wealth is based upon their 4,000 Norfolk acres around Raveningham and 10,000 acres in

Lincolnshire. They also own a valuable art collection including some fine English watercolours.

Contact: Sir Nicholas Bacon, Bacon Charitable Trust, Raveningham Hall, Norwich, Norfolk, NR14 6NS. Tel: 01508 46206.

TIMOTHY COLMAN

£3,000

PREFERENCE: Norfolk, churches
AGE: 64
WEALTH: less than £20m
TRUST LINKS: Timothy Colman Charitable Trust
COMPANY LINKS: Eastern Counties Newspapers

The most recent accounts for the **Timothy Colman Charitable Trust** show a drop in the total amount donated from around £11,000 in recent years to only £3,000 in 1992/93. This was distributed through a large number of small donations, directed mainly at charities operating in Norfolk. There was also some preference for religious causes – the larger donations included £500 to Bixley Parochial Church Council (where Colman lives), £250 to the Church Urban Fund and £200 to Kirby Bedon Church. A gift of £500 was also made to an individual, the purpose of which is not specified. The higher grant total reported in previous years was also predominantly focused on charities operating in East Anglia, and in 1991/92 included £3,000 to the Theatre Royal Appeal, £1,000 to both the Norfolk Society and St Margaret's Trust in Kings Lynn. The trust was set up by Colman in 1962 with a bundle of shares in the Reckitt & Colman food company, and now holds assets worth over £200,000.

Timothy Colman's close links with Norfolk are also apparent in his other activities. Apart from living in the county, he is also pro-chancellor of the University of East Anglia, chair of the trustees of Norfolk and Norwich Triennial Festival, and chair of the Royal Norfolk Agricultural Association. His wider charitable interests are obvious in his role as trustee, and past chair, of the Carnegie UK Trust – one of the major grant-making trusts in the country. On the business front he is chair of the Eastern Counties Newspapers group – of which his family are major shareholders – and is a non-executive director of Anglia Television and former director of both Reckitt & Colman plc and Whitbread, the brewers.

Contact: The Administrator, Timothy Colman Charitable Trust, Messrs Coutts & Co, 440 The Strand, London WC2R 0QS. Tel: 0171 753 1000

ROLF SCHILD
and family

£3,000

PREFERENCE: general
AGE: 70
WEALTH: £35m-£50m
TRUST LINKS: none found
COMPANY LINKS: Huntleigh Technology

Rolf Schild and his family control just over half of the shares in the public Huntleigh Technology group. This Luton-based company manufactures specialised medical equipment, including a mattress designed to prevent bedsores – the scourge of long-stay hospital patients and a major drain on the resources of the NHS. Given their strong holdings in the company and Rolf Schild's role as chair, the charitable donations of

£3,000 made by the company in 1991 could be considered as coming indirectly from their own coffers. The grants made by Huntleigh are decided by the company's management committee. We were informed that charitable gifts made personally by the Schild family are private and for specific causes.

Contact: Rolf Schild, Huntleigh Technology plc, 310-312 Dallow Rd, Luton, Bedfordshire, LU1 1TD.

PADLEY family

£3,000 ~~NEW~~

(but see below)

PREFERENCE: Lincolnshire area
AGE: 43
WEALTH: £35m-£50m
TRUST LINKS: G W Padley Memorial Trust
COMPANY LINKS: G W Padley Holdings

As Bernard Matthews (qv) is to Norfolk, so are the Padley family to Lincolnshire – both made their fortunes through poultry processing. The family company was started by the husband and wife team of George and Doris Padley, who drove their truck from farm to farm in Lincolnshire buying live chickens to sell on at the large markets, until they were able to set up a highly profitable automated chicken plucking line.

In 1987 George and Doris were involved in a car crash in Majorca, which left George dead and Doris badly injured. In order to commemorate George Padley, the family set up the **G W Padley Memorial Trust** in 1990, with an initial sum of nearly £16,000. Its founding trustees were Doris Padley and her sons David and Steven. This trust has general charitable purposes,

with a particular emphasis on the relief of poverty in the county of Lincolnshire. It is not possible to give any further information on the activities of this trust as there are no accounts on file at the Charity Commission.

The family still has total ownership of the firm, G W Padley Holdings Limited, which is now run by the eldest son, David, who personally controls most of the shares. His mother still takes an active interest in the company as director, and she also holds one-quarter of the shareholding. The company made charitable donations of around £3,000 in 1990, the last year for which figures are available, with a preference for locally based organisations.

Contact: Mr D G Padley, G W Padley Memorial Trust, c/o G W Padley Holdings Ltd, Anwick, Sleaford, Lincs, NG34 9SL. Tel: 01526 832661.

DRAPER family

£2,500 ~~NEW~~

PREFERENCE: general
WEALTH: £20m-£35m
TRUST LINKS: Draper Tool Company Limited Charitable Trust
COMPANY LINKS: Draper Tool Company

The Draper family own a major stake in the Draper Tools group, mainly via non-charitable trusts. The company is based near Southampton, and until recently was the main sponsor of the city's Premier League football club. In 1985 the firm established the eponymous **Draper Tool Company Charitable Trust**, with John and his late father Norman Draper as founding trustees. The last accounts on file show it to have an income of only £455 in 1990, although it had previously received an annual £5,000 covenant from Draper Tools. The donations of £2,500 made in the year were split up into a large number of small grants to general causes, the largest of which were £1,000 to Trustees of Jason, £150 to Age Concern, and £100 to both Barnardo's and Guide Dogs for the Blind.

In response to being a sent copy of the above entry, the trust's solicitors commented that some of the information contained was inaccurate, although they did not provide any further details or corrections. They also noted that the trust is being run down because of the changes in tax law.

Contact: Mr T F Q Hedley, Solicitor, Draper Group Charitable Trust, 109 Leigh Rd, Eastleigh, Hants, SO50 9DR. Tel: 01703 611133.

DAME CATHERINE COOKSON

£2,000

(but see below)

PREFERENCE: general, medicine, North East
AGE: 87
WEALTH: £20m-£35m
TRUST LINKS: Catherine Cookson Trust
COMPANY LINKS: none

Best-selling novelist Dame Catherine Cookson has drastically curtailed her more public donations, which she made through an eponymous charitable trust. She felt that she was receiving too many requests for help, and had formed the opinion that, 'Britain has become a nation of beggars. I like to help but it has gone too far' (*Times*, 3/8/92). She made the decision to wind down the trust

because of the adverse impact that dealing with enquiries had upon her health and that of her husband: 'The people who send them don't know what they are doing to us. Every day we have several letters pleading for money. It's very distressing and the strain is just too much.'

Cookson had set up the **Catherine Cookson Trust** in 1977 to help deal with the requests she received from charities for financial help. Over the past six years, the trust has donated a total of £400,000 to various causes, funded primarily by royalties from Cookson's 1987 book *Bill Bailey's Lot*, the rights of which are vested in the trustees. Major grants have included £100,000 to Sunderland Polytechnic to fund research into arthritis and rheumatism, £40,000 to Pilgrim Street Trust in Newcastle, and £25,000 to both South Shields Postgraduate Medical Centre and Hexham General Hospital Golden Jubilee Appeal Fund. Some support has also been given to literary causes, such as £20,000 to the Library Campaign, and Cookson is vice-president of the Royal Literary Fund. By 1992/93, however, the trust had assets of £33,000, made a single donation of £2,000 to St Michael's Hospice in Hastings, and had a paltry income of £500.

The charitable gifts which Dame Catherine has made in the past through her trust reflect her strong connections with the North East, where she was born and grew up in abject poverty. She has drawn upon many of her childhood experiences when writing her books, which are amongst the most popular at libraries across the country. She is now a multi-millionaire thanks to her writing prowess, and although she may be no longer be making large donations to charities through her eponymous trust, it is unlikely that her support has dried up altogether but is instead made through less publicised channels.

In response to our draft entry, the administrators of the trust informed us 'that Dame Catherine Cookson does not approve of the publication of unauthorised articles such as that you propose…and considers that they give a garbled and misleading account of matters which are her private concern. In particular your so-called "wealth estimate" can only be a wild guess, is very wide of the mark, and must not be used. No further information will be disclosed.'

Contact: Mr D Hawkins, Catherine Cookson Trust, 20 Eversley Rd, Bexhill-on-Sea, East Sussex, TN40 1HE. Tel: 01424 210530.

PETER JOHNSON

£2,000

PREFERENCE: not known
AGE: 55
WEALTH: £75m-£100m
TRUST LINKS: none found
COMPANY LINKS: Park Food Group

Peter Johnson is managing director of the successful public Park Food Group, which puts together and sells mail order hampers. He owns nearly three-quarters of the company's shares, so whilst we have been unable to trace any charitable trusts registered in his name the £2,000 donations made by his firm in 1990/91 can be viewed as coming indirectly from his own coffers. Johnson is also chair of Tranmere Rovers FC, and like many others in this book has pumped a substantial chunk of his fortune into improving his favourite team's fortunes. He was also involved with a bid to take over control of another Merseyside club, Everton.

Contact: Secretary to the Managing Director, Park Food Group plc, Valley Rd, Birkenhead, Merseyside, L41 7ED. Tel: 0151 633 0566.

JOHN RITBLAT

£2,000

PREFERENCE: Jewish causes, elderly people, art, youth, education
AGE: 58
WEALTH: £35m-£50m
TRUST LINKS: John Ritblat Charitable Trusts No.1 and No.2, Manchester Square Charitable Trust
COMPANY LINKS: British Land Group, Conrad Ritblat Sinclair Goldsmith

John Ritblat is renowned for his strong opinions and his continued survival in the notoriously tough property market, and he currently runs the British Land investment company. He has appeared to have a sixth-sense when it comes to anticipating booms and slumps in prices, a trait which no doubt attracted that other master of timing, George Soros (qv), with whom British Land has entered into a joint venture to invest £1 billion in property for Soros' Quantum Fund.

Ritblat is active in the non-profit sector, with diverse interests ranging from conservation, through education, to art. He is a member of the Prince of Wales Royal Parks Tree Appeal Committee, and in the past has been involved with London Zoo's development trust. On the education front, he is director of the Hall School Trust, deputy chair of its governors, and a member of London Business School's governing body. He is also a member of Business in the Community's governing council. Ritblat clearly believes that travel broadens the mind – he was a founder sponsor of Young Explorers' Trust and has sponsored the Royal Geographical Society – and shows his wider concern for youth welfare through an involvement with the London Federation of Boys' Clubs and membership of NSPCC's financial development board. He puts his surveyor's training to good use as honorary surveyor at King George's Fund for Sailors. As an avid collector of art, it is not surprising that Ritblat is one of the Tate Gallery's Patrons of British Art.

He also gives some financial support to various causes through his trust, the **John Ritblat Charitable Trust No.1**. He set up this trust in 1971, and in recent years it has received assets and income to the sum of nearly £50,000 from the **Manchester Square Charitable Trust**. This is another charity with Ritblat as a trustee, and in 1990/91 it made a donation of £43,000 to the Weizmann Institute, of which Ritblat is a director and member of its executive committee. The other trustee of the Manchester Square Charitable Trust is Colin Wagman, who is also a trustee of Ritblat's first trust. The John Ritblat Charitable Trust itself appears to have been relatively quiet on the grant-making front, with donations totalling under £2,000 in 1991/92, directed mainly at Jewish charities. Another trust bearing Ritblat's name registered at the Charity Commission is the **John Ritblat Charitable Trust No.2**, but there are no accounts on file since its inception in 1971. A letter from the trust's representatives dated 1979 states that 'there have been no activities on this particular Trust from inception to date' – although this may not still be the case fifteen years later.

The various listings of the rich in this country seem to have overlooked Ritblat's personal fortune, although he did appear in *Esquire* magazine's recent survey of the 'secret rich'. His wealth comes from a relatively small stake in the property investment company British Land, of which he is chair and managing director, and from his interest in the estate agency Conrad Ritblat Sinclair Goldsmith. He is a keen sportsman, and has been involved with recent Olympic Appeals. He is also an expert skier, is in the St Moritz Cresta Club, and in the past has been vice-president of the British Ski Federation and sponsor of the British National Ski Championships.

In response to us sending a copy of the above entry, Mr Ritblat's representatives told us that 'the information is grossly inaccurate, despite the fact that much of it is within the public domain', but they gave no indication as to the precise nature of these inaccuracies.

Contact: John Ritblat Charitable Trust No.1: Mr C B Wagman, Trustee, 10 Cornwall St, London, NW1 4QP. Tel: 0171 486 4466. Manchester Square Charitable Trust: Mr C B Wagman, Hobson House, 155 Gower St, London, WC1E 6BJ.

PAUL GASCOIGNE
£1,500

PREFERENCE: general
AGE: 27
WEALTH: less than £20m
TRUST LINKS: Paul Gascoigne Charitable Trust
COMPANY LINKS: none

Football whizzkid Paul Gascoigne seems to be permanently in the tabloids thanks to his antics both on and off the pitch. Arguably one of the most gifted players in recent times, he has been struggling to consistently regain match fitness because of the serious knee damage he incurred during his infamous tackle in the 1991 FA Cup Final. This injury didn't prevent his £5.5 million transfer from Spurs to the Italian club Lazio, which topped the £2 million his former club paid to obtain his talents from Newcastle United. He receives a substantial salary from Lazio, and is involved with various product endorsements including Lotto football boots.

In January 1992, Gascoigne set up the **Paul Gascoigne Charitable Trust** to make gifts to general charitable causes, but as yet the trust remains relatively small. In 1992/93 it had an income of £6,000, derived from donations presumably from Gascoigne himself, and made grants to charities of around £1,500. Whilst the beneficiaries were not listed, the trust has reportedly directed some support to children's causes and cancer research charities.

Gascoigne himself told the *Independent on Sunday* that his philanthropic impulses have been strongly influenced by the children's TV programme *Blue Peter*: 'It provided my first contact with the world of charity, and I've been hooked ever since.'

Contact: Mr L S Lazarus, Paul Gascoigne Charitable Trust, Arram Berlyn Gardner, Holborn Hall, 100 Grays Inn Rd, London, WC1X 8BY. Tel: 0171 753 5511.

VISCOUNT COKE

£1,300 **NEW**

PREFERENCE: welfare, arts, wildlife, Norfolk
AGE: 57
WEALTH: £35m–£50m

TRUST LINKS: Viscount Coke's Charitable Fund
COMPANY LINKS: none

Viscount Edward Coke, the son and heir of the 6th Earl of Leicester, is in the classic asset rich/cash poor position encountered by many aristocratic landowners. He owns over 26,000 valuable acres of Norfolk countryside around his stately home, Holkham Hall, but over the past decades has had to sell some of the family's art treasures in order to pay death duties and maintain his property. Most notable was the 1980 sale of a manuscript by Leonardo da

Vinci, which was purchased by Dr Armand Hammer for over £2 million.

The Viscount has felt able, however, to divert some money into setting up a small charitable trust, **Viscount Coke's Charitable Fund**. He established this fund in 1979 with the purpose of relieving poverty amongst ex-employees and parishioners in areas local to the family estate, and to make donations to any charity, although the British Red Cross Society, the RNLI, the Mental Health Foundation, and Mencap are all specifically mentioned. By 1991/92 the trust had relatively modest assets of nearly £11,000 which generated an income of £1,300 which was distributed via three donations to the RNIB's 'Looking Glass' appeal (£1,000), the Theatre Royal Norwich Trust (£250), and Norfolk Victims' Support Scheme (£50). In most previous years the grants total was a little higher, helped by income from annual concerts which each raised around £1,000-£2,000, although in 1991/92 it seems one was not held. The largest single donation made by the charitable fund in recent years was a gift of £6,000 to the Game Conservancy Trust, of which Viscount Coke is a trustee.

Contact: Viscount Coke's Charitable Fund, Messrs Fladgate Fielder, Heron Place, 3 George St, London, W1H 6AD.

VISCOUNT PORTMAN
and family
see below

PREFERENCE: see below
AGE: 60
WEALTH: £100m-£250m
TRUST LINKS: Viscount Portman's Charitable Trust
COMPANY LINKS: none

Viscount Portman inherited his title from his uncle, who died in 1967, along with interests in the non-charitable trusts which hold the Portman family's land in central London. Because of the limited information available on the accounts filed at the Charity Commission, it is not clear whether he also took over control of **Viscount Portman's Charitable Trust** which the previous Lord Portman had set up in 1963 with an initial cash settlement of £15,000. The aim of this trust is to help fund the maintenance and upkeep of the Portman Memorial Chapel in St Martin's Church, Bryanston, Dorset, and also to pay an annual sum of £300 to the League of Friends of Blandford Hospital. In 1991, the trust had assets of £74,000 which produced an income of £8,000, but the only donation made was £300 to Blandford Hospital League of Friends.

Portman has something of a racy past. In his younger days he was a racing driver, and a love of fast cars appears to run in the family's blood as his son, Alex, has also taken up the sport. The Viscount is an acquaintance of Nigel Mansell (qv), and reportedly bought one of his Grand Prix car's spoilers at a charity auction for £1,000.

Contact: Trust Officer, Viscount Portman's Charitable Trust, Salisbury Diocesan Board of Finance, Church House, Crane St, Salisbury, SP1 2QB. Tel: 01722 411922.

LORD EGREMONT
£1,000 NEW

PREFERENCE: West Sussex, Cumbria
AGE: 46
WEALTH: £20m-£35m

TRUST LINKS: Egremont Charitable Trust, Lord Egremont's Charitable Settlement

COMPANY LINKS: none

Like many other aristocrats in this book, the 2nd Lord Egremont has a substantial wealth based on land and art – his family owns some valuable art treasures along with over 15,000 acres in Cumbria and around Petworth House in West Sussex – but apparently little loose cash. As a result, the gifts made through the two family charitable trusts are relatively small-scale, even though Egremont is actively involved with a number of charities on a personal basis.

The larger of these two grant-makers is **Lord Egremont's Charitable Settlement**, of which Lord Egremont was a founding trustee when it was set up by the his late father in 1969. The trust received £50,000 from the executors of the late Lord Egremont's will in 1977, and has now built up assets of over £200,000. In 1991/92 it made three grants totalling just over £6,000, dominated by a £6,000 gift to the Village Weavers, which left £3,000 of income undistributed. The grant total for this trust has fluctuated between £1,000 and £10,000 over the past five years, and major donations have included £9,000 to Impact in 1990/91 and £5,000 to the West Cumbria Hospice in 1987/88.

The other trust, the **Egremont Charitable Trust**, was established by the current Lord Egremont in 1981 with a cash endowment of £1,000. In 1987 Egremont signed a four year covenant to pay £2,500 net each year to this trust. As a result, in 1991/92 the trust had capital to the value of £14,000 and made a single donation of £1,000 to St Anthony's School. In previous years the amount donated has ranged from nothing to £3,000 in 1990/91 when three grants of £1,000 went to Petworth Cottage Nursing Home, Courtlea Amenity Fund, and Petworth Parochial Church Council.

Both of these trusts thus appear to have a preference for supporting causes in West Sussex and Cumbria, areas where the Egremont family has extensive landholdings.

Lord Egremont's other charitable activities are mainly confined to conserving various aspects of our heritage. He is a member of the Royal Commission on Historical Monuments, chair of the Friends of the National Libraries, and a trustee of the British Museum and the Wallace Collection. He is also a trustee of Henry Smith's Kensington Estate Charity, one of the ten largest grant-making trusts in Britain, which supports health and social welfare causes. The correspondent for his trust commented that Lord Egremont's contributions to charity amount to "considerably more' than the estimate we have given above.

Contact for both trusts: Mr T Wardle, Estate Office, Petworth House, Petworth, W Sussex, GU28 0DU. Tel: 01798 42502.

BRIAN KINGHAM
£1,000

PREFERENCE: not known
WEALTH: £20m-£35m
TRUST LINKS: none found
COMPANY LINKS: Reliance Security Group

Brian Kingham is chair of the Reliance Security Group, and owns around three-quarters of the shares in this alarms and security business. Whilst we have been unable to trace any grant-making trusts registered in his name, his firm made charitable donations of £1,000 in 1991/92.

Contact: Reliance Security Group, Surety House, 81 Chester Square, London, SW1W 9DR.

EARL OF LICHFIELD

£1,000 NEW

PREFERENCE: general, Staffordshire

AGE: 54

WEALTH: less than £20m

TRUST LINKS: Lichfield Charitable Trust

COMPANY LINKS: none

Lord Lichfield is one of our most famous professional photographers, having produced pictures both of the Royal Family and of rather more scantily clad models for various corporate promotional calendars. Although by no means the richest person in this book, with a wealth his representative estimated at less than £2 million, he does divert some of his earnings to good causes via the **Lichfield Charitable Trust** which he set up in 1977 with an initial settlement of £5,500. In 1991/92 this trust had assets of £16,000 due to a further £10,000 Lichfield introduced in the year. This capital supported donations totalling just over £1,000, which went to a wide variety of charities, ranging from wildlife conservation groups such as WWF, through to various medical and health organisations such as St John Ambulance. Youth welfare was also funded, as were causes local to Lichfield's residence, Shugborough Hall in Staffordshire.

Lord Lichfield is actively involved with a number of voluntary bodies, both overseas, nationally and in the West Midlands. He is a patron of Acorn Children's Hospice, The Foundation for Conductive Education and the Woodland Trust. He is also a council member of VSO and vice-president of Birmingham Royal Institute for the Blind. His former wife, the Countess of Lichfield, formerly Lady Leonora Grosvenor, is sister of the Duke of Westminster (qv).

Contact: Major J R Haszard, Lichfield Charitable Trust, Ranton Abbey, Lawnhead, Stafford, ST20 0JQ. Tel: 01785 282659.

DUKE OF ATHOLL

£900 NEW

PREFERENCE: health, wildlife, Scottish charities

AGE: 62

WEALTH: £100m-£250m

TRUST LINKS: Duke of Atholl's 1987 Charity Trust

COMPANY LINKS: Westminster Press

The 10th Duke of Atholl, George Iain Murray, is aiming to obtain more in grants from the public purse than he has ever given away from his own pocket via his grant-making trust. He is hoping that the restoration of gardens at his stately home to their former glory will attract several hundred thousand pounds of support from Scottish Heritage and government bodies. Despite his substantial wealth his own donations made through his charitable trust appear rather restricted, perhaps indicative of an 'assets rich, cash poor' position.

Atholl owns a large tract of land around Blair Castle, the family home in Perthshire – fitting credentials for a past president of the Scottish Landowners' Federation. Falling land prices north of the border have recently reduced his wealth, although this may be offset by receipts from visitors to the castle, which attracts around 170,000 visitors a year paying £4 each. The Duke claims it is the most popular in Scotland having gained fame during its starring role in the TV series *Strathblair*. He also has a second home in London, where he worked as chair of the publishers Westminster Press from 1974 up until last year.

In common with many titled landowners, the Duke lends his name to a number of charities, but appears to give relatively little direct financial support from charitable trusts registered in his name. He is closely connected with several organisations north of the border, notably as president of the Scottish Wildlife Trust and vice-president of the National Trust for Scotland, and his Highlands estates help explain his position as vice-president of the Game Conservancy Trust. On a wider front, he is also vice-president of two national charities, the Thomas Coram Foundation for Children and the Marie Curie Memorial Foundation, and was chair of the RNLI in the 1980s.

The Duke makes some donations through the **Duke of Atholl's 1987 Charity Trust**, whose assets consist of £43,000 worth of Pearson shares. The Duke has close family connections with Pearson – his uncle is Viscount Cowdray (qv), who is principal shareholder and president of the publishing to banking group. These investments generated the majority of the trust's £2,000 income in 1990/91, of which just over £900 was distributed as grants to various organisations. The recipient of the largest gift of £300 was the Marie Curie Memorial Foundation (see above), with St John's Kirk in Perth receiving £150, and the Highland Society of London £125. The remaining donations were all very small, and were directed to a variety of causes, notably Scottish and wildlife charities. A previous time-limited trust which was set up in 1968 to distribute its income to charity for twenty years, the Duke of Atholl's Charity Trust, was terminated in 1988.

After we had sent a copy of this entry for checking to the trustees of the Duke's charitable trust, we were informed that 'the facts as asserted are, in a number of respects, incorrect and misleading', although in which respects they did not say.

Contact: The Duke of Atholl's 1987 Charity Trust, c/o Secretary of the Cowdray Trust, 10/12 Cork St, London W1X 1DA.
Tel: 0171 439 9061.

PETER HINCHCLIFFE
£500 NEW

PREFERENCE: general, North West
AGE: 47
WEALTH: £20m-£35m
TRUST LINKS: Hinchcliffe Foundation
COMPANY LINKS: Iceland Frozen Foods

Peter Hinchcliffe is deputy chair and joint managing director of Iceland Frozen Foods, the company he set up with Malcolm Walker in 1979. Having taken over Bejam, its former rival run by John Apthorp (qv), this Deeside based company is now a leading retailer of frozen produce and, increasingly, other foodstuffs.

Hinchcliffe still has a valuable stake in the company, although has frequently sold small chunks, including half a million shares for £1 million in 1992. Some of the proceeds of these disposals may find their way to the **Hinchcliffe Foundation**, which was established by Peter Hinchcliffe in 1988 with the sum of £1,000. Currently, this charitable trust has a rather limited financial impact –

by April 1992 it had built up assets of over £34,000, but during the previous three years had made donations totalling less than £6,000, of which £5,000 went to Eaton Hall Design in 1989/90. The foundation's most recent accounts for 1991/92 show an income of only £800 and a solitary donation of £500 to Chester Childbirth Appeal.

Contact: Mr P H Taylor, Hinchcliffe Foundation, Bullivant & Co, State House, 22 Dale St, Liverpool, L2 4UR. Tel: 0151 227 5671.

MUCKLOW family

£250

PREFERENCE: general, medicine, welfare

WEALTH: £50m-£75m

TRUST LINKS: Mucklow Charitable Trust Ltd

COMPANY LINKS: A & J Mucklow

The Mucklow family may not be instantly recognisable to many of us, but in the West Midlands they are well known from their activities in the building and property sector. The family firm A & J Mucklow was set up by Albert and Jothan, uncle and father of the current company chair. It started off building houses before branching out into property, and it is now the leading factory landlord in the region.

The only grant-making trust we have been able to find registered in the family's name is the **Mucklow Charitable Trust Limited**, a charitable company which was founded by Jothan Mucklow and his wife Florence in 1978. Both of the founders have since passed away (Jothan in 1985 and Florence in 1992) and the current directors include

Albert Jothan Mucklow and Allan John Mucklow. The trust has a relatively restricted impact, however, as its annual grant total has never exceeded £800. In 1992 it held assets of £22,000 which produced an income of £1,500, and donations of only £250 were made.

Contact: Mr Albert J Mucklow, Mucklow Charitable Trust Ltd, Haden Cross, Halesowen Rd, Cradley Heath, Warley, West Midlands, B64 7JB. Tel: 0121 550 1841.

KEN MORRISON and family

£150 NEW

PREFERENCE: general, Yorkshire

AGE: 62

WEALTH: £250m-£500m

TRUST LINKS: Ken and Edna Morrison Charitable Trust, Wm Morrison Supermarkets plc Charitable Trust, Wm Morrison Enterprise Trusts Nos. 1 and 2

COMPANY LINKS: Wm Morrison Supermarkets

The **Ken and Edna Morrison Charitable Trust** was endowed in 1987 with 200,000 shares in Wm Morrison Supermarkets. Readers in Yorkshire, where the chain is based, will appreciate that that makes a tidy fortune in itself. The market value of the trust's assets was in fact some £900,000 in 1992, although grants made in the year came to only £150, following £300 in the previous year. Age Concern, Marie Curie Cancer Research and Sight Savers received £50 each.

The only sizeable donation that appears to have been made by the trust to date is a £100,000 gift made to

Bradford Girls Grammar School in 1987/88. This was financed by the sale of part of the trust's shareholding. Whether or not the trust has it in mind to make more donations of this size and is accumulating investment income to that end is unclear, but the capacity is certainly there.

The Morrison supermarket chain, one of the top performing companies in the country, also has its own **Wm Morrison Supermarkets plc Charitable Trust**. This made donations totalling £20,000 in 1992/93 and although no information on the beneficiaries was available, it is likely that the money went to charities in the Yorkshire area. There are also two Wm Morrison Enterprise Trusts, although the first trust now seems to exist primarily as a conduit for donated funds to the second. A total of £78,000 was spent by the No. 2 Enterprise Trust in 1992/93 on the organisation of training in business and enterprise skills, particularly concerned with self-employment. Ken Morrison is a trustee of all these trusts.

Fierce competition in the supermarket sector may have recently hurt both profits and the share value of Wm Morrison, of which Ken and his family own nearly 40 per cent, but if any of the major chains can survive the ride intact it ought to be this one. Meanwhile, the Ken and Edna Morrison Charitable Trust continues to grow.

Contact: For Ken and Edna Morrison Charitable Trust: Gordons Wright & Wright, Solicitors, 14 Piccadilly, Bradford, West Yorkshire BD1 3LX. Tel: 01274 733771. For Wm Morrison Supermarkets plc: K Ounsworth, Hilmore House, Thornton Road, Bradford, West Yorkshire BD8 9AX. Tel: 01274 494166.

SIR ANTHONY JACOBS
£140 NEW
(but see below)

PREFERENCE: Jewish causes, the Liberal Democrats

AGE: 62

WEALTH: £35m-£50m

TRUST LINKS: Jacobs Charitable Trust

COMPANY LINKS: BSM Group

Well-known for his backing for the Liberal Democrats, Sir Anthony Jacobs is also a supporter of charities through the **Jacobs Charitable Trust** which he set up in 1972, the year before he joined BSM. There are, however, no recent accounts on file for this trust at the Charity Commission, which is presumed to be still active. The 1977/78 accounts record assets of £1,400 and donations of only £140, although we would expect that this figure has grown substantially in recent years. In the period 1973-76 the trust made grants totalling £13,000, mainly to Jewish and Israeli causes. We were informed by Sir Anthony that: 'At the present moment and probably until the end of this year or early next year, there is no requirement to publish the accounts of charitable trusts which explains why there is none on record since 1978.'

Sir Anthony Jacobs made his fortune thanks to learner drivers. He steered the driving instruction company, the British School of Motoring, from strength to strength until he sold most of his shares for around £40 million in 1990 in order to retire. The BSM Group was floated on the stock exchange last year, and Sir Anthony took this opportunity to sell some more of his remaining holding, leaving him with only 4.5%.

Sir Anthony requested that we 'do not publish my name or any data concerning my supposed wealth or philanthropy.' He also commented that significant donations may be given by Gift Aid.

Contact: Sir A Jacobs, Jacobs Charitable Trust, 9 Nottingham Terrace, London, NW1 4QB.

SIR EUAN ANSTRUTHER-GOUGH-CALTHORPE

PREFERENCE: not known

AGE: 27

WEALTH: £50m-£75m

TRUST LINKS: none direct

COMPANY LINKS: none

Sir Euan, the 3rd Baronet of Elvetham, inherited his title and his wealth from his grandfather in 1985. He is now the proud owner of a large slice of leafy Birmingham around the Edgbaston cricket ground, along with several other investments in America and on the Continent, and some valuable art treasures. The family's landholdings have their origins in the 1700s, when an ancestor, Sir Richard Gough, used the proceeds of his tradings in South East Asia to buy Edgbaston Manor for the princely sum of £20,000.

What was not passed down from his grandfather, however, was control of the **Elvetham Charitable Trust** (also known as the Elvetham Charities), which had been set up by the 2nd Baronet in 1972. Other than this family link, Sir Euan has no direct connection with the Elvetham Charitable Trust. It currently has assets of over £370,000 which generate an annual income of around £25,000. In 1991/92 donations of £43,000 were

made, but in 1992/93 this fell to only £2,500. Whilst the recipients of these donations were not specified in the trust's accounts, there is a stated preference for charities working in the medical, welfare and environment sectors. The trust particularly concentrates its efforts on the Birmingham area, where the family owns property; and on Hampshire, where the family has an estate at Hartley Wintney. One of the trustees of the Elvetham Charitable Trust is John Austen Anstruther-Gough-Calthorpe, who is Sir Euan's uncle and also his heir.

Contact: The Secretary, Elvetham Charitable Trust, Belmore Park, Upham, Hampshire, SO3 1HQ.

LORD ARCHER

PREFERENCE: not known

AGE: 54

WEALTH: £20m-£35m

TRUST LINKS: none found

COMPANY LINKS: none

Perhaps Lord Jeffrey Archer's best known charitable involvement was his stint as chair of the Simple Truth organisation, which raised a worldwide total of £57 million for the Kurds. Of this, £14 million came from this country – £10 million from the government and £4 million in donations from individuals and companies. He is no stranger to professional charity fundraising. After studying for an education diploma at Brasenose College Oxford, he set up a company – Arrow Enterprises – which arranged cash generating events for various causes.

We have not, however, been able to trace any charitable trusts registered in his name through which he might make personal donations. He did, however, redirect to charity the

£550,000 damages he received from the *Daily Star* and *News of the World* following his famous 1986 libel case.

Lord Archer's life story is almost as extraordinary as one of the plots from his best-sellers. After running for his country, he was a fresh-faced Tory MP in the early seventies. He left the House in 1974 with debts of £427,000 which took him several years to pay back. He turned his hand to writing, with his first novel *Not a Penny More, Not a Penny Less* published in 1975. Each successive book has contributed larger amounts to Archer's bank balance, with reported advance sales of £3 million for his latest, *Honour Among Thieves*. Along the way he has also found time to maintain an active involvement with politics as deputy chair of the Conservative Party in the mid-eighties, although he was passed over for the post of chair of the party in a recent cabinet reshuffle.

Contact: Lord Archer, Alembic House, 93 Albert Embankment, London, SE1 7TY.

DUKE OF ARGYLL

PREFERENCE: Scotland, youth
AGE: 56
WEALTH: less than £20m
TRUST LINKS: none found
COMPANY LINKS: Beinn Bhuidhe Holdings

A former New York stockbroker, the Duke of Argyll appears to be in the position faced by many members of the British aristocracy, as his wealth derives from land assets held by his family rather than from a more easily accessible source. Accordingly, we have been unable to find any charitable trusts registered in his name at the Charity Commission, although the Duke is involved with several

causes in Scotland and is president of the Royal Caledonian Schools and the Argyll Scouts Association. On the business front he is director of several Scotch whisky distilleries, including White Heather and Glenlivet, and chair of Beinn Bhuidhe Holdings.

Contact: Duke of Argyll, Inverary Castle, Inverary, Argyll, Scotland, PA32 8XF.

MICHAEL ASHCROFT

PREFERENCE: education
AGE: 48
WEALTH: £50m-£75m
TRUST LINKS: ADT Education Trust Ltd
COMPANY LINKS: ADT Group

Like a number of the other self-made millionaires in this book, Michael Ashcroft has supported the government's City Technology College initiative. The company he runs, ADT, has given substantial help for one of the colleges which has been set up in Wandsworth. The firm's assistance has been channelled through the **ADT Education Trust Limited**, which was established in 1990 as a charitable company with Michael Ashcroft as one of the subscribers.

The Wandsworth 'ADT College', as it is now known, opened in September 1991, and in that year received £7.8 million of its capital funding from the Department of Education compared with £1 million from the ADT Group. The college has recently agreed to pilot the government's wholly school-based teacher training programme.

Ashcroft's fortune has been variously estimated at around £50-£60 million in recent wealth listings, although he stated that the figure we have given above is inaccurate. His worth stems from involvements with a substantial business empire – ranging from business services and office cleaning, through orange juice, to home security and car auctions – which centres around the overseas-based ADT Group. Away from the world of industry, he is also chair of the trustees of the Community Action Trust, the crime prevention organisation.

Contact: ADT Group plc, Prospect House, The Broadway, Farnham Common, Slough, SL2 3PQ. Tel: 01753 645622.

LORD BARNARD

PREFERENCE: not known

AGE: 70

WEALTH: £20m-£35m

TRUST LINKS: Lady Barnard Memorial Fund

COMPANY LINKS: none

Lord Barnard controls a large tract of land around the family seat, Raby Castle in County Durham. He has strong charitable links with the region. He has been involved with the regional branches of the British Red Cross Society, St John Council, Scouts Association, and the Royal British Legion. He is currently president of Teesdale and Weardale Search and Rescue and Durham Wildlife Trust, and until last year was vice chair of the national British Red Cross council.

The only grant-making trust we have found registered in his family's name is the rather old **Lady Barnard Memorial Fund**, which was set up by a previous Lord Barnard back in 1918 in memory of his wife. It was originally endowed with £1,000 in government war loan stock – a considerable amount in those days. By 1990, however, the fund held

assets of only £266 and made total donations of a meagre £60.

In response to us sending him a copy of the above entry, we were informed that Lord Barnard felt that it 'does not reflect the up to date position very well, where charitable giving is not necessarily through Charitable Trusts but by Covenant and Gift Aid'.

Contact: Lord Barnard, Raby Castle, PO Box 50, Staindrop, Darlington, County Durham, DL2 3AY. Tel: 01833 660751. Lady Barnard Memorial Fund: Mr M J White, Clerk to the Trustees, Watsons, 8 Newgate, Barnard Castle, County Durham.

MARQUESS OF BATH

PREFERENCE: see below

AGE: 62

WEALTH: £35m-£50m

TRUST LINKS: none found

COMPANY LINKS: Longleat Enterprises

The Marquess of Bath is not your typical member of the aristocracy. He painted a series of erotic murals in the late sixties which are now on public show, he has been involved with what the *Sunday Times* describes as numerous 'wifelets' over the years in addition to his wife Anna Gael, and he has stood as a Wessex Regionalist candidate for the European Parliament. At present, however, he is Liberal Democrat whip in the House of Lords. Bath inherited the title from his father in 1992, having previously been Viscount Weymouth for most of his life, and he lives at Longleat in Wiltshire. This stately home is famous for its lions and labyrinths, and more recently the Centre Parcs leisure complex in its grounds.

The only charitable trusts with

which we have been able to link Lord Bath's family are two rather ancient education foundations, which were established by an earlier Viscount Weymouth in 1905 and have a current annual income of only around £50 each.

We were informed that Lord Bath did not wish to feature in this directory, as he makes regular donations to several chosen charities, but prefers to keep details about the recipients and the amounts private. He also felt that this entry would encourage even more 'begging letters' than he already receives, and it is impossible to respond to them all.

Contact: Marquess of Bath, Longleat House, Warminster, Wilts, BA12 7NN. Tel: 01985 844400.

BEATTIE family

NEW

PREFERENCE: West Midlands
WEALTH: less than £20m
TRUST LINKS: James Beattie Charitable Trust
COMPANY LINKS: James Beattie

The Beattie surname is well-known in the West Midlands thanks to the efforts of the late James Beattie, who built up the eponymous Wolverhampton-based chain of department stores and made his fortune.

Charities in the region benefit from a charitable trust set up by James Beattie in 1972, initially called the Perton Charitable Trust. It has since been renamed the **James Beattie Charitable Trust** and is the only charitable trust we have found which is currently registered in the family's name. James Beattie initially endowed the trust with 5,000 shares in his company, which it still holds along with other assets together worth £124,000. These generated an income of £9,000 in 1992/93 of which £5,000 was distributed to charities. Given James Beattie's strong links with the area, it is not surprising that the beneficiaries of these grants were located mainly in Wolverhampton and the West Midlands, including Abbeyfield (Wolverhampton) Society and Wolverhampton YMCA which both received £750, and Wolverhampton Diabetes Trust which got £500.

Whilst the trust is currently relatively small, when he died in 1988 James Beattie left it one-fifth of his net estate in his will. This should enhance the trust's assets to the tune of £1.5m-£1.75m, hopefully in 1994/95, with a subsequent increase in the amount available for charitable donations. However, appeals from individuals will still not be funded.

Contact: Mrs J V Redshaw, Trustee, James Beattie Charitable Trust, PO Box 12, Bridgnorth, Shropshire, WV15 5LQ.

DUKE OF BEAUFORT

PREFERENCE: churches, health, youth, Avon
AGE: 66
WEALTH: £50m-£75m
TRUST LINKS: Beaufort Charitable Trust
COMPANY LINKS: Marlborough Fine Arts

David Robert Somerset, the 11th Duke of Beaufort, is perhaps best known for the horse trials held at his Badminton stately home. He inherited the title and the house from his cousin in 1984, and also took charge of the **Beaufort Charitable Trust**, which was established by the 10th Duke in 1968, and of which the present Duke was a founder trustee. The trust's relatively modest assets of £22,000 in stocks and shares are soon to be supplemented by a cash legacy of £25,000 from executors of the 10th Duke's will. In 1991/92 the trust made donations totalling £3,165, with over two-thirds directed towards Kington Church in a single donation of £2,500. The only other grant of any size was £150 given to the Rehabilitation and Medical Research Trust. The rest were very small and directed at general charities, with an emphasis on those located in the Avon area, or dealing with wildlife and young people.

The Duke's wealth is derived not only from over 52,000 acres of land around Badminton, but also from an art collection which includes two paintings by Canaletto worth £8m. His interest in art also extends to his business interests – he has been chair of the art dealers Marlborough Fine Art since 1977. His most notable foray into the corporate world, however, was his participation in the £13.5 billion bid for the BAT cigarette conglomerate in 1988 with two other members of the mega-rich – Sir James Goldsmith (qv) and the Australian Kerry Packer. Clearly, someone who mixes at such a high level cannot be short of either business acumen or financial assets.

The present Duke and Duchess are both involved with a handful of charities. The Duchess is president of the National Star Centre for Disabled Youth and vice-president of the Abbeyfield Society, but received most press attention for a recent charity abseil down the Gloucestershire Royal Infirmary at the age of 64. The Duke is a patron of the Brooke Hospital for Sick Animals. He also reportedly subsidises the Beaufort Hunt to the tune of £100,000 each year. Does the Brooke Hospital take injured foxes?

Contact: Mr J R Whateley, Trust Administrator, Messrs Lee & Pembertons Solicitors, 45 Pont St, London SW1X 0BD. Tel: 0171 589 1114

SIR DEREK BIBBY

PREFERENCE: Liverpool
AGE: 72
WEALTH: £20m-£35m
TRUST LINKS: D J Bibby Trust Fund, Bibby Trust Fund, Lady Bibby Trust Fund
COMPANY LINKS: Bibby Line Group

The private Bibby Line Group, a shipping company based in Liverpool, is almost totally controlled by the Bibby family. The family patriarch, Sir Derek Bibby, is now president of the company but no longer sits on the board, having handed over the reins to his son Michael. Sir Derek is also chair of Birkenhead Boys' Club.

There appear to be at least three charitable trusts registered in the family name at the Charity Commission, but we have not been able to find much out about them because of the limited information on file. The **Bibby Trust Fund, D J Bibby Trust Fund and Lady Bibby Trust Fund** were all established back in the early sixties by Sir Derek's parents, with Liverpool Council of Social Service as the trustee. We have been unable to find any indication of their current size or scope.

Contact for all funds: Mr E Murphy, Chief Executive, Liverpool Council of Social Services, 14 Castle St, Liverpool, L2 0NJ. Tel: 0151 236 7728.

NIGEL BROWN
and family

PREFERENCE: various counties in the North and Midlands

AGE: 48

WEALTH: less than £20m

TRUST LINKS: Brown Butlin Group Charitable Foundation

COMPANY LINKS: Brown Butlin Group

Whilst information concerning personal charitable donations made directly by Nigel Brown was not available, the company controlled by his family has recently established the **Brown Butlin Group Charitable Foundation** through which to make donations. This grant-making trust was set up in 1991 with an initial settlement of £1,000 from the Lincolnshire based Brown Butlin Group which markets agricultural chemicals. The foundation's deed of settlement restricts it to the support of organisations which educate the public in agriculture or preserve agricultural artefacts, or which are involved in the conservation of the rural environment and landscape. Its area of operation is also limited to the various counties in the North and the Midlands. These restrictions reflect the nature of the company's products and its client base. However, for technical reasons this foundation is in the process of being wound down.

The Brown family owns three-quarters of the shares in the successful Brown Butlin Group. Nigel Brown himself is a major stockholder and chair of the company, and is also non-executive director of Newark Preparatory School.

Contact: Mr K J Matthews, Brown Butlin Group Charitable Trust, Brook House, 42 Manor St, Ruskington, Sleaford, Lincs, NG34 9EP.

ANDREW BROWNSWORD

PREFERENCE: Bath and South West, medicine, children

AGE: 46

WEALTH: £100m-£250m

TRUST LINKS: Brownsword Charitable Foundation

COMPANY LINKS: Hallmark, incorporating Andrew Brownsword Collection

Perhaps in anticipation of his future wealth, Andrew Brownsword has recently established the **Brownsword Charitable Foundation**. This grant-making trust, which is still very much in its early days, was set up in 1992 with Brownsword and his wife as founding trustees. It mainly supports local causes operating in Bath and the South West, where its founder resides, and has given grants to various hospices and cancer charities, as well as organisations dealing with the welfare of young people. At present there are no accounts on file for it at the Charity Commission, but given Brownsword's burgeoning wealth this foundation is clearly one to watch out for in the future.

If you have ever bought a birthday card, it is a fair bet that you will have contributed to the rapidly expanding fortune of Andrew Brownsword, who only last year entered the *Sunday Times Top 400 Rich* list at number 50 and is not yet listed in *Who's Who*. In 1989 his company, the Andrew Brownsword Collection, acquired Gordon Fraser, the leading brand-name in the greetings card market. During the following few years, takings soared as the company grew into Britain's largest card maker — good news for Brownsword who owned four-fifths of the firm's shares. In its continuing search for further profits, the company diversified its operations into book publishing and a wider variety of merchandising.

In a transaction largely carried out away from the bright lights of publicity, this company has itself recently been purchased by Hallmark Cards, having received the blessing of the Monopolies and Mergers Commission. It is thought that the sale price was in excess of £200 million, and Brownsword got the job of Hallmark's UK and Ireland chief executive as part of the bargain. All this is not bad for someone who started out in the industry because he liked his £12-a-week summer job as a delivery van driver so much that he did not return to polytechnic to finish his catering course.

Contact: Bob Calleja, Personnel Director, Brownsword Charitable Foundation, James Street West, Bath, BA1 2BS. Tel: 01225 444544.

LADY SHEILA BUTLIN

PREFERENCE: disability, youth, elderly people
AGE: 64
WEALTH: £35m-£50m
TRUST LINKS: Bill Butlin Charity Trust
COMPANY LINKS: none

Lady Butlin continues her late husband's philanthropic activities as trustee of the **Bill Butlin Charity Trust**, which he had established in 1963. Billy Butlin was knighted for his generosity – in the early 1970s he told the *Daily Mirror* that he had given half of his earnings away to charity. This trust now holds assets of over £1.5 million, the proceeds of which supported donations of £119,000 in 1990/91. These were directed mainly at charities dealing with disabled children, the elderly and the needy.

Lady Butlin was the third, and last, wife of the holiday camp magnate Sir Billy Butlin. He had arrived in Britain from Canada with £5 in his pocket, but proceeded to build up the famous leisure business which he sold for a fortune to the Rank Organisation in the 1970s. She had started working as a bar supervisor at Butlin's Pwllheli camp, and had rapidly progressed up the company hierarchy to become director of its travel division. As their paths crossed, the working relationship developed into a personal relationship, and eventually the two married in 1976. Sir Billy died in 1980, leaving a large share of his £100 million fortune to his wife. Lady Sheila continues to live quietly in the Channel Isles, where the couple had moved for tax reasons.

Contact: Darren Win, The Bill Butlin Charity Trust, c/o Rawlinson & Hunter, 1 Hanover Square, London W1A 4SR. Tel: 0171 493 4040.

EARL OF CARNARVON

PREFERENCE: Hampshire & Berkshire
AGE: 70
WEALTH: less than £20m
TRUST LINKS: none found
COMPANY LINKS: Newbury Racecourse

The Seventh Earl of Carnarvon is closely involved with the pursuit of horse-racing, as the Queen's racing manager, chair of both the Newbury Racecourse company and the Equine Virology Research Foundation, and past president of the Thoroughbred Breeders' Association and the Amateur Riders' Association. He is active with a wide range of organisations around the family seat, Highclere House near Newbury, including positions as chair of the Basingstoke and North Hampshire Medical Trust, president of Hampshire and Isle of Wight Naturalists' Trust and Hampshire Association for Care of the Blind, and past president of Basingstoke Sports Trust. On a wider scale, he is also vice president and past chair of the Game Research Association, and chair of the Standing Conference on Countryside Sports. Past involvements with economic planning in Hampshire and the South East are reflected in his role as chair of the Standing Conference on London and the South East Regional Planning Authorities.

The family is also famous because of the current Lord Carnarvon's grandfather, who was involved with archaeologist Howard Carter in the famous excavations of King Tutankhamun's tomb earlier this century. The apocryphal story would have us believe that the former Lord Carnarvon died as a result of the Pharaoh's curse afflicting those who disturbed the burial site.

Contact: Lord Carnarvon, Milford Lake House, Burghclere, Newbury, Berkshire, RG16 9EL.
Tel: 01635 253387.

of the North Sea Oil exploration boom of the seventies. In 1985 he was co-founder of the **Cluff Foundation**, a charitable company whose objects were the relief of poverty and sickness, the furtherance of religion and education anywhere in the world, and promotion of the arts and sciences. It also cited certain charities which were to benefit, namely: NSPCC, National Association for the Welfare of Children in Hospital, Blue Cross, National Library for the Blind, Fauna Preservation Society, and Grenadier Guards Benevolent Fund. The foundation has lain dormant over subsequent years, with no income or assets. It was dissolved as a company in March 1991 but is still a registered charity. We have not been able to trace any other active grant-making trusts registered in Cluff's name.

Cluff, who once owned the *Spectator* magazine, is currently chair and chief executive of Cluff Resources. He owns only a small stake in the business, and estimated his personal wealth at between £4 million to £5 million. He is also a trustee of the Anglo-Hong Kong Trust and chair of the Youth Cancer Trust.

Contact: Mr J G Cluff, Cluff Resources plc, 58 St James's St, London, SW1A 1LD. Tel: 0171 493 8272.

JOHN GORDON (ALGY) CLUFF

PREFERENCE: children, animals, welfare, general
AGE: 54
WEALTH: less than £20m
TRUST LINKS: Cluff Foundation
COMPANY LINKS: Cluff Resources

John Gordon Cluff, universally known as 'Algy', made his fortune on the back

STANLEY COHEN

PREFERENCE: general
AGE: 66
WEALTH: £50m-£75m
TRUST LINKS: Cohen Family Foundation
COMPANY LINKS: Queensway Securities, Betterware

Through his Queensway Securities investment company, Stanley Cohen has generated money though his own abilities through various interests, including a stake in the Platignum pen business. However, he has become a very wealthy man largely thanks to his son, Andrew Cohen (qv), who has steered the Betterware direct sales home products group to success and considerably enhanced the value of his father's holdings. Stanley Cohen is a non-executive director of this business. In the summer of 1993, four members of the Cohen family sold a 13% stake in Betterware for £31 million, leaving them with around half the company's shares. Stanley Cohen and his wife reduced their personal holdings from 29% to 22.5%, netting around £15 million. It is likely that a portion of this money will have found its way into the **Cohen Family Foundation**, which Stanley Cohen established in 1992, with him and his son Andrew as co-trustees. Because the foundation is relatively new, at the time of writing there were no accounts on file for it at the Charity Commission. It was set up with the broad aims of supporting general charitable causes.

Contact: Cohen Family Foundation, S J Berwin & Co, Solicitors, 222 Grays Inn Rd, London, WC1X 8HB. Tel: 0171 837 2222.

SIR HUMPHREY CRIPPS
and family

PREFERENCE: Northants, education, health, heritage, churches
AGE: 77
WEALTH: unknown
TRUST LINKS: Cripps Foundation
COMPANY LINKS: Pianoforte Supplies Ltd, Velcro Industries

Sir Humphrey Cripps chairs Pianoforte Supplies, a Northampton based company which provides components for the motor industry, and the American company Velcro Industries which manufactures the fastening strip of the same name. In 1955 he set up the **Cripps Foundation** with his late parents Sir Cyril and Lady Cripps. By 1991/92 the foundation had an income of £1 million obtained mainly from covenants from various unspecified companies – although in the previous year they were Pianoforte Supplies, Pianoforte Supplies (Manufacturing) and Tonelodge – and made donations totalling £1.7 million.

The Cripps Foundation appears to have a strong preference for causes with which Sir Humphrey has some personal connection or involvement. Major grants made in the year 1991/92 included: £1.3 million to Northampton High School for Girls, of which Sir Humphrey has been a governor; £287,000 to Queens' College Cambridge, of which he is honorary fellow, although he graduated from nearby St John's College; and £50,000 to Peterborough Cathedral, of whose trust he is a member. The remaining donations were directed to churches and to a variety of medical, education, youth and elderly organisations operating in Northamptonshire. Sir Humphrey is also chair of the foundation trust at Northampton School for Boys, trustee of the University of Nottingham's Development Trust, and member of the trust for All Saints Church, Northampton. A major project supported by the foundation in previous years, and over which Sir Humphrey still presides as trustee, has been the Cripps Postgraduate Medical Centre at Northampton General Hospital.

After a draft of this entry had been sent for checking to the foundation, we were informed by Sir Humphrey's son, Edward Cripps, that 'it is misleading to attribute to Sir Humphrey the charitable donations of the Cripps Foundation'. On the basis of press reports, we had initially given Sir Humphrey's wealth as between £75-£100 million, but his son told us that this was a 'gross exaggeration' and that his total asset holdings amount to less than 1% of our estimate. Edward Cripps also expressed his belief that there should not be any entry for Sir Humphrey Cripps in this book.

Contact: The Secretary, Cripps Foundation, 8th Floor, Aldwych House, 81 Aldwych, London, WC2B 4HP. Tel: 0171 242 2444.

DEREK CROWSON

PREFERENCE: general
WEALTH: £35m-£50m
TRUST LINKS: Derek Crowson Charitable Trust
COMPANY LINKS: Crowson Fabrics

Derek Crowson has one of the highest executive salaries in the UK, and over the past two years has received total payments of over £5 million from the company he runs, Crowson Fabrics, which makes furnishing material. It looks like some of this money will soon be going to charity via the **Derek Crowson Charitable Trust**, which he set up in 1993 to support general causes. As yet, there are no accounts for this trust on file at the Charity Commission, so it is not possible at present to anticipate its donations policy or the total amount it might give.

Contact: Mr J R Hughes, Derek Crowson Charitable Trust, 116 High St, Uckfield, East Sussex, TN22 1QH. Tel: 01825 761555.

DUKE OF DEVONSHIRE
and family

PREFERENCE: heritage, Sussex, Derbyshire, general
AGE: 74
WEALTH: £100m-£250m
TRUST LINKS: 10th Duke of Devonshire's Charitable Trust
COMPANY LINKS: none

In common with some of the other wealthy aristocrats in this book, the Duke of Devonshire and his family make fairly substantial donations through a charitable trust. Of this total, a major chunk is redirected towards the upkeep of the family seat 'for the public benefit', in their case Chatsworth House in Derbyshire.

The **10th Duke of Devonshire's Charitable Trust** was set up by the present Duke's father in 1949 with 1,600 ordinary £20 shares in the Eastbourne Waterworks Company. Although a founding trustee, the current Lord Devonshire now has no direct link with the charitable trust. However, his son and heir, the Marquess of Hartingdon, is one of the current trustees, and as such is a steward over its considerable £7 million asset base. This generated an income of nearly one-quarter million pounds in 1992/93 and permitted donations of £144,000. As in previous years, the major recipient of the trust's largesse was the **Chatsworth House Trust** (see below) which in 1992/93 received £60,000, and in 1990/91 benefited to the tune of an exceptional £1.3 million. The remaining grants were focused primarily on charities and educational establishments operating in Derbyshire, West Yorkshire and Eastbourne, where the family holds the land that is the basis of their wealth. These included £25,000 to RNLI Eastbourne, of which the Duke is president, £8,000 to Pilsley CofE School, £5,000 to Keighley Cadet Corp, and £4,000 to Eastbourne War Memorial Housing. Other more general gifts included £5,000 to the Ian Gow Memorial Fund and £1,000 to the Pornography and Violence Research Trust.

The Chatsworth House Trust, a charitable company, was set up in 1981 by various subscribers including the Duke and his wife, and the Marquess and Marchioness of Hartingdon. These four are also members of its council of management, which also includes banker Rupert Hambro. Its principal activities are given as 'the maintenance and preservation of this property [Chatsworth House] and opening it to the public'. Aside from donations from Devonshire's charitable trust, the main component of its 1992/93 income was the £1.7 million revenue from visitors to Chatsworth, although this was not sufficient to pay for its running costs of over two million pounds. Shortly after it was established, the Chatsworth House Trust took an assignment of a 99 year lease of the house and its essential contents, along with 1,575 acres of land including the garden and park surrounding the house, at an annual rent of £1. The Duke of Devonshire subleases a private suite within Chatsworth House, at a rent assessed every five years by independent chartered surveyors.

Aside from financial support, the Duke is involved on a personal basis with a large number of causes. He is connected with various organisations working with the disabled, as president of the National Association for Deaf Children, East Midlands Mencap, and Chesterfield & District Society for the Deaf, and vice-

president of RADAR. He is also active in the welfare of the young and elderly as patron of Methodist Homes for the Elderly, vice-president of Help the Aged, and president of Derbyshire Boy Scouts Association and Chesterfield & North Derbyshire NSPCC. Other involvements include positions as chair of the Diocese of Bradford Church Buildings Appeal, and vice-president of Action Research, Cancer Research Campaign, Arthritis and Rheumatism Council, Ex-Services Mental Welfare Society, National Council for One-Parent Families, the Animal Health Trust, and the Council for the Preservation of Rural England. His wife, the Duchess, is vice-president of the Rare Breeds Survival Trust, and his son the Marquess of Hartingdon is a vice-councillor of the Cancer Research Campaign.

Contact: 10th Duke of Devonshire's Charitable Trust, Messrs Currey & Co, 21 Buckingham Gate, London, SW1E 6LS. Tel: 0171 828 4091.

DICK FRANCIS

PREFERENCE: racing charities?
AGE: 73
WEALTH: £20m-£35m
TRUST LINKS: none found
COMPANY LINKS: none

Dick Francis has produced a string of more than thirty best-selling horse-racing thrillers on the trot, at the rate of around one per year. His previous and successful career as a jockey is unfortunately best remembered for the infamous occasion when his mount Devon Loch, one of the Queen Mother's horses, lost its footing within sight of the Grand National finishing post when way ahead of the field and virtually assured of victory.

We have not been able to trace any

grant-making trusts registered in Dick Francis' name. A possible indication of his charitable preferences can be found, however, in the pages of *Comeback*, his 1991 novel. The leading character, Peter Darwin, whose family benefits from the Injured Jockey's Fund after the death of his jockey father says that 'Whenever I gave anything to charity from then on, it was to the Injured Jockeys' Fund', which is also described as 'a marvellous organisation.'

When contacted, Dick Francis's manager, Felix Francis, replied that his client is no longer a resident of the UK and so did not wish to be included in this publication.

Contact: Dick Francis, c/o Andrew Hewson, John Johnson (Authors' Agent) Ltd, Clerkenwell House, 45/47 Clerkenwell Green, London, EC1R 0HT.

DAVID GREEN

PREFERENCE: not known
AGE: 48
WEALTH: £50m-£75m.
TRUST LINKS: founding trustee of Tangent Charitable Trust
COMPANY LINKS: Colefax & Fowler, Carlton Communications

Like his younger brother Michael (qv), David Green's wealth is derived mainly from his stake in Carlton Communications, the company they set up jointly. He is no longer actively involved in its day-to-day operations, but sits on the board as non-executive director to keep an eye on his £40 million stake in the company. Instead he runs Colefax & Fowler, a high class furnishings and wallpapers group. He is chief executive of this firm, and holds £2 million worth of shares. However, the recession has not spared Colefax, and in 1993 it was in the red to the tune of nearly half a million.

We have found no evidence of charitable gifts made by David Green through trusts registered in his name. Although he was one of the co-founders of the **Tangent Charitable Trust** along with his brother (see entry for Michael Green), he now has no formal connection with it. He resigned as a trustee in 1986, the year he retired as director of Tangent Industries, the private company upon which the brothers had built their fortune. Even Colefax and Fowler gives relatively little – only £9,600 in 1991.

Contact: Colefax & Fowler Group plc, 39 Brook Street, London, W1Y 2JE. Tel: 0171 493 2231.

PETER GREENALL
and family NEW

PREFERENCE: general
AGE: 40
WEALTH: £100m-£250m
TRUST LINKS: Greenall Foundation
COMPANY LINKS: Greenalls Group

The Hon. Peter Greenall, eldest son and heir to Lord Daresbury, accepts that his family's wealth comes with certain strings attached, as he told the *Times*: 'You have the responsibilities of wealth and position, and you have to be involved' (26/6/93). He may choose to express this involvement through the **Greenall Foundation**, which he set up in 1992 to support general charitable causes, with himself and his wife as founding trustees. The only accounts on file at the Charity Commission are for the six month period after the foundation was set up, and they record a donated income of £17,000 but show that no charitable gifts had been made.

A London Business School graduate, Peter Greenall is now managing director of the pubs and hotels Greenalls Group, having sat on the board for nine years. The company owns the famous Belfry Hotel and golf course, and is planning to set up a national golf academy there for amateurs and professionals. His concern for the community is reflected in the actions of the family firm, which has been going for over three hundred years. It is an active contributor to charities local to its sites, which Peter Greenall says 'isn't just bleating concern – it's that people will feel better about Greenalls and go to the pubs more if they are proud of us' (*Times*, 26/6/93).

The Greenall family owns 16% of the shares in the company, and this stake is the basic source of their wealth. Peter is the family member with the highest profile, and chairs the Warrington Victims' Appeal Fund, which was set up after the 1993 IRA attack in the town where the Greenalls Group is based. He is also chair of the Aintree Racecourse, and no doubt was glad to preside over the smooth running of the 1994 Grand National following the previous year's debacle. Gilbert Greenall, Peter's brother, is a qualified medical doctor, adviser to the Overseas Development Organisation, and non-executive director of the Greenall Group.

The Greenalls Group also produced another family fortune last year when it bought the Devenish chain of pubs in the South West. The chair of Devenish, Michael Cannon, along with his family received around £25 million for their 13% stake in the company. We have not yet been able, however, to trace any charitable trusts registered in their name.

Contact: Mrs N L Campbell, Greenall Foundation, Hall Lane Farm, Daresbury, Warrington, Cheshire, WA4 4AF. Tel: 01925 740212.

ALBERT GUBAY

PREFERENCE: religion in the North West
AGE: 63
WEALTH: £100m-£250m
TRUST LINKS: none found
COMPANY LINKS: sold Kwik Save

Albert Gubay is very much a 'hands-on' businessman, and despite his fortune is still frequently to be found working at the site of his latest construction project. He has amassed his wealth mainly through a series of deals associated with retailing. In particular, he helped re-write the retail rulebook through the Kwik Save chain of 'limited line discounters', which have basic displays and a relatively restricted product range, but whose keen prices are now causing concern to the major supermarket groups. Since selling his interests in the Kwik Save group, he first went into overseas retail but more recently has become involved in property investment and development. He has overseen the building of a luxury hotels and leisure complex on the Isle of Man for an American company. He has also set up the Celtic Bank on this island, where he lives in a tax exile which he reckons has saved him millions of pounds. He has suggested that he might move to Switzerland in the near future as it is even more money-friendly.

Although we have been unable to trace any charitable trusts registered in Gubay's name, he set out his philanthropic intentions very clearly in a recent Hunter Davies interview: 'I wasn't bought up a Catholic. I was bought up nothing, but in the last few years, since my mother died, I go to church every Sunday. I've already built a church and given them it. I'm going to leave half my money to the Church. Liverpool diocese probably. I think they do good – teaching people right from wrong' (*Independent*, 30/6/92).

So it looks like the Church in Liverpool could eventually benefit to the tune of several hundred million pounds.

LORD HANSON

PREFERENCE: medicine, education, youth
AGE: 72
WEALTH: £35m-£50m
TRUST LINKS: Hanson Research Trust
COMPANY LINKS: Hanson

Lord Hanson, the most feared businessman of the eighties and one of the most politically fêted, is set to retire in 1997. What he will then do with his famed energy and his millions is anyone's guess, but on past evidence charitable activities may feature but will not top the list.

The Hanson-related donations that we have uncovered all stem from Hanson plc, the Anglo-American industrial conglomerate that Hanson runs with his partner Lord White, and in which he holds a stake of less than one per cent. Donations from Hanson plc in the UK totalled £894,000 in 1992/93, out of pre-tax profits of over £1 billion, and also included funding for the British Sports Trust for the Hanson Leadership Award of over £125,000 in that year. A commitment of £1 million over five years has been made to the National Youth Theatre. The company has also contributed £500,000 to the Royal College of Surgeons. In 1978 the company founded the **Hanson Research Trust** which maintains a fellowship in surgery at the University of Oxford. The 1993 accounts for the trust record expenditure of £25,000 on University of Oxford fellow and student costs and note that the current Hanson fellow is working on plastic surgical reconstruction.

Hanson Industries, the company's US arm headed by Lord White, also gives sizeable donations. In 1994 a gift of $1 million was made to the American Red Cross to provide support for victims of floods in the Mid West, following a similar donation for the benefit of victims of the San Francisco Earthquake and Hurricane Hugo. In the gentler nineties such donations may have gone some way to mitigating the tough, union-busting reputation with which Hanson has been characterised in the US. The president of the American Red Cross was quoted as saying, helpfully, 'We especially appreciate the fact that a transnational company should come to the aid of Americans in need'.

Lord Hanson himself is a member of the court of the Royal College of Surgeons of England and a fellow of the Cancer Research Campaign. He has in the past been described as a supporter of cancer research, but whether this is a reference to the Hanson Research Trust (above) is unclear. If Hanson was a substantial supporter of cancer causes it would not be surprising: Hanson's younger brother, champion show-jumper Bill Hanson, died from cancer at the tragically young age of 29. A new biography of the industrialist by Alex Brummer and Roger Cowe suggests: 'The loss of his brother was to prove the most formative event of [Lord] Hanson's life. It left scars that colour his views even today.'

One other trust, the **Hanson Educational Trust**, was set up by Lady Hanson in 1977 to support students. Its 1993 accounts reveal a £4,400 trust fund and donations in the year of £1,000 which contributed to the university expenses of a student.

Contact: Nicola Blyth, Charities Administrator, Hanson plc, 1 Grosvenor Place, London SW1X 7JH. Tel: 0171 245 1245.

SIR JACK HAYWARD

PREFERENCE: heritage

AGE: 70

WEALTH: £50m–£75m

TRUST LINKS: Hayward Foundation

COMPANY LINKS: Grand Bahamas Development Corp; Freeport Commercial & Industrial Ltd

Surprisingly for someone who has earned the nickname 'Union Jack' for his passionate support of all things British, this Wolverhampton born entrepreneur has made his home, and most of his considerable fortune, in the Bahamas. The self-imposed exile is not without its drawbacks – Sir Jack even exported a pub to the island of Grand Bahama, but no doubt the beer did not travel very well!

Sir Jack's love for this country and its past achievements is reflected in his charitable activities. He is heavily involved with the conservation and preservation of Britain's maritime history as honorary life vice-president of the Maritime Trust, and vice-president of the SS Great Britain Project, having bought Brunel's ship and gifted it to the nation over twenty years ago. Although outbid by Americans when he tried to save the Queen Elizabeth cruise liner and London Bridge, in 1969 he also bought the island of Lundy in the Bristol Channel for the nation, and he is still vice-president of the Lundy Field Society.

Sir Jack has no personal charitable trust, and there often seems to be some confusion between what he does with his personal money and what the trustees of the Hayward Foundation choose to support. The **Hayward Foundation** was established in 1961 by his father, the late Sir Charles Hayward, with shares in his company Firth Cleveland. Sir Jack is only a trustee and we have therefore not listed its grants under Sir Jack's personal donations. The foundation currently has a substantial asset base of nearly £20 million (none of it from Sir Jack), which permits grants of around £1.3 million per year. A major recipient of grants has been the Centre for Policy on Ageing, which received a quarter of a million pounds from the foundation in both 1988 and 1989, which it used to fund improvements in voluntary residential homes for the elderly. Other causes which have benefited include hospitals, the environment, the elderly and people with disabilities. The **Charles Hayward Trust** set up by Lady Hayward, Sir Charles' late wife, makes annual donations of around £600,000, but Sir Jack has no formal links with this trust.

Hayward inherited a sizeable fortune upon his father's death, but much of his wealth has been subsequently generated by continuing his family's development of Freeport, a boom town on Grand Bahama Island in the Bahamas, which is controlled by his two companies: Grand Bahama Development and Freeport Commercial & Industrial. He owns half of the island, as well as its main airport. He has also recently set up a joint airline venture, Laker Airways (Bahamas) Ltd, with Sir Freddie Laker, which flies American tourists to Grand Bahama Island.

Even though he lives on this tax haven, Sir Jack shows few of the trappings of luxury displayed by many multi-millionaires, and has a self-confessed parsimonious streak: 'I am terribly mean' (*Daily Mail*, 14/3/94). He has also compared his fortune, unfavourably, with other people who grace these pages: 'So much of it is on paper. It can go up in smoke. I don't know how much I am worth. I mean, I own a lot of land in the Bahamas that has not been exploited. It's all in the future. I am no Paul Getty. Nor for that matter am I a Jack Walker. More of a Lionel Pickering' (*Daily Mail*, 14/3/94). In *Who's Who*, the first recreational activity given by Hayward is 'promoting British endeavours, mainly in sport.' This would help explain his massive injection of an amount variously estimated at between £10m-£20m into Wolverhampton Wanderers, his local football team when growing up in the Midlands. He has said he will 'throw money at the club until the men in white coats come to take me away' (*Birmingham Post*, 27/12/93). He often travels half-way around the globe to support his team, which is now chaired by his son Jonathan.

We do, however, have a final word of warning for any fundraisers who might be thinking of approaching Sir Jack personally – he has a reputation for leaving all mail unopened!

Contact: Sir Jack Hayward, Seashell Lane (PO Box F-99), Freeport, Grand Bahama Island, Bahamas.

LORD HOWARD DE WALDEN
and family

PREFERENCE: racing charities, Saffron Walden

AGE: 82

WEALTH: £250m-£500m

TRUST LINKS: Saffron Walden United Charities

COMPANY LINKS: none

One of the oldest of Britain's aristocratic families and one of the richest, the family of Lord Howard de Walden owns some 100 acres of prime real estate in London's W1. Lord Howard de Walden also holds the distinction of having his name attached to one of the oldest trusts to appear in this book: **Lord Howard de Walden's Charity**, which was set up under the will of one of his ancestors in 1797. The Charity has since been subsumed under the Saffron Walden United Charities, and produced an income of £187 (sic) in 1992.

This does not exhaust the charitable activities of the Baron, however, who is a renowned racing enthusiast, having been senior steward at the Jockey Club three times, with a Derby-winner to his name (Slip Anchor, 1985). He recently put up his horse Gisarne to be raffled on behalf of the Racing Welfare Charity, although the filly will return to him at the end of her racing career.

Now in his eighties, Lord Howard de Walden stepped down as chair of his main property vehicle, Howard de Walden Estates, in 1992. In addition to the London properties, he has a 3,000 acre estate in Berkshire and some 30 racehorses. His four daughters are co-heiresses to the family fortune: the Hon Mrs Czernin, the Hon Mrs Buchan of Auchmacoy, the Hon Mrs White, and the Hon Mrs Acloque. The eldest, Mary Czernin has been noted for her charitable work. She is married to Joseph Czernin, who himself is of impeccable stock: *Debrett's* records that he is a son of a Count of the Holy Roman Empire with the predicate 'Hoch und Wohlgeboren (High and Well-born)'.

Contact: Lord Howard de Walden, Avington Manor, Hungerford, Berkshire.

LADY (P D) JAMES `NEW`

PREFERENCE: literature, religion, churches and Christian causes, conservation, welfare

AGE: 73

WEALTH: less than £20m

TRUST LINKS: P D James Trust

COMPANY LINKS: none

If you were introduced to a Mrs Phyllis Dorothy White you would probably not bat an eyelid. However, if you were then informed that she is better known as Lady P D James you would no doubt recognise the name of one of the country's foremost writers of detective thrillers, whose best known creation is Inspector Adam Dalgleish. Like several of the other novelists in this book, such as Dame Barbara Cartland and Ken Follett (qqv), she has a grant-making trust registered in her name at the Charity Commission.

● ARTS & ENTERTAINMENT GIVERS

Cameron Mackintosh	£1,903,000
Andrew Lloyd Webber	£1,200,000
Richard Attenborough	£219,000
Anthony Hopkins	£148,000
John Cleese	£60,000
Ken Follett	£40,000
John Gielgud	£22,000
Barbara Cartland	£16,000
Catherine Cookson	£2,000
Lord Lichfield	£1,000

The **P D James Trust** was set up by Lady James at the start of 1993 with herself and her two daughters as trustees. From the first accounts on file at the Charity Commission we are not able to give any indication of its likely size, although we are informed that it is not yet fully funded and cannot respond to unsolicited appeals. It intends to focus support on the promotion of education, especially in English language and literature; the relief of the poor, aged and infirm; the conservation and protection of the environment; and finally, the promotion of Christianity and the preservation of English churches. This latter purpose is not altogether surprising, as Lady James lists 'exploring churches' as a recreation in *Who's Who*.

Lady James has been involved more widely in the field of the arts as past member of both the Arts Council's Literature Advisory Panel and the British Council's Literature Committee. She was also a governor of the BBC from 1988-93. Her solicitors informed us that their client would much prefer that her entry did not appear in this book.

Contact: Mr F W O'Shea, P D James Trust, Maxwell Batley Solicitors, 27 Chancery Lane, London, WC2A 1PA. Tel: 0171 405 7888.

LORD LAING
and family
see below

PREFERENCE: business responsibility

AGE: 71

WEALTH: £100m-£250m

TRUST LINKS: none found

COMPANY LINKS: United Biscuits

Lord Laing is a familiar face in charitable circles as it was he who first floated the idea of launching in Britian a Per Cent Club, where businesses give a percentage of their profits to charity. United Biscuits, where Laing was chair for 18 years until 1990, gave away £902,000 in 1992, compared with pre-tax profits of £209 million. The company, where Lord Laing is now life president, bakes nearly half the biscuits in the country, and the Laing family still holds a small stake.

Lord Laing was chair of Business in the Community until 1991, and was a champion of corporate community involvement. He told a group of business leaders: 'While profits are of course an essential operating requirement of business they are not its sole purpose – the ultimate responsibility fo business is to serve society.' Laing himself has receded from public life over the last two or three years, stepping down as president of Goodwill and the Weston Spirit, and as joint treasurer of the Conservative Party. His recreations are listed in *Who's Who* as gardening and walking.

Contact: Graham Parker, secretary to the appeals committee, United Biscuits (Holdings) plc, Church Road, West Drayton, Middx UB7 7PR. Tel: 01895 432100.

LEVY family

PREFERENCE: youth, medicine, Jewish causes

AGE: 54

WEALTH: £20m-£35m

TRUST LINKS: Joseph Levy Charitable Foundation, P L Levy Charitable Settlement

COMPANY LINKS: Shaftesbury

Peter Levy, chair of the public property group Shaftesbury, is included in this book largely due to the efforts of his late father, who made a fortune out of London property development after the war, and proceeded to establish what is now a major grant-making trust.

Joseph Levy set up the **Joseph Levy Charitable Foundation** in 1965 with general charitable objects, and with several other Levy family members, including Peter, as trustees. It now has a considerable asset base of just under £10 million, which in 1991/92 generated an income of over three-quarters of a million. The donations made by the foundation tend to be concentrated on charities concerned with young people or health and medicine, and Jewish organisations. In the year, it made grants of £878,000, including a major gift of £132,000 to the London Federation of Boys' Clubs, which is a regular recipient, and £113,000 to the Admiral Nurse Service. Other large donations went to a variety of causes, such as the Jewish Welfare Board (£50,000), Alzheimer's Education and Training (£28,500), Muscular Dystrophy Group (£25,000), Stackpole Trust (£25,000), Friends of Hebrew University Jerusalem (£21,000), and the British Technion Society (£20,000). The Cystic Fibrosis Research Trust, of which Peter Levy is chair and trustee, was the recipient of a £64,000 gift and has received other substantial donations in previous years.

Peter Levy has a smaller, but more personal, grant-making trust of his own, the **P L Levy Charitable Settlement**, which he set up in 1979. In its most recent accounts, for the year 1990/91, the trust records assets of only £11,000 and no donations, although an interest free loan of £5,000 was made to the North Western Reform Synagogue.

Contact: Joseph Levy Charitable Foundation: Dr S Brichto, Director, 11 Waterloo Place, London, SW1Y 4AU. Tel: 0171 930 4606. P L Levy Charitable Settlement: Mr N W Benson, Lewis Golden & Co, 40 Queen Anne St, London, W1M 0EL. Tel: 0171 580 7313.

CELIA LIPTON

PREFERENCE: medicine

AGE: 67

WEALTH: £50m-£75m

TRUST LINKS: none found

COMPANY LINKS: heiress

British-born Celia Lipton inherited a massive fortune when her husband, the American inventor and industrialist Victor Farris, died in 1985. Whilst he was alive, she was an active charity fundraiser, and she has since continued in the same vein. In 1989 she reportedly gave £1 million to the American Foundation for AIDS Research set up by actress Elizabeth Taylor. Her wealth has not been decreased substantially, however, because it is regularly topped-up with royalties from her husband's inventions, which include the cardboard milk carton.

Lipton has greasepaint in her blood. She is daughter of Sydney Lipton, a band-leader of the Forties, and trod the stage of the London Palladium in her teens. She uses the name Celia Lipton in preference to her married name. *Business Age* magazine reported that in 1986 she spent quarter of a million recording an album entitled *The London I Love*, which despite heavy advertising reputedly sold less than 400 copies.

SIR SYDNEY LIPWORTH

PREFERENCE: general

AGE: 63

WEALTH: less than £20m

TRUST LINKS: M S Lipworth Charitable Trust

COMPANY LINKS: past involvement with Allied Dunbar

Sir Sydney Lipworth, like his former partners Joel Joffe and Sir Mark Weinberg (qqv), made his fortune when he sold his stake in the Hambro Life assurance company to BAT in 1984. Despite his wealth he avoids most of the trappings of the mega-rich, and he is not a great accumulator of personal possessions.

Like his ex-colleagues he is actively involved with the voluntary sector, giving both money and time to various causes. Two years after he attained his wealth, Lipworth set up the **M S Lipworth Charitable Trust** with an initial cash injection of £1,000 in order to support general charitable causes. Because there are no accounts on file at the Charity Commission for the trust, it is not possible to determine the level of its total grant-making or the types of organisation it prefers to fund.

Aside from this trust Lipworth holds frequent dinner parties to help raise money for charities, and is also personally involved with several causes. He has a clear love of art and music, and expresses this through positions as chair of the Philharmonia Orchestra, trustee of the Royal Academy's Trust, and past-governor of Sadler's Wells Foundation. He is also member of the Breakthrough Breast Cancer Research Trust's advisory panel, and is closely involved with his former-company's programme of community support as trustee of the Allied Dunbar Charitable Trust.

Since leaving Allied Dunbar, this South African from a Jewish Lithuanian family has gained repute as chair of the Monopolies and Mergers Commission. Lipworth resigned from this post in 1993 to become a QC, and has also taken on the role of chair of the DTI's Financial Services Taskforce. He is also chair of the Financial Reporting Council, deputy chair of National Westminster Bank, and a non-executive director of Carlton Communications.

When contacted, Sir Sydney stated that he would prefer not to appear in this publication, and requested that we withdraw this entry.

Contact: Sir Sydney Lipworth, M S Lipworth Charitable Trust, 41 Lothbury, London, EC2P 2BP.

EARL OF MANSFIELD

PREFERENCE: Scotland
AGE: 64
WEALTH: £35m-£50m
TRUST LINKS: see below
COMPANY LINKS: Crown Estate

The Earl of Mansfield finds himself in the classic 'asset rich yet cash poor' position faced by many of Britain's aristocratic landowners. His substantial acreage around the much visited Scone Palace in Perthshire constitutes a fortune which is not easily realisable, although it does produce earnings from fishing and shooting rights. Whilst he has no grant-making trusts listed in his name with the Charity Commission, he does have one registered with the Inland Revenue in Scotland. We were, however, unable to obtain detailed information for this trust.

The Earl was involved with a number of charities north of the border in the seventies, including the Scottish Association for Care and Resettlement of Offenders, the Scottish Association of Boys Clubs, and the Scottish Branch of the Historic Houses Association. He is currently a trustee of the Wildfowl and Wetlands Trust, and president of the Scottish Country Dance Society. On the business front, Mansfield is a director of the public companies American Trust and General Accident, as well as several other firms including Ross Breeders. He is also first commissioner and chair of the Crown Estate, which administers the hereditary Land Revenues of the Crown, and manages property in the whole of Britain as well as the foreshore and seabed around our coast.

When contacted, the Earl of Mansfield commented that he took considerable exception at appearing in this publication.

Contact: Earl of Mansfield, Scone Palace, Perthshire, Scotland, PH2 6BE.

BERNARD MATTHEWS

PREFERENCE: youth, environment, arts, Norfolk
AGE: 64
WEALTH: £35m-£50m
TRUST LINKS: none found
COMPANY LINKS: Bernard Matthews

Bernard Matthews is famous for pronouncing that his various turkey products are 'bootiful' in TV adverts for his eponymous public company. The company still operates from Great Witchingham Hall, a Jacobean mansion near Norwich and donated £85,000 to charities in 1991, with a preference for local causes in areas where it operates, and for children's charities, environmental organisations and the arts. Despite his obvious close links, we have not included the company's gifts in the figure for Bernard Matthews' known charitable donations, as he personally owns less than half of the shares in the firm. Also we have been unable to find any charitable trusts registered in his name at the Charity Commission.

Contact: J G Brown, Company Secretary, Great Witchingham Hall, Norwich, Norfolk, NR9 5QD. Tel: 01603 872611

ROBERT MURRAY

PREFERENCE: general, Yorkshire?
AGE: 47
WEALTH: £20m-£35m
TRUST LINKS: R S Murray Charitable Trust
COMPANY LINKS: sold interests in Spring Ram, Sovereign Capital

Robert Murray co-founded the kitchen furniture business Spring Ram with Bill Rooney in 1979. After a decade of supervising the company's growth, he left in 1990 and has since sold shares in the company for a total of £30 million. He has recently established the **R S Murray Charitable Trust**, to offer support to general charities.

As it was only created in July 1993, there are no accounts on file for this trust at the Charity Commission, and so it is not possible to assess either its potential size or its preferences. However, given Murray's strong links with Yorkshire, where he lives and where Spring Ram was based, it would not be surprising if some donations were focused on the county.

Contact: Mr R S Murray, R S Murray, Charitable Trust, Crayke Court, Church Hill, Crayke, York, YO6 4TA.

NICKERSON family

PREFERENCE: education, agricultural research, Lincolnshire
WEALTH: less than £20m
TRUST LINKS: Joseph Nickerson Charitable Foundation, Joseph Nickerson Heather Improvement Foundation
COMPANY LINKS: Nickerson Group Rothwell

There are five separate charities registered under the Nickerson family's name, all of which were established by the family patriarch, the late Sir Joseph Nickerson. Two of them – the Joseph Nickerson Benevolent Trust and Joseph Nickerson Husbandry Award – have now been wound up, but the rest of them appear to be going strong. When Sir Joseph died in 1990, he made substantial bequests in his will to these charities. As the administration of his Estate is not finally complete, however, certain of these bequests have not been made, so the total picture is not yet shown in the accounts. The details of the three active charities are as follows:

The **Joseph Nickerson Charitable Foundation** was set up by Sir Joseph in 1978, and its principal objectives are confined to charitable activities within the village of Rothwell and the old county of Lincolnshire. Its accounts for the year 1992/93 show assets of £105,000, and an income of £25,000. This supported charitable expenditure of £11,000 and a loan of £3,500 to the **Joseph Nickerson Rothwell Memorial Trust**. The charity takes an active interest in the people, both young and old, living in Rothwell by arranging adventure holidays for the young and outings for the elderly residents, as well as helping students from the local area with their higher education costs.

The principal objectives of the Joseph Nickerson Rothwell Memorial Trust are to establish, maintain and open to the public a gallery detailing the life and times of Sir Joseph Nickerson. In his will he bequeathed the trust a house, The Villa, Rothwell, as well as a large number of personal items of memorabilia to be displayed in the gallery. This memorial is now complete, but is open to the public only six times during the year. As detailed above, the trust has received loans from the Joseph Nickerson Charitable Foundation, and it restricts its expenditure to the maintenance and development of the gallery, including property alterations, pictures and framing, carpets and furnishings. In 1992/93 the trust spent just over £8,000 to this end.

The last of these active charities is the **Joseph Nickerson Heather Improvement Foundation**, which aims to support and promote research into the better use and co-ordination of resources in upland Britain, and particularly heather growing areas. A number of research projects have been sponsored, and the foundation is currently financing the production of a video dealing with the full annual cycle of heather maintenance and re-generation. In 1992/93 this foundation had assets of £59,000 and an income of only £6,000, but still managed to fund research projects to the tune of £43,000.

The Nickerson family's fortune stems from two main agricultural businesses which were created by Sir Joseph. Shares in the Nickerson Group Rothwell, whose principal subsidiaries are Cherry Valley Farms – the duck products firm – and Cotswold Pig Development Company, are still owned by non-charitable trusts established for the benefit of Sir Joseph's family. He also set up the Nickerson Seeds businesses which were sold to the Shell Group in the 1970s. Throughout his life, Sir Joseph managed to reconcile a strong interest in conservation of wildlife and the countryside – he was a founder member of the WWF – with a love of shooting which earned him the nickname 'Partridge Joe'. He found out what it was like to be on the receiving end, however, when he was famously 'winged' by Lord Whitelaw whilst bagging game. His son Charles Nickerson is manager/agent of the consortium which owns the village of

Brookenby, which was converted from an old Lincolnshire RAF base. Charles told the *Guardian* that he is trying to create a pleasant environment in this settlement: 'I might not be a philanthropist and my intentions might seem feudal, but I was going to plant a lot of flowers and I wanted to set standards'.

Contact: Joseph Nickerson Charitable Foundation: The Secretary, Estate Office, Rothwell, Lincoln, LN7 6BJ. Tel: 01472 371371. Joseph Nickerson Heather Improvement Foundation: P R C Braithwaite, at the same address.

CLARICE PEARS
and family

PREFERENCE: education, general, South East

AGE: 60

WEALTH: £100m–£250m

TRUST LINKS: Pears Family Charitable Foundation, William Pears Group of Cos. Ltd Trust Fund

COMPANY LINKS: William Pears Family Holdings

The Pears family controls the private William Pears group, which operates in the commercial property market and is run by Clarice Pears and her sons. In 1975 the **William Pears Group of Companies Limited Trust Fund** was set up in order to advance the education of pupils at the City of London School by the provision of scholarships and bursaries. The Charity Commission has no record of the trust's current income or expenditure.

There is also a more recent grant-making trust, the **Pears Family Charitable Foundation**, which was established by Clarice Pears in 1991, with Mark and Trevor Pears as original trustees. The accounts for the period to March 1993 show the foundation to be inactive, with no income and no donations made so far. It was set up to support general charitable organisations, but will benefit the South East in practice.

Contact: William Pears Group of Companies Limited Trust Fund, Mr M J Sant, Bursar, City of London School, Queen Victoria St, London, EC4V 3AL. Tel: 0171 489 0291. Pears Family Charitable Foundation: Mr Trevor Pears, Clive House, Old Brewery Mews, Hampstead, London, NW3 1PZ.

DUKE OF RICHMOND
and family

PREFERENCE: Sussex
AGE: 64
WEALTH: £35m-£50m
TRUST LINKS: see below
COMPANY LINKS: Goodwood Group of Companies

The Richmond estate includes the stately home of the same name near Chichester in West Sussex, along with 12,000 acres in the county. The Duke of Richmond, a chartered accountant, is chair of the 'glorious' Goodwood race course. He himself maintains that his personal wealth is only £1 million, that he is not the owner of the pictures and furniture in Goodwood House, and that he is also neither the owner or principal shareholder in the Goodwood Estate Co Ltd which owns the land and buildings on the estate.

His charitable activities appear to be focused mainly upon organisations active in Sussex. He is Chancellor of the University of Sussex, president of Sussex Rural Community Council, the Chichester Festivities, and St Catherine's Hospice Crawley, chair of the trustees of Sussex Heritage Trust, and past chair of the Chichester Cathedral Development Trust. He is also involved with several Christian causes, and was a member of the General Synod and of the World Council of Churches. On the business front, he is chair of the Goodwood Group of Companies, Dexam International Holdings, and John Wiley & Sons, and he is president of the South East England Tourist Board.

When contacted, the Duke of Richmond stated that the amount of cash he has available to give away is 'very small', and that he has a small charitable trust which he does not publicise because of the number of appeals he would thereby receive. We were unable to obtain any further details about this trust. He also expressed a desire to have his name deleted from this publication.

Contact: Duke of Richmond, Goodwood House, Chichester, W Sussex, PO18 0PX.

LORD ROTHSCHILD

PREFERENCE: arts, homelessness, mental health, disability, London
AGE: 58
WEALTH: £250m-£500m
TRUST LINKS: J Rothschild Group Charitable Trust, J Rothschild Assurance Foundation, Caritas
COMPANY LINKS: St James's Place Capital, J Rothschild Assurance

Lord (Jacob) Rothschild is the son of the brilliant late Victor Rothschild, scientist, banker, government adviser and MI5 officer. He chose, however, to pursue a career outside the family-controlled bank and set up an investment vehicle, now known as St

James's Place Capital, in the seventies. More recently, he teamed up with his old friend Sir Mark Weinberg (qv) to set up the life assurance company J Rothschild Assurance, a subsidiary of St James's Place Capital.

Credited as the man who secured the Sainsburys' support for the National Gallery extension when he chaired the Gallery's board of trustees in the eighties, Lord Rothschild is also responsible for some charitable giving of his own, albeit through his companies. The donations budget of St James's Place Capital, a leader in the field of corporate giving, is managed by the **J Rothschild Group Charitable Trust**, which made donations totalling £134,000 in 1993/94. Of this, £32,500 was spent on mental health and disability (ranging from a donation towards the cost of employing a development worker in Tower Hamlets to a specialist charity involved in design and manufacture for disability) and a similar amount on problems of youth (from the Southwark Youth Project to a school for children with little or not sight. There were also small grants to a wide range of groups in London. The trust also gave some support to disaster appeals and to causes in which the shareholders and staff of the company took an active personal interest, and makes a point of supporting 'neglected' causes. Lord Rothschild himself is one of the three trustees.

Lord Rothschild is also a trustee of a charitable trust named **Caritas**, which was settled by a relative, James A de Rothschild. Caritas made grants totalling £131,000 in 1991 to a range of medical, Jewish and arts organisations.

Lord Rothschild's new life assurance business and his business links with Sir James Goldsmith (qv), particularly in the area of gold mining, have kept him in the news in recent years. At the end of 1993 his partner

● FINANCE SECTOR GIVERS

Martyn Arbib	£4,090,000
Julian Hodge	£1,000,000
Robin Fleming	£732,000
Evelyn de Rothshild	£605,000
Joel Joffe	£286,000
Henry Hoare	£224,000
Mark Weinberg	£103,000
Cayzer family	£53,000
Colin Frizzell	£10,000

Sir Mark Weinberg set up a new trust named the **J Rothschild Assurance Foundation**, probably to be the giving arm of the new company. It is too early to say how large the foundation is likely to be, but its income is estimated on registration documents at £30,000 a year.

Contact for the J Rothschild Group Charitable Trust: Mrs Diane Lovegrove, St James's Place Capital plc, 27 St James's Place, London SW1A 1NR. Tel: 0171 493 8111. For the J Rothschild Assurance Foundation: M Cooper-Smith, J Rothschild House, Dollar Street, Cirencester, Glos GL7 2AQ. Tel: 01285 640302. For Caritas: c/o Saffery Champness, Fairfax House, Fulwood Place, London WC1V 6UB.

MARQUESS OF SALISBURY

PREFERENCE: Hertfordshire and Dorset, general
AGE: 77
WEALTH: £75m-£100m
TRUST LINKS: Salisbury Pool Charity
COMPANY LINKS: none

The Marquess of Salisbury owns the magnificent Jacobian mansion Hatfield House, which was built by

BRITISH SCHOOL OF OSTEOPATHY
1-4 SUFFOLK ST., LONDON. SW1Y 4HG
TEL. 01 - 930 9254-8

241

his ancestor Robert Cecil, the first Marquess, in the early 1600s. His family also hold property in central London, along with 13,000 acres of land in Hertfordshire and around their other home, Cranborne Manor, in Dorset. Salisbury's father, the previous Marquess, made provisions in his will to set up the **Salisbury Pool Charity** when he died in 1972. The charity was registered in 1976, with the current Lord Salisbury and his eldest son, Viscount Cranborne, as co-trustees. The last accounts on file at the Charity Commission, for 1984, list assets of £36,000 providing an income of £6,000. In that year grants of £4,500 were made to a variety of general causes in Hertfordshire and Dorset, as well as medical, youth, and educational organisations and churches. The Charity Commission's database gives a 1992 income of £19,000 for this grant-making trust, which we reckon would fund donations of at least £15,000.

● GIVING BY ARISTOCRATS

Earl Cadogan	£179,000
Duke of Northumberland	£100,000
Marquess of Cholmondeley	£52,000
Marquess of Northampton	£52,000
Earl of Aylesford	£45,000
Marquess of Tavistock	£26,000
Earl of Bradford	£17,000
Lady Willoughby de Eresby	£16,000
Earl of Derby	£14,000
Lord Margadale	£12,000
Viscount Ingleby	£11,000
Earl of Harewood	£10,000

Lord Salisbury is involved on a personal basis in the voluntary sector as president of the British Deaf Association and the BVA Animal Welfare Foundation. In the same vein, his wife, the Marchioness, is patron of the Animal Welfare Trust. Aside from these charitable activities, he is also a founder and member of the editorial board of the right-wing journal the *Salisbury Review*.

Contact: Mr M R Melville, Secretary to the Trustees, Salisbury Pool Charity, Hatfield House, Hatfield, Herts, AL9 5NF. Tel: 01707 251592.

LESLIE SILVER

PREFERENCE: general, probable preference for Leeds and Yorkshire
AGE: 69
WEALTH: £20m–£35m
TRUST LINKS: Leslie Silver Charitable Trust
COMPANY LINKS: sold holdings in Kalon Group

If Leslie Silver ever feels like painting the town red he won't have to look very far to find supplies. The Leeds based Kalon paint manufacturing company, which he built up over a period of 45 years, is a leading supplier to DIY retailers and the decorating trade. He started the firm, then called the Silver Paint and Lacquer Company, just after the war with a gratuity received for his stint in the airforce. Under his careful stewardship, this initial investment of £250 had increased in value to over £25 million by the time Silver retired and sold his stake a few years ago.

In 1991 he founded the **Leslie Silver Charitable Trust** with the aims of supporting general charitable activities. To date, the beneficiaries have been charitable organisations in which Mr Silver takes a particular interest and this policy is likely to continue. For this reason, we have been advised by the trustees that grants to individuals are unlikely to be made. Given Mr Silver's strong links with Leeds and West Yorkshire it is proabablethat his trust will direct some support to causes active in the area. Mr Silver's highest profile connection is as chair of Leeds United FC, but on a wider front he is also chair of the board of governors at Leeds Metropolitan University.

We have been asked by his solicitors to make it clear that Mr Silver did not wish to be included in this book and that he does not welcome unsolicited appeals of any kind.

Contact: Mr I J Fraser, Trustee, Leslie Silver Charitable Trust, Robson Rhodes, 40 Great George Street, Leeds, LS1 3DQ. Tel: 0113 245 9631.

SIMPSON family

PREFERENCE: general
WEALTH: less than £20m
TRUST LINKS: Simpson Family Charitable Trust
COMPANY LINKS: sold holding in DAKS Simpson Group

The Simpson family used to own just over half of the shares in their well known eponymous London store, until they sold out in 1991 to a Japanese company, receiving around £20 million.

In the year before the sale, family member Georgina Andrews (née Simpson) and her actor husband Anthony established the **Simpson Family Charitable Trust** with general charitable purposes. Its accounts for the period to April 1991 record the transferral to the trust of 5,000 shares in the DAKS Simpson Group from Georgina

Andrews, which have since been sold. The accounts give no indication of any donations having been made by the trust in the year, so it is not possible to state whether it has any particular preferences.

Georgina Andrew's solicitor stated that she would very much prefer that we made no reference to her in this book.

Contact: Simpson Family Charitable Trust, Messr MacFarlanes (ref: TRV/ 514429), 10 Norwich St, London, EC4A 1BD. Tel: 0171 831 9222.

PHILIP SMITH

PREFERENCE: general
AGE: 48
WEALTH: less than £20m
TRUST LINKS: Philip Smith's Charitable Trust
COMPANY LINKS: W H Smith

The Honorable Philip Smith's wealth is derived from his valuable shareholding in the W H Smith retail company, established by previous family members over two hundred years ago. The Smiths now have little involvement in the day-to-day running of the firm, although Philip is a director.

In 1991 he set up **Philip Smith's Charitable Trust** through which to make donations to general charitable causes. At the time of writing, no accounts were on file at the Charity Commission for this trust so we have not been able to assess its size or the types of causes it supports.

Contact: Mr M Wood, Philip Smith's Charitable Trust, Bircham & Co Solicitors, 1 Dean Farrar St, Westminster, London, SW1H 0DY. Tel: 0171 222 8044.

COUNTESS OF SUTHERLAND

PREFERENCE: heritage
AGE: 73
WEALTH: unknown
TRUST LINKS: Sutherland Trust
COMPANY LINKS: none

Like many of the other rich aristocrats in this book, the Countess of Sutherland has set up a charitable trust to help preserve the family home 'for the benefit of the nation'. There are in fact two charities registered in Sutherland's name, although one appears to be largely inactive.

The **Sutherland Foundation** was set up by the Countess in 1981 with 145,000 shares in a company called Trentham Garden Limited. Over the next two years these shares were sold for a total of £199,000, the bulk of which was transferred to the **Sutherland Trust**, leaving the foundation with only £6,000 in assets. The Sutherland Trust had been established by the Countess in 1982 with her husband and son amongst the founding trustees. Its aims include the preservation of historic buildings for the benefit of the nation and the advancement of public education in such buildings, as well as general charitable objectives. The 1991 accounts for the trust show that it holds the chattels of Dunrobin Castle and the Gardener's Cottage, which are valued at around £1 million, and it had an income of £7,000 generated by dividends and interest on other assets. The main expenditure for 1991, as in previous years, was £15,000 on 'insurances', presumably for Dunrobin Castle. Donations made to other charities by the trust were nil in 1991 and 1990, and only around £500 in 1989 and 1988.

Dunrobin Castle is Countess Sutherland's family home in Scotland, where she sits as Chief of the Sutherland Clan. The source of the family's wealth is the land it holds around the Castle, running to many thousand acres. The Countess is chair of Dunrobin Castle Limited, and a director of the *Northern Times*.

After sending a draft copy of this entry, we received a reply from Lady Sutherland's son, Lord Strathnaver, who commented that: 'The Sutherland Trust has its hands full looking after Dunrobin Castle and does not have large sums to give to other charities. In all these circumstances I would have thought that the best course of action is to withdraw the entry about my mother altogether. She, the Sutherland Trust and the rest of my family are not a useful source of funds for the sort of people who will be reading your book.'

Contact: Lord Strathnaver, Sutherland Trust, Sutherland Estates Office, Golspie, Sutherland, Scotland, KW10 6RR. Tel: 01408 633268.

DAN WAGNER

PREFERENCE: not known
AGE: 30
WEALTH: less than £20m
TRUST LINKS: none found
COMPANY LINKS: MAID

Dan Wagner may have been tempting fate last year when he wrote a letter to *Business Age* magazine following his inclusion in their list of wealthy individuals. After expressing his surprise at being represented he commented that: 'The expected flood of letters pouring through my letterbox has failed to materialise. Let's hope it stays that way because I'm a sucker for good causes.'

His charitable impulses should be well funded in the future, as Wagner looks set to be one of a new generation of information technology multi-millionaires. His recently floated company, MAID plc, offers an innovative on-line computer information service which facilitates access to a wide range of databases.

Contact: Dan Wagner, MAID plc, The Communications Building, 48 Leicester Square, London, WC2H 7DB.

PETER WATERMAN

PREFERENCE: general appeals
AGE: 47
WEALTH: £35m-£50m
TRUST LINKS: Stock Aitken & Waterman Charitable Trust
COMPANY LINKS: PWL (Pete Waterman Limited)

The song-writing and production triumvirate of Stock, Aitken and Waterman were the men behind many of the pop hits of the eighties. They were responsible for bringing us the singing soap stars Kylie Minogue and Jason Donovan. At the height of their success in 1988 the trio established the eponymous **Stock Aitken & Waterman Charitable Trust**. The major recipient of donations from the trust has been the Hillsborough Disaster Appeal Charity Fund, which received a total of £380,000 in 1989 and 1990. Only four other donations were made by the trust in these two years, the largest being £35,000 to the Daily Star Royal Marsden Hospital Appeal. This trust appears to be funded by the proceeds from charity records and concerts, such as *Ferry 'Cross the Mersey* (a celebrity record for Mersey Aid/ Hillsborough Disaster Appeal), and SAW Goes to the Albert (a concert in aid of the Royal Marsden Hospital). Waterman has also been involved with numerous other charity

recordings, such as Band Aid's *Do they know its Christmas?*, *Let it Be* (Ferry Aid), *Help!* (Comic Relief), and *Let's all Chant* (Help a London Child).

Pete Waterman is the best known of the three, due to his frequent stints as a television presenter. He also has built up a considerable fortune from his music interests via his company PWL, and a joint venture with Warner Music. As a former British Rail fireman, he has rekindled old memories by spending over £1 million on a collection of vintage steam locomotives, which he has renovated and keeps on railway sidings near Crewe. In the same vein, he recently acquired the rights to run rail charter services, and there have also been press reports that he is a potential bidder for the royal train, if it is privatised by Railtrack.

Contact: Stock Aitken & Waterman Charitable Trust, Taylor Joyston Garrett, 10 Maltravers St, London WC2R 3BS.

DUKE OF WELLINGTON

PREFERENCE: wildlife, conservation, service charities
AGE: 78
WEALTH: less than £20m
TRUST LINKS: none found
COMPANY LINKS: none

The 8th Duke of Wellington is a direct descendant of the Iron Duke who defeated Napoleon at the Battle of Waterloo. The grateful nation rewarded this victory with Stratfield Saye, a beautiful stately home and estate in north Hampshire, which remains the family seat and whose restoration and preservation is the aim of the Stratfield Saye Preservation Trust, a registered charity. The present duke is still closely involved with the military life as colonel-in-chief of the Duke of Wellington's Regiment.

The Duke has an extensive range of voluntary sector activities, mainly focused on causes connected with animals, the environment, agriculture and the military. In the past he has held positions as president of both Game Conservancy, the Rare Breeds Survival Trust, the Council for Environmental Conservation, and as vice-president of the Zoological Society of London and trustee of the UK branch of the WorldWide Fund for Nature. He is currently president of the Atlantic Salmon Trust and vice-president of the Kennel Club, trustee of Lawes Agricultural Trust and the Centre for Agricultural Strategy at the University of Reading, and governor of Wellington College. His links with the army are apparent as member of the Queen's Trustee Board of the Royal Armouries, and national vice-president of the Royal British Legion as well as president of the charity's south-east section.

Despite these considerable personal involvements with various non-profit organisations, we have been unable to find any charitable trusts registered in the Duke's name, which is no doubt indicative of the 'asset rich, cash poor' position so typical of our aristocracy.

Contact: Duke of Wellington, The Wellington Office, Stratfield Saye, Reading, RG7 2BT.

DUKE OF WESTMINSTER

PREFERENCE: welfare, education, general, in London and the North West

AGE: 42

WEALTH: over £500m

TRUST LINKS: Westminster Foundation

COMPANY LINKS: Grosvenor Estate Holdings

As is the case with many of the aristocrats in this book whose fortune is founded on landholding, public records reveal only limited charitable donations made from the pocket of Gerald Cavendish Grosvenor, the Sixth Duke of Westminster, often cited as Britain's richest man. Unlike many other aristocrats, however, he does appear to be very active in business: it was recently announced in the press, for example, that the Duke's main property vehicle, Grosvenor Estate Holdings, was taking a 20 per cent stake in UK Realty Partners, a new Anglo-American venture which intended to invest up to £500 million within five years in commercial property in the UK.

The Duke does chair the board of the **Westminster Foundation**. This is a grant-making charity set up and endowed by his father, the Fifth Duke, in 1974, but with the support and encouragement of the present Duke. Donations made by the foundation totalled £1,025,000 in 1993, compared with an income of £830,000 which came mainly from investments. In the previous year, over half of the donations by value went on social welfare causes, but the fields of medicine, youth, education, the arts, conservation and the church also got a look in. The British Red Cross in London received £45,000; Centrepoint, Soho, £40,000; the Passage Day Centre £35,000; and the Queen Elizabeth Gate Appeal, the Cardinal Hume Centre and Youth Clubs UK £25,000 each. Grants of £20,000 were made to Westminster Abbey and to the Industrial Society. Business in the Community, of which the Duke is a director, received £22,500.

The foundation's spending power increased substantially after 1990 when the block of shares in Grosvenor Estate Holdings with which it had been endowed were sold to the Sixth Duke of Westminster's

1971 Settlement for £14.3 million. Putting this money into a wide portfolio of investments has released a considerable income stream for the foundation.

Westminster's directorship of Business in the Community is only one of a block of voluntary appointments that occupies six square inches in *Who's Who*. Most of his spare time, however, is spent soldiering in the territorial army, where he commands a regiment of 600 men in the Queen's Own Yeomanry. Westminster's involvement with regimental charities and others suggests he may well donate substantial amounts other than through the foundation set up by his father. He reputedly contributed £150,000 to the Manchester 2000 Olympic Bid – which he chaired – and has also been acknowledged by name as a donor to other charities, including the 21st Century Trust, a research body.

Westminster's other reported donations were made to the Conservative Party. But he fell out with the Party over the poll tax, being sufficiently outraged by its unfairness to increase the wages of his employees to offset the cost of the tax. He remained a member until 1993, however, when he resigned in outrage at the Tories' leasehold reform legislation which threatens to eat a chunk out of the Grosvenor Estate's freehold of 300 prime acres in Mayfair and Belgravia.

Any dent the Duke of Westminster's wealth suffers as a result of leasehold enfranchisement will not be too deep. In addition to the prime London estates, the Duke owns some 140,000 agricultural acres, including his 11,000 acre estate at Eaton in Cheshire, and property interests in Australia, Vancouver, and some 25 cities in the US. The Duke regards himself very much as a steward of this property for

future generations. When pressed in a recent interview in the *Guardian* (27/9/93) to estimate how much he was worth in total, he refused to be drawn. 'We are rich in terms of property and the quality of property. It is not something that frankly concerns me. Never has. Not interested in material things. Honestly. It would drive me bonkers if I thought too deeply about it – woke up during the night thinking, say, £100 million had been wiped off our value. I sleep well.'

Contact: Mr J E Hok, Secretary, Westminster Foundation, 53 Davies Street, London W1Y 1FH. Tel: 0171 408 0988.

WESTON family

PREFERENCE: medicine, education, general

WEALTH: over £500m

TRUST LINKS: Garfield Weston Foundation, five other specialist Garfield Weston trusts

COMPANY LINKS: Associated British Foods

Like some of the other wealthy families in this book, the Westons' philanthropy stems principally from an earlier generation. In this case the great philanthropist was W Garfield Weston, father of Garry and Galen Weston, respectively the current magnates of the UK and Canadian halves of the Weston empire.

In the later part of his life Garfield Weston established at least seven grant-making charities, including the mighty **Garfield Weston Foundation**. He rebuilt the bread business his father, George Weston, had started in Toronto and served as Conservative MP for Macclesfield during the war. An early donation went to the government: £100,000 to the Spitfire Fund set up to replace lost fighter planes. The Anglo-Canadian tycoon also had extensive interests in South Africa, where he was a vigorous supporter of the old order.

By the time Garfield Weston died in 1978 there were Weston trusts for St Paul's Cathedral, Westminster Abbey, and the New University of Ulster, as well as a Garfield Weston Boy's Club Trust and a Garfield Weston Trust for Research into Heart Surgery attached to Charing Cross and Westminster Medical School. The last two trusts were still pulling in an income of well over £100,000 in 1993. All these trusts were funded by the Garfield Weston Foundation. Another trust, the Garfield Weston Irish Foundation, was however removed from the Charity Commission register in the early nineties.

The Garfield Weston Foundation is now one of the UK's biggest. It made grants to over 700 charities totalling nearly £8 million in 1992/93. Hospitals, medical research, education, the arts, social welfare and youth were the main fields supported but there was also a large number of small grants to a very wide range of charities. The biggest awards included £1 million to the Thrombosis Research Institute and £500,000 each to Marie Curie Cancer Care, UMIST, and the Royal Commonwealth Society Library.

Nearly all the foundation's assets are held in two companies, George Weston Holdings and Wittington

Investments, both holding companies in a business empire which includes Associated British Foods and Fortnum and Mason (Wittington is the name of the mansion Garfield Weston acquired by the Thames). Subsidiary companies in AB Foods also make a number of corporate donations to charity, but appeals to head office find their way onto the desk of the foundation.

The current chair of AB Foods, and of the foundation, is 67-year old Garry Weston (his full name, confusingly, is Garfield Howard Weston). A sober character, Garry has a reputation in the City of playing the long game, and sees himself primarily as a business manager rather than a wheeler-dealer. He is not known for his extravagance, but he was a loyal supporter of Margaret Thatcher and continues to make major donations to the Conservatives.

Garry's younger brother Galen runs George Weston Ltd in Canada, a £1 billion baking to supermarkets to chocolate operation, as well as holding a major stake in AB Foods. Known as a polo-playing socialite and friend of Prince Charles, Galen Weston is involved with a number of charities including United World Colleges (of which Charles is president). In 1994 he was also spotted in London at an event for the International Sacred Literature Trust. Married to a former model from Ireland, Hilary Frayne, the couple have spent very little time in Ireland following a failed IRA attempt to kidnap them in 1983.

1994 saw the planning of a financial restructuring of the Weston empire in order to facilitate tax and inheritance planning for the family. The deal is to give George Weston Holdings sole ownership of Associated British Foods, with the independent shareholders transferring their stake from AB Foods to the holding company, enabling accumulated dividends held by George Weston Holdings to be released at a lower tax liability. The Weston family and the Garfield Weston Foundation, which currently hold just under two-thirds of AB Foods, may benefit by up to £130 million from the deal.

With Garry Weston obviously planning for the future, the other question centres on who will succeed him in the next few years. In the business world there has been a lot of speculation, often to Weston's annoyance, about the prospects for two of his sons, Guy and George, but charities may be more interested in one of his daughters, Sophia, who has been working for the foundation. In any case, the inter-generational transfer of some of the UK's most famous businesses, one of its largest foundations, and a very, very large sum of money, may yet provide new impetus to the family's philanthropy.

Contact: Harold W Bailey, Garfield Weston Foundation, c/o G Weston Centre, Bowater House, 68 Knightsbridge, London SW1X 7LR. Tel: 0171 589 6363.

LORD WOLFSON

PREFERENCE: education, health, arts and humanities in UK and Israel

AGE: 66

WEALTH: £100m-£250m

TRUST LINKS: Wolfson Foundation, Wolfson Family Charitable Trust

COMPANY LINKS: Great Universal Stores

Lord Wolfson of Marylebone is a very rich man by any standards, but would have been considerably more wealthy if he and his father had not given so much of the family fortune away. The late Sir Isaac Wolfson, who died in 1991, was a great philanthropist and various charitable causes are still reaping the benefits of his largesse through two grant-making trusts.

The larger and slightly elder of these two trusts is the **Wolfson Foundation**, which Sir Isaac established in 1955 with his wife and son Leonard (now Lord) Wolfson as founding trustees. Lord Wolfson is still actively involved with the foundation as chair of the trustees. It is now one of the largest grant-making charitable trusts in Britain, due to its substantial shareholding in Great Universal Stores. The Wolfson family controlled this public company for sixty years, but this changed when the firm's non-voting ordinary shares were enfranchised in September last year. The foundation now holds only 6.6% of Great Universal Stores' ordinary shares, but this holding was valued at £406 million earlier this year. The foundation's massive asset base, worth £467 million in total, generated an income of £14 million in 1993/94 which funded donations of £12.6 million.

In the previous year grants of £8.6 million were made by the Wolfson Foundation, which included support for a number of education, medical and arts projects. The largest gift of £750,000 went towards the Wolfson City Technology College, which is to receive a total of £1.1 million. Another major chunk of £480,000 went to pay for student accommodation at Wolfson College, Oxford, and a further £221,000 went to the University to cover the cost of eight academic posts as part of a £1 million grant from the foundation. Two other centres of further education, Huddersfield Polytechnic and University College of Wales received £120,000 and £100,000 respectively towards their buildings maintenance programme. On the medical front, the Institute of Preventative Medicine at St Bartholomew's Hospital received a total of £1 million, of which one-quarter was paid in 1992/93, and the Royal Marsden

Hospital's new children's cancer unit was awarded £0.5 million. Four large gifts of around £100,000 each went in support of the following museums and galleries: the V&A, the National Gallery, the National Arts Collection Fund and the National History Museum.

Lord Wolfson is also chair of the **Wolfson Family Charitable Trust**, which was set up by Sir Isaac in the 1970s. By March this year the trust's investments were valued at nearly £45 million, which produced an income of £4.2 million against which grants of £3.6 million were made. Its objects restrict it to the support of medical and surgical research, and the advancement of education and religion. Fittingly, its largest grants in 1992/93 were £250,000 to Wolfson-Hilliel Primary School, £125,000 to the Royal Marsden Hospital (part of a £500,000 donation for the new children's cancer unit), and £100,000 to the Sunshine House special needs school in Northwood. The trust also made smaller gifts to museums and universities. Donations in the UK were overshadowed, however, by those made to various causes in Israel which received two-thirds of the grants-total. The main recipient was the Weizmann Institute which received US$700,000 (about £440,000) for research scholarships and laboratory modernisation.

Lord Wolfson took over his father's mantle as managing director and chair of the massive Great Universal Stores company back in 1962. Its core activities are mail order and credit, and it has five non-executive directors including carpet magnate Sir Philip Harris (qv). Lord Wolfson is also a patron of the Royal College of Surgeons. The family wealth comes from their stake in the company, much of which is held in various non-charitable trusts.

Contact for both Wolfson Foundation and Wolfson Family Charitable Trust: Dr Barbara Rashbass, Barrister-at-Law, 18-22 Haymarket, London, SW1Y 4DQ. Tel: 0171 930 1057.

INDEX